the world

the world we create

FROM GOD TO MARKET

TOMAS BJÖRKMAN

First published in 2019 by Perspectiva Press

ISBN 978-1-912892-59-4

Also available as an ebook
ISBN 978-1-912892-48-8

Typeset by seagulls.net
Cover design by Miroslav Šokčić
Printed and bound by Clays
Project management by whitefox

Perspectiva Press

Soul food for expert generalists

CONTENTS

PART 2: OUR SOCIALLY CONSTRUCTED WORLD

PART 3: GOING BEYOND GOD, SCIENCE AND THE MARKET

PREFACE

We seem to be living in a strange state of growing cultural estrangement and disorientation today. We struggle to find convincing answers about who we are as individuals, as a society and as humanity for that matter; which values we should espouse, what is true and what is fake news, and what on Earth we are headed towards - and thus, what kind of future society we should build. We live in a time of fast-paced, deep-seated changes, but many of us are not at all able to understand what is going on and what they should do. This collective confusion and lack of direction is arguably one of the primary reasons for the widespread sense of insecurity and anger that turned into the UK's attempt to withdraw from the European Union and the election of Donald Trump as president of the USA.

The pervasive value vacuum of our time can make it hard to see any greater meaning with our existence, what the value of our shared society and culture is, or why we should bother getting involved in making the world a better place. We may then get caught up in our own little, private world's illusion of happiness and retreat to an innocuous existence wrapped up in ourselves, our daily chores and needless consumer choices.

At the same time there are many who realise we cannot continue as we do today. We are destroying the environment and depleting our natural resources at a frightening pace; and while stress and depression are epidemic in the rich world, people in the poor world continue to die from curable diseases and malnutrition. And even though we as a global community are getting richer every day, we are also getting more and more unequal, locally as well as globally, which poses a serious risk to our future wellbeing in terms of violence and political instability.

As a father, I really don't know what to say to my children when they wonder how the future will look. Will their lives be as comfortable and peaceful as my own generation's? That should not be impossible if we act today and change the present course. But will we turn the boat around in time? Are we making the right decisions today? Long-term decisions? The previous generations' mistakes will undoubtedly cost the next. The question is just how much, and what we are going to do about it.

It is no wonder that many people are worried and scared. Sadly, simple answers to complex problems often become very appealing to our emotion-driven Stone Age brains when we are upset. And when there are no clear, common value systems, and when liberal democracy and the market no longer deliver the basic security and prosperity we seek, regressive ideas which were previously held in check suddenly begin to appear attractive to many. Primitive ideas such as fascism and racism get a new chance when we look for simple explanations instead of asking complex questions.

We also see increased religious interest of an equally pathological kind in many parts of the world. Christian fundamentalism expands in the United States, and many European nationalists see Vladimir Putin as a saviour from the threat of Islam and multiculturalism. The Muslim parts of the world are themselves the scene of a religious renascence not so different from that in the United States and Europe: a fundamentalist, xenophobic and totalitarian religious belief that often has political ambitions.

And when neither the political establishment, our scientific institutions, nor the market provide any potent responses to these complex issues, then we have a serious problem.

So are there any convincing alternatives to the simple answers of fascism and fundamentalist religion? I believe there are. And that is what this book is about.

Despite the gloomy introduction I'm somewhat optimistic about the future. Not only do I believe there is a fairly decent chance of overcoming the challenges ahead, I also believe we have many promising opportunities to create a future that is significantly better than the present – and indeed, this may be the only way to solve any of the major problems we are faced with today.

BRIEF OUTLINE OF THE BOOK

This book is divided into three parts: Part 1 takes our past as the canvas with which to paint a picture of relentless evolutionary change; Part 2 connects that to our socially constructed and market-oriented present; and Part 3 conjectures on how to steer these dynamics towards a better future.

We begin our journey in Part 1 by going all the way back to the Big Bang, and from there outline a developmental and evolutionary systemic view on everything from the formation of stars and planets, over the emergence of life and its burgeoning complexity at each successive stage, right up to human societal and cultural development across history. The central idea in Part 1 is that humanity has progressed through four fundamentally different stages of experiencing and interpreting the world, that which I call 'thought perspectives', and that at each stage a new symbolic invention in our wordview has been seen as the highest authority on truth and justice. The historically most important of these have been God, Science and the Market.

Part 2 takes the grand historical narrative from Part 1 as its point of departure and zooms in on the most recent thought perspective and its highest authority: postmodernism and the market respectively. The extent to which our society and culture – our *collective imaginary* – are shaped by social constructions, which we often remain unaware of or take for granted as natural, given facts, is one of the most central points in Part 2. The contemporary account of the postmodern condition and the dominance of the market is thus approached from the perspective of a socially constructed world. The purpose of this is to see the market as a social construction – not a fact of nature – that postmodernism unwittingly has made our highest authority, and to realise that a 'free' market could be very different from the one we have today.

Part 3 proceeds from the contemporary context of postmodernity's market-induced malaises in Part 2 by turning our gaze towards an increasingly complex world that the fragmented symbolic Universe of the present fails to properly handle. Part 3 sees considerable engagement with the field of psychological development. The central tenets here are that human minds develop through stages of cognitive complexity, that this also applies to adults, who under favourable conditions can advance to more complex stages of thought and perception, and that it is absolutely necessary to meet the challenges of our times that we all develop our ability to see the world in more nuances, depth and complexity if we are to ensure a successful transition to a sustainable society. The point is, to understand and manage an increasingly complex world, our inner complexity needs to match the outer complexity of our world. As the world grows more complex, so must we as individual thinking creatures – along with our social institutions and the narratives about reality that we tell ourselves and others. The last chapter thus explores how we can 'co-create' a new 'metanarrative' so that we can free ourselves from the inadequate thought perspectives of the present and their dated or limited authorities: God, Science and the Market.

The World We Create is a title with two different meanings. The first is the realisation that the world we experience and interpret is always a creation of our own consciousness. The other is the insight that many parts of our world are created by collective human process: the social construction of reality, of our collective imaginary. Accordingly, both of these ideas will be underlying themes throughout the entire book.

ACKNOWLEDGEMENTS

This book is in many ways the result of a co-creation process over more than ten years. So many people have contributed ideas, perspectives and suggestions for literature and theories that in some way or the other have shaped the final result. I wish to thank them all. Claes Nordén and Harry McNeil provided important feedback at an early stage. Ekskäret Foundation has proved an invaluable arena, and I would like to thank all who have contributed with interesting conversations and seminars, not least Jan Henriksson, Erik Fernholm, Caroline Stiernstedt Sahlborn and Göran Gennvi. Much inspiration has also been gained from similar talks within the Club of Rome. I especially wish to thank Nora Bateson, Carlos Alvarez Pereira and Maja Göpel for the insights they gave me about complex systems.

During the work with the Swedish original edition, four people were indispensable: Emil Ejner Friis, Kristina Elfhag, Daniel Görtz and Lene Andersen have all through valuable conversations and insights – along with specific improvements to the text – made contributions without which this book would not have been possible.

For the work with the English edition (which is not a direct translation of the original Swedish edition, *Världen vi skapar*, but more of an improved second edition) I would like to thank John Wright for providing a first translation and Emil Ejner Friis for making the substantial improvements and additions to the original text I felt were needed. I would also like to thank Giuseppe Dal Pra for proofreading the book and for the contributions he has made to the notes and the introduction chapters.

Finally, I am grateful for, and humbled by, the overwhelming positive reactions I received following the release of the original Swedish edition. I wish to thank everyone who has contacted me. It has encouraged me to improve the book even further, and convinced me that it is one that is needed in the world today.

Tomas Björkman
January 2019

INTRODUCTION

What is the great narrative of our time? The shared vision of the future to guide our collective efforts towards societal improvement? In today's hypercomplex, globalised reality, where religion, national identities and the major political ideologies of yesteryear have lost their sway over public imagination, what is the next big story we as global citizens can tell ourselves and each other about the society we live in, its purpose and why we should see each other as members of the same society in the first place? What's our shared story?

Every society needs to address these questions. Sadly, convincing answers are currently few and far between. Excessive focus on identity politics and a postmodern disdain for *metanarratives* have left us divided and without common direction. In particular, we lack an overarching narrative to connect the many smaller ones: a powerful metanarrative to serve as a new foundation for our shared society that we are all co-authors of.

This book has been written in search of such a narrative; and given the requirements of making it as foundational and all-encompassing as possible, we shall begin our journey by approaching the biggest story of all: the creation of the Universe and life's blossoming in a very small corner of it. The purpose of this perspective from the grandest scale imaginable is to provide a less fractured account of the world and our place in it; to see ourselves and others as integral parts of a world greater than the sum of its parts and to see that we are all inescapably co-creators of this world.

On one front this book is an exercise in integration, which necessitates straining somewhat to bring so many apparently disparate and specialised areas into coherence. But the risks of appearing foolish are minor in comparison to the rewards of more meaningfully, expansively and engagingly framing our great story – and catalysing new perspectives on an ideally greater future.

CO-CREATING THE WORLD

Upon setting out on this journey towards a new metanarrative it is fruitful to grapple with our current condition and dilemmas, to ask how we can speak of a 'world *we* create'. How is it you and I – mere points in a sea of rising and falling expectations, conventions, laws and the worldviews they spring from – can dare to create the world? A better world? Are we not on a planet more crowded, confusing, rapidly paced and chaotic than ever before? Doesn't our impending reckoning with uncontrollable forces such as climate change, nationalism, inequality and ever more advanced technologies preclude such creative optimism?

I argue it does not. Indeed, it must not. The very same issues above also carry great rewards for us all, should we see them from a more comprehensive perspective and act on their promise. In order to see why, we will chart the history of our Universe, our evolution, our thinking and our becoming, right up to our present predicaments. I wish to show how we have not only faced similarly dire challenges before, but that our ability to overcome them when they appear most critical is what makes us human in the first place. In appreciating this, we can look towards enhancing our agency as we have done many times before – to become co-creators of a world we want, not just one we stumble into.

The world is a vast interacting system of unfathomable complexity and chaotic processes that may appear way beyond our influence as individuals or collective. As contemporary co-creators it can thus seem as if we barely hold the creative force needed to act at all, let alone with poise, form and confidence. However, the world – the world that *we* create – has always been bewilderingly complex, breathtakingly chaotic and inescapably destined to develop along trajectories we cannot unchoose. But at the same time the world is vividly ours. We cannot control or steer, but we can – and every day do – influence this complex process in different directions. We do have choices. We do need to make choices and exercise both individual and – even more difficult – collective agency.

This book is therefore a book about systems and systems thinking. About different kinds of interconnected dynamic complex systems acting on different time scales and with completely different properties and makeup. And still all interconnected and interdependent. We will be studying systems on a *personal level*, on a *collective level* and on a *universal level* and be interested in how they interact and relate to each other and what tools we need to develop in order to understand them.

This book is also about our human place amongst these systems and our individual and collective ability – and responsibility – to influence the development of these systems: to influence the development of ourselves and our world. It is important to understand that this is not a question of choosing between influencing these systems or not. We *are* influencing all these systems daily, whether we are aware of it or not. We live in the Anthropocene. It is now time that we become aware.

This book has thus arisen from a seeker's intuition. It probes expansive questions, skirting the horizons of our tentative understandings, with an eye towards systemic change. This need for change – and a constant questing for not only more accurate, but also more fruitful answers – drives much of the inquiry in this book. It is in the service of shaking the reader's perhaps well-worn perspectives in a productive fashion that our history is followed from the Big Bang to the present – hopefully carried with enough conceptual drama and empirical evidence to draw the reader into a coherent and vivid narrative about the developmental processes leading to the world of today that convincingly unveils the reader's role and agency in the one of tomorrow.

The developmental junctures throughout human history, evolutionary leaps in a way, have often been the result of our own decisive responses to overwhelming odds.

It is high time for another.

But before we move on to the Big Bang and the evolution of the Universe, of life and of consciousness, a few key concepts used throughout this book to understand the development of systems deserve an introduction: chaos, complexity, self-organisation and emergent phenomena.

ORDER AND CHAOS

The human mind relentlessly attempts to make sense of our highly complex and chaotic world by searching for neatly ordered patterns amidst the messy reality we encounter. 'Order and chaos shape all our attempts to understand our world,' the historian David Christian has argued, 'in part because we are built to see complex structures.'[1] Hence, order manifests itself in our mental world through an innate instinct for pattern recognition. Our capacity to determine the regularities of risks and chances, where there is likely to be danger and where we might find opportunities, has been vital for our survival and thus been refined to ever-greater sophistication by evolutionary pressures. Order helps us define structures and events and to make realistic expectations. Order is what we can say to understand, the things we can explain, what makes sense to us.

Chaos, on the other hand, applies to everything else. Often, it is likened to the primordial, undifferentiated whole; the teeming, terrifying everything that precedes our naming and boxing off. Chaos is all of that which we perceive as devoid of form or pattern, the irregularities we cannot predict, the things beyond our mental grasp that mystify us and appear irreversibly foggy to our prying, limited perspectives. Of course, what is seen as chaos depends on the perspective. As David Christian puts it, 'any definition of chaotic behaviour depends on the scale of inquiry. Phenomena which at a lower level of analysis appear to be chaotic may display more order when viewed from a higher, more all-embracing perspective.'[2] Historically, intellectual progress has therefore been characterised by new perspectives from where order has become visible in what previously appeared as chaos. The branch of mathematics known as 'chaos theory' that made it possible to formally study complex phenomena that could not be accounted for with the traditional tools of science has thus been a continuation of this development towards making order out of chaos.

Chaos theory largely revolves around creating models to make sense of seemingly random occurrences by identifying how they comport with underlying universal patterns. These models can be applied to a wide array of complex chaotic systems, such as the weather, the market, neural networks, etc., whose behaviour cannot be predicted with linear models of cause and effect due to the high complexity of such systems. Chaos theory emphasises that even the smallest initial condition can lead to widely diverging outcomes, the so-called 'butterfly effect' (the notion that the flapping of a butterfly's wings in one part of the world with time can lead to a chain of events causing a tornado in another part). The behaviour of complex chaotic systems is in theory fully determined by their initial conditions, but the impossible task of taking all of these into consideration makes a linear conception highly inadequate at predicting future outcomes since all the chains of cause and effect determining the behaviour cannot be accounted for. Complex chaotic systems are therefore only chaotic to the extent that they in practice remain unpredictable, which is sometimes referred to as 'deterministic chaos'.[3] In theory, no random occurrences affect their behaviour.

Chaos theory cannot provide us the same kind of solid predictions about chaotic systems that traditional scientific methods can about more linearly observable systems. But the attention to how initial conditions, even the most minuscule, potentially can affect chaotic systems, may (with the help of a wide array of sophisticated non-linear mathematical tools pertaining to feedback loops, attractors, fractals and other complicated inquires) give us a better understanding of the *possible* trajectories along which they may unfold.

So, despite its name, chaos theory is not so much a theory about chaos as it is a way to find subtle strands of order in what only on the surface appears chaotic and entirely unpredictable.

* * *

Chaos is key to understanding how complexity emerges and develops, as we will see in the following sections and the next chapter, and thus deserves an appreciation that might strike the reader as somewhat detached from their usual expectations of chaos. But order and chaos, in diametric opposition, should be recast by our highest faculties. Just as in the sciences, we should feel confident in finding order in chaos, and indeed, the necessity for chaos to feed into and renew our orders. It is through patterns ordered across space and time that we see the emergence of highly complex phenomena such as life, consciousness and culture. Their order over time and space is qualified in chaotic environments, and it is from this multifaceted interplay that complexity arises.

Complexity: The Third Scientific Revolution

The study of complexity can according to the physicist and systems scientist Yaneer Bar-Yam be seen as the investigation of 'how relationships between parts give rise to the collective behaviors of a system and how the system interacts and forms relationships with its environment.'[4] As such, it is not a field like that of chemistry or biology, studying a delimitated area of reality, but more like a method that can be used in a number of different areas of inquiry. In a way, it is, as Neil Johnson has described it, an 'umbrella science', or a 'science about sciences'.[5]

There is no commonly agreed-upon definition of the term 'complexity', but it is generally used to describe something with many diverse parts interacting with each other in varying and distinct patterns. The term is also used as a measure of development, to define how complex a certain structure is in relation to another. It is important to note that 'complexity' should not be confused with 'complicated'. Roughly speaking, 'complexity' refers to qualitative aspects (the particular ways things are ordered), 'complicated' merely quantitative ones (the number of things in interaction with each other). Complex structures can be recognised by their ordered structures, like that of a piece of fabric. If it is more like 'spaghetti', then we should not use the term 'complex'.

The scientist and mathematician Warren Weaver argued that complexity can be seen as a 'third scientific revolution'.[6] The first revolution was that of *mechanics*, now referred to as 'classical mechanics', which made it possible to study the linear relations we know from Newton's equations. (Note that when I talk about linearity it not only refers to what in mathematics is known as 'linear functions', it even includes exponential functions. On a logarithmic scale the latter can actually be plotted as a linear increase.)[7] Classical mechanics studies that which with certainty occurs (a rock falls to the ground when dropped, a still billiard ball will move when hit by another, etc.). *Statistics* (or statistical mechanics) brought the second revolution about by facilitating the study of complicated chemical processes by adding up a large number of likely events. This method also proved very useful in the social sciences and can be used to determine the probability of everything from dying in a car crash to winning the lottery. The third revolution of complexity is the study of the dazzlingly unpredictable that occurs all the same, like the emergence of life forms, a category 5 hurricane, a new thought perspective, etc. Such events cannot be predicted linearly or statistically since their emergence is determined by factors that will never enter such models.

The roots of complexity science can be traced back to the 1950s with cybernetics' attempt to understand self-organisation and the research of chaos theory, that it is closely associated with, in the 1960s and '70s. In 1984 a major step was taken when the Santa Fe Institute was founded, which has now become a world centre for complexity research. Salient for the success of this research area has been the access to increasingly powerful and cheap computers. Through data-simulations we can now better understand the dynamics of complex and chaotic phenomena such as meteorological developments, financial markets, or neural networks like our brains.

The order we fail to perceive in such chaotic systems with more linear conceptions can from a complexity perspective reveal patterns we otherwise would not have considered. This can improve our knowledge of a wide selection of poorly understood phenomena and thereby has the potential to function as a bridge between many different scientific disciplines. It is thus a telling sign that Stephen Hawking a few years ago in a newspaper interview said, 'I believe that this century will be the century of complexity science.'[8] Truth be told, I am inclined to agree with him.

Simple, Complicated, Complex and Chaotic Systems

The area of inquiry in complexity science can be said to lie somewhere between the seemingly opposite poles of order and chaos. This can be illustrated in the following diagram:

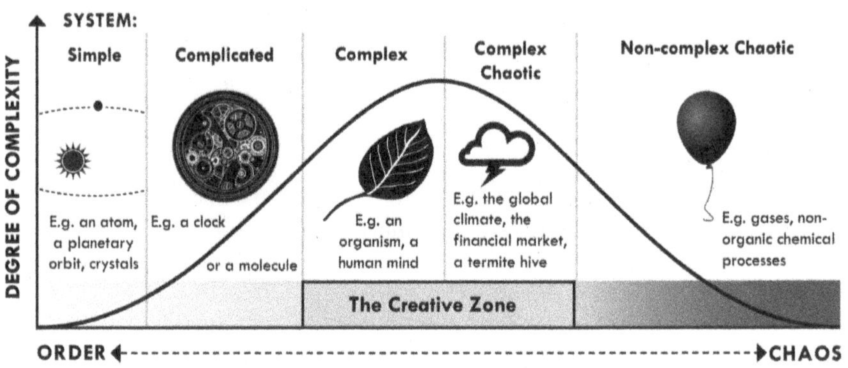

Various types of systems. From simple to chaotic.

Simple systems consist of simple, linear cause and effect connections that can be accounted for by classical mechanics. *Complicated systems* are a little harder to study with such methods, but they can be analysed linearly by studying each part in isolation and then investigating how they are connected. This has traditionally been where natural science has functioned best. Newton's great contribution was to take the complicated solar system and divide up the movements of the planets into simple linear relations through a number of reductions. He assumed the Sun had such a large mass compared to the planets that we could disregard their mutual gravitational influence and see the system as a simple two-body problem. Newton thus reduced a complicated system to a couple of simple systems that can be easily grasped mathematically. And in contrast to many other such reductionist attempts, this one worked fairly well. It most often works to the fifth decimal place.

Ever since Newton, much of science has revolved around picking apart and reducing complicated systems to simple, linear relations. This makes them easier to work with and fit into mathematical equations. But physics would quite soon discover that there were many phenomena that refused to be reduced in this way. *Non-complex systems* like gases or non-organic chemical processes, for example, consist of large agglomerations of atoms or molecules that move and interact with each other rather randomly. Studying all the individual particles' movements is impossible, so the solution was then to treat the problem statistically. However, when we want to study seemingly randomly behaving phenomena with more complex patterns than those of simple agglomerations of gases or chemical processes statistics do not suffice, and neither is it meaningful to reduce these to simple systems. This is where chaos theory and complexity science enter the picture.

Complex systems differ from complicated ones by being more open. A clock is a relatively closed system. Apart from its source of energy, whether that is kinetic or electrical, its parts interact with each other without any influence from the outside. Complex systems, on the other hand, are in a constant interplay with their surroundings. An organism can only maintain its structure by a continuous exchange of matter and energy between itself and its environment. This makes it more complex than a clock since there are more factors to consider, and also more unpredictable. Although it is impossible to account for all of these factors, the processes that occur do behave in accordance with a number of rules relating to the organism's attempt to maintain its overall structure, or a 'will' to survive if you like. These rules can be used to predict its actions within a certain margin of probability, or at least narrow down the number of possible outcomes we should consider.

Such rules, however, do not apply to complex systems such as the weather, the global market and other similarly decentralised systems since they do not contain a regulatory core of self-maintenance dictating every part to preserve its structure. The overarching structure in these systems is merely the result of the sum of all the individual components' agency and their mutual interactions. To differentiate the two kinds of complex systems I have chosen a separate term for the latter: *complex chaotic systems* (but for brevity I will just use 'chaotic systems').

The terms 'complex system' and 'chaotic system' are often used interchangeably, and rarely is any analytic distinction made between what I refer to as 'complex chaotic systems' and 'complex systems'. Financial markets and organisms are commonly treated as the same type of systems, but I believe it is important to differentiate between the two. So keep in mind that the distinction here is not common practice.

The fundamental difference is, as mentioned, that a complex system has a regulatory centre of agency that governs all of its constituent parts. Chaotic systems have no such centre. Although both types of systems should be seen as wholes greater than the sum of their parts, *how* they are wholes differ. A human being, for example, is not just a whole in the way its constituent cells give rise to a body, but something else: namely its *consciousness*. It is therefore erroneous to compare the way human beings give rise to the greater whole of a society with that of cells in an organism. The behaviour of the cells in an organism are governed in a deliberate manner by a higher-level faculty, which even has created them with the sole purpose to maintain the overall system. And if the system disintegrates (dies), so do the cells. A society, however, cannot be said to create its inhabitants just as little as it can be said that the only purpose of each and every individual is to serve the interests of the system (ideally, it should be the other way around). They have their own personal agency and goals, which often can be in direct opposition to that of society. And if a society collapses, its former citizens can continue to live outside it. For this reason, a human constitutes a centrally governed and self-maintaining whole with an agency in a way a society does not. In contrast to complex systems, chaotic systems contain many *independent* self-regulated entities acting according to, often surprisingly, simple rules that generate greater systemic patterns.[9]

Chaotic systems are also less rigid and more open than complex ones. A complex system cannot deviate too much from a certain order without breaking completely apart. A few disruptions to an organism's order are often enough to kill it. Chaotic systems can on the other hand take a number of forms and still remain a coherent system. In this way they can be said to be more chaotic than a complex system since there are simply so many ways it can organise itself and still remain a whole. Paradoxically, however, the chaotic systems are from the perspective of chaos theory simultaneously more deterministic (in theory, that is, as mentioned before), since there is nothing but the initial conditions to affect its outcome. So even though the complex systems appear to have fewer possible trajectories due to their more rigid structure, their higher-level agency in terms of a self-maintaining centre makes their behaviour impossible to predict since this governing whole cannot be inferred from any of its parts, not even in theory.[10]

Self-organisation and Emergent Phenomena

The structure of chaotic systems emerges through a process known as 'self-organisation' that is the result of the way their individual components (in human systems we usually talk about agents), in accordance with sets of rules determining their responses, interact with each other and the environment. The properties of the system as a whole emerge through the sum of all the components' individual and largely autonomous actions without any centrally governed coordinating mechanism.

A good example is how ants build a nest: Each ant acts according to very simple rules and has no idea of the big picture, but together they create a system with many functions that manifests itself as an ant colony. Similarly, a flock of birds has a pace, a form, density and direction that does not exist in any of the individual birds. Instead, the fluctuating structure of the flock arises from the simple behavioural rules each bird, each component, acts in accordance with. The dynamics of the market is similarly the result of such mechanisms. No one makes any conscious decisions about how it shall behave on the overarching level. There is no plan, but this does not mean that the market is aimless. The sum of all the objectives each and every agent pours into the system propels it in a certain, chaotically deterministic direction.

The entire world is an ocean of complex systemic synergies arising from the individual behaviour of countless parts acting in accordance with simple rules that only on the overarching level take on chaotic properties. From the simple behaviour of trillions of individual particles in the atmosphere giving rise to volatile weather phenomena, over evolutionary pressures in ecosystems causing erratic fluctuations in animal populations, to the millions of buyers and sellers who generate the ever-changing dynamics of the market forces daily; everywhere it is a question of synergies that continually form and self-organise themselves into chaotic – but not random – patterns.

However, once in a while something truly unpredictable happens when a chaotic system spontaneously organises itself in a way that suddenly gives it novel properties that cannot be deduced from studying the properties and past behaviour of the system, nor from any of its components – 'surprises', so to speak. Hereby the system has transformed itself into a new – *emergent* – phenomenon, an entirely new order of existence.

Historically we have found it hard to imagine such a spontaneous, emergent genesis, and it has been convenient to bundle it up with a God – or an invisible hand – as an organising principle. However, today we have the prerequisites to understand how self-organising processes can bring about emergent phenomena without involving anything magical or seeing them as extremely accidental coincidences. There is nothing strange at all, neither a mysterious force of creation, nor an equally enigmatic randomness. When an emergent phenomenon of higher-level complexity is brought into existence, it is simply because ever more varying units in increasing numbers interact and develop increasingly varying relations and patterns. These new relations and patterns can in turn – propelled by order and chaos – form emergent phenomena on a higher level of complexity, which function in accordance to other rules than those governing the system's components or the preceding lower-level state.[11]

Every emergent phenomenon exhibits behaviours that cannot be deduced from its components. In fact, emergence is *defined* as the spontaneous occurrence of new systemic properties that cannot be found in those of the emergent system's individual components. Only when a 'surprise' like this occurs that cannot be predicted from the rules governing the behaviour of the systems' components can we talk about an emergent phenomenon. As the evolutionary biologist Ernst Mayr has argued, '[chaotic] systems almost always have the peculiarity that the characteristics of the whole cannot (not even in theory) be deduced from the most complete knowledge of the components, taken separately or in other partial combinations. This appearance of new characteristics in wholes has been designated as *emergence*.'[12] So whereas the behaviour of chaotic systems in theory is deterministic according to chaos theory, complexity science adds the crucial exception that this does not apply when they give rise to emergence. A new level of complexity is always the result of such non-deterministic events since the emergent whole they bring about cannot be deduced from that which gives rise to it.

What constitutes an emergent whole is also how we can distinguish one level of complexity from another. But without a clear conception of the qualitative aspects of developmental complexity we can easily draw erroneous conclusions. The conventions of our language permit us to talk about a phenomenon being more complex than another in purely quantitative terms and to the degree we can comprehend them, for example when we say that a large computer system is very complex and the fly disturbing us while we try figuring out how it works is a rather simple creature. But this is not a meaningful way of using this term in a developmental fashion. Given its properties of being an organism, the fly, buzzing around in simple patterns (that we may quickly decipher, so as to disintegrate it into its molecular components and carry on our work), belongs to a higher *level* of complexity than the computer.

Scale should not be used to determine the level of complexity either. The entire Universe may due to its sheer size appear vastly more complex than an ant, but the latter belongs to a higher level of complexity than any of the structures of the former which only consist of inorganic matter. This is because the ant just like the fly constitutes a whole that gives it emergent properties that are nowhere to be found in the inanimate world. The ant contains the qualitative levels of complexity of atoms and molecules since it is made of these components, but it also contains additional complexity in virtue of being an organic creature. In a similar fashion a molecule is more complex than an atom because it contains all the properties of the atom *and* additional complexity from the particular order of its atomic components.[13]

It is important to stress the term 'deduced' when we say such linear inferences cannot tell us anything about the properties that emerge on a higher level of complexity. If we accept a reductionist approach it is not conceptually invalid to say that complex structures consist of nothing but their parts, but it is theoretically incorrect that we can deduce the properties of an emergent phenomenon from its parts. It simply remains to be seen how even the best knowledge about the properties of atoms alone can predict the behaviour of a molecule or how we can use chemistry to predict those of an organism. The notion that everything 'fundamentally' is made of nothing but subatomic particles is therefore as simple-mindedly reductionist as it is theoretically inadequate. Being an expert on particle physics will not help us explain how air particles can form tornados, how carbohydrates and amino acids can assemble into life forms, or how neurons can bring about poetry and algebra. These are all phenomena whose emergence cannot be deduced from the components giving rise to them, and neither can the former be reduced to the latter. And if we wish to give a comprehensive explanation of a human being, accounting for the biological processes of each and every body part and how they are connected simply does not suffice since humans belong to a level of complexity above that of biology. We remain organic creatures, just as much as humans and single-cell organisms remain chemical processes, but we are also something more than this. We are cultural beings. We are interdependent systems within larger systems within an interconnected whole.

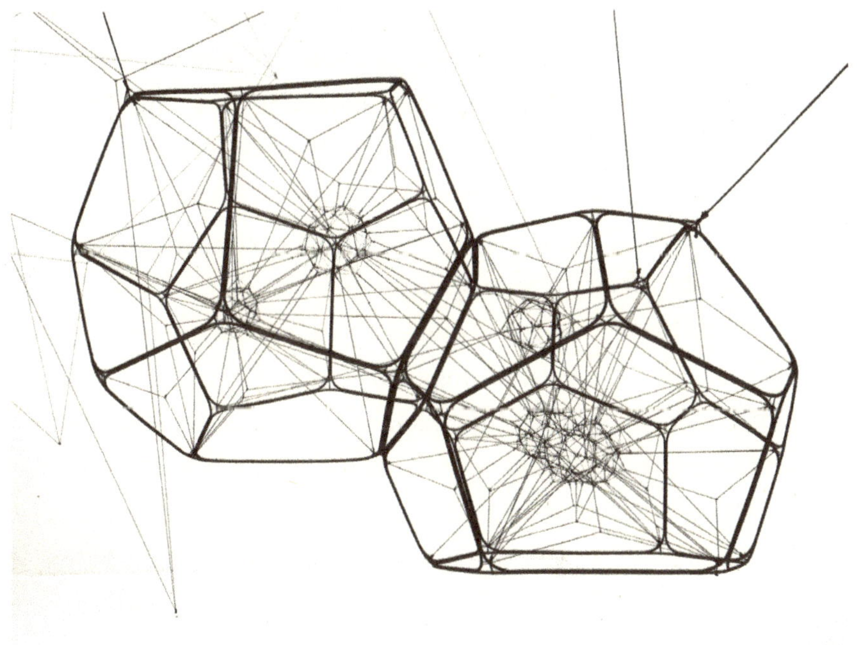

Systems within interconnected systems. Installation by the Argentinean artist Tomás Saraceno, San Francisco Museum of Modern Art, 2017. Photo by author.

* * *

A holistic and developmental picture thus arises from complexity. While it might have been apparent to many that sociology makes little sense collapsed into particle physics, a prejudice for physics remains apparent in many other fields. This 'physics envy', the result of a desire to reduce and analyse (literally, break down into constituent parts), can lead us astray in dismissing fields of inquiry that originate from higher levels of subtler and subtler emergence. Complexity science helps to formalise the intuitions that something is missing from a purely reductionist account, and gives us the immense advantage of a rigorous global level of analysis; that is, one that takes the whole and engages its behaviours, structures and dynamic synergies in their own right, without attempting to crush them into the strictures of more 'fundamental' disciplines.

From a perspective of chaos and complexity, we can commence a paradigm shift away from the one-eyed focus on analysis and reduction, but without getting mired in a converse narrow focus on mere holism and synthesis which tends to overlook specifics. With this way of thinking we can place ourselves somewhere in between the components and the entirety, the particular and the universal, and realise the beauty in the diversity that thrives on the edge of chaos.

A perspective of and from complexity is needed to comprehend patterns manageably, amidst an impossibly large picture. In a globally distributed, economically and informationally connected civilisation like ours, finding patterns we could not otherwise see might not only be useful for purely material gains, it may even prove essential for the transition to a new – and hopefully more graciously endowed – thought perspective.

Humanity's adaptability, and the speed with which our thinking can follow the dynamics of complex systems on the edge of chaos, give us more than hope for change. They allow us to comprehend and consciously consider our direction and, as part of a natural and flowing world around us, swim in life-giving currents of growth.

PART 1

The Great Thought Perspectives

INTRODUCTION TO PART 1

Throughout history, the ever-increasing complexity of the world has repeatedly prompted us to revise our understanding of reality, the intellectual tools we use to make sense of it and the narratives at the core of our culture. Mostly, the alterations we make to our intellectual tools and symbol systems are merely piecemeal adjustments to accommodate a few analytic incongruities here and a couple of societal changes there. But every now and then the many small changes add up and reach a tipping point in which even our most central symbol systems, the overarching metanarrative, appear utterly out of tune with current reality. Historically, this has often coincided with what I call a phase transition, or a paradigm shift, to a new *thought perspective.*

A 'thought perspective' is the overarching, foundational view of the world that shapes more or less our entire way of thinking: how we interpret symbolic and sensory information, including our own thoughts, what kinds of narratives we tell ourselves about the world; how we relate to others, how we organise society, how we work, even how we have sex. A thought perspective is the glue that holds our inner world of symbols together and gives them meaning.

You can think of a thought perspective as the frame through which we collectively make our worldviews cohere. Others would perhaps make do with simply calling them worldviews, but for me it is not only about *seeing* the world in a certain way. It is just as much about *how* and *what* we can think. Thought perspectives contain symbol tools – updated 'software' for our brain – that enable us to *think* in new ways.

'Paradigm' is another term that may appear closely analogous to 'thought perspective', and it remains a useful one I sometimes use in my talks since most people already know the word. It would not be incorrect to refer to a thought perspective as a paradigm, but since everything that can be described as a paradigm is not the same as what I mean when I talk about thought perspectives, I concluded it would be better to use a separate term. To be more specific: in this book, thought perspective refers to one of four different developmentally dependent, overarching ways of thinking. They are as follows:

- The *animist* thought perspective: Emerged *c.* 50,000 years ago during the Stone Age. Characterised by animistic and magical beliefs, an occupation with a spirit world and no differentiation between physical and mental reality. Still present among some indigenous populations today.
- The *religious or pre-modern* thought perspective: Emerged *c.* 800 BCE at different locations across the central axis of Eurasia, in some aspects as early as 2000 BCE in Egypt and Mesopotamia, but to its fullest extent only blossoming after 500 CE with the consolidation of the great moral religions such as Christianity, Islam or Buddhism. Characterised by transcendental ideas of salvation, divine law and the rationalisation of mythology in accordance with universal theological principles. Still dominant in many developing countries and in certain areas of the West.
- The *rational* or *modern* thought perspective: Emerged *c.* 1500 CE in Europe during the Renaissance, but in some aspects in its proto-variant as early as 500 BCE in Greece. Blossoming only in the nineteenth and twentieth centuries. Characterised by rationalistic and scientific thought, notions of progress and material growth, emancipation of the individual from arbitrary religious and

political control, and human rights and democracy. Remains the most dominant thought perspective today.

- The *postmodern* thought perspective: Emerged in the twentieth century in the West, though some aspects appeared in the late eighteenth century. Characterised by a critique of rationalism, progress and established power relations, concerns with issues such as the environment, gender and race, and a highly relativistic and pluralistic perspective. Yet to fully blossom and become the most dominant, but highly influential in much of intellectual life in the West today and particularly common among the educated classes.

As you can see, a thought perspective is a category both distinct from and containing what we usually refer to as worldviews or paradigms, i.e.: Christians and Muslims arguably have different worldviews, but both see the world from the religious thought perspective; Newtonian and Einsteinian physics remain two different scientific paradigms, but both belong to the rational thought perspective. In this way, you can think of thought perspectives as a kind of 'meta-paradigms'.

So, when I use the term 'thought perspective', I only refer to one of these four and a future fifth one to be presented in Chapter 13. This, however, does not mean that I reject that it could make sense to add a few others, or that we can talk about certain in-between phases.

Although they may overlap to some degree, more or less every adult person on the planet can be said to adhere to one of these thought perspectives, and there is no society where one of these is not the most dominant. This, however, does not mean that all of humanity uniformly sees the world from one of only four perspectives, or that everyone adhering to the same thought perspective thinks alike. Despite the homogenising effects of globalisation, there still remains a vast multitude of different *symbol worlds* that give every culture its own unique views, values and habits of thought.

The term 'symbol world' is used for the more localised symbol systems of different religious affiliations, national cultures, scientific communities and so on. Both thought perspectives and symbol worlds are *symbol systems*, but whereas 'thought perspective' refers to a developmentally determined way of thinking and acting that follows a particular logic at a certain level of societal complexity, transcending all cultures if they reach this level, 'symbol world' refers to the specific symbol systems that we are all conceptually and culturally situated within by the particular community, or communities, we are part of. The emergence of thought perspectives is deterministic in the way they are shaped by how thought itself is structured. This gives them universal properties that with necessity appear when certain conditions are present. Symbol worlds largely emerge from random historical developments that can shape the specific languages, aesthetic traditions, customs and other features of a community in a number of unique and particularistic ways.

So even though the symbol worlds of different societies around the world are overlapping more and more in our globalised age, Britons and Japanese people, for example, can still be said to live within two very different symbol worlds. This often makes it challenging for these people to understand each other. Yet the fundamental way of thinking, the metanarrative pertaining to each culture (market-liberal democracy, scientific inquiry, secular, etc.), is largely identical in Britain and Japan. Both are modern countries where the rational thought perspective is dominant. Persons from Britain and India may communicate more easily (given the countries' shared colonial past), but the former will usually have more in common with someone from Japan in terms of reasoning, values and attitudes since the religious thought perspective still remains the most dominant in India. The degree to which our symbol worlds overlap may thus determine how well we can have meaningful dialogues, but the thought perspective we adhere to is more crucial to our thinking and behaviour.

* * *

The emergence and development of thought perspectives is a central theme in this book, and it has largely been written from a conviction that we currently are at a critical phase transition from one thought perspective to another. But as history teaches us, such developments are highly unpredictable – especially if we do not come to grips with the peculiar dynamics between determinism and chance, order and chaos.

Chapter 1

FROM THE BIG BANG TO HOMO SAPIENS

Our Universe is a merciless place. It is governed by a law-bound force exerting a destructive tendency that over time breaks down all physical structures, creating chaos out of order. Scientists call it 'the second law of thermodynamics'. Simultaneously, a complementary self-organising tendency, determined by strange chaos mechanics, constantly gives rise to locally increasing order and complexity, thus creating order out of chaos. Chaos and order are the core of the evolutionary processes that have brought everything into being and, eventually, will break everything apart. Things are born, they die, and from the destruction of one sort of order, new orders are born in a continuous process towards locally higher levels of complexity.

The human being and its mind are results of this cosmic evolutionary creation process. We are the most complex entity we know of to have emerged from the Universe's propensity towards self-organisation. Mind arose from organic matter, which emerged from complex chemical compounds, which again was the result of physical processes that began before matter, space and time even existed as distinguishable entities. All the way from atoms, to molecules, to organic cells, to thinking creatures such as ourselves – pondering how it's all connected, and stubbornly asking what it's all good for – we see a developmental process of self-organisation towards higher levels of complexity where each step is intimately related to each other.

We are thus all the result of events that can be stated in terms of physics, chemistry and biology. However, to understand the human being we cannot solely rely on the explanatory models provided by the natural sciences. The human being is a creature of such high complexity that we need qualitatively different symbol systems to grasp it such as psychology, anthropology and sociology. Yet, we should still include the biological, physicochemical and astronomical aspects in our creation story if we want to understand who we really are.

I thus propose that we go beyond the 'intellectual apartheid' that prevails between the natural and human sciences, and that we approach the human being and its culture and society from a perspective that goes all the way back to the birth of the Universe. History from this grandest perspective of all can help us put our anthropocentric notions aside so that we can obtain a more universal and comprehensive perspective on reality, history and ourselves. This can enable us to see how the physical and cosmological processes that began with the Big Bang follow general evolutionary principles that also apply to how we as persons and how we collectively as societies develop.

In fact, we will through the book be moving back and forth between three scales of evolution and development: the *personal scale*, the *collective scale* and the *universal, cosmic scale.*

THE BIG BANG AND THE UNIVERSAL EVOLUTION

We begin our story on the *universal scale* with the Big Bang almost 14 billion years ago. This is as far back as we can trace and imagine the world. From a single point of extreme density and heat, where space, time and matter still do not exist as separate dimensions, this primordial state suddenly expands at an astronomical speed. During the first milliseconds, the smallest components of matter emerge, elementary particles that soon thereafter form the first atomic nuclei, which around 400,000 years later start to bind electrons so as to form the very first simple atoms: hydrogen and helium. Something new and more complex is thus born from something less complex; an *emergent phenomenon* whose whole is more than the mere sum of its parts.

An atom is namely not just a bundle of elementary particles and electrons. It has new properties (e.g. mass, malleability, boiling point) that did not exist in any of its constituents prior to forming the atom.

The emergence of more complex structures from less complex ones has characterised the evolution of the Universe ever since the Big Bang: from elementary particles, to atoms, to molecules and finally to organic cells. At every stage in this continuous development towards higher complexity, each emergent phenomenon brings novel properties into existence that cannot be predicted, deduced from or reduced to what came before[1] – 'surprises', so to speak.

So what causes this to happen? One of the driving forces behind the Universe's propensity towards self-organisation is *gravity*. Around 400 million years after the Big Bang, enormous clouds of matter begin coalescing under the force of gravity. What emerges are, however, not just dense balls of atoms, but yet another emergent phenomenon: stars.

As gravity pulls atoms increasingly closer together, the pressure and heat in the centre goes up and eventually reach a point where the simple hydrogen atoms fuse into heavier and more complex helium atoms. This is an emergent property of stars that could not have been deduced from or be reduced to an individual atom.

The Universe was a very dark place prior to this. But the fusion process generates a residual product in the form of radiation – light – which is thrust into the Cosmos. The emergence of fusion also gives rise to higher complexity on a smaller scale. Many of the first stars are very large, much larger than our sun. Accordingly, the gravitational pressure and the heat they produce are also much higher, which make the fusion process faster than in smaller stars. Consequently, the gigantic stars run out of hydrogen more rapidly, which makes them collapse under their own weight. When this happens, pressure and heat increase drastically, causing the remaining matter to fuse into even heavier and more complex atoms, such as oxygen, carbon, iron, and many of the other elements we know from the periodic table. The outburst of energy from this process is so great that the star eventually explodes into what we call a supernova. The newly formed complex atoms are thus ejected far into space along with residues of hydrogen and helium.

This is where we find the origins of our solar system. Some 4.6 billion years ago, a huge cloud of debris from an ancient supernova begins to contract, which from the shockwave of another supernova nearby triggers the process leading to the formation of our sun. The sun makes up about 99.9% of all matter in our solar system; the remaining 0.1% belongs to its eight orbiting planets and other smaller objects in the solar system. Matter blasted out from the early formation of the Sun coalesces into these planets shortly after the Sun's formation. The lighter materials end up farther away from the Sun, forming the large gas planets such as Jupiter and Saturn, while the heavier materials end up closer to it, forming the rocky planets such as Venus, Mars and our own planet, Earth. Once again something more complex has emerged.

Yet gravity is not the only early source of complexity in the Universe. The effects described by quantum mechanics also play a decisive role. Without going into further detail on this complicated branch of physics, it suffices to emphasise the major discovery of quantum mechanics, namely that subatomic particles behave quite irregularly. This had a crucial effect on how complex patterns formed after the Big Bang. Because subatomic particles behave rather chaotically, they did not spread out evenly along a deterministic and linear course but varied slightly in their individual trajectories and thereby ended up at different distances from each other. Though minor at first, the irregularities on the smaller scale thus shaped the overall structure of the Universe by forming higher densities of particles in some areas and lower in others. With the expansion of the Universe, the empty space that appears between matter is therefore rather asymmetrical, which makes it possible for the force of gravity to form points in space with higher complexity, and vast areas with no complexity at all: vacuum, empty space. In what appears to be a fundamental principle, complexity in one point is always the result of, or at the expense of, less complexity in another.

The after-effect of this asymmetrical expansion of the Universe can to this day be observed as the small temperature differences in the cosmic background radiation. This is a sign of the varying densities of particles in the early Universe from which stars and galaxies would later form. Accordingly, the cosmologist Max Tegmark has suggested that 'the cosmic microwave background is to cosmology what DNA is to biology'.[2]

The tiny temperature variances can be seen in this famous NASA image:

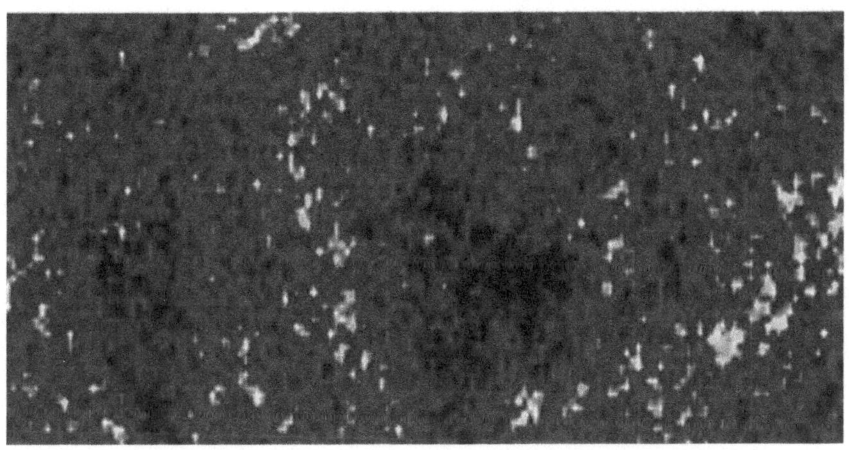

NASA's depiction of the cosmic background radiation – an image of the birth of the Universe.[3]

At first, the Universe is a hot and dense place in a state of near thermodynamic equilibrium, but as it expands and cools its initial symmetry is broken.[4] This is decisive. The breakdown of symmetry is crucial for the transition towards higher levels of complexity precisely because complexity is characterised by being non-symmetrical. In a completely symmetrical Universe, no further complexity than a uniform cloud of particles would be able to form. Had it not been for the random behaviour of particles described by quantum mechanics, the Universe would merely consist of a homogeneous soup of hydrogen and helium atoms. A uniform gravitational field simply would not have had anything 'to work with', so to speak. However, because the irregularity of subatomic particles made them bounce around space in a slightly uneven manner following the Big Bang, over time these initial minuscule irregularities added up so as to form greater density in some points and less in others. From here, gravity begins to draw matter even closer together which eventually leads to the formation of stars, galaxies and finally planets such as our own Earth.

It may appear as if complexity is predetermined, but the irony is that complexity is the result of the Universe not being *entirely* predetermined. The point is, while everything is predetermined on the larger scale (objects in space move in conformity with regularities that can be accurately predicted with mathematical models), it is the other way around on the smaller scale, where individual particles' behaviour is quite chaotic and therefore not entirely possible to predict. The dynamic between these two sides of physical reality is the basis for all further development and complexity. In addition, it also says something about development and history in general: our world is inherently chaotic and it is impossible to predict everything, but at the same time there appear to be regularities and patterns that determine the overall course – the difficulty is to differentiate the two when we want to make sound predictions about where it's all going.

* * *

This world of star systems and physical matter is a world that I am very familiar with. Before I started my career as a finance entrepreneur, I studied particle physics during the 1980s in Uppsala and wrote my Master's thesis at the University of Sussex on mathematical models for medium-heavy atomic nuclei. It is a world of objective parameters such as mass and speed. This is a perspective that is highly suited to experiments and one that can be described in elegant mathematical formulae

– so elegant indeed that physics for a long time was the science that all other sciences tried to imitate.

However, physics cannot explain all there is to the world. In the Milky Way there are no social constructions such as money, matrimony or countries. Nor are there consciousness, objectives or meaning – merely blind forces. But on a small planet in a distant part of one of the many billions of galaxies, a new emergent phenomenon has begun to develop that is so complex that it cannot be described in terms of physical processes alone. What happens here differs so radically from the physical processes to have occurred up to this point that we need to complement the scientific models we have used to describe the creation of the physical Universe with new symbolic language systems, such as chemistry and biology, to properly address the higher complexity at these stages.

LIFE'S BATTLE AGAINST ENTROPY

We now find ourselves on Earth around 4.5 billion years ago. This planet came to orbit its star at a close enough and adequately far distance to provide the optimal 'Goldilocks' conditions[5] for life. Here, it is neither too cold nor too hot for complexity to evolve further. However, Earth is not yet a hospitable place, but a semi-fluid hot mass that is slowly solidifying. Collisions with space materials bring with them important chemical elements from which the much later creation of plants, animals and humans can emerge. Frequently occurring volcanic eruptions make the surface of the Earth an even more inhospitable place, but they add gases to the atmosphere that are vital for all organic matter later on. The surface of Earth is still a crude and barren place, but in the sea, chemical processes are now occurring from which life will later arise. This new emergent phenomenon – life – is so different from anything before that it appears as if it almost breaks the laws of physics.

The nineteenth-century physicist Sadi Carnot made the discovery that energy never disappears, but just changes the forms in which it exists.[6]

This observation is the basis of the law of the conversation of energy, also known as 'the first law of thermodynamics', which states that energy can be transformed from one form to another, but that the total energy in an isolated system is constant. Energy itself is always conserved, so to speak. The *second* law of thermodynamics states that in closed systems, such as the Universe, the amount of *free* energy, the type of energy that can perform 'work', tends to dissipate over time. In closed systems, all energy differentials will sooner or later diminish. This leads to a Universe that is increasingly less ordered, less complex, as it moves towards a state of total thermodynamic equilibrium. At the same time there is a steady increase in the amount of unusable energy known as 'entropy', the radiation or heat we can observe by the aforementioned cosmic background radiation. The vast empty space that emerged and has continued to expand after the Big Bang has accordingly been described as a gigantic 'entropy dumping ground'.[7] The fact that the Universe is constantly expanding entails that it will become increasingly colder since the heat needs to spread out over an ever-larger area. So as the Universe is constantly moving towards equalising all heat differentials, it is thereby, in a way, 'dying' a slow heat death.

How closed systems over time move towards thermodynamic equilibrium can be observed by how a star has its greatest effect initially, only to later cool off. The same phenomenon can be seen in the way hot bathwater cools, for instance, or more generally in the way any amount of mass over time tends to acquire the same temperature as its surroundings after the initial influx of energy has ended. The second law of thermodynamics also applies to matter: biological entities are constantly battling the fate of being equalised and reduced to their atomic components. Without the constant influx of solar energy to the earth, no life could have developed.

Human societies are also subject to the destructive force of entropy. To keep these complex and highly asymmetrical structures from falling apart, a constant input of external energy, such as fuel and food, is needed. All complex entities depend on the continuity of energy differentials to fuel their asymmetrical structure, and they are all faced with the equalising tendency of the second law of thermodynamics, which will eventually dissolve them into their less complex constituents.

As such, it would seem as if the equalisation of all differentials in the long run would make the Universe less ordered, more chaotic. Entropy would go up while complexity would diminish. However, this is obviously not the case, as complexity evidently has increased locally consistently after the Big Bang. Somehow, the drive towards disorder creates novel forms of order. But how is this possible?

First of all, gravity ensures that matter is assembled in higher densities in certain parts of the Universe despite its constant expansion. The second reason is the peculiar way complex structures, especially organic ones, use energy. The second law of thermodynamics applies to all closed physical systems, but as the physicist Erwin Schrödinger pointed out in his influential book *What Is Life?*, it does not apply in the same way to the open systems that we call 'life'.[8] Obviously, all lifeforms cool off, or die, without any influx of energy from the outside. But since they are 'open systems' and have intricate mechanisms to take up energy from outside themselves they can thereby counter 'the arrow' of history and over time be built up instead of broken down. Complex structures therefore need a constant throughput of energy to help them 'climb entropy's remorseless down escalator';[9] and the higher the level of complexity, the more energy is required. Complex creatures like mammals require more energy than less complex ones like insects, and complex biological organs like brains likewise require more energy than other body parts. A human brain, the most complex entity we know of, is accordingly the most energy-consuming phenomenon in relation to size.[10] This principle also applies to human societies: Complex industrial societies require much more energy than simple farming societies. Without fossil fuel, or any equally powerful energy source, our society would grind to a halt. It thus appears as a general rule that the larger and the more complex a phenomenon, the greater the energy flows. As such, complex entities do not really counter the second law of thermodynamics, they actually speed up the process of entropy yet further. This seems to apply to all stages of complexity; the more complex, the faster the pace of entropy.

In this way there is an ironic twist to how life counters the ruthless law of entropy. Complex forms of lifeless matter, such as stars and planets, are in a dynamic steady state and tend to be very close to thermodynamic equilibrium because the energy needed to retain their structure is relatively limited. As such they generate entropy relatively slowly. But more complex entities such as life are in states much further from thermodynamic equilibrium.[11] Accordingly they need far more energy to maintain their highly asymmetrical structures. Being far from equilibrium is simply so demanding that higher energy throughputs are required, which also necessitates higher levels of entropy. In organisms, energy is processed at a much faster pace than in stars, which also entails that entropy is exuded at a faster pace in the former than the latter. To maintain its complexity, life in turn speeds up entropy by transforming high-quality energy forms into lower forms such as heat. On all levels of complexity this pattern unfolds. During every step in the energy chain – from the fusion process in the Sun, to photosynthesis in plants, and finally to the metabolism in animals and humans – ever more 'usable' energy is consumed and exuded into increasingly 'unusable' forms. The transformation of free energy into unusable forms of heat is much faster in stars than in clouds of space dust, and in biological creatures this process is even faster. Complexity thus speeds up the pace of which the second law of thermodynamics works towards its final destination: a Universe without order, a state of equilibrium where all free energy has been consumed and only a left-over in the form of cosmic background radiation remains.

What Is Life?

Life is such a decisive emergent phenomenon that it represents a transition from a less complex to a more complex level of development. Life acts in ways not observed in the physical (non-biological) Universe, and in accordance with new rules that cannot be deduced from what came before.

Instead of losing energy over time, as with stars and hot bathwater, living systems have the capacity to gather energy from the outside and thereby maintain and even increase their complexity. Life is therefore not merely a cluster of complex molecules to be described in terms of chemistry alone, it is something more. We now need new explanatory measures such as biology and the theory of evolution.

But what is life exactly? The Nobel prize-winning physicist Erwin Schrödinger famously stated that we cannot break it down to a checklist. Neither metabolism, reproduction nor any other specifics like these are sufficient to define life since we always end up with exceptions that can be observed elsewhere in the non-organic world. Instead, he argues that we should look at how life on the overall systemic level differs significantly from other phenomena, for instance how '[t]he unfolding of events in the life cycle of an organism exhibits an admirable regularity and orderliness, unrivalled by anything we meet with in inanimate matter'.[12] Accordingly, life is above all characterised by being *significantly* more complex than anything else in the known Universe.

It is fair to say that life constitutes a higher level of complexity due to the increased number and variety of building blocks, number of connections and interactions between them, and the sequencing of these constituents which far exceed anything else observed in the Universe. But there is more to life than its mere *quantitative* aspects in regard to complexity. We need to remember that what sets one stage apart from another is not only scale, but more crucially, that new rules and properties emerge on the higher level of complexity that cannot be deduced from its predecessor.

The foremost *qualitative* aspect is first of all that life must constantly tap into matter and energy flows from outside itself in order to exist and multiply. This is the newest addition to the game, so to speak. In extension of this, the capacity of life to deliberately maintain and further develop its complexity is another crucial distinction. Under the merciless circumstances of constantly having to find new sources of energy and survive the 'hurricane of energy flowing through them',[13] to quote David

Christian, organisms consistently come up with new ways of relating to their environment that lead to new levels of complexity with no parallel in the inanimate world. As mentioned, this also entails that living organisms produce entropy at a much faster pace. Whereas stars emit relatively little entropy in relation to size, and only in the form of radiation, organisms in comparison emit very high amounts of entropy in the form of heat, but, as something new, even in the form of matter. In order to maintain their complexity, biological organisms must extract matter from their surroundings, break it down, and release the excess materials into the environment. Plants produce relatively little material entropy, but animals produce a whole lot more in order to maintain their complex and energy-expensive muscles, brains and digestive systems. In organisms, entropy therefore not only takes the form of excess heat, it also takes the form of molecular disintegration of matter that would otherwise have taken much longer to occur. In organisms, molecules, such as carbon dioxide and carbon hydrates, are dissolved into their lesser components at a much faster rate than they would have been in an entirely sterile environment. Again, the higher complexity of life coincides with an acceleration of entropy.

More entropy is the price we pay for our complexity, and observations of lifeforms in relation to their level of complexity seem to confirm that higher levels always entail larger amounts of entropy. This has been supported by the astrophysicist Eric Chaisson, who has argued that the level of complexity of various entities, to some extent, is proportional to the level of energy flowing through them (and thus the capacity of the entity to sustain itself against the pressure of entropy), evident by measuring the free energy rate density in units of energy per time per mass.[14] It has been revealed that the power density of a plant is 450 times denser than that of the sun, a human body 10,000 times denser, and a human brain contains a power density roughly 75,000 times larger (again, in relation to size). As such, the entropy produced by a human brain is roughly 75,000 times larger than that of the sun.[15] Quite remarkable when we think about it.

In addition, a notable property of life is how well it handles these energy densities. Life can handle far denser energy flows than stars without breaking apart (or exploding), which allows it to climb farther and faster up the thermodynamic down escalator by 'sucking orderliness from its environment',[16] in the words of Schrödinger (again, more complexity in one point always entails less in another). Because this is a very difficult task, life has accordingly developed ever more complex ways to withstand the energy flowing through them. A hallmark of living organisms is namely their abilities of self-preservation, and the various complex strategies they develop to do so. The way in which lifeforms retain their recognisable patterns over time from the assimilation of the environment is a feature that distinguishes them from inanimate objects. In theory, life would be able to outlive the Sun, given that it finds new sources of energy in the Universe. Life is able to retain a stable and coherent pattern, both in form of bodily function and as structure across time, which no other entities are capable of. That is, life can replicate itself, stars can't.[17] A star can only 'attempt' to maintain its equilibrium, in a rather undeliberate fashion, while a living organism has *proper agency* in the way it deliberately strives towards continuing its existence.

This peculiarity of life also relates to one of the major differences between the physical and the biological regime: *form* and *function*. Whereas stars and planets can undergo differentiation in *form*, only biological regimes can do so in *function*. Here we need a new way of talking about the world that is fundamentally different from that we have used to describe innate phenomena; a new symbol language to accompany physics and chemistry: biology. To talk about stars as having the function to keep the galaxy together does not make much sense. But when it comes to biology it makes perfect sense to talk about function. One of the most fundamental questions in biology is namely what function a part of a certain organism has in order to maintain its complexity and keep it going. Function is thus one of the new emergent properties that life brought into existence.

The fact that organisms constantly need to extract matter and energy from the environment is one of the new rules in the game of cosmic evolution. And to play along, living creatures need to develop ever more efficient and sophisticated functions to accomplish this. Life is subject to the deterministic rules of physics just like anything else, but unlike inorganic entities, they operate according to somewhat more open-ended rules of change. Biology is on the most fundamental level as law-bound as physics and chemistry, but the rules on this new stage of complexity are quite different and allow for structures further from equilibrium than in the inanimate world. Yet, to ensure their continued existence and proliferation, organisms need to obey the rule that *extreme precision* is required. The mechanisms to facilitate the delicate task of handling large energy flows must be highly fine-tuned and accurate, mere approximation is rarely good enough.[18]

The precision required has no parallel in the inanimate world. A rock can be ordered rather randomly without any noteworthy changes to its properties, but living organisms will break down due to the slightest deviation from a certain order and thus immediately turn into dead matter that soon disintegrates into its less complex constituents. This, however, also makes them exceedingly more fragile. As such, we find the basis of yet another change to the game. With life, a new factor of change comes into being: *natural selection*. Because organic lifeforms are so fragile and constantly risk elimination before they get a chance to reproduce, a process of constant innovation and adaptability to the destructive forces of the environment come to define the development of change on Earth hereafter.

The Emergence of Life on Earth

Around 3.5 billion years ago, biological life starts to emerge out of the physical and chemical prerequisites that prevail on the early Earth. Precisely how the first forms of life arose we do not know, but the Universe has, as we have seen, a tendency towards spontaneous self-organisation. The emergence of life is an almost immediate event. This suggests that given the presence of unique Goldilocks conditions, the emergence of life may have been somewhat determined. This does not mean that evolution has any pre-planned direction – chance is still at play – but it is reasonable to propose that photosynthesising organisms and later multicellular organisms would eventually emerge from the first biological molecules, given that the circumstances remained favourable. In this sense, the trend towards higher levels of complexity seems to be 'determined', and life can be seen as the mere continuation of the same process that began at the Big Bang. But that only holds true in regards to the more general path. It was not predetermined that mammals would evolve into brainy, cultured creatures such as ourselves. Had it not been for the natural catastrophe that wiped out the dinosaurs, it is not improbable we would have had highly intelligent lizard creatures flying to the moon. In its particularities, life could have evolved along a multitude of different paths. The random primordial event that gave all subsequent life forms the particular basic cellular design they all share today could have been slightly different, with vastly different-looking creatures as a result. Chance always plays a role, and as such it was not predetermined that we would have five fingers instead of four or two brain halves instead of four quarters. But it was probably destined to happen that once the first lifeforms had appeared, sooner or later they would start forming multicellular organisms and crawl onto land. Again, the determination on the larger scale and chaos on the smaller seem to shape the development of life as well as the larger Universe in general.

With the emergence of life, we will need to view the development of complexity through the lens of natural selection that Darwin was among the first to see. However, 'selection' is perhaps a poor choice of words since no one exactly 'selects' which organisms are to survive. Survival is determined by a blind logic, so as an alternative to 'selection' we might view evolution as the extinction of less adapted lifeforms through a process that has also been called 'non-random elimination'.[19] Evolution is blind, but not aimless. Its simple laws lead to constantly better adapted forms of organic complexity being determined to develop over time.

Yet, the logic of evolution actually began before the emergence of life. In the years following the Earth's formation, a primordial soup of random chemical processes begins to form complex molecules in the oceans. Initially, chance determines which elements are to coalesce into new chemical compounds. Most of these quickly vanish, but among the many random processes a few create more stable by-products than others. As early as this point the logic of non-random elimination starts to work; a logic that, as with the formation of stars and planets, builds on principles of determinism on one hand and chance on the other. The chemicals not sufficiently well adapted to their environment vanish, while those proving robust enough to withstand the iron law of entropy become the basis for further development of increasingly complex molecular combinations. Some of these are the first hydrocarbons, chains of hydrogen and carbon, and simple amino acids, which later become the basis of all subsequent lifeforms.

From these developments, the first self-replicating molecule emerges, RNA, which accordingly has been proposed to be the first primitive form of life.[20] RNA is eventually replaced by more complex DNA molecules, which prove even more efficient in storing information in the cell and thus favour the emergence of even greater biological complexity.[21] The informational capacities of DNA illustrates how biological evolution is the result of *learned experiences*; a more deliberate process than that regarding the formation of lifeless matter, since properties that ensure survival and reproduction are stored in the DNA's code through processes of non-random elimination. DNA is in this way a sophisticated transmitter of information containing those experiences – experiences about what works and what doesn't – which are passed onto future generations.

A good way of imagining the process of evolution, and illustrating the interaction between chance and determinism, is through the thought experiment of an ape randomly punching away on a typewriter. In order to get a complete Bible, we would probably have to wait an amount of time surpassing the expected lifespan of the Universe. But if we add one crucial rule, namely that every time the ape types a correct letter it will be locked in while every time it hits a wrong one it will disappear immediately, we could expect a Bible within a decade.[22] In a similar fashion, nature creates a host of random entities that immediately vanish, but once in a while something new appears that is fit for survival which then gets locked in and made available for further development. Evolution is therefore not just random (although it depends on chance), but determined by the law-bound nature of non-random elimination of unfit structures.

With the genesis of life, we now for the first time in the known Universe have something that creates new copies of itself. This revolution also entails that the pace of development starts to accelerate – a circumstance that appears at every stage of complexity. The initial development of complex chemicals is rather slow. But the emergence of the first RNA chains considerably speeds up the pace at which new and ever more complex entities emerge, and with the emergence of DNA and the later blue-green algae that give rise to photosynthesis, evolution on Earth accelerates dramatically. The algae start to produce large quantities of oxygen that gradually alter the Earth's atmosphere. Since oxygen facilitates greater turnovers of energy, and since higher complexity always requires higher levels of energy, the organisms that adapt to use this new fuel in their metabolism thus attain the possibility of developing even higher levels of complexity. With oxygen, life on Earth henceforth enters a new stage of faster-paced evolution than ever before.

On a knife's edge between entropy's movement towards chaos and evolution's creation-process towards increased order and complexity, on the edge between symmetry and constantly increasing asymmetric structures, single-cell organisms start to lump together into multicellular organisms around 1.7 billion years ago. Thereby the evolution of higher forms of life has definitively taken off. All daughter organisms will however have the exact same DNA and the same vulnerabilities. So if something threatens a particular type of life, all organisms are threatened simultaneously. Only random mutations lead to changes in the DNA, but most of these are either detrimental to the organism or ineffective. Evolution therefore progresses rather slowly in anticipation of favourable mutations. This, however, starts to change around a billion years ago when more advanced organisms that reproduce sexually through combining parts of their DNA from two different hosts start to emerge. In this way there is much greater variation in the offspring, of which some may prove exceedingly favourable. This development really speeds up evolution. Instead of 'waiting' for random occurrences to lead to better adapted organisms, sexual reproduction allows for the most suitable properties from various individuals to be 'chosen' by the law of natural selection, and the least suitable to be non-randomly eliminated.

Following the emergence of sexually reproducing multicellular organisms, the next revolution occurs around 450 million years ago when life moves up on land; initially plants, followed by animals a little later. The first lungfish evolve with time into enormous lizards, and dinosaurs dominate the surface of the planet for millions of years until they are eradicated in a major natural catastrophe 65 million years ago. This is, however, not the end of complex life on land. As with previous natural catastrophes, complexity increases rapidly after even this great mass extinction. Small but hardy organisms, sufficiently adapted to survive the harsh conditions prevailing after the catastrophe, take over the niches handed down to them and quickly spread across the globe. One such group of species are the mammals. After the extinction of the dinosaurs, these small creatures are suddenly able to evolve into larger and more complex species, of which one of these eventually evolves into us, Homo sapiens. But in order to understand the success of our species, we must first take a look at our prime asset, our brain, and explore what it is that made the mammal brain so well-adapted for surviving and thriving in comparison with the less complex reptile brain.

CONSCIOUSNESS AS AN EMERGENT PHENOMENON

The brain is intimately connected to one of the greatest mysteries of all time: consciousness. But although it is very fundamental to our personal experience of the world, we have always had a hard time explaining what it really is. Much of human intellectual history has been devoted to the question of consciousness and existence: from the great world religions, over philosophy, spiritual practices, and to modern neuroscience, all have tried to create coherent narratives that attempt to explain this fundamental property of existence. Science has always had great difficulties explaining this phenomenon or even defining it, often resorting to rejecting the matter as pure speculation and irrelevant to how the world really works. Still, it remains one of the most fundamental phenomena of our world and continues to puzzle humans to this day and age.

The evolution from matter, to life, to mind is as perplexing as it is fascinating. When and where did consciousness emerge? What is its function? And how do we adequately analyse it? All are intrinsically difficult questions to which we essentially just have speculations to base our inquiry on. That however should not stop us from pursuing the matter. After all, consciousness is a phenomenon present to us throughout all stages of being; available for further investigation from the very focal point of our own private perspective on existence. Consciousness can therefore be observed, and results can be deduced from our investigation of existence itself. To some degree it can even be said that consciousness is the basis of all existence, or that it is existence.

But let's begin by pursuing the matter in scientific terms. The evolution of brains probably followed the same patterns of development as other organs through the merger of individual and hitherto autonomous cells. The sensors in single-cell organisms, primitive sensors registering food and danger, may have evolved ways of communicating with each other as multicellular organisms evolved and started a process towards a division of labour between cells. These primitive systems of sensory cells working together to create appropriate reactions to stimuli could have created the first form of consciousness. Having capacities to accurately create images of the surrounding world would have had great advantages. So as long as there was an evolutionary pressure and a positive reward in terms of survival and reproduction to achieve even more reality-congruent images of the world, evolution would allow for increasingly higher levels of mental complexity.

Consciousness can be said to be the capacity to feel sensation. Even without the capacity for self-awareness, consciousness is the ability, in the words of Nicolas Humphrey, 'to have affect-laden mental representations of something happening here and now to me'.[23] This was a monumental transition that allowed complex creatures to contemplate and reflect on their surroundings. It opened up the possibility to create mental images of the world, analyse situations, and make decisions on a preferred course of action. It made it possible to control large complex bodies and move intentionally to achieve results to a degree that is completely out of reach for organisms without such data-processing organs.

Even the worm registers its environment. With the aid of a nerve centre with a few hundred neurons it reacts to the environment accordingly. A neuron, or nerve cell, is the nervous system's most basic unit and is responsible for the reception and transmission of nerve impulses. The nerve signal consists of an electrical impulse that runs through a nerve cell which is relayed to the next. We may call the accumulation of these nerve signals a form of proto-consciousness; a consciousness consisting of sensory impressions, attention and motivation.[24]

Reptiles have somewhat more advanced life-adjusting mechanisms than worms. The reptile brain governs the motor control of the body and processes sensory impressions such as sight, smell, taste and hearing. The lizard, with its reptile brain, has an active sense that can focus its attention and register the outside world. In this directed attention, the lizard can register the part of its surroundings that calls it to attention, only then to react, for example attack or flee from a threat, something the worm cannot do. It is, however, the case of an instinctive, pre-programmed reaction, not a conscious choice. On the next level in the brain's evolution there are further neurons formed on the outside of the reptile brain, making up the limbic system, which can be found in mammals and birds. They still have a reptile brain, which holds the most basic life-sustaining parts, but the limbic system that encloses it should be understood as something new, not just a larger reptile brain. The limbic system gives rise to emotions, such as fear, excitement and anger, which further regulate the organism's behaviour. The limbic system thereby complements the reptile brain's basic life-sustaining impulses. Because of the limbic system's introduction of these completely new phenomena, emotions, which cannot be derived from the earlier impulses, it is possible to talk about the limbic system as an emergent phenomenon that constitutes yet another developmental step in terms of complexity. Mammals also have advanced memory functions thanks to additional neurons that form the area of the brain called the cortex. With this, they can remember and retain images in their mind. For instance, even if the cat a dog is chasing disappears around a corner, the dog is capable of continuing the chase. It has a preserved image, a memory, of the cat that has disappeared from view. Mammals can with these memory functions also learn new things about their environment, for example where food usually can be found, in contrast to more primitive species that exclusively have to rely on senses such as smell and taste in order to find food in a constant here and now.

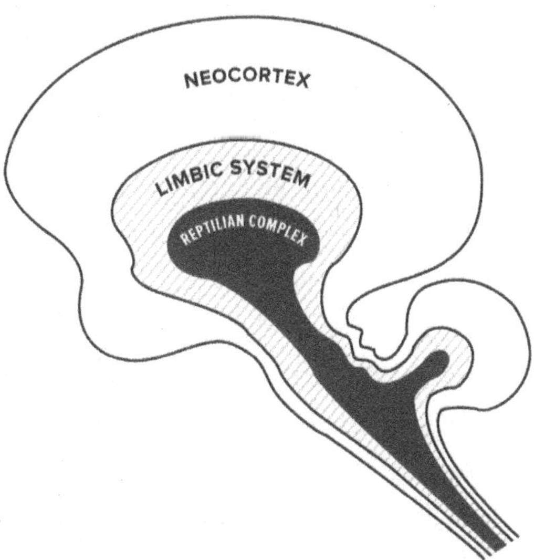

The human being's tripartite brain.[25]

The cortex is the basis for a first inner world, which we can see in the way mammals play, dream and have inner motivations. A mammal can use trial and error and through curiosity learn what various behaviours lead to. Mammals, such as the dog, have in their inner world conceptions of things and phenomena that need not be present, but can be motivated by and driven towards something thanks to this inner conception, without something visible having occurred in the environment. This is a decisive difference from what we see in reptiles, which are only instinctively driven away from or towards external stimuli.[26]

We have with the first mammals definitely reached so far in evolution that we may speak of an advanced form of consciousness that resembles that of our own. It is still not a self-aware consciousness, but a consciousness all the same. Now, thanks to the inner conceptions that can motivate the animal independently of immediate external circumstances, objectives have arisen in the Universe. Objectives are something completely new – a new type of reality, an inner reality. Objectives do not exist in the physical world, but they produce very tangible results that can be observed in the way that creatures blessed with these mental constructs succeed in manipulating their surroundings to their advantage.

Our inner reality is something that is extremely difficult to approach in scientific terms. The philosopher Ernest Nagel has in his famous paper 'What Is It Like to Be a Bat?' proposed that consciousness is what it is to *be* something, what it *feels* like to be a conscious creature. He uses the example of a bat because the sensory capacities of these animals, using echolocation, or bio-sonar, for perception, are so utterly out of reach for humans to a degree that we cannot even imagine what it is like to be a bat. We simply have no point of reference. Nagel's approach is a direct attack on material reductionism, the position that conscious organisms are nothing more than the sum of their material constituents; that everything about them can be deduced from the description of the physical processes in their brains and bodies. But mental phenomena as a subjective quality means that consciousness cannot be explained without reference to 'the subjective character of experience.'[27] This renders a purely objective approach of consciousness highly inadequate since it does not attempt to describe the subjective properties that ultimately should be the subject of analysis. Subjectivity itself is a variable that, per definition, is not accounted for in exclusively objective analyses.

If we use the definition of consciousness as that of having experiences, we may infer from empirical observations what is experienced in the inner world of other organisms. By looking at the evolution of cognition, we can investigate how organic entities on various stages of complexity react to their environment and appear to process data. From such inquiries we may conclude that the behaviour of organic cells seems to express a kind of pre-conscious form of protoplasmic irritability and that plants react to sunlight and soil compositions in ways that indicate the presence of some sort of rudimentary sensation. The behaviour of reptiles shows that they probably have a form of sophisticated perception, and mammals appear as if they (as in the above example of a dog chasing a cat) have a capacity to form mental images in their minds. However, all these properties are inner qualities that objective science, by definition, cannot say anything about. From our empirical methods we can only observe that living creatures react in accordance with certain patterns. What it is actually like to *be* the given entity we observe, however, what it is like to *have* that sensation of irritability, impulse or feeling, this we can only deduce from the experience of having similar sensations ourselves. Scientifically we can only observe the emotional *responses*; the emotion itself remains out of reach to us as scientists. As famously stated by Bertrand Russell, our brain is known exteriorly 'by description', but our mind is solely known interiorly 'by acquaintance'.[28] Only the former is addressed by natural science.

But that should not lead us to despair. Even if we do not have access to the stream of consciousness of another person, we can still from their emotional response deduce what is 'going on inside' because most of us possess many of the same emotional capacities. If a person is crying, for instance, you can recall the emotion associated with having the same response yourself and conclude that it must be similar to what the other person is experiencing right now. The same goes for the deduction of experiences in lower-level organisms. As famously stated by the writer Arthur Koestler: 'When a man lies down on the psychoanalyst's couch, a horse and an alligator lie down with him.'[29] By this he means to say that we are governed by many of the same impulses and emotions as animals since we contain the very same reptile brain and limbic system that we share with other animals. However, this also means that we may have some of the necessary 'insider-knowledge' to understand what goes on in their minds. Being the most complex creature on Earth, and being the result of several stages of transcendence from all those preceding, less complex stages of biological evolution, we have on each stage not only transcended those earlier stages, but also *included* what came before (evident in the similar physical structures in human and animal brains). Accordingly, we find within ourselves traces of all these preceding inner worlds and have good reasons to conclude that our impulses for aggression, sex and hunger must be similar to those in reptiles, and that the emotional affection we can feel towards others may not be that different to what a complex mammal may experience towards its offspring. After all, given the similarities in our nervous systems, the sensation of pain we all experience from physical harm probably does not differ that much from animals. An animal may not be able to comprehend the emotional pain affiliated with deep existential anxiety, but since the human mind contains all the earlier levels of mental complexity, we probably have internal acquaintance with most of the emotions and impulses of other animals. As such, it is not entirely unreasonable to suggest that we can draw sound conclusions about the workings of consciousness in general from our own acquaintance of having one of these devices installed ourselves.

Our capacity to relate to the inner workings of others also seems to be a hardwired evolutionary feature of the human mind. Most humans have this capacity, which is often referred to as empathy: the intuitive understanding of the subjective state of others. This is not only beneficial for drawing sound conclusions regarding consciousness as such, but is also, as we will see in the following, a capacity of crucial evolutionary importance to highly social beings such as ourselves.

THE ADAPTABLE PRE-HUMANS

Five to six million years ago, apes swing from tree to tree in the forests of Africa, eat fruits and plants and sleep protected from predators in the tree crowns. Life in the trees requires good coordination between hands for gripping and stereoscopic vision in order to navigate the three-dimensional environment. This in turn requires large brains and generates an evolutionary pressure towards increasingly larger and more complex brains. Hands with opposable thumbs will later prove extremely well adapted for manipulating objects and creating tools.

Within the course of a few million years, the formation of an enormous rift valley through the African continent results in new mountain ranges and great rivers that cut off the ape populations from each other. The climate changes drastically in the eastern part, where the forest recedes and leaves space for dry savannahs. The eastern ape populations quickly adapt for survival in this inhospitable environment. Now they cannot live in the trees and eat fruit as their cousins in the west, but are forced down onto the ground to wander long stretches in search of food. This accelerates the development of a new species of apes and creates evolutionary pressures to favour individuals who are able to move on two legs which is more energy efficient. This feature may also have protected the first hominids from heat and predators as they could no longer find shade or seek refuge in the trees. Upright walking reduces the surface of the body that is exposed to direct sunlight and having a field of vision at a higher elevation helps detect predators at longer distances. But most importantly, perhaps, standing on two legs means that their hands become free for toolmaking and the domestication of fire.

With time, these early pre-humans learn to hunt. Meat is more energy-dense than plants and enables the development of smaller stomachs, as great amounts of plant material are no longer necessary for survival. Smaller stomachs are also necessary in order to better walk upright and require less energy so that even more fuel can be released to the brain. Increased social coordination of the hunt also requires larger brains (as snatching leaves and fruits is less intellectually demanding than hunting), so in a positive spiral of constantly smaller stomachs, better upright walking, growing brains and improved hunting skills, these creatures are rapidly evolving into something we might call humans.[30]

As pre-humans a few million years ago, we are living in small groups that provide us better chances of survival. Survival depends on greater levels of cooperation than before as hunting, food gathering and defence against predators is a more elaborate endeavour on the African savannah than in the tree crowns of the jungle. Social coordination is conducted with simple signals such as body movements and sounds, probably akin to what we can observe among chimpanzees and gorillas. We are inventive and evolve in accordance with the growing demands of the new environment. Several new species of pre-humans evolve in Africa at the same time. Some of these are capable of using simple utensils such as sharp rocks around three million years ago. We are then able to more efficiently scrape off meat from bones, and the extra nourishment provides further energy for the development of even larger brains.

In these pre-humans there is rage, fear and joy; feelings that we share with other mammals. But the pre-human brain develops even further in the more emotively specialised cerebral hemisphere. With this, we get the ability to entertain more advanced inner conceptions separate from the current environment. We gain a basic understanding of cause-and-effect, we learn new things by imitating others, and use trial and error to learn from our mistakes. In addition, the inner conception of the world enables a mental 'trial' of potential actions, and having more exact and detailed models of reality favours survival.[31]

The Brains of Pre-humans

Two and a half million years ago, a period of ice ages, frenetically coming and going, subjects our species to manifold privations such as chill and drought. As a consequence of these insecure and highly unstable conditions, evolution powers ahead with full force and only the best-adapted survive. Individuals with more developed cognitive abilities gain crucial advantages vis-à-vis others less fortunate, and the evolution of more complex brains accelerates further. The brain measures around 600 cm^3 and a third stage in the evolution of the brain can be said to have begun. The cerebral cortex has now been developed and we have thus acquired greater capacity for memory, language and attention. The two hemispheres of the brain increasingly divide up tasks between them and we become ever more adept at producing tools with the aid of our improved motor skills and our minds' greater capacity for strategic thinking. Previously we just picked up stones from the ground, but now, stone fragments, wood and bones are processed to create even more refined tools.

The prefrontal cortex inherited from apes, which expands most significantly throughout human evolution, is the part of the brain associated with tool making. Apes are capable of using simple tools like putting a stick into a termite hive or cracking nuts with stones. But the larger-brained hominids have left archaeological remains in the form of stone tools of a far greater complexity than any other species. Tool use seems to have caused selective pressures for larger brains and improved eye-brain-hand coordination. Behavioural changes may have started a process of positive feedback where the larger-brained, better-coordinated individuals increase their chances of survival by acquiring better tool skills, which at the same time, through a mechanism known as sexual selection, impel females to mate with the most skilled males. The more skilled individuals then have more offspring and this over time increases these mental capacities in the genetic makeup of the entire species.

Another such feedback loop is sociability. The capacity to manage many social relations likewise requires larger brains. Bigger-brained hominids may have had better social skills, more sexual partners and higher status in the social hierarchy. In addition, they were probably also better at handling the political relations of the group, solving conflicts, gaining access to food, etc. These are all capabilities that increase the chances of having more offspring. Since larger brains and better social skills are both linked to the capacity for language skills, this may even have created a third evolutionary feedback loop towards more sophisticated forms of language.[32]

It is thereby group processes, our capabilities of relating to other humans, that propel the evolution of the human species forwards; and as such, not only traits that benefit the survival of the individual, but also those that increase the odds of survival for the group as a whole that evolution favours. When our ancestors could hold several relations in mind, group size could be extended from tens of members, in principle an extended family, to upwards of hundreds of individuals. This gives the group certain advantages, as the division of labour can expand, as well as evolutionary long-term advantages of having access to greater genetic diversity. But since we now live in larger groups it also becomes increasingly important to be good at handling social relations, to understand what other individuals feel and what their intentions might be. Those who in addition have well-developed language abilities receive further advantages in the social competition for food and mating partners, and thereby more offspring, hence spreading these desirable genetic abilities into the larger gene pool over time.

Around 1.8 million years ago, our brain's size has grown to around 800 cm^3. Effectively managing the increasingly complex social life has become ever more important, but there is yet another development of our social skills that is just as crucial, one that can be said to be more 'in depth' in our understanding of other human beings. Not only do we see a greater awareness of the 'breadth' of human society, with further understanding of the intricate social constellations of the group, but a greater awareness of its 'depth' occurs as well. At this stage, we start gaining insights about others as sentient creatures. This development of our mental world can be described as one of acquiring models of others' inner worlds, known as 'theory of mind'.[33] It entails a basic understanding of others' perspectives, the crucial insight that others have feelings, thoughts and intentions. This becomes more important as the social complexity of the group increases and survival depends on delicate cooperation with other group members.

Empathy thereby becomes a distinct human ability of crucial importance for our species' further evolution. With this we can understand if someone else is in pain, or in need of something. We can 'feel' with another person, and 'com-passion' impels us to show consideration towards others, which thereby benefits the group as a whole. This is epochal. As we begin to have conceptions of others' inner worlds, we come to understand others well before we attain a proper understanding of ourselves. For survival, it is namely more important to understand what goes on in other people's minds than in our own. Thus, as a species, we actually become conscious of others long before we become self-conscious. Strength, speed and stamina are still critical, but the capacity to understand our fellow humans' intentions and needs grows in importance.[34]

HOMO SAPIENS

Under the many environmental and social pressures, our brain evolves rapidly. A new sub-branch of hominids, Homo sapiens, turns up in Africa around 200,000 years ago. The brain in Homo sapiens is now around 1,400 cm^3 and consists of upwards of 100 billion neurons. At this stage of development, we now have creatures who are physically quite similar to contemporary humans. From here on only minor biological changes will occur; not that biological evolution suddenly has ceased, but it progresses incredibly slowly compared to the cultural changes that will occur hereafter.

All human beings that live today are, with the exception of a few biological changes such as skin colour or lactose tolerance, genetically almost identical to these early humans. We might say that the 'hardware' is complete; now it is mainly the 'software', the programming, which will be developed further. All later development can be said to belong to a completely new regime, that of culture, a developmental step in complexity beyond the biological. It is a new stage of complexity that, just like biology, will accelerate the pace of evolution to a hitherto unseen speed, and introduce completely new rules.

We are the result of millions of years of biological evolution, and still to this date we are part of it. Biologically we are adapted to a Stone Age environment rather than the urban environment most of us live in today. New branches of psychology have realised the significance of our Stone Age origin in order to understand the human being of today: Evolutionary psychology studies how behaviour and emotions can be explained by our origin on the African savannah, and new investigations in health psychology take into consideration how people are influenced by a modern environment and lifestyle to which we are yet to evolve biologically sufficient adaptations. We are, for example, not adapted to sitting still for long periods, having access to abundant sources of sweet and fatty foods, or living in an urban environment with millions of strangers.

At some point in our mental evolution we become self-aware. Being self-aware is to witness one's own inner world. As mentioned, the ability to interpret others' inner functioning only arrived with evolution, since we needed to manage our social relations. But in this process, we also realise that others have an inner conception of ourselves, not just of our body, but as persons with an inner world. This helps us become self-aware, just as the child discovers itself as a separate entity through reflections of its parents. Now we start to reason around *what* we feel, believe and want instead of simply feeling, believing and wanting without any thoughts about why we do so.

With the emergence of self-awareness, we take a first step out of the total symbiosis with nature and realise in a totally new way that we exist as individual persons. Leaving the symbiosis with nature is expressed in the Bible as the expulsion from Paradise. We realise that we are naked since we have become conscious of ourselves, and we can feel shame and guilt.

Self-awareness is an emergent phenomenon that cannot be reduced to its earlier components; it is not an advanced type of impulse, and neither is it merely a new kind of emotion. With this development, evolution creates something completely new: a creature that is aware of itself and that can reason about its existence. With this, a new level of freedom also arises. Thus far, all creatures have merely possessed a will. The worm cannot will anything other than to dig in the soil, and reptiles have no other choice than merely reacting to the impulses they experience. But with the emergence of human beings and their complex neocortex, the instinctive will can now view itself and for the very first time choose something else. This degree of freedom is, however, not something that we humans necessarily possess from birth. It is largely a degree of freedom that needs cultural support in our environment in order to develop its full potential, as we shall see in the following chapters.

Complexity is arguably related to freedom. A defining feature of higher levels of complexity is, as mentioned in the Introduction, the way higher-stage structures limit the autonomy, the freedom, of their lower-level constituents. Organisms limit the way molecules can move around, that is, within the overarching structure of the cell; the trajectories of individual molecules are limited to behave in strictly specific ways to perform the highly precise tasks that ensure the overall structure of the organism. In a similar fashion on the next level of complexity, multi-cellular creatures limit the autonomy of cells and make them perform particular tasks. But at the same time the subjection of lower-level entities also gives the higher-level entities greater freedom to manipulate their environment. There are simply more things high-complexity entities can do than lower-complexity entities can.

But high complexity not only gives us more freedom to manipulate our environment, it also entails higher freedom to govern ourselves – and thereby, we might also say, greater responsibility. We can create future objectives that motivate and propel us forwards. But these are often in conflict with our immediate wishes. Our immediate lower-level impulses may impel us to move in one direction, but our higher-level mental faculties may convince us that we need to go in another to better fulfil our overall intention. This can often be quite difficult. In order for us to stick to our intentions we need fortitude and mental power that only can be derived from our higher-level faculties, which again often need careful cultivation.

Only the human being can decide to go against its immediate impulses without any external factors to force its behaviour. We may want to follow our immediate impulse and eat all the fish we have caught at once, but if we realise that it is detrimental to our overall intention of staying alive we can decide to save some for the winter. Our biological instincts still play a role, but with this ability we have become something other than just biology. We have become cognitive creatures that can check and govern our biology through the power of thoughts. We have developed the ability to prefer a future need over a present one. We can choose between our present self and a future self. Although other animals prepare for the winter and perform tasks to benefit them later on, these appear to be merely instinct-driven behaviours. As far as we know, humans are the only creatures who deliberately plan for the future and repress their immediate desires to favour a future goal. But since such behaviours are not derived from inert instincts, because they need to be learned, the extent of which we manage to postpone our desires and go against our immediate inclinations is largely determined by our social structures, our moral systems and the shared values of the group to discipline our behaviour. Other social species have mechanisms to impel group members to comply with the overall wellbeing of the group, but humans are the only one that use non-physical means, commonly shared mental structures, to do so; and those groups that have developed the most sophisticated and efficient measures have likewise been the most successful ones. Step by step, millennium by millennium, human societies have created ever more efficient measures to control their desires and instincts and to increase the discipline of its members. This is quite remarkable, as it has occurred without any noteworthy changes to their biology.

* * *

Two hundred thousand years ago, we are biologically fully developed modern people, but we still live in a ruthless natural environment as an animal among others with threats at every corner. Around the same time the climate deteriorates as another ice age begins. These privations bring our species close to extinction. Groups of maybe just a few thousand survivors make their way to southern Africa. These particularly harsh circumstances probably lead to yet another evolutionary spur in our mental and cultural evolution. The people that remained were probably the ones with the most creative solutions and the greatest cognitive capacity since they found ways to handle the difficult conditions. It is probably under these demanding circumstances that our symbolic thinking 'fast-tracks' towards its current capacity and our language becomes more complete.[35]

The tens of thousands of survivors that remain around 75,000 years ago are the ancestors of us all. This little group of Homo sapiens disperses through Africa and out into the wider world. Around 60,000 years ago we reach Asia via the Arabian Peninsula, and then further on to Australia. When the ice retreats back north, we wander into Europe. This part of the world is already occupied by our hominid cousins the Neanderthals who have emigrated from Africa a few hundred thousand years earlier, but now they are rapidly being out-competed by the newcomers. A little further on we also spread to America as the first larger land-based creature since this continent was separated from the rest of the world.

The human being's adaptability is a key factor in explaining why we succeeded with this. We can live on food from the vegetable kingdom as well as from the animal kingdom, and we can survive in many different climates and under various ecological circumstances. The most important factor for our adaptability is, however, that we rely on our thoughts, that we use tools, and that we have language for social interactions.

But even though we have inhabited most of the planet's climate zones for thousands of years, we are biologically speaking still tropical creatures. Our preferred environment lies within a temperature range between 20 and 30 degrees Celsius, similar to the dry and stable climate of the East African rift valley, a Goldilocks condition in which we thrive and one we attempt to recreate wherever we settle by constructing shelter. But the savannah is still our ancestral home. Not rarely have modern people expressed a primordial feeling of belongingness to the African savannah when visiting it for the first time.[36] As such, it is striking how we seem to have tried to recreate this landscape in our parks and backyards: grasslands dotted with single trees. Not dense forests, jungles or swamps, but savannah-like landscapes seem to be the environment where we feel most comfortable and at peace. A hundred thousand years of evolution in other climates have not been enough to distance us from our original home in Africa.

The next chapters will be devoted to how these 'Africans' evolved, not biologically, but culturally.

Chapter 2

THE HUMAN BEING CREATES CULTURE

We do not know exactly when, but at some point between 200,000 and 40,000 years ago, the human being progressed to a level of complexity that made it, for lack of a better term, a *cultural* being. Other creatures can be said to possess some form of culture, if what we mean is a degree of social organisation, community-specific means of communication or customs unique to a particular group, but Homo sapiens is the only species that has created works of art, advanced symbolic languages, and what we usually refer to as shared belief systems, narratives, rituals and artistic expressions that characterise any human society. The unique symbolic world spaces that every human society possesses are manifestations of an emergent phenomenon exclusive to our species that can best be described as *culture*.

It is this start of a new developmental path, coupled with a number of nascent technologies, which will lead to empires, world literature, the atomic bomb and the Internet in just a few tens of thousands of years. All this in turn totally changes our conceptual worlds, values, economic prerequisites, environments and gender roles in the process. With the emergence of culture, evolution shifts into a higher gear of rapid change. We move now from the *universal scale* of cosmic and biological evolution to the *collective scale* of cultural evolution and development.

THE REVOLUTION OF THE UPPER PALAEOLITHIC

Archaeological investigations reveal that the pace of technological progress quickens about 50,000 years ago and that novel phenomena, such as art, start to appear. These developments are so radical that they have impelled scholars into terming it the 'revolution of the Upper Palaeolithic',[1] with Jared Diamond calling it 'our Great Leap Forward'.[2] Archaeological evidence from this period and beyond shows a sudden burst of technological progress and a flowering of human culture, evident in hitherto unseen cave paintings and richly crafted artworks that in comparison make the earlier period appear crude and rather primitive. Something spectacular and radical happened in the Upper Palaeolithic that makes it appropriate to talk about a developmental transition from one stage to another.

Homo sapiens were not the only humans on Earth. Long before our migrations into Europe and Asia, these lands had already been occupied by other human species for hundreds of thousand years. Like us, they used fire, crafted simple tools and used spears for hunting. In itself this highly complex behaviour constitutes a developmental revolution, one that made the hominids very successful as a species and helped them colonise a large proportion of the planet. Yet it is perhaps more the degree of sophistication that makes this human trait so remarkable. Tool use is not exclusive to humans, and even though no other animals have learned how to control fire, other non-human species have demonstrated highly complex engineering skills, such as the construction of hives and river dams, that humans only surpassed after the emergence of agriculture. The ways in which our Palaeolithic ancestors and hominid cousins manipulated their material surroundings is testimony to a very high level of development, but these advances do not represent as much a novelty as that of the development of culture that followed.

At the time before this revolution of the Upper Palaeolithic, Homo sapiens are not particularly more successful than other human species. The material conditions of our ancestors are very much the same as those of their hominid cousins. They rely on the hunting of wild game, crafting of tools, and use of bonfires to prepare their meals and keep warm. But then something astonishing starts to happen: we begin to create works of art. This truly deserves to be treated as a revolution, not only because art was an entirely new phenomenon, but also because of how suddenly artworks appear all over the world in the archaeological records from this time on. The appearance of art coincides with the rapid expansion of Homo sapiens across the globe, and during the same period we also see an equally rapid increase in the pace of new developments in tools. These demonstrate the underlying proliferation and expansion of information networks, made manifest in the material and social practices of early humans.[3]

We only have the material archaeological remains to give us a hint about what actually happened. We know that technological development started to progress much faster compared to the period before, that human numbers expanded and that humans colonised most of the Earth, and that they replaced all other hominids and eventually settled in areas where no other species of humans had lived before, such as the Arctic regions, Australia and finally the Americas. Why this particular sub-branch of the human family suddenly managed to do all this is something the emergence of art and the way in which it coincides with these other developments may give us an answer to. It appears as if something truly novel appeared in their inner, mental worlds.

From around 50,000 BCE, art appears more or less simultaneously in all regions of the world with the first settlements of humans in these areas. One of the most impressive and characteristic types of artistic expressions of the era are the famous cave paintings. These have been found all over the world and are remarkably similar, indicating a common origin and perhaps even a common culture shared among people across large distances.[4]

The oldest discovered paintings are estimated to be 40,000 years old and have been found in both Europe and the Indonesian island of Sulawesi. With carefully extracted pigments, made of red and yellow ochre, hematite, manganese oxide and charcoal, caves around the world have been skilfully

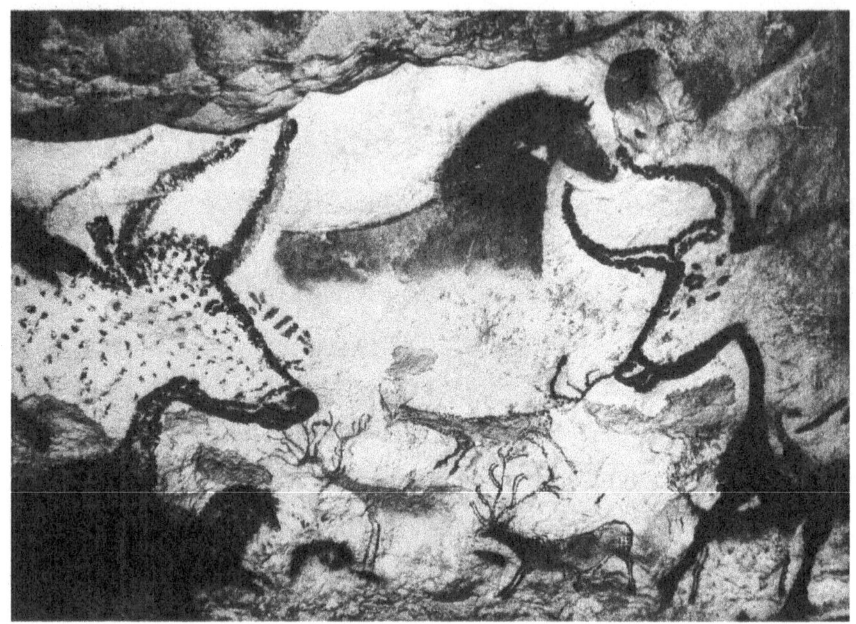

From the Lascaux Cave in south-eastern France, dated to around 17,000 years BCE. The most common motif is large, wild animals on the move in various scenarios. Photo: Wellcome Images.

decorated, indicating the awakening of some kind of increased complex consciousness.[5] The famous paintings of the Lascaux Cave in France have even urged Jared Diamond to argue that anyone seeing these amazing works of art would conclude that the people who made them 'must have been as modern in their minds as they were in their skeletons'.[6]

We do not know who made the famous cave paintings, or why they made them. Even if these depictions of animals may appear as lifelike and aesthetically pleasing to us as they did to our ancestors, we cannot with certainty know what exactly they meant either. The only thing we can conclude is that the people who made them had acquired a capacity to create something that had never existed before.

Astonishing as they are, these cave paintings are not nearly as remarkable as the new mental worlds they indicate the presence of. What is new is that a living organism – the human being – now succeeds in placing parts of its conceptual world in enduring outward depictions. We obviously do not know what went on inside our ancestors' minds, but some crucial threshold must have been reached since they had suddenly developed the mental capabilities to create these refined works of art – and, not least, thought it important enough to dedicate the time and effort to express themselves artistically. This points to a rich inner world of imagination beginning to emerge in our ancestors, or at least only now manifesting itself in the physical world.

Suddenly a mind has arisen that not only tries to make accurate mental representations of its surroundings, but one that begins to create new mental representations of things that do not necessarily exist in the physical world, and even desires to recreate these in its surroundings. The human mind is unique in the way that it does not seem to be content with making mere mental representations of the world, but is a world in itself that even has a yearning to make representations of its own creation in the outside world. Art is a very tangible result of this inclination, a feature that is shared by all human societies. Yet this is only a surface phenomenon. The human mind strives towards creating meaningful social realities and narratives that it can share with others, and art is merely one among many activities in which humans can do this.

The human being expresses their inner conceptual world not just through objects and images, but also through dances, songs and rituals. In this way, knowledge, concepts and stories can more easily be shared with others and passed on to new generations. This externalised conceptual world is also more robust; it endures over time irrespective of its creators. We might even say it takes on a life of its own beyond the biological human being, and works in accordance with completely new rules.

First, biological evolution created the human, then the human created culture. This is largely an undeliberate act of creation, an emergent phenomenon that arises from, but in many ways can be said to transcend, the biological regime.

Fundamentally, culture is constructed through symbols and comprises everything that we humans have created: everything from technology to language, narratives, religion and societal systems. Culture is constituted in a more general sense by certain shared thought structures, in which symbols are created, shared and pieced together in new ways. It is this creative process that constitutes this new cultural world, which here will be referred to as our *symbol world* or our *collective imaginary*.[7] It is the creative and symbolic dimension of the social world, the dimension through which we human beings create our ways of living together and our ways of representing our collective life which tie a society together and the forms which define what, for a given society, is 'real'.

This world is an emergent world unto itself that cannot be reduced to its material or biological constituents. It is born out of human imagination, and to understand it, we must explore its foundation: human symbolic language.

THE EMERGENCE OF SYMBOLIC LANGUAGE

The features from the Upper Palaeolithic that archaeologists consider signs of a new stage in human development are 1) new ecological adaptations accompanied by the entry into new environments different from those of Africa and the Middle East, 2) new technologies such as more refined and precise stone and bone tools, often in the form of standardised blades, 3) evidence of networks of exchange over considerable distances, 4) and finally, indirect signs of symbolic activities evident in the remains of artworks.[8] The latter was probably a result of humans' newly acquired capacity for advanced symbolic language.

We do not know exactly when human language emerged. Some scholars put it as recently as 100,000 years ago, claiming it to be a unique property of Homo sapiens, while others believe it to have appeared as far back as 2 million years in our hominid ancestors.[9] Remains of pigment processing dating back 250,000 years suggest that the capacity for symbolic thought was present from a very early age since such substances do not have many practical applications. However, it is the time around 100,000 years ago that has been described as a 'linguistic big bang'.[10] When we look at the remains of our ancestors, it then appears clear that whether our brain's current capacity for advanced communication emerged before or after this, it is the last 100,000 years that have seen the greatest consequences of this radical transformation. It is not unlikely that it would then have taken some additional time after the biological wirings were in place to develop many of the words, symbols and concepts that made the revolutionary developments of the Upper Palaeolithic possible.

A unique feature of human language is the use of symbols. In other non-human species, representations of the external world rely on the detection of similarities and correlations between objects and events. Bacteria, as a crude example, can react to all manifestations of warmth and light in one way, and cold and darkness in another; that is, they can detect similarities and react in a specific way to all occurrences of that sort. More advanced beings, such as mammals, exemplified by Pavlov's dogs, can react to correlations, for example the sound of a bell, and connect it to certain events, such as the presence of food. However, both forms rely on 'one-to-one' correspondences between internal and external events. What humans are capable of is moreover to react to symbols which not only refer to things in the external world, but also whole collections of similarities and correlations so as to manufacture whole inner worlds of complex realities in their minds. This kind of symbolic thinking is a very advanced capability. It requires that the mind keeps its representations, in the form of similarities and correlations, in the background, while other parts distil their conceptual essence into symbolic form. Shifting our attention from concrete appearances to more abstract kinds, or more specifically, going from separating indexical links between signs and objects to organising set of relations between signs, requires a lot of brain processing power. This explains why the threshold dividing concrete thinking from symbolic was so difficult to reach, and why it only appears to be our species with our exceptionally large brains that has been able to acquire such symbolic modes of representation.[11]

But size is not everything. Advanced language also requires the capacity to quickly make symbolic gestures and sounds, and the capacity to process these at an equally rapid pace in order to comprehend them. Not only did the biological brain need to evolve advanced capabilities to accommodate the rudimentary forms of symbolic communication – language itself – the symbols used in communication needed to evolve as well, in order to become more delicate and precise. This was probably a process of co-evolution involving positive feedback loops in which non-random elimination ensured that the individuals with better language-processing brains would increase their chance of reproduction, while, at the same time, the societies with more complex and refined symbols collectively would be more successful.[12] Whereas a biological threshold was probably reached more than a hundred thousand years ago, a cultural juncture, that being the development of a critical level of complex symbols, was most likely only to have been reached 50,000 years ago, evident in the sudden rapid developments associated with the revolution of the Upper Palaeolithic.

It has been argued that since cultural developments started to accelerate without any further increase in brain size, a 'new cognitive factor had obviously been introduced into the equation', which then would make our capacity for continuous symbolic innovation our most prominent characteristic.[13] From this point the evolution of our socially and symbolically constructed *collective imaginary* really took off.

THE COGNITIVE REVOLUTION

The revolution of the Upper Palaeolithic also coincides with what has been called the 'Cognitive Revolution' between 70,000 and 30,000 ago.[14] This was a defining moment in the evolution of life so radical in comparison with what had come before that the historian Yuval Noah Harari has called it 'the point when history declared its independence from biology'.[15] A rephrasing would be that *memes*, rather than *genes*, become the dominant factor of change on Earth. We will return to the theory of memes at the end of this chapter.

Up until this time, biological change in the genome had been the predominant factor determining the behaviour of organisms. Homo erectus manufactured and used stone tools, but the design did not change for 2 million years until they went extinct.[16] This suggests that their capacity to use tools was largely genetically determined; and without any substantial genetic changes, their behaviour would probably not have changed either. Homo sapiens, on the other hand, has not experienced any major genetic changes for the last 100,000 years, but their behaviour has changed drastically. This means that they must have gained some cognitive abilities to transcend their genetic dispossessions, so as to go beyond these and into a mental space of memetic mutations.

It is common to think about this change in either biological or cultural terms, but most likely it was a combination of the two interacting in a positive spiral towards more complex thinking and behaviour. The most widely accepted theory has to do with language, arguing that some kind of mutation changed the inner wirings of the brain so as to facilitate more complex ways of communicating and handling symbolic information. However, this ability alone does not suffice to explain the radical changes it caused; it is equally important to explain what was done with it. Harari suggests that our ability to talk about others, 'gossip' that is, is what makes our complex social organisation possible. To obtain reliable information about who is to be trusted, who is a freeloader, who is allied with whom and who is sleeping together is very important when handling social relations effectively above a certain size. In larger groups, this information can be just as (or sometimes even more) important than where there is food or where there is danger. It is also from gossip we see the emergence of one of the first moral systems. When we talk about someone as being lazy or dishonest it is not only an objective assessment of that person's qualities, it is foremost an intuitive feeling of moral indignation, which then gives us the urge to tell others about that person. By doing so we unconsciously create common perceptions of right and wrong, we tell others what is expected from them, and we attempt to arouse feelings of shame and guilt in the person we are gossiping about so as to alter their behaviour and keep them from harming the group. This is probably a hardwired evolutionary form of behaviour, evident by the fact that people often get a feeling of immediate pleasure from talking about the wrongdoings of others. We do this without thinking much about it, but the result is that it helps to keep people within certain mutually agreed conventions so that they do not harm the greater good of the group. Moral indignation, or gossip, has thus been argued to be an 'anti-cheating technology'[17] in foraging societies; one that works even today.

The ability to gossip helped Homo sapiens to organise larger and better-informed groups than those of other hominids, and even apes, who seldom reach numbers above fifty. But gossip's organisational capacity has an upper limit of just above 150 individuals.[18] Most people are not capable of handling more than 150 social relations, and sociological research shows that groups almost always start to face organisational difficulties above this limit. Readers are invited to consider the disparity in quantity between their social media connections, and their social circle of whom they semi-regularly keep up with.[19] So how come we are able to organise millions or even billions of people in today's globalised society? The secret and crucial cognitive ability to explain this mystery is the second important development of the Cognitive Revolution: the capacity to imagine things that do not exist in the physical world. Before this time, humans were capable of communicating about physical entities such as a lion, another person, or a river, but somehow Homo sapiens developed the ability to talk about the *spirit* of the lion, the *soul* of a diseased relative, or the river as having some kind of *magical* abilities. As far as we know, we are the only species that has been able to speak about things we cannot see, smell or touch.

The new emergent phenomenon was, in one word, 'imagination'. Here it is important to keep in mind that imaginations are *not* the same as false ideas or lies. Even chimpanzees can lie (it has been reported that chimps have falsely warned other group-members about danger, only to make the others flee into the trees so as to get the fruits on the ground themselves).

No, imaginations are narratives about things beyond the physical world that nonetheless harbour some kind of meaning or message, stories that are able to convey truth values about non-physical entities. Our ability to speak about imaginations is perhaps the most unique feature of our language compared to those of non-human animals, and probably also our deceased hominid cousins. As such it is not only that we imagine things that are not there, but that we do so collectively. Believing in common narratives and myths, and in the power of rituals and symbols, gives us an unprecedented flexibility to collaborate efficiently in large numbers.[20] Myths give us the ability and inclination to help others we do not even know because we believe those strangers to be part of an extended, imaginary community – an extremely powerful ability. Consider, for example, the great poetic narratives of Abrahamic religion, or the 'American Dream' today. The human societies who have created the most trustworthy narratives – with rituals, symbols and other forms of social reality – and managed to convince the largest numbers of people of their place within such *collective imaginaries*, have historically also been the most successful. Such collective imaginaries can have immense social value, enhancing organisational capacities. The myth of the nation can organise millions of strangers through feelings of belonging and believed mutual bonds; the same applies to narratives about a company, legal systems and so on. But neither nation-states, companies, nor legal systems exist in the physical world. Nonetheless they have concrete consequences and are perceived to be real by the ones who live within these imaginaries. Accordingly it would be wrong to dismiss them as just lies, fantasies or fake news. They make it possible for millions of individuals, who are essentially strangers, cooperate peacefully and hence create organisations beyond the limit of a mere 150 individuals. Our modern world is filled with these socially constructed imaginaries – money, laws, religions, human rights, nations and so on – and it is highly unlikely that we would have evolved to the present level of complexity and organisation without them. But these modern imaginaries do not exist beyond the narratives we tell each other about such things.[21]

So besides ascribing magical abilities to physical entities or talking about the spirits of the dead, our species also becomes capable of talking about themselves, and of equal importance, the communities they lived in as spiritual entities. Our societies thus became something more than just a group of people. The tribe, the clan or any other larger group of individuals grew to be perceived as spiritual entities, bound together by narratives, myths and ideas perceived as greater than the sum of each and every individual. We become able to see our human organisations as something beyond what meets the eye, and collectively we assured each other that they were just that. Our ancestors' fictional beliefs got transported into myths, rites, songs and dances that all constituted an important social framework, or social glue, which made it possible to coordinate the social behaviour of large groups of people – and that only become possible because these beings had developed a cognitive ability to imagine invisible worlds in their minds. Gossip was capable of organising groups of 150 individuals, and still does so today, but collective imaginaries can organise far larger numbers, essentially billions – as long as we kept believing in them.

COLLECTIVE IMAGINARIES

These imagined invisible worlds we share with each other are sometimes also called 'social imaginaries'. These have been defined by John Thompson as 'the creative and symbolic dimension of the social world, the dimension through which human beings create their ways of living together and their ways of representing their collective life.'[22] The collective imaginaries that bind our cultures together are thus intersubjective entities that manifest themselves in our shared symbol world. They are, as has been proposed by Manfred Steger and Paul James, 'patterned convocations of the social whole' that determine the ways in which we imagine our social existence. These are deeply seated within our cultural context and provide us with pre-given understandings that we often do not reflect upon.[23] So even if we should not equate the collective imaginaries that shape our understandings and assumptions about our cultural context with the social constructs that make up our more concrete societal institutions, they can still be seen as a kind of subtler, implicit form of institution, by the way in which they create systems of meaning to govern and shape our social structures.

The theory on collective imaginaries draws considerable inspiration from Sartre's idea of 'the imaginary'. Imaginaries are what we intend them to be, he argues; they are imaginary objects that appear to us as perceptions that we tend to treat as if they were real.[24] But in a physical sense they are not real perceptions: they are not derived from external phenomena that we pick up with our senses, but are mere mental constructs that we perceive with our minds. Yet this does not mean that we are deluding ourselves to mistake fiction for facts, according to Sartre. Ultimately, we do know that they are not real in any physical sense, that they are simply things we create in our mental space, but nevertheless we still ascribe certain 'essences' to these mental objects, which we then establish as truths by confirming with each other that they are very real indeed. As Cornelius Castoriadis has written, social imaginaries 'are the laces which tie a society together and the forms which define what, for a given society, is "real"'.[25] What is real in the cultural regime is therefore something we ourselves decide.

The ability to treat these imaginaries as 'real', knowingly aware that they are our own creations and thus subject to change if we come up with something better, is crucial to our cultural development. We need to perceive them as 'real' to make them work, but at the same time we need to keep in mind that they are realities that we imagine, collectively, and that they can be changed so as to better address the ever-changing circumstances and challenges we are faced with. The cultural stage of evolution thus entails a higher degree of freedom than the former biological one. This higher freedom gives us the possibility to choose to act as if these fictions we create together are real. This also entails a higher degree of intentionality, one of the new rules of the game that emerges with culture. We are no longer limited to merely react to whatever nature throws at us; culture puts us one step ahead of the game, from where we can proactively throw the ball back in nature. In this way the imaginary worlds we create are not just made from externalities that are fused into our consciousness, rather, as cultural beings we create the world from our intentions and transfer them onto the external world. On this new level of complexity, humans thus refused to merely be part of a larger creation process; with our advanced mental capacities and sophisticated social devices we stubbornly insisted on becoming co-creators of the world.

THE POWER OF CULTURE

The ability to create collective imaginaries, as well as form and understand abstract mental images, symbols and concepts, opens up a whole new world of existence. In the words of Fred Spier: 'In contrast to the dominant mechanism for adaptation in biological evolution, in which change comes as a result of genetic variation, humans do it by changing their image of the surrounding world – called culture – and by adjusting accordingly.'[26] Perhaps most importantly, humans seek to change their environment according to this new inner world, according to their own desires and newly gained visions about how it *ought* to be.

One of the most iconic pieces of evidence of our ancestors' newly won mental capacities is the so called *Löwenmensch*, or 'lion-man', ivory sculpture found in Germany in 1939. Not only does the figurine reveal that both lions and elephants (woolly mammoths) lived in Europe at the time, the strange half-human, half-animal motif also reveals that the artist had the cognitive ability to imagine something that did not exist in the physical world. Putting a lion head on a human body testifies to the creative and imaginative power of the artist. Once again, we do not have the slightest clue about the artwork's meaning, but something quite peculiar must have been happening in the minds of our ancestors. It reveals that humans have now embarked on a path toward increased symbol-use and that their

Löwenmensch figurine (Dagmar Hollmann/Wikimedia Commons).

minds and cultures have developed to an entirely new level of thought. The appearance of anthropomorphic motives may suggest the emergence of shamanistic beliefs, that humans had begun to believe in supernatural beings, and that these artefacts played a role in some early religious shamanic practices during the Upper Palaeolithic.

Admittedly we only have material remains to base our analysis on, but we have good reasons to believe that the abovementioned artefacts are the material manifestations of a rich culture that began to develop at this time. One of the universals shared by all human communities, and something that seems to be unique to our species, is the performance of song and dance.[27] Celebrations, rituals, song and dance and common myths have been observed in all human communities and served as a social glue to keep larger groups together, maintain the peace and sustain collaboration across several groups.[28] As such, we have good reasons to believe that the same applied to our Palaeolithic ancestors.

In the face of the hard realities of life, people have always sought consolation and emotional expression in gatherings, rituals, art and music. We do not know how this phenomenon came about, but it is as with many of the other features described here probably a result of the Cognitive Revolution. To rhythmically move together while vocalising the same shared words is an effective method to strengthen social bonding, create mutual support and resolve quarrels. It is even capable of creating a sense of community between people who are essentially strangers to each other, but do not feel that way because they know the same dances and songs. This can generate social coherence above the threshold of 150 individuals. It can also mobilise organisational capacities against a perceived other (for example, a marching song or battle cries). Song and dance are inherently connected to the invisible fictions or myths of a society, our social imaginaries and hence one of the practical applications of our cognitive ability to imagine things that do not exist in the physical world.

Through narratives, we place our inner ideas and emotions in an outer reality. They may manifest themselves in works of art, rituals and new spoken words, but these are merely superficial aspects of the shared symbol worlds we create and recreate; a worlds that only exist between us – between subjects, hence 'inter'-subjectivity. Essentially, the basic components of these worlds are narratives. Through the narratives that we tell ourselves and others, our otherwise random and chaotic symbol world is given structure and meaning. Narratives create the structure that our social world needs to survive.[29]

Through fortifying narratives with cultural expressions, the human being transfers its inner world to the outer in order to share it with others. So in the same way that Pablo Picasso in his famous painting *Guernica* attempted to shape a visual representation of the horrors of war and what war means to us as humans, the creators of the Lascaux paintings, we may surmise, probably wanted to depict what the hunt meant to them. Art is a way of transcending our current language. Through various artforms we can exceed the symbolic language's existing limitations and widen the horizons for what we can say by creating new symbols to express ourselves. In many ways, art is an important stimulus in the development of our symbol world. Hereby language finds new ways to relate to an ever more complex reality, enabling our movement into higher levels of abstraction.

So how, then, does this creation of new symbol worlds come about? The human being is prone to create ever more new conceptions; conceptions about existence and other things considered important enough to be conveyed to others. If a conception or idea gains ground, it becomes part of our common reality; through practice and action, it becomes embodied, and the idea is strengthened by being repeated, by an increasing number of people embracing it, and in turn putting it into symbol systems where it is functionally relayed to future generations. The ideas become a natural part of society, where they are expressed in the form of rituals, stories and belief systems. For new generations, the conceptions soon become a self-evident part of existence. What are actually only ideas and thought constructions are then perceived by later generations to be as given as natural phenomena. Symbolic language is the prerequisite for this process.[30]

Money, for example, which is only an idea, has become an integrated part of our symbol world and therefore functions as legal tender. Despite the fact that it may just be a case of ones and zeroes in a distant computer system, we all experience money as something very tangible, natural and often necessary. Even if we as individuals might understand that money is just part of our collective imaginary, we are still painfully dependent on them in our current society. Only an act of *collective agency* – that we all decide to change our shared belief system – can take us out of the collective grip that money (or nation-states, etc.) holds us in.

Biological evolution created our language ability, but later it is the human being itself who, with the aid of symbolic language, creates new symbolic realities and symbol worlds. Ultimately, language and narratives do not just create our interpretations of the world, they also constitute the very foundation of our social reality. The symbol world helps us create order among our experiences and gives meaning to existence. Through such central phenomena as money, the market, nation-states, marriages and presidents, we realise how important the symbol world and our collective imaginaries are for our human existence, as these phenomena only exist there and not in the physical world. Cities, cars and atomic bombs would never have existed either without our symbol world. Symbol worlds are something uniquely human and a valid reason for arguing that humanity belongs to a higher level of complexity in evolution.

Our first kind of such symbol worlds was a belief system, a worldview – in my words, thought perspective – that has later been termed 'animism'.

THE ANIMATED WORLD

Humans strive to understand and see coherent patterns in an otherwise chaotic and unpredictable world. We have according to Jeremy Lent a 'patterning instinct'.[31] We constantly attempt to create meaningful narratives in order to gain a feeling of balance and control and to avoid inner chaos, but also to predict outcomes in order to help our chances of survival. In this regard, we are no different to our Palaeolithic ancestors.

The fierce and unforgiving forces of nature are a daily concern in the Stone Age. When natural phenomena affect us, we try to manufacture explanations. However, without any scientific knowledge of the mysterious behaviour of nature we only have our inert human intuitions to rely on. As a highly social species we thus apply our capacity to understand the inner world and intentionality of other humans onto the natural phenomena and then ascribe them anthropoid (human-like) capacities. As nature is given intentionality, the great intellectual project of our Palaeolithic ancestors thus becomes an elaborated attempt to *anthropomorphise* and *enchantificate* their surroundings.

The word 'animism' is derived from the Latin 'anima', which roughly translates into 'breath', 'spirit' or 'life', and is often the name used to describe the religious or spiritual worldviews of many indigenous populations today. These are considered similar to those of our pre-agrarian ancestors. Animism is a term for different worldviews in which human as well as non-human beings are believed to possess some kind of spiritual essence or soul and where the actions of animals are intentional, planned and purposive. Often even inert objects and natural phenomena are believed to have intentions and wills of their own.

Animist thought is characterised by the conception that there is no distinct separation between the spiritual and the physical world; that the whole world, both the subjective realms of the mind and the physical Universe, are bound into webs of kinships. Often such worldviews include the idea that certain individuals, families or entire lineages are related to particular species of animals. This kind of thinking can be described as 'totemic' and harbours a sense of belonging and close kinship with the natural world. Sometimes kinship even extends to plant life and weather phenomena, which are also considered to have magical animistic capabilities. The supernatural world is seen as an accessible realm with beings one can interact with, almost like a separate tribal territory, and the means to access this world are believed to be various rituals and symbols. By giving gifts to the spirits, in the form of ritualised sacrifices, for instance, one can improve relations, and it has even been observed that people have believed they could marry into the spirit world. In many ways they seem to have believed they could interact with the spirit world in similar ways to that of other people; that humans and spirits were part of the same social reality and that the natural world had anthropoid qualities.[32]

It has been argued that animists do not see themselves as separate from their environment and that the natural world is not something to be grasped intellectually as an object external to one's self.[33] They identify with the world and feel that they are both within and apart from it at the same time. Among other things, this makes the hunter aware of himself and what he is doing while simultaneously taking in the viewpoint of his prey and feeling as one with it.[34] Such a capacity may indeed have proved very effective and increased the chances of success. A spiritual, or intellectual, life preoccupied with the spirits of the animals and the imitation of these in animistic rituals may not have been a purely religious matter, but also a means to increase the hunter's abilities by ascribing intentionality to animals so as to better predict the behaviour of wild game. By applying our well-developed human capacity of 'seeing' the inner perspective of others, hunters can avoid scaring animals away and sometimes even lure them into traps. With the success of this kind of thinking, it is thus tempting to apply it to the rest of nature: 'If we can attract prey, maybe we can even attract rain, and if it is possible to make animals not attack us, maybe we can even make the rest of nature treat us in more benign ways.' In our need of understanding our surroundings we begin to see the world as full of intentions to be interpreted and influenced in the same way as other humans.

If we dream about the dead or the wild animals, or simply just fantasise about them, it can appear as if we are meeting their spirit. From that, it is easy to imagine that we live in a world imbued with invisible spirits and magic. What characterises this worldview is the lack of division between nature and mind, objectivity and subjectivity. Not only are humans seen as an integral part of nature, there is not even any clear distinction between the interior lives of the mind and the exterior physical world; everything is equally part of the same reality, and all have an effect on our lives.

Along with wild game, even the forest, the sun, the wind and the rain are given subjective qualities. Spiritual life is preoccupied with attempts to understand and affect the intentions of all the creatures and phenomena of the natural world. This is evident in artworks and myths where animals and natural phenomena are given central roles with wills of their own and human-like qualities, as well as in ceremonial sacrifices with the purpose of appeasing the spirits of nature. The world is enchanted by spirits and it is as important to be on a good standing with these just as it is with other humans. When catastrophes occur, it may also be easier to live with the belief that nature is 'angry' than to concede that it was just plain bad luck. This increases social cohesion further and thus the chances of survival.

In a state of not knowing the difference between the subjective and objective worlds, phenomena in the inner world can seem as tangible as phenomena in the external. The dream of a dangerous beast can invoke the same amount of fear as an encounter with one in the physical world, and to explain the meaning and intentions of such mental encounters would then seem just as important as dealings with the physical ones. It is thus with great effort that humans struggle to interpret such dreams and visions, often considered important messages from the spirits, and through rituals, dances and states of ecstatic trance attempt to strengthen the relation to this invisible world. The shamans or wise old people are seen as mediators between the worlds who are considered to have particularly good relations to the spirits and thus become authorities in society. This is a social structure that will become the basis for later social hierarchies with priests on top and a division of labour where some are given intellectual tasks. The initial perception of natural phenomena as the embodiment of various spirits will later develop into more elaborated belief systems with various gods. Often it is the trustworthy spirit of the sun that becomes the basis of later sun gods, supreme gods in pantheons of hierarchically ordered gods, that even later evolve into the more abstract perceptions of God or supreme divine principles that we know from later organised religions. But these ideas have their beginning in the animistic perceptions of the world; perceptions to be derived from deep within the human psyche that are probably the result of projections of our subconscious mind made conscious through dreams, visions and states of trance.

Among animists, everything is interpreted in terms of an invisible inner world, a world of magic. Yet magic is in this context not to be understood as nonsense and make-believe, but as a first explanatory model for cause-and-effect. Understanding that things have a *cause* is a very important intellectual breakthrough for humankind, and to conclude that something happens because of magic is after all better than no explanation at all: If there is a cause, maybe we can change things in our favour.

The animist thought perspective is easy to acquire through emotions and imagination and seems to be embedded deep within the human psyche. It is a way of thinking that is derived from our 'hardwired' social cognitive capacities and therefore something that does not need a long theoretical education to be learned. According to the famous psychologist Jean Piaget, this animistic enchantification of the exterior world is an early stage of thinking that is also evident in the cognitive development of children.[35] All children seem to go through this phase, and it is not a coincidence that we initially attempt to anthropomorphise the physical world since human relations account for some of our first and most important experiences with it. We thus take those first experiences with the world and attempt to apply them onto other phenomena. It is common that children ascribe intentions to physical objects: for instance, if a child hits its foot on a chair it may cry out that the chair is 'stupid' for causing it pain. Similarly, we sometimes hear children give anthropoid explanations to physical phenomena, for example that the moon rises at night time to say goodnight. This shows how fundamental animistic thought, with its attribution of conscious life to nature, is. Ascribing intentions, good or bad, to natural phenomena is the first way of interpreting nature before we have learned anything else, and it predates any elaborated belief system with supernatural beings. The rain is believed to be an irregular free-floating spirit that is difficult to control, sometimes benign, sometimes malevolent, and the sun is seen as a supreme being with the intention of providing us light and warmth.

Animism is our earliest thought perspective, a pre-rational form of thinking that entails the entirety of existence becoming permeated by this invisible world's consciousness and magic.[36] Animism initially constitutes the human being's total base of interpretation within which reality could be understood and managed. It is here we find some of the first traces of human culture and see the first major developments of a spiritual life beyond the mundane. The invisible spirit world is the first comprehensive intellectual system the human being develops in order to orient itself in existence. There is no division between phenomena such as culture, religion and politics. These are differentiations that are only crystallised later. Everything is interpreted within a completely different frame of reference, which we today would regard as a fantasy world, where the border between the inner and outer, fantasy and perception, possible and impossible, is very fluid. However, as modern humans we should under no circumstances disparage our Stone Age ancestors' attempt to attain understanding of the world. They reflected upon their mental worlds of dreams, fantasies and fears, and they were thinking about the outer world with plants, animals and the overpowering forces of nature. They understood that both the inner and the outer world influence us, and just like everyone else they had a need to piece together an understanding of their total existence's cohesive whole. Through animism, humanity created a culture and conceptual world that provides a model of how the world might be interconnected, as well as furnishing methods to influence existence. The growing conceptual world and the ideas we have built around it are thus the foundation for our continued cultural evolution.[37]

With animism, magic truly conquered the world – and the souls of those who obtained its strange secrets. This mode of thought was in fact so effective that it out-competed all other human lifeways to an extent that no pre-animistic societies have survived into the modern era, or even very long into the Upper Palaeolithic for that matter. The gains of having a rich artistic tradition, delicate spiritual practices and sophisticated narratives about the world gave the societies who embraced this kind of thinking some crucial social capacities that – as a matter of Darwinian logic – increased the odds of survival to a degree that within a few thousand years, all human societies had either moved on to the animist thought perspective or died out from the competition of more successful animistic ones.

* * *

The reasons for the radical changes brought upon the planet by humans should not be looked for in the human body alone, but in the way in which humans organise themselves. Somehow, some kind of threshold was crossed when humans, after slowly evolving over millions of years, suddenly transformed the face of the earth in the matter of, in evolutionary terms, an almost insignificant number of generations. It has been argued that it probably has something to do with our particularly well-developed capacity to learn[38] – one of the defining traits of our species. Even though other species, especially mammals, also have the capacity to teach their offspring certain things, in most other species, experience is lost when an individual dies. Because non-human animals do not have any symbolic means to transfer knowledge across generations, information thereby fails to accumulate over time. What made humans breach this developmental threshold is the capacity for language and symbolic thought. Human language, David Christian has argued, 'allows more precise and efficient transmission of knowledge from brain to brain. That means that humans can share information with great precision, creating a common pool of ecological and technical knowledge, which in turn means that for humans, the benefits of cooperation increasingly tend to outweigh the benefits of competition.'[39] Humans contribute knowledge to a common pool that survives the death of the individual, which can be accessed by others and thus accumulate knowledge and skills non-genetically from generation to generation.

A distinctive feature of humans is hence their ability to learn collectively. Christian accordingly believes this is why it is crucial to understand humans, not by comparing individual humans with individual chimpanzees, but by comparing groups of humans with other groups in the animal kingdom. We need to investigate the 'collective brains' that millions of humans have developed over many generations, he argues.[40] After all, very few of the countless human-made artefacts we surround ourselves with and the methods of social organisation that we live and work with could have been invented by a single individual during their very short lifespan. Our complexity can therefore not alone be explained by the fact that we as individuals are a little more intelligent than chimps and the other hominids that we out-competed. Indeed, given the larger brains of the Neanderthals, we cannot with certainty establish that we in fact are the species with the greatest amount of raw brain power to have walked the Earth. Our success has more to do with what we did with our intelligence, most notably socially. That we ended up as vastly more creative than the Neanderthals is therefore, as pointed out by Christian, because of the way in which we managed to share knowledge within and between generations.[41]

So with the emergence of the culture-creating human we thus have a new object of investigation, something that completely changed the further trajectory of evolution, namely the mental artefacts transferred from one human mind to another.

MEMES: CULTURE'S EVOLUTIONARY MECHANISM OF CHANGE

With the emergence of culture and our collective imaginary, things start to change at a much faster pace compared to the previous developments in Earth's history. But how can we explain this increased speed? The development of the physical Universe progressed very slowly. When life arose, the biological evolutionary processes unfolded much more rapidly than the physical ones before. With the genesis and development of the human being's symbol world, the speed of development increases further. Critical changes in complex biological organisms often take thousands of generations over hundreds of thousands or millions of years to come about. Substantial cultural changes in our symbol world can, on the other hand, occur over one or two generations.

A simple way of understanding how our symbol world allows for such fast-paced development is through the concept of 'memes', originating from Richard Dawkins' book *The Selfish Gene* (1976). Dawkins argues that cultural and technological evolution is driven by memes, which he considers the smallest components of our symbol world. He sees them as mental equivalents to the genes of the biological world, though non-material symbolic entities that only exist in our minds.[42] Just like a gene, a meme is to be understood as a self-replicating unit of transmission, but instead of replicating through the gene-pool, memes propagate through our minds. They are units of cultural information, the knowledge and skills humans non-genetically pass from individual to individual across generations, such as signs, ideas, thought systems, etc. On a smaller scale a meme can be a word, a song or a tool, and on a larger scale an entire language, a religion or a scientific discipline. Whenever a song, a word or an idea originating from someone else has been transferred by 'injecting its memetic DNA' from one individual to another, the meme can be said to have been successfully reproduced.

In this regard, memes appear to behave much more like viruses than genes. Memes can be very contagious – just think about that song on the radio you cannot get out of your head.[43] When that happens, the meme can be said to have injected its DNA into your brain and hence managed to use you as a vessel for its reproductive ends – and thereafter you might even infect someone else by whistling the song in their proximity. This viral dynamic occurs much faster than any proliferation through a gene-pool, which explains the fast-paced development of culture contrary to the slow evolution of biological bodies. Because memes are not transmitted through biochemical processes, but through signs and language, they can escape the bio-physical constraints of genetics. The meme is therefore not dependent on slow random mutations and natural selection in the form of annihilation of biological individuals, but can spread much faster from one living person to another.

Memes are, however, like genes, still subject to evolutionary pressures. Only the memes that consistently manage to spread to large numbers of people over time will survive in the end; and in order to do so they need some competitive edge in relation to the environment, and to other memes. It can be a type of tool that proves exceptionally useful for survival, or it can be a certain type of behaviour, a thought or an attitude that gives its host society an advantage in relation to nature or other societies. If the meme is not competitive, it either dies when superior memes are adopted or it dies with its host when its competitive disadvantages cause the culture that has embraced it to be destroyed by others with superior memes. Even the song that is stuck in your brain is subject to these evolutionary pressures: In order to consistently inject its memetic DNA into our brains, it needs to provoke stronger emotional rewards than some other song currently on the radio; and with time it is gradually out-competed by new and superior songs that more sufficiently resonate with our emotions.

This does not mean however that only the 'fittest' memes will spread at any given moment. Rather, over time, it is more probable that memes better adapted to the current situation will prove victorious and survive to reproduce another day. Religions and ideologies can survive for a long time, even in face of memetically superior ones, but with time they are likely to succumb to symbol systems that address the current problems of the age more adequately. Societies and cultures that do not adopt new superior memes often vanish. Individuals and societies who succeed in the transmission to better adapted memes can avoid the negative consequences of having obsolete memes and thus eventually out-compete those who have not.

Memes, like genes, also do not always copy perfectly, but may change over time, or *mutate* in other words. They can even merge with other memes and consequently create entirely new meme structures. But memes do not act as randomly as their biological equivalents either. New memes do not emerge as random mutations from which only a few give its host an advantage, but rather emerge in the minds of human beings as a conscious response to their environment. This further explains why the speed of cultural development is so much faster than biological evolution: humans do not need to wait for nature to randomly come up with an advantageous meme; as active agents we can develop them ourselves as answers to certain problems. With culture, we do not need to wait for advantageous genetic mutations to appear in a lucky host and wait for everybody else to go *non-randomly* extinct. With culture, we can simply change our behaviour by *selecting* a more fitting course of action.

This does not mean, however, that inherently uncompetitive memes do not appear. Despite being the result of conscious activity, memes have still not been entirely free of 'faulty mutations', so to speak. People have always come up with ideas and solutions that did not work out very well but were still chosen nonetheless. Just like particular malevolent viruses can emerge in nature, extremely pathological memes may also appear (such as suicide cults), but the iron law of natural selection, or non-random elimination, will inevitably weed out such developments in the end – if a virus or a meme kills its host before it can be transferred it is, logically, 'game over' for that meme. Nazism, for example, proved to be a most unfavourable memetic mutation, not only to the world as such but even to its host culture. Evolution put it out of existence in the course of only thirteen years.

Some memes have proved so advantageous that they have endured for millennia, while others have only been competitive for a shorter period and ultimately declined when conditions changed. The steam engine automobile, the Soviet planned economy and the élan vital theory are all memes that proved too faulty to pass the test of time (sustainability is a key factor in determining the pathology of a meme just like a gene). Yet, some do not survive due to pure chance, such as the Betamax, Manichaeism or the decimal clock, while others proved rather successful for a long time, such as the horse buggy, the Islamic Caliphate and the Doctrine of the Four Elements, but eventually were out-competed just like the Neanderthals. A lot of factors determine the success of memes – chance is sometimes one of them when other equally competitive memes are present – but in the long run they are all subject to evolutionary pressures, and in the end the less advantageous will simply not be reproduced any more.

* * *

The rapid developments during the last few thousands of years have not been caused by biological evolution, but by an evolution of our symbol world. Ever since memes appeared, they have been the primary cause of change on Earth due to the sheer speed through which they can transfer information and the immense power they wield in relation to the physical world. In the same way DNA replaced RNA because of the former's greater informational capacities, memes replaced DNA as evolution's leading force because of their even greater capacity to transfer knowledge and experiences across generations. With the emergence of memes, the primary carriers of evolutionary information were no longer body-bound, but non-physical entities to be found within the impalpable and volatile world of symbols. This, however, did not mean that the effects on the physical world would be any less tangible. On the contrary. The higher flexibility and propensity to change that prevails within the realm of symbols caused changes so dramatic, and at an unprecedented speed, that within a few thousand years, a mere blink of an eye in biological evolution, the surface of the Earth would be altered beyond recognition.

With the new player in town, symbolic language, human beings ventures onto a dangerous and beautiful path as evolutionary co-creators to change the world in accordance with the imaginary constructs of their collective minds.

Chapter 3
THE GREAT CHANGE

About 16,000 years ago, the glaciers start to move north and the environmental conditions in the Middle East begin to change. The animals we rely on also move north as the climate becomes drier, and 13,000 years ago it becomes ever harder to find wild wheat, which has now become an important part of our diet to compensate the loss of wild game. This impels us to learn how to cultivate the wheat and catch the animals that remain without eating them all at once. Drought also causes more people to live together in the increasingly fewer fertile square metres available. Without anywhere to go, as most of the land is already occupied, we settle down as farmers and shepherds.

The emergence of agriculture entails a revolution by virtue of the vastly greater energy consumption of a single species, in total and per capita, and the massively greater number of people it brings into existence. The increase in the share of bio-matter subject to a single species is spectacular. The pace at which these developments take place is also, compared to those of the preceding foraging regime, very rapid. Instead of hundreds of thousand years, these developments happen in just a few thousand.

Humans start to sustain themselves in ways that depart significantly from any other species before. The crucial change is the way in which we alter our relation to nature by deliberately transforming it to serve our needs. Until this point, every living species has simply lived off whatever resources nature could provide. And even if living organisms have always changed the environment and other species in their surroundings, when humans start to domesticate plants and animals it is the first time a species seeks to do so deliberately and with so great efficiency.

This novel mode of production, however, not only changes the way we sustain ourselves, it also brings equally revolutionary changes to the ways in which we organise society. Agricultural production makes it possible for human numbers to grow far beyond what any naturally occurring resource could sustain. And in these densely populated sedentary communities, entirely new ways of organising social relations emerge as a result. As societies get larger and more productive, they also get far more socially stratified, and with time, more centralised as well. In a few thousand years, agricultural production gives birth to complex, literate civilisations with well-organised bureaucracies, cities with inhabitants that think and act very differently from their foraging predecessors and powerful elites that control large armies to control these people and keep outsiders at bay. When the first pyramid-building civilisations appear in the Middle East, a second chapter in the development of the agrarian regime begins – and with that a qualitatively very different way of life.

THE LIFE OF THE SEDENTARY

Agriculture is a very powerful meme system. The societies who embrace this meme system will not only secure their own survival, but, as their numbers soar and they expand into virgin lands, even ensure the memetic proliferation of agriculture across the planet.

After emerging in a few regions, agriculture spreads to most of the world through a complex process – a combination of migration, diffusion and local invention and reinvention; often along new or existing networks of exchange.[1] After the first emergence of agriculture in the Middle East, it appears independently in at least six other locations: China, Papua New Guinea, Mesoamerica, the Andes, Sub-Saharan Africa and parts of India. So, given that it emerged autonomously in so many different regions not yet connected with each other, agriculture appears to be a universal developmental feature, not just a fluke, which seems to occur when certain societal and ecological preconditions are met. In all these regions, agriculture first appears in hilly areas with subtropical climates, suggesting that such environments provide the optimal Goldilocks conditions for agriculture to emerge from scratch.[2] In addition, we also see the emergence of nomadic societies, usually consisting of a few hundred people, that follow the animals' movements and subsist on cattle rearing, as well as trade – and war – with the sedentary farming communities.

In many areas, the emergence of agriculture is far from an immediate event, but co-exists with traditional hunter-gatherer lifestyles, to which agriculture is only a supplement to foraging, for thousands of years.[3] This is not strange. Even if agriculture can support larger populations than foraging, and hence out-compete these lifeways in the long run, foragers have good reasons to resist the transition. Early agriculture brings new forms of stress and disease: Less varied diets, overwork, bacterial and viral infections and famines are endemic in farming communities, and from skeletal remains we see a sudden increase in teeth problems and skeletons grow to be shorter on average. Life expectancy and child mortality do not improve either and violence seems to have increased as well.[4] These circumstances have led Yuval Harari to call agriculture 'history's biggest fraud'[5] and David Christian to conclude that it 'did more to depress standards of human welfare than to raise them'.[6] It has even been theorised that the earlier life of foragers was the 'original affluent society', one in which 'all the people's wants are easily satisfied'.[7]

With the transition to agriculture, we have to exchange the somewhat freer hunter-gatherer lifestyle for a more toilsome sedentary existence tending our crops. No longer do we freely roam the lands. The arguably more gratifying hunting life is replaced by backbreaking farm-work and a monotone diet largely consisting of starch while leisure time declines considerably. In addition to these noteworthy deprivations, women also get a particularly raw deal. Agriculture generally favours male dominance, so as a consequence women have to give up some of the freedoms they enjoyed in the foraging regime. This is partly a result of the higher birth rates agrarian life brings about. Young children do not need to be carried around any longer, and the new grain-based diet shortens birth intervals so that children can be weaned from an earlier age. When females breastfeed children for shorter periods of time, the risk of getting pregnant increases accordingly (breastfeeding causes a considerable delay in the return of ovulation after pregnancy). The abundance of energy-rich grain diets also makes females reach puberty earlier, thus raising the prospect of even more babies. Contrary to the nomadic lifestyle, where children remain a burden for a much longer time, the additional births are even encouraged since children can contribute to the agrarian household economy from a younger age.[8] Consequently the number of humans grows rapidly following the Agricultural Revolution.

With time, the sedentary way of life makes people forget the intricate knowledge of nature that had helped them survive as hunter-gatherers. Sedentism becomes a trap. Once people have got accustomed to an agrarian lifestyle they can no longer go back. Not even if they wanted, or if conditions allowed for it, since they have now lost the skills required for a successful life as foragers. In most cases, however, there is no going back either way, because of the growing number of mouths to be fed. In a development known as 'path dependency',[9] the increased amount of food leads to more births, which again increases the demand of more extensive agriculture, so as to further increase birth-rates in an ever-continuing upward spiral.

Naturally, people are tempted by the larger amounts of food that can be acquired from agriculture and the security of growing their own food supply. But since the life of farmers is a more toilsome and demanding existence, and since humans rarely engage in the many difficulties a transition to an entirely new form of life entails when the contemporary is able to sufficiently meet their needs, the transition to agriculture is unlikely to have been entirely voluntary. Necessity, rather than free choice is most likely what makes us become farmers in the first place. A shortage of resources, competition from other humans, and no other ways to ensure survival are probably what spur the first human societies to adopt agriculture.

With agriculture, we start to influence the natural environment to a greater extent than before. We begin to consciously alter our ecological surroundings in ways that better suit our needs. Since only a few select animals and plants are useful to us, these are prioritised in favour of others, which results in a decline in untamed natural complexity. As such, the increase in human complexity is directly linked to decreased biological complexity – corresponding with the universal rule, that high complexity in one part of the Universe results in lower complexity in another.

In order to fuel the increase in human complexity, the extermination of many species follows, along with soil erosion and deforestation, which in some parts of the world even cause local climatic changes. Sometimes the depletion of the natural environment even deteriorates living conditions to the degree that agrarian societies collapse from time to time when ecological boundaries are transgressed. Another type of horror afflicting humanity is new diseases. Since we live closer to one another and to our animals, our villages become hotbeds for the spread of microbes and viruses. Many of our diseases, which we are immune to today, are mutated animal diseases. These would later have disastrous consequences for the peoples outside Africa and Eurasia, where they did not have access to domesticable animals and thus did not develop immunity to their diseases.[10]

The relationship between humans and nature starts to fundamentally change. Our ambition to reshape the natural environment gives us a growing sense of separation between the natural and human worlds. The feeling of connection and belonging to nature, prevalent among foragers to this day, gradually diminishes and is replaced by a feeling of alienation towards nature and a sense of the natural world as indifferent and sometimes even hostile towards us.[11]

The new agricultural living conditions catalyse the development of new ways of thinking and acting. The old animist thought perspective is no longer sufficient. To survive, we must develop our culture. We can no longer rely on magical happenings, but need to unravel the mysteries of nature to decide when it is time to sow and harvest. This fundamentally changes our perceptions of nature and reality as we have to adapt our lives to the cyclical rhythms of agricultural production. The first forms of calendars are invented, which may have entailed some of our first formal conceptions of time. To help us determine the right time for sowing and harvest we start giving greater attention to celestial constellations, which start to play a stronger role in people's imagination. With the emergence of increasingly powerful leaders, this may help explain the transition from spirit beings in nature to powerful gods tied to celestial objects. As in hunter-gatherer societies, the worldview of early agrarian societies is concerned with spirit beings with great supernatural powers inhabiting the natural world. Thereafter, with the transition to more advanced forms of agriculture, these narratives become much more institutionalised.[12]

New forms of social conduct and self-discipline are also required in the agrarian regime since the work in the fields requires greater efforts and social coordination; especially since we can no longer consume all the available food when we feel like it. Forward planning and retaining rather than immediately consuming all the available food is a major break with previous modes of production and consumption – and thought. We must learn to become more disciplined and overcome our immediate needs and impulses. Humans' immediate and instinct-given impulses have to be repressed, and the way evolution has adapted the human mind to a life of hunting and gathering on the African savannah must be transgressed. Even the human body has to transgress its evolutionary limits as the hardships of monotonous, backbreaking farm-work, to which it is ill-suited, has to be endured as well. This conduct has to be learned; new memes have to be developed as such acts of self-restraint cannot be derived from instinct. Norbert Elias has pointed out that the new sort of self-discipline that agrarian society demanded, to a considerable degree had to be instilled by external constraints. This circumstance, he argues, may have given rise to a new class of priest-chiefs, perhaps descending from shamans, who, with the aid of new religious beliefs and practices, provide binding solutions to the problem of self-discipline by instilling this kind of behaviour in people.[13]

New social imaginaries are required, and it is crucial that we agree on them as truths, that we believe them to be real. Groups with strong priest-chiefs and effectual narratives may then have prospered more than those without, which as a matter of evolutionary logic causes this kind of social structure to become dominant.

The Emergence of Cities, States and Empires

About 5–6,000 years ago the first city-states appear in Mesopotamia and Egypt, and a little later in the Indus Valley and China. Cities are crucial to the emergence of states by their very nature as concentrators of power. They bring together authority and labour previously diffused over a large area into a single node of power, while they simultaneously create needs for novel measures of power projection and labour coordination as they grow and new organisational problems arise. So as the need for central regulation increases, and measures are taken to accommodate this, so do the available resources for central authorities too.

Most early states emerge in river valleys often surrounded by almost inhabitable lands and near subtropical mountain areas where agriculture was pioneered thousands of years earlier. That states do not emerge in these areas, in many regions escaping central control up until modern times, is probably due to the difficulty for armies and bureaucrats to operate in such mountainous environments. Instead it is in the nearby river valleys, where conditions for irrigation are present, that we see the first instances of state-like structures. Irrigation requires large amounts of cooperation that are only feasible through strong organisations, which accordingly prompts the need for central regulation.[14] The flat plains, rich soils and rivers suitable for irrigation projects thus explain that state-like regimes first emerged in the densely populated urban regions in southern Mesopotamia and Egypt.

Cities also often emerge at the centre of networks of exchange. Accordingly, southern Mesopotamia happens to be located between two resource-rich areas, the northern arc of the Fertile Crescent and the Persian Gulf, and thus becomes a hub region in this early far-reaching network. As regional networks of exchange gradually become larger, more diverse and more complex, new hierarchical structures begin to appear with large cities at the centres, where wealth, knowledge and people are concentrated in ever-growing numbers. The outlying regions thus begin to depend on some subordinated niche within the new networks of wealth and power – which further increases the centrality and wealth of the major cities. In addition, the increasing aridity in the Middle East may have forced people into the narrow straits of fertile land along the two rivers of Mesopotamia and along the Nile in Egypt, increasing population density and thereby the size of cities further.[15]

Cities are more than large villages in that they are the first wholly humanised environments. Cities are characterised by having large numbers of people who themselves do not engage in farm work but nevertheless are supported by the surplus production of agriculture. This makes new forms of complex division of labour and specialisation possible, such as full-time artistry and trade. The new agrarian cities are hotbeds for novel memes to emerge. The organisational issues that appear as society grows larger, the new living conditions in the urban environments and the growing number of people, goods and ideas that circulate in the cities, all contribute to the creation of new memes and higher levels of complexity. The growing complexity that emerges in the dense centres of the cities can be likened to the way in which the pressure in a star gives rise to more complex atoms; as the 'gravity' of the city pulls in 'matter' from afar, new memes are forged in its centre. That is, as growing numbers of people and goods are caught in the gravitational field of the city and brought to its centre, the density of these resources in a single location henceforth allows for increased social and technological complexity to develop.

As agriculture develops and spreads over a larger area and the population grows accordingly, settlements come ever closer to each other and coalesce with time into larger societies. The cities become powerhouses that gradually extend their influence and power in the region. The surrounding villages are soon subordinated by the exchange hubs that they trade with, and eventually the biggest and most powerful cities extend their power to other smaller cities, creating political structures approaching the form of territorial states. With this development, human complexity has entered a new stage. We get a denser weave with ever-increasing complexity in evolutionary cultural development disseminated via memes. With the closer connections between cities we also start to see the languages of powerful cities become dominant in a larger area, whereby memes can spread more easily. We can communicate with, be inspired by and ourselves influence others in a wider common sphere than ever before.[16]

But a shared language entails more than the ability for us to talk to each other. Of equal importance is the way in which it makes it possible to live in common cultures where we share the same symbol world, even with people we do not know personally. Our symbol world grows larger and the number of people who contribute to our collective learning process goes up so as to further the development of new levels of technological, social and cultural complexity. This also makes it possible to create social imaginaries, myths and narratives that extend to ever-larger numbers of people.

With the emergence of the first city-states in southern Mesopotamia around 3200 BCE, Sumerian society has become so large and complex that relations cannot be managed within the animist kinship way of thinking. New class structures start to emerge, categorised by occupation and city of origin. But kinship continues to be important among the lower levels of society, and symbolic forms of kinship survive in religious thinking.[17] In parallel with the emergence of ranked hierarchies among humans, so do elite gods with equal demands of appropriate respect begin to appear; and to honour these, special buildings are erected for them. In all the locations we find monumental architecture it is evident that powerful leaders existed so as to coordinate the labour-intensive work of erecting such structures. This is both a sign *and* an instrument of power since leaders can thereby inspire awe in the gods, but also in themselves by being the ones who deal directly with these powerful beings.[18] State religions often become cultural regimes to foster social cohesion and legitimise the authority of rulers. The narratives of state religions are usually based on notions of supernatural forces and symbolic kinship with rulers portrayed as descendants of the sun or the moon and fathers (or sometimes mothers) of their people. These religions become dominant in the new public spheres of the cities, while the older farmer religions remain important at the local level. The differentiation into state and popular religions coincides with the differentiation of social life into a public sphere, dominated by males, and a subordinated domestic sphere where women are increasingly secluded.

As the cities grow, more and more people have to live in close proximity with people that are not kin and with whom they do not share personal relations. New moral guidelines on how to deal with strangers are therefore needed. State elites thus begin to formulate laws and forge overarching state identities with the aid of religions and bureaucracies. The result is what Benedict Anderson has called 'imagined communities', since people become capable of feeling some kind of shared identity with others they do not know personally.[19] Our ability to forge social imaginaries is thereby used to create new identities that are better suited to the new conditions in complex agrarian societies.

Eventually the territorial states evolve into what we sometimes refer to as 'civilisations'. With these, we now have even larger societies and cities with hundreds of thousand inhabitants. New symbolic conceptions are thus created to address the new conditions. The civilisations begin to create new myths about themselves, imaginaries about their divine origins, their rulers' right to govern, and people's subordinated role within these structures. The narratives of these social constructs, which are reproduced across generations and memetically evolve to ever-higher levels of sophistication, make us imagine the civilisations we live in as communities we rightfully belong in. These social imaginaries are purely fictitious, they only exist in our minds, but since we collectively assure each other that they are true, in cultural, symbolic terms they become real – real as in there is actually something in our minds that corresponds to what we consider a civilisation, and real as in the very measurable and tangible results these social constructions bring about in the physical world. With the emergence of civilisations, humans start to behave in ways that would not have been possible without such social imaginaries. Civilisation is a new stage in our cultural evolution, but that does not necessarily mean that it is 'better' than the earlier societal forms (as sometimes implied by the use of the term 'civilised'). It simply means that it is a more complex, and more efficient, meme system, which accordingly will spread across the rest of the world, either through imitation or conquest. As in the biological evolution, the new and more efficient meme out-competes all other life ways – and those who do not adapt, either die or become subordinated. The world becomes increasingly 'civilised', but truth be told it is far from the most civil development altogether.

A NEW POWER ORDER

The growing surplus of food makes it possible to support a number of specialists to engage in non-agrarian activities, such as priests, bureaucrats, artisans or other things requested by the power elite. The new specialisations are an important prerequisite for city life and further cultural growth. The increased specialisation of work functions also creates a hierarchical structure with a middle class above the primary producers and below the rulers. The growing division of labour creates higher levels of wealth, but it is far from equally distributed. The difference between poor and rich grows larger, and people's social status within the new hierarchies, usually preordained from birth, tends to determine the terms of life to a greater extent than individual skills.

New productive regimes, such as agrarian civilisation or capitalism, always tend to create more elitist structures, concentrating wealth, power and status in the hands of fewer people. But this is a sad requirement to sustain the growing complexity at the initial stage of such developments.

Generally, without the concentration of power, social complexity cannot function or develop to higher stages. Complex human societies simply require that someone has the necessary means to govern these structures efficiently and keep them from falling apart. For civilisation to emerge and sustain itself, resources need to be amassed in a central node. Because complexity is characterised by asymmetry, and because higher complexity entails equally higher asymmetrical structures, the source of this uneven distribution of entities must be derived from somewhere. In the case of civilisation, that source is the natural environment and the farmers who extract resources from it. For a new emergent phenomenon to emerge, it is essential that it has sources of energy from where it can 'suck orderliness' from its surroundings, to use a phrase from chapter 1, so as to fuel its complexity. As a result, it inevitably creates entropy, and thus less complexity elsewhere. With civilisation this entails an impoverished environment, and population, which arguably may have been better off without it. In later stages of societal developments, we do see the emergence of counter-tendencies, new levels of complexity to address the problems created by the previous iterations. But initially, whenever a new productive regime is developed, it is characterised by growing concentrations of power and wealth controlled by a few – the new structure simply cannot emerge without it.

People have good reasons to resist such developments, and in many cases some have even succeeded for a surprisingly long time as evidenced by peoples in areas with terrains too difficult for central authorities to efficiently operate. But in most areas where agrarian societies developed there were considerable pressures towards centralised organisation. There can be many advantages for communities to remain autonomous and loosely organised; yet, if a society does not succeed in allocating power to efficiently managed nodes of government, it runs the risk of losing out to those who do – and as a consequence become subjected to centralised power nevertheless, however, in a subordinated position instead. So as a matter of Darwinian logic, following the emergence of civilisation 6,000 years ago, the strongest nodes of concentrated power begin to swallow their weaker neighbours and eventually grow into vast empires. Complexity goes up and great civilisational advances are made in and near the centres of power, but so are injustices, oppression and the scope of violence expanded.

A New Economic and Political Structure

The economic organisation during the Stone Age is built on mutual interactions where people help each other, as in a family, and share whatever food is acquired with the other members of the tribe. We do so without expecting to receive a precisely measured corresponding compensation later on because it is simply the most efficient way to ensure our survival. This system has been described as the 'gift economy', a system with social reciprocity as its engine.[20] We bestow gifts on each other which helps the group survive, but also functions as a social glue to keep it together. Gifts as well as sacrifices are a way of appeasing both humans and gods in the age of animism. The exchange of gifts is ritualised and embedded deep into our social imaginaries, moral systems and customs that make up our shared symbol world.

This, however, starts to change with agriculture. Those who work hard on their patch of land tend to develop a sense of ownership and want to protect it. We thereby get more extensive forms of ownership, new notions about what's mine and what's yours, and become more reluctant to share everything equally with our neighbours – especially if we perceive of them as lazy or less diligent than ourselves. After all, farm work is tedious and backbreaking, not as much fun as hunting, so those who work the hardest start feeling entitled to keep what they have produced by the sweat of their brow. In addition, sedentism allows for far more wealth to accumulate, since things do not need to be carried around any more. Our sweat and toil thereby endows us with far more possessions than before. Both these factors have great economic and political consequences.

Economically, we begin to see steeper gradients of wealth since some farmers turn out to be more skilled than others. But not only quantitative changes appear like that of growing differences between rich and poor, even qualitative changes start to occur in our social relations as the growing economic complexity gives rise to entirely new classes and occupations: artisans, soldiers, religious specialists and slaves, all with great differences in social status within the newly stratified social structure. Most profound is perhaps the change to the status of our leaders, who now emerge as a separate class, rather than just a group of particularly competent and trusted individuals in the tribe.

Politically, growing social and economic complexity, which requires that some get the task of coordinating work and distributing the produce, enables them to sustain themselves exclusively from the surplus of others. They can thereby increase their power by specialising in things other than food production, for instance organised violence, which among other things gives them control of the grain, a most lucrative specialisation. The reason this becomes possible is because the growing population densities and the new concern with private property bring a particular issue to the forefront: security. With that, a new social logic – the quest for security through means of organised violence – starts to completely reorganise social relations. As a result, we see the emergence of elites whose main occupation is in the security business. This makes it possible to establish a new and more organised power order that persists until the late Middle Ages. This order entails that whoever has the military power to control and defend a certain area can unilaterally decide how the yields of the land should be distributed. For apparent reasons, without any sufficient military measures, people cannot resist what is to be done with their resources. The grain surplus that remains, after the peasants have received enough to survive and sow the fields, can then be used by the ruler as they please. The gift economy of foragers is thus replaced by an economic system based on the principle of redistribution. Some of the surplus is used for the rulers' own luxury consumption, but most of it is used to support the soldiers that defend the land and control the farmers.

For all the local differences, and despite being initially unconnected, states around the world begin to exhibit very similar characteristics. This is likely the result of the equally similar conditions and challenges that occur when societies grow larger and more complex. All agrarian states become highly stratified societies with elites monopolising organised violence and taxation through means of armies, religion and bureaucracy, and with an urban middle class specialising in artistry and trade.

All around the world, agrarian civilisations always contain three (at a minimum) levels of management and exploitation.

First. At the bottom are the primary producers such as farmers, fishers and other extractors of natural resources. Many of these are slaves, which is another near-universal feature of agrarian civilisation. The primary producers are usually organised around traditional principles of village life, similar to that of the early agrarian era before the emergence of civilisation, but with the exception that they are now subject to an overarching hierarchy of rulers and tribute takers (who can also draft farmers in case of war).

Second. Above the village level we have local elites, nobles, priests and so on, mitigating relations to the centre of power. These local power brokers extract resources by taxing the primary producers of the villages, but usually do not interfere further in their life.

Third. Above these local elites are where we find the sovereign rulers of the state, such as kings (and sometimes queens). These rely on the resources extracted by the elites on the local level. Sometimes, with the emergence of empires, there are even rulers above the level of kings: emperors, shahs and the like. But the outlined structure with primary producers at the bottom, a ruler at the top, and a middle level of power brokers in between is a universal feature of all human civilisations in the agrarian regime (also sometimes referred to as the feudal system).[21]

How to Seize Power in Agrarian Civilisation

But how did a few people manage to subdue large numbers of farmers? We know that nomads will usually resist individuals attempting to assume power over them, so how did early agrarian leaders overcome this initial resistance?

In the beginning, farming communities must have willingly surrendered some control of resources and labour to trusted leaders as a measure to combat the problems caused by the increased population density and social complexity.[22] It is unlikely that leaders could have managed to assume power in a community by means of coercion alone, since they would have lacked the resources to do so initially. So power must have grown out of some sort of consent-based social structure, like that we know from foraging communities, where leaders are chosen by their merits and where their authority ends when they do not benefit the community any longer, or a better candidate becomes available.

As security becomes an increasingly urgent issue, a higher authority to curb the growing violence becomes necessary. Thenceforth, in order to defuse internal conflicts and protect people from outsiders, people willingly give up some of their freedoms, in particular the use of violence, delegating political authority and the necessary means to carry it out to trusted leaders in order to benefit the community as a whole. The construction and maintenance of irrigation projects is another way in which political authority is more or less voluntarily delegated to a central figure, as these endeavours are impossible without the delegation of power to a strong and cunning leader. Such endeavours usually require further measures of political authority than those traditionally ordained to an early agrarian big man or chieftain in order to coordinate joint labour efforts efficiently and redistribute resources peacefully. So to accommodate these new productive efforts, more resources and political authority than before start to be concentrated in smaller, centralised nodes of power from which the first small state-like structures emerge. For the chieftains to become kings, they have to develop new means of achieving political precedence. This is as much a political as it is an economical matter.

Following the Agricultural Revolution, the economy gradually evolves from first a traditional system of gift-giving (known from hunter-gatherers and horticulturalists), via, second, a form of tributary system (observed among early agrarian horticulturalist big-man societies and chieftains) to, third, a system of taxation (or plunder, depending on the degree) that we know from state-like structures. Gift-giving prevailed in the foraging regime and was characterised by tribal members living in intimate, reciprocal relationships of mutual trust in which resources by necessity were shared to satisfy everyone's needs. In a setting where food is scarce and people are free to simply wander off if they disagree, a leader does not have any other means to secure political authority than the trust he is able to instil in his own personal leadership skills. In addition, the livelihood of nomadic tribal societies depends on everyone getting enough to eat, which requires a communal effort that can only be achieved by considerable amounts of trust that everyone does their part and shares whatever surplus they may fairly obtain with everyone else. This changes to some extent when societies become sedentary and grow larger. As the intimate relationships of a few band members wane in favour of the larger and considerably less personal agrarian societies, the need for a central figure of authority to manage the economy grows larger. However, the tributary system among horticulturalists is not as unequal as the title of a big man or chieftain may suggest. Although village members usually hand over most of their surplus to a leader, such authorities for the most part only keep a small fraction to themselves since their primary task is to redistribute society's resources fairly, for instance by organising lavish feasts and giving out gifts. In fact, the political power of the big men relies on their abilities in pleasing their people, and the 'bigness' of such an authority figure is usually proportional to the size of the gifts he is able to bestow on others. The tributary system of exchange is thus an extension of the traditional gift, or sharing, economy of hunter-gatherers in which the gift-giving part has just been centralised to a single leading figure and institutionalised in the form of tributaries (meaning that social and cultural measures have been instilled to enforce society's expectations of handing over surplus goods to a central figure).

Initially, military means to achieve this remain secondary to the various cultural measures, the charisma of leaders, and the ability of these to instil trust. However, as people become sedentary farmers and food production rises along with the size of the population, the main concern of getting enough to eat gradually wanes in favour of security from other people. Accordingly, the big men and chieftains come to increasingly draw their authority from their military abilities. But at this stage it is just as important to secure the peace as it is to win military battles, of which the former is often achieved by appeasing neighbouring tribes with gifts, which can sometimes turn them into allies. The tributary economy thus works in close tandem with the older gift economy. With time this may lead to the consolidation of several villages under the authority of a single chieftain, who then gains the necessary resources to organise and supply regular armies. Eventually, the tributes people more or less voluntarily handed over to their leader in virtue of the trust he could instil turn into outright taxation in fear of the military consequences if they refuse. The amount of organised violence to be marshalled by a leader in a horticultural setting is rather limited, but as agriculture gets more productive, the ability to muster large armies becomes more feasible – which changes the game of political and economic power completely.

As chieftains become kings, they now have to worry less about public opinion and more about military competitors. They can now keep a larger fraction of society's economic surplus to themselves as long as they keep their armies adequately equipped to suppress the population and fend off invaders. As a consequence, social inequalities grow rapidly. The productivity of societies grows significantly throughout the agrarian era and, by extension, the military capacities of leaders as well.

What distinguishes state formation from the earlier evolution of the agrarian regime is that it, with the words of David Christian, 'marks a critical transition from personal relations to impersonal power, and from power over things to power over people.'[23] People tend to be hesitant towards handing over the fruits of their labour to someone that is not family. But a well-liked and trustworthy individual who is widely respected in a local community, and who is believed to manage resources in a way that benefits the greater good, can convince us to give away our possessions willingly. This, however, becomes more difficult to achieve when societies grow larger and more impersonal. Humans like to give each other gifts, but they usually do not like paying taxes; and handing over resources to a person we have not even met is almost impossible without some means of coercion. So apart from centralisation, another central characteristic of states is the increasingly impersonal aspect of power they bring along. Power distances grow as societies become larger, and the chains of command expand greatly. In the new agrarian regime, it suddenly becomes common for people to never personally meet the individual who is in charge. This is something that greatly differs from the earlier power relations among hunter-gatherers, which relied on personal relations and reciprocal trust.

With the growing centralisation of power, distribution becomes lopsided towards the elites who control the redistribution and a privileged class of specialists. The latter's highly sought-after skills often give them a disproportionally large share of society's surplus in comparison with the primary producers. Such specialists are responsible for a high number of novel material and cultural achievements, but only a small fraction of the population is to benefit. The vast majority remain farmers who only participate in the new cultural regime of agrarian civilisation by providing matter and energy to keep the states and the lifestyles of the elites going. The only thing they get in return is protection, but at the price of heavy taxation. Farmers are often pressed to the margin of subsistence, and poor harvests, wars, diseases and plunder repeatedly make their life miserable. Yet as they are tied to the land and usually do not have any sufficient means of physical force, they cannot escape the situation. The authority and resources they initially granted their leaders, by varying degrees of public consent, prove to be a trap that is used to further enhance the elites' grip on power.

The Subordination of Women

We also see a substantial change to our gender roles. The traditional division of labour among hunter-gatherers, where women primarily gather while the men go hunting, makes for a relatively equal relation of power between the sexes, since both males and females are important for producing food. But with the new conditions in agrarian society, women increasingly find themselves in a subordinated position.

The first less complex form of agriculture is often termed 'horticulture' and differs from agriculture proper by the fact that it does not entail ploughs, draft animals and manure. Instead, work in the field is conducted with simple sticks or hoes to plant seeds and clear out weeds. As a logical extension of the traditional gender roles in foraging societies, this work is mainly performed by women. But when farming becomes a much heavier job with the introduction of the plough and large animals, it is transferred to the physically stronger males. Since power relations favour those providing the all-important calories, men accordingly get more powerful vis-à-vis women. This explains why more or less all agricultural societies tend to be patriarchal. Men's newly gained role as 'breadwinners' furnishes substantial power status at home, no matter how far down the social ladder they are in society at large, as long as they provide their wives and children with the necessities to keep the household going.

Women also get increasingly burdened by more childbirths, as mentioned, and since sedentary lifestyles need to address the problem of increased material entropy – garbage that is – even more time and effort need to be spent on domestic duties. But taking care of large numbers of children and performing housework is an effective way of getting excluded from the circles of power – which are simply not located within the domestic domain of child-nurture, cooking and cleaning. As society becomes larger and more complex, and as the growing surplus of agricultural production makes it possible to support a number of new occupations, a new public sphere emerges outside the household with new opportunities for wealth and power. Since women are effectively secluded from this domain, they are likewise cut off from the resources and social positions it can provide. Their domestic duties simply do not allow them the privilege, and time, to devote themselves to a single specialised task outside the household.

That this also includes new specialised roles from which to obtain unprecedented levels of wealth and power, now becoming the exclusive domain of men, further reinforces patriarchal structures and sentiments in society at large. That men end up dominating the most economically and politically powerful occupations, while women end up with ever more children and garbage to dispose of, thus simply strengthens the idea that men should rule and women should prepare their meals. In combination, these factors push women further into the domestic sphere, while men begin dominating the public sphere – and that's where the power is.

With higher specialisation, the social and productive life-world of humanity splits into two distinct spheres where the domestic sphere ends up in a more precarious situation, as it increasingly relies on the resources provided from the public sphere. Basically, women end up in need of more outside assistance, and men are the ones to give them that. As such, men gain the upper hand: if a man leaves his wife and children, the family risks starvation, but the man himself, however, does not rely on his wife for his immediate survival. Under the new conditions, one could no longer just gather what one needed from nature, but relied entirely on agricultural products. And since that was provided by the public sphere that men came to dominate, women ended up in an unequal power relation of dependence towards the men. This circumstance, sometimes referred to as 'patriarchy', would remain unshaken until the later industrial age. Assisted by modern inventions such as birth control, electrical household appliances and ready-made food products, along with the circumstance that men's superior physical strength no longer mattered, women could gradually gain access to the public sphere and thereby retain a more equal status – a process that is yet to reach its completion.

THE REVOLUTION OF WRITTEN LANGUAGE

Of all the new memes to emerge in agrarian civilisation, writing is perhaps the most innovative and the one to most radically change our symbolic world. The invention of writing has been termed by John Wright as 'the second information revolution'.[24] The first was spoken language itself, and there is little doubt that both 'technologies' did indeed revolutionise not only how information is handled, but also the overall complexity of human life.

Writing is an essential tool for the management of large, complex civilisations. It gives us the ability to externalise our ideas in a more efficient and precise way, which agrarian civilisation can use to coordinate the joint efforts of people to an extent not possible before. Written language gives us the possibility of developing much more complex collective imaginaries. Without any means of transmitting and storing information in material form, societies could not have evolved much further than that of an advanced chieftain. It simply could not have been feasible to govern large empires without any further information technologies than oral language, evidenced by the fact that all major agrarian civilisations have had some means of externally recorded information (be that knotted strings, as used by the Incas, or more conventional methods of sign-use) to control and organise people, matter and energy.[25]

Power and information go hand in hand, and because the handling of information often entails control of larger amounts of complexity and power, the ones working with symbol analysis have usually been ascribed higher status than those performing manual labour. Gaining a monopoly on information eventually becomes as important to states as the monopoly on violence, and its importance has increased up to this day. What characterises those in power in complex civilisations is not their physical strength, but their access to important information that others do not have. The most powerful societies have likewise been the ones who most efficiently handled information.

Initially, written symbols were used for bookkeeping and not to record speech. Only later would they evolve to handle more abstract concepts and emotional messages. It is thus a telling sign of the nature of civilisational progress that the oldest text we have been able to decipher is that of an ordinary receipt of 29,086 measures of barley from the ancient city of Uruk. Curiously, the first name of a person we have from recorded history is thus not that of a king or a conqueror, but merely a humble accountant named Kushim, who signed this document.[26] The ancient writing system of Sumer, commonly considered the oldest, is initially merely a system of accounting. One of the main reasons that we have such plentiful evidence of this ancient system is because of the coincidence that it was engraved into tablets of durable clay. It is, however, given the conditions in early agrarian civilisations, probably not a coincidence that the oldest systematised writing system we know of is one of recording debts and financial transactions. The needs of recording past debts and financial transactions are simply much more urgent in ancient civilisation than that of recording poems or tales; and given the complexity of such activities, the former has been much more likely to emerge before the latter.

When we study the clay tablets of ancient Sumer, it becomes obvious that credit systems are in fact a very old invention, one that predates coinage,

Cuneiform, one of the earliest systems of writing, was invented by the Sumerians in the late fourth millennium BC. Photo: Wikimedia Commons.

which only emerges several millennia later. Even though silver is the official currency of ancient Sumer, silver does not circulate in Sumerian society and is not used for everyday transactions (just as gold was not used back when the US dollar was pegged to the gold standard). The value of goods is compared to its perceived worth in silver, but peasants and merchants are not required to pay their taxes or debts in silver and can pay in almost everything else of value. So even if silver is nominally the currency, signs engraved into modest clay functions as the de facto currency – and, as in any modern market economy later on, most transactions in Sumer are based on credit.[27] These tablets of clay function as IOUs. They are often traded, and as such they are the first historically recorded instance of money anywhere in the world. This circumstance reveals what has been increasingly obvious since the modern world relinquished its dependence on precious metals: that money, basically, is nothing but promissory notes, or debt in another word; notions of how much the holder of an IOU is deserving of.

Promissory notes have repeatedly served as money, as periods of crisis again and again have revealed when cash flows dried up.[28] Taverns have always had credit systems, even in ancient Sumer, and such notes have often been traded and used as a currency. It is thus revealing that money, when it is invented in ancient Sumer, emerges from the first known instance of debt recording anywhere in the world.

In a way, we can say that money is 'written into existence'. We need to keep in mind that money is not a physical object, like that of coins, for instance, with any intrinsic worth of its own. Money is simply information, and as such an information technology that only becomes possible with the invention of writing. With this technology we can make records of people's past labour and estimate its value as judged by society. Spending money is an informational act that sends a signal to confirm one's wants to the people involved in satisfying them.[29] A difference between exchanges involving money and simple bartering, for example precious metals for other goods, is that money often has a value above the perceived value of the metal itself – and most often, money has functioned without any involvement of precious metals or any other valuable materials at all. As an information technology (one involving information about who owes what to whom, or more specifically how much the debt of a person is worth in relation to others), money can be seen as a kind of IOU – and IOUs, contrary the expectation of returned favours as those prevailing in a gift economy, require writing to determine their actual worth.

By writing down debts, the trust barrier between strangers can also be overcome. This is necessary in the large and dense societies of the later agrarian era, where we do not know each other as well as before but still enjoy a high enough level of security to conduct peaceful transactions with one another. With debts in writing, it makes it harder for borrowers to deny the existence of a loan or for lenders to exaggerate it. Yet such contracts only have any value in societies with a monopoly on violence to defend these claims. When money does not have any worth on its own, such as clay tablets as opposed to precious metals, its value is only as high as the level of organised violence to defend it. If the recordings of debts are not supported by military means to collect it if a borrower refuses to pay, then they are essentially worthless. And only when someone defends the value of a legal tender with organised violence can its value exceed that of the metal or other materials it is made of. We thus see how the state and its means of organised violence, and the invention of writing and of money, which at first were more or less the same thing, make up two of the most central memes of civilisation.

But the state and money are more than a coercive measure of control and an informational system of economic organisation respectively. They are very much social imaginaries, purely mental constructs that first become 'real' when enough people believe in their truth claims. Only when we begin to act as if they were real entities, and bestow them with some kind of 'essence' in our symbol world can the myths of the state and money become effective organisational principles in society – and we need to do so collectively. We need to confirm with each other that they are real, that they are more than just imagination, and those societies to do so most effectively also become the most powerful. This requires further means than purely administrative ones. On a systemic level there are certain limits to how well the state can affect our behaviours by coercion alone and how much trust can be instilled in a currency that is essentially made of worthless numbers. Hence, we need a cultural dimension to make these imaginaries believable, some set of shared symbols and narratives to make us forget for a moment that they are purely fictitious. With the emergence of civilisation, there are thus great efforts put into making states and money integral parts of our symbol world. Religion, art and rituals are used in ever more sophisticated ways to prop up these social constructs with meaning – and beauty. The myths of the state and money will become so integral to our understanding of the world that we eventually cannot imagine the world without them. Over time they become self-evident, naturally given facts that few ever question, or ponder their purely imaginary nature; and eventually, the invention of writing itself proves a most effective tool to enhance these social imaginaries in our shared symbol world as myth can now be put into writing and saved for future generations.

In the beginning, writing was, as mentioned, only used for accounting purposes and other administrative measures for which it had been invented, what has been termed 'sectorial literacy'. But later it penetrates into the central core of our culture, which then gives rise to what has been called 'cultural literacy'. When that happens, our writing systems become much more advanced. We go from systems where individual signs are used to signify material objects, for instance a silver ingot or a bundle of barley, to a system where signs are used for the sounds in our spoken language. This dramatically increases the utility and efficiency of written language. Instead of having to write and interpret a great number of signs, a limited number of syllables is sufficient, which also provides more flexibility and precision. This opens up entirely new ways of relating to our symbol world. According to Jan Assmann, this form of writing 'restructures not only thought but also, under certain cultural circumstances, the whole network of relations between human beings, man and society, man and cosmos, man and god, and god and cosmos'.[30] This is because, as he elaborates, writing serves as 'a special kind of symbols that bestow visibility to the invisible, stability to the volatile, and wide dissemination to the locally confined'. Oral language, on the contrary, 'uses sound-symbols that are invisible, volatile, and locally restricted'.[31] What writing and literacy on this level accomplish is thus the opening-up of a whole new way of relating to the world, a way in which aspects of reality, hitherto invisible and difficult to grasp, can be scrutinised and brought under the control of human beings.

With writing it also becomes possible to record and archive past events and thus produce history. Because history has the capacity to document the doings of kings and conditions created by humans, not only gods, it will eventually dispel and replace the old mythology of the early agrarian religions. Disregarding the actual validity of such records, written historical memory has a verifiability and truth value about past events that exceed those of myths. And in these records, the actions of humans take precedence from those of gods.[32] With this development we see a first step towards a more rational and secular worldview, though it will take more than a couple of thousand years of mythical and religious thinking before a fully rational worldview emerges in the later centuries of the second millennium CE.

Parallel and largely connected with the growing complexity of human societies, the capacity to store and transmit information has increased enormously, both in volume and range, while the costs have gone down. This appears to be a general law of history, and one that has resulted in an ever-greater ability to learn from others and manipulate matter and energy, from which further complexity and divisions of labour, but also increased social inequality, have been the consequences. With writing, our 'collective brain' has grown larger.

With written language, cultural development will also progress much faster. Writing allows for the pace of development to speed up as new ideas and information can more easily spread and accumulate across generations and geographical boundaries. Written language will thus have great significance for the human being's continued cultural development. A community can only hold a certain number of stories and myths alive in oral tradition, but with writing it becomes possible to ensure a more exact and undistorted transfer of a greater number of narratives and the construction of a much richer and more diverse symbol world. This facilitates one of the most decisive developments in human history that will be the topic of the next chapter: organised religion.

Chapter 4

THE HUMAN BEING CREATES GOD

During the first millennium BCE, the growing complexity and size of agrarian civilisations make it ever harder to organise society. A growing number and wider range of conflicts of interest arise between classes, cultures and powerful individuals, both within the centres of power and across longer geographical distances. As the empires expand, the newly added and culturally diverse provinces far from the centre have to be kept tightly within a larger framework – and at peace. At the same time, discontent among the large urban underclasses are growing into a serious issue for those in charge. Social cohesion is of greater concern than ever; and as a means to remedy the situation, we create God.

Previously, conflicts within a community could more easily be mediated since they revolved around family members and others in the small village with whom we had personal relations, and upon whom we were often mutually dependent. But in the densely populated cities of agrarian civilisation, we live with people to whom we are not related and whom we do not know personally. We are now surrounded by strangers with whom we may not even share the same symbol world. This creates new societal challenges. Ancestor cults no longer suffice. New narratives are required to keep everything from falling apart.

Kings and emperors also need novel ways to legitimise their authority, and the best way to do so is to seize the perceivably powerful magic of the spirits and claim it as their own. Thus, with the help of the new invention of writing, the existing animistic beliefs are transformed into coherent and formalised belief systems more in tune with the larger and more socially stratified societies. 'Magic' thus becomes 'myth' in the hands of a highly specialised religious elite, and the new divine narratives create shared symbol worlds that provide the necessary social glue to keep people together within communities that are largely imagined. On the one hand this serves the needs of those in charge, but on the other it also serves the overall stability and coherence of the much larger societies now stretching beyond the family and the clan. Gods transform us into brothers and sisters of the one true faith, but by the same token the rulers who monopolise these myths also obtain the spiritual means to legitimise their authority.

THE EMERGENCE OF ORGANISED RELIGION

In the large cities of the late agrarian era a great degree of uncertainty lingers regarding the question of how we should deal with the many strangers we are suddenly supposed to live with. How do we make sure that people who are no longer related and do not know each other personally treat each other with a minimum of respect and kindness? One possibility is, of course, to create laws so that people can be punished for their violations of others. But this is not enough. Ethical guidelines, which are not dependent on external control measures, are just as necessary. If people only exhibit pro-social behaviour under the direct threat of force, they are likely to break the rules as soon as they believe they can get away with it. Coercing people to behave nicely is also a very resource-intensive endeavour. As such we need new beliefs, religious convictions, to exert internal control as well. Organised religion has the capacity to transform our wills so that we not only act ethically to avoid punishment in our earthly life, but also behave well towards others to please the gods, generate good karma, and so on. And it can make us refrain from harming others in order to avoid divine punishment or secure ourselves a good position in the afterlife.

It is of utmost importance that the state creates a shared symbol world and a shared identity if people are to co-exist peacefully and cooperate efficiently. Organised religion (exactly because it is *organised* and thus has a much greater capacity to influence a larger number of people than that of a traditional animistic belief system) has the ability to create common and more expansive symbol worlds, social imaginaries that are shared by many people who do not know each other. The shared identity provided by organised religion enables us to see each other as part of a larger family. If we know the same narratives, songs and customs we feel that we have much more in common, which helps us to better avoid misunderstandings and conflicts.

Religion permeates culture in agrarian civilisation and regulates most things in life, both in private and public. Religion and legislation are usually the same, with the former providing ethical guidelines for how we should treat others. It also offers more specific codes of conduct for various everyday problems. Religious narratives can inspire us and provide role models to help us overcome many of life's challenges, which in turn can make us more resilient and well-functioning as individuals, and as societies. Religion is thus a source of mental strength and societal coherence.

This contains a highly evolutionary dimension: cultures that succeed in making people treat each other well and follow rules and thought patterns that are conducive towards positive societal and personal development have a greater chance of survival than others.[1] Just as in nature, where the most suitable genes ensure their own as well as their host's survival and dissemination, societies in which a favourable cultural, memetic mutation is rooted likewise increase their chances of survival and expansion. The new way of viewing the spirit world that organised religion offers does just that. Societies with strong religious sentiments increasingly win economic and military competitions with others. And as the advantages of having an organised religion become clearer, the incentives of developing such symbolic systems become all the stronger. As civilisations grow larger and more complex, we thus see the emergence and proliferation of new religious symbol systems all over the agrarian world.

But as the expansion of the great empires and increasing inter-regional trade bring a growing number of different peoples and various symbol worlds into contact with each other, the practical question arises: how shall we relate to each other's gods? Who can lay claim to the religious truth? Whose god is the right one? And who bears religious claims to political authority? These important issues need to be resolved to make the increasingly larger states cohesive.[2]

The diplomatic solution is to add others' gods to one's own. As such, organised polytheist religions emerge with sets of gods in pantheons: institutionalised and, often, hierarchically ordered systems of gods with specific powers and functions. Usually the god of the politically dominant actor becomes the leader and most powerful, while the gods of conquered peoples come to represent subordinate roles. The god of a coastal people relying on fishing and maritime trade may become the god of the seas, the god of farmers may become the god of fertility, and the god of a fierce warrior tribe may become the god of war. Many new professions also see the light of day, with every guild getting its own god. These are all accepted and incorporated into the growing pantheons as long as the god of the central city is acknowledged as the god above all gods. It is also common that every city has its own god, and through the pantheon, the different cities' symbol worlds are interwoven in ways that facilitate trade and other forms of cooperation. Polytheism facilitates encounters with more distant cultures, since their gods and myths can be included in the overarching religion.[3] These solutions also demonstrate how interactions with other cultures can spur creativity and lead to an extension of one's own culture.

However, with time the many different and often contradicting myths and local beliefs begin to cause a considerable amount of conceptual confusion that prompts more universal explanations. At this point, society has evolved so far beyond its humble beginnings that the old myths increasingly start to appear hopelessly outdated and out of tune with the higher complexity of the current social reality. The old narratives lose their trustworthiness and intellectual validity as thinkers begin to question the established customs and culturally inherited truths of their own society, speculating on whether there could be some higher truths applying to all cultures and all people and if society could be organised in much better ways. These circumstances are at the core of what would later be called the 'Axial Age', the age when the great civilisations' various symbol worlds emerge: cultural superstructures that permeate the everyday life of the majority of the world's populations to this day.

THE AXIAL AGE

The 'Axial Age' is a term coined by Karl Jaspers for the period *c*. 800–200 BCE when, supposedly independently of each other, various intellectual and spiritual traditions emerged in the great centres of civilisation across Eurasia.[4] According to Jaspers, the developments of the Axial Age have their origins in the increasing tension at the time between various centres of power both within and between states: a development that can be interpreted in prevalent (and it may be added socially unsustainable) conditions characterised as the 'struggle of all against all'. Under these circumstances, individuals as independent social units emerge to challenge the prevailing state of affairs and confront the thinking of the majority and the elites. Old ideas, customs and conditions are questioned and finally liquidated, which led Jaspers to characterise the Axial Age as an age of 'reflection', openness to 'new and boundless possibilities', and of man raising 'himself above his own self'. It is the age of 'transcendence', 'the ethicisation of religion', and an age characterised by the struggle of *logos* versus *mythos* – an age to bring a new self-understanding of the human being vis-à-vis the world into existence.[5]

The Axial Age overlaps with the Iron Age. The economic, agricultural and urban growth that followed from the introduction of iron and the equally important technologically disruptive qualities of iron weapons cause increased political turmoil and warfare in both the East and the West. The many uncertainties of this transition have been argued to relate to the new intellectual and spiritual developments of the Axial Age. Changes of this magnitude, in combination with the perception of crisis, usually exert (evolutionary) pressures to develop new forms of social organisation. It thus seems to be no coincidence that the Axial Age also coincides with the Warring States period in China, the political disruptions caused by the introduction of iron weapons into the Middle East and the equally politically volatile situation on the Greek peninsula during the time of the Greek philosophers. However, in order for profound rethinking to appear in the midst of political and societal crisis, the existence of suitable arenas for thinkers to develop and articulate new ideas is required, as is a written medium for this to be conducted within. This requires a certain degree of autonomy from political power. Accordingly, the great Axial thinkers are all to be found in cultures with highly developed literary traditions, and often in the periphery of the dominant political centres.[6]

Until the first millennium BCE, even as state power increased, religions tend to be local or regional in their claims and influence. Religions are used to legitimise state power, mobilise loyalty and justify tribute taking. Even if smaller regional deities are incorporated into larger ones as the empires expand, religions usually remain regional affairs with particularistic claims tied to a certain dynasty or political entity and with ethnocentric promises of protecting a particular people. Not until the Axial Age do the first universal religions appear. Even while these religions are associated with particular dynasties or empires, they proclaim universal truths and validity to all people.

During the Axial Age there is a widespread critique of the 'might makes right' logic of agrarian society. As trade increases within and beyond the borders of the empires, and societies become more commercialised, a growing number of different peoples and distinct cultures co-exist and interact with each other in myriad ways. Exposure to a multitude of different and alien customs, beliefs and ideas thus stimulates intellectual and cultural life, but it also erodes dominant myths and established convictions, which causes tensions and new problems to arise. New ideas start to emerge and both political and intellectual challengers begin to erode the existing base of power. The old myths and political legitimacy of the established political order are scrutinised from a more critical point of view, while novel ways are sought to address the emotional needs of people and the hardships of life in agrarian civilisation.

Initially, the answers do not emerge within the centres of power, but among 'righteous rebels'[7] at far enough distance to criticise the authorities, yet close enough to enjoy the intellectual advances made by agrarian civilisation and to sufficiently affect it. What starts as a revolt against the establishment is, however, eventually adopted by the empires themselves to provide them with the necessary moral legitimacy, while the rebels gradually become part of the new established order. In the end, the rulers agree to subject themselves to the new moral order in exchange for staying in charge. They relinquish their claim to divine exclusiveness and accept the role of merely being the divine's mediators and foremost representatives on Earth. With the invention of divine law, rulers must govern in accordance with higher moral principles not even they stand above, and they only uphold their political legitimacy as long as they do so. And with the 'invention' of the soul not only are the elites considered to have heavenly qualities, now everybody has a piece of divinity within them. An agreement is reached that rulers retain their higher status within the realms of the earthly and mundane, but in heaven everybody is on a more equal footing – sort of.

The developments of the Axial traditions are, as mentioned, largely associated with the growth of the vast empires at the time in which people of diverse beliefs and cultures are governed by the same political entity. As such, it is probably not a coincidence that Zoroastrianism (the first major universal religion) appears in the Achaemenid empire, the largest at the time, and the first to control the entire hub region of middle Eurasia, covering a large array of different languages, religious traditions and cultural customs. The exchange networks of Eurasia grow rapidly during the first millennium BCE, which can be seen in how the Axial traditions travel along these growing links between civilisations. Not only Zoroastrianism, but also Manichaeism emerges in the Iranian lands of the Achaemenid Empire. These religions are, however, soon to be replaced by intellectual and spiritual traditions from a bit farther west: initially the Greek philosophies during the period known as Hellenism, following the conquest of Alexander the Great, and somewhat later with Christianity and Islam, which evolve from the Near Eastern Hebrew religion of Judaism. To the east, in India, Buddhism emerges and travels along the Silk Road to China, where Confucianism and Taoism are already developing around the same time. All of these symbolic systems differ from the previous religions and cults by their universal claims and critical stance towards the current societal and religious conditions.[8]

Some religions have supernatural overtones, such as Christianity and Islam, while others, such as the moral teachings of Confucius, do not. Hinduism, for instance, grows out of an early state religion, but most such early state traditions are abandoned during the Axial Age. All of the Axial Age religions share some novel characteristics: they make universal claims and have written orthodoxy or canon, making them more complex in nature. This is a structure that serves the ruling elites as only they can coordinate such advanced religious services. The moral teachings of the new Axial religions are the result of, and highly adapted to, the perceived needs of the large urban populations that appear at the time. The religious needs of farmers remain the same, however, as their productive relations with nature do not change. This causes tensions to arise between religious elites in the cities and rural inhabitants, whose religious sentiments remain tied to some kind of supernatural nature. In many religions this leads to a great deal of compromise between agrarian and urban religiosity.[9]

Although most of the new moral religions are the result of private enterprise, the states generally abandon their old belief systems when a sizable number of people, usually in the cities, convert to such religions (or are conquered by people who adhere to such powerful, universal faiths). It is highly advantageous for state elites to ally themselves with the new religions, since the universal claims and elaborate moral teachings can be used to legitimise their claims to power and because they possess the capacity to unite peoples of many different ethnicities to a much greater degree than earlier state religions.

The universal teachings of salvation become an efficient means to satisfy the emotional and spiritual needs of people, but also to govern them more efficiently. With the Axial wisdom teachings, philosophies and moral religions, civilisation obtains the necessary cultural superstructure to ensure stability and social cohesion, and in effect, the continuous development of their complexity. These traditions eventually become the new cultural foundation of society, replacing the older cults and pantheons. By virtue of their universal appeal they manage to include many different ethnicities and distinct cultures, so as to eventually mould them into the great world civilisations we know today. Eventually they spread beyond the borders of the empires that initially gave birth to them, and many even survive the collapse of the empires themselves, expanding relentlessly until they finally encounter other Axial traditions with equally universal aspirations – which often causes violent conflicts to erupt.

The increased social cohesion gives the societies who embrace an Axial tradition a substantial competitive edge – not least on the battlefield. Those who believe the one true God stands beside them in combat increasingly win the battles. Universal religion is a powerful meme, a symbol system and a way to organise the collective imaginary no empire in the millennia to come can be without.

THE AXIAL AGE: HONING REFLEXIVE HUMAN BEINGS

A decisive feature of the Axial Age according to Dalferth, as quoted by Jaspers, is 'man's reaching out beyond himself by growing aware of himself within the whole of Being'. In this process 'man becomes certain of transcendence', and 'thereby becomes human in a new and decisive sense' because '[i]t is impossible for man to lose transcendence, without ceasing to be man'.[10] In other words, the human being becomes capable of transcending its current state of being, and thus in that process becomes something else. The human being reaches a new level of psychological development, so to speak.

God, or similar notions of the divine, are increasingly seen as something recondite and separate.[11] Abrahamic monotheism, at this time Judaism, and Buddhism both emphasise that the divine is reached beyond language and the body.[12] Now we try to separate our mind from the material and worldly in order to attain the divine. Within Buddhism, asceticism is used as a method to attain transcendent experiences, while the material world is regarded as trivial. In Greece, Plato creates the dualist distinction between body and consciousness that has characterised European thought ever since. With the Axial Age we seek to rise above nature. Hence, we start to wage a battle against the body's desires and impulses. We develop an existential consciousness, becoming aware of the human being's nature and prerequisites. Through this we acquire new tools for reflecting upon the suffering that life brings.

The Axial Age also entails a radically new way of thinking that manifests itself in three main principles in particular:

- Every person is an individual with a personal soul or spirit.
- There is free will.
- We have personal responsibility.

This was something new. Prior to this, common people were not necessarily believed to have a soul or a piece of divinity within them. This was usually reserved for the elites. In addition, individual free will and responsibility were not central to the older religions and cults. In the old Judaic religion, for instance, God measures virtues at a societal level and distributes collective rewards and punishment based on how good a *society* the Jews had built. In many of the Axial religions, however, God measures how we behave at an individual level and hands out individual rewards and punishments.

The god concept is generally formed so that it fits into the spirit of the times and the new ethical ideals.[13] The image of the enraged god, formed by the bellicose cultures before the Current Era and who was the god of his flock, thus has to give way to a more moral and caring, individually oriented god. It is possible to follow this development from the older parts to the newer ones in the Old Testament. The god concept is developed into a god we can have as a role model and a good ideal. So to meet the demands of the time, religion will now focus on the human being's inner world, our responsibility towards others and higher ethical ideals. In this way, Judaism is gradually transformed during the Axial Age as the god of the Jews takes on more universalistic characteristics. In Greece, from the sixth century BCE, the old vice-laden gods are increasingly questioned by philosophers, while similar developments occur in India during the same period.

The institutionalisation of shared symbol worlds that the Axial traditions bring about also helps to extend our moral behaviour to a wider sphere. A shared identity and a commonly agreed-upon morality make it easier to expand the scope of our solidarity. Personal relations of trust and pre-conventional morals are sufficient to keep smaller groups together, but to make us more inclined towards treating strangers more ethically we need something to give us the necessary discipline and self-control. We need to start taking control of our instinctive emotions and impulses, and to mobilise our will power to fight our immediate inclinations. We have to learn how to take a step back and think before we carry out an act instead of just acting on impulse; here moral religion plays a central role in the cultivation of such mental capacities.

It is also now that we begin to distinguish ourselves from nature and start to regard ourselves as something apart from it. The Axial Age is, as mentioned above, the age of 'transcendence'. From the original animism, where we have been part of nature, we now separate our mind from the material and worldly in order to attain the divine. Instead of having gods with human flaws and weaknesses, particularly noticeable in the Greek tradition, the divine becomes an elevated ideal instead. We seek to rise above nature and our instincts, which are not appropriate in larger societies, and the old gods fortified with human failings do not offer a reliable precept. The god concept becomes more elevated, recondite and separated from nature, more 'transcendent'.[14] Through willpower the human being attempts to wage a battle against the body's biological limitations to reach the higher ideal that God or similar universal divine entities represent, with our new faiths helping us to cultivate these capacities.

When we talk about 'faith', it should not be understood as faith in a particular religion or god, but rather what Jaspers call 'philosophical faith', as '[f]aith in God, faith in man, faith in possibilities in the world'.[15] As such, faith is not mere superstition or arbitrary naive beliefs in things not grounded in nature, but a level of consciousness that enables us to go beyond our immediate instincts and inclinations to a place where we can establish a belief in the validity of visions not perceptible to the naked eye. This should be regarded as cognitive progress. Only by enabling faith in one's capacity to see beyond the mundane is it possible to set forces in motion to realise the possibilities only visible in a transcendent realm of symbols and ideas. By trusting the mind's truth claims, even though they are not grounded in mundane reality, humans can change the world according to their wishes. This is actually a precursor to the acclaimed anti-faith doctrine of rationality, which would not have been possible if it was not for the faith in the inner eye's capacity to reach sound conclusions above the realms of mundane reality.

The Axial Age thus brings a 'quest for transcendence' into existence that should be seen as what has been called a 'humanizing force of human history'[16] – a process that enables us to move beyond one state of being to one where we become more conscious and more capable of taking responsibility for our own development. From earlier traditions, the myths of the human's or the god's voyage to an inaccessible, invisible world is transferred to the new. This can be seen as an inner search for something beyond the mundane. Jesus, Buddha and Muhammed come to represent hero figures who recognise that our existing conceptions of the world are insufficient.

The hero is driven to leave his home and his old self, venturing into the world to attain new insights with the support of an invisible world. The hero then returns with these new insights to his people.[17]

With the Axial Age the human mind discovers itself as a world of its own; a distinct realm vastly different from the mundane natural and human environment it exists in. And when this happens it enables the human being to go beyond, 'transcend' that is, its immediate inclinations, emotions and prejudices and view them from a distance. What hitherto had been *subject* becomes *object* so that we can critically and methodologically examine the subjective part of reality – and thus, ultimately alter it. This is what sets this stage of human development apart from its prior: whereas the natural world and spirit world previously appeared to be part of the same unquestioned, all-encompassing reality, now the spirit world is something distinctly separate, something 'higher'.

The constantly growing and increasingly complex societies continuously bring forth new demands on people's ability to relate to both others and themselves, leading to major changes in religiosity during the Axial Age. Within such new religious practices, it is no longer considered sufficient to exercise rites, conduct sacrifices and the like. Instead, religion calls upon us to gaze inwards and discover ourselves to attain greater clarity.[18] As it was written on the forecourt of the Temple of Apollo at Delphi: 'Know thyself'. And as Socrates once famously stated: 'The unexamined life is not worth living.'[19] The new philosophies and religions offer methods and mental tools for reasoning about our inner world; tools that help us in developing our self-consciousness. Through these we explore our consciousness and try to govern our will.

An example of new symbol tools for this level of self-consciousness, with roots in the Axial Age is the widespread emphasis on virtues. In all the world religions and wisdom traditions we see a celebration of *virtues* that are considered morally desirable, such as humility, generosity, chastity, patience, fairness, courage and temperance. Among the *vices* to avoid there are such as greed, gluttony, laziness and so on. Through the virtues we receive guidance as to how we should be as humans, and what we should avoid. We start to use concepts that describe new comprehensive meanings. Thus, as we gain access to these new abstract concepts, the actions, thoughts and emotions, which previously had not been subject to conscious reflection, now become possible to think about and reason around.

What all the major world religions have in common is that they have moral and ethical guidelines in relation to other people. An example of this is the 'Golden Rule'. The gist of this principle is that you should treat your neighbour as you would like to be treated yourself. This idea develops simultaneously in various parts of the world, in parallel with a more moral highest principle in the form of a god or a divine semblance, which can serve as a paragon and an ideal. There is an emergence of religions that do not merely require that we satisfy the needs of some god or other to gain favours in our earthly life, but rather require that we treat our fellow humans as we want to be treated ourselves in order to reap rewards in the afterlife.

Buddhism distinguishes itself from the Western monotheist religions by lacking a god concept. Instead it focuses on an absolute state of being. But this, too, is based on moral and ethical guidelines in relation to other people. Buddhism proposes careful guidance to how we can systematically develop our consciousness. One example is the Noble Eightfold Path, which is an endeavour to think and live correctly to attain Nirvana. The Noble Eightfold Path focuses on wisdom in perception and thought, ethics in speech, action and way of life as well as meditation to increase attention and concentration. In polytheist Greece, the dramas shed light on the human being's emplacement in the world by showing the conscious and well-considered choices the hero must make to engender empathy and compassion with other people.[20] In China, Confucius also emphasises virtue and caring for others through his wisdom teachings.

Through these new methods and precepts, we seek to reflect upon and adapt ourselves vis-à-vis that which is prescribed as more desirable. Through culture and new social imaginaries, we now get an opportunity to influence our own will. We try to influence our own consciousness, emotions and reactive patterns through relating to higher ideals of what is right and good. Religion systematises our ability to wish for something different and better. Our ability to consciously govern our thoughts, actions and will is also necessary for our society to survive and to thrive, as society benefits greatly from citizens able to control their will.

FAITH AND REASON – *MYTHOS* AND *LOGOS*

Around 400 BCE, in previously peripheral Europe, there has now arisen a civilisation that in terms of complexity and development can be measured against, and later even surpass, the old civilisations in the Middle East. In wealthy Athens, a philosophy develops that will become the touchstone of Western thought. In this tradition, reason is given great focus, which, two thousand years later, will constitute the foundation of a completely new thought perspective: the rational. The more philosophical and reason-oriented thinking is usually called *logos* after the Greek word for 'word', 'reason' and 'logic'. The Greeks see a close connection between thinking and the word, which is also reflected in their language.[21] The objective of human thinking, according to Greek philosophers such as Aristotle, is to understand the innermost principles of existence through reason. Everything in the physical world is considered animated by an intrinsic purpose, an inner principle. Hence the physics of antiquity still retains vestiges of animism's subjectivity. With Aristotle, the doctrine of 'teleology' is developed, in which every part of reality is thought to carry an inherent *telos*, after the Greek word for 'objective' or 'purpose'. Things are still considered to have an inner world with inherent objectives and meanings. But in contrast to animism's capriciousness in the essence of nature, *telos* is conversely a specific law-bound property which, in accordance with the spirit of the age, can be made comprehensible through human reason. The tree or the rock both have their specific *telos* that imply their meaning and objective. Aristotle's approach is empirical: He studies and tests physical reality, and attributes his observations to teleology. Thus, if a stone is dropped and falls to the ground, Aristotle infers that this is the stone's *telos*. The concepts of *telos* and *logos* will follow us through the Western history of ideas, as we shall see further on in this book.

Prior to the Axial Age, a *myth* was seen as a story – a fairy tale – which helped us learn and understand something. There was no reason-based thinking that took a position on whether what was stated in the myth was accurate in a physical or historical sense. Myths are important since humans have a need for meaning-creating narratives to anchor our symbol worlds and keep ourselves and our societies together. Myths do not necessarily need to be historically accurate in order to be meaningful. However,

Raphael's painting The School of Athens from 1511. Plato is pointing upwards towards the realm of reason and ideas. Aristotle is pointing downwards towards the realm of empirical experience. Two different perspectives on the world that will be in competition up until today. Photo: Wikimedia Commons.

with the Axial Age's rational culture, our thinking receives new features in the form of critical questioning and higher demands for factual accuracy. Where it had previously been sufficient that we received guidance and support in the myths, it is now important that they are also historically accurate. The new religious symbolic systems all strive towards universal, generally applicable explanations, but still base their stories on a mythology. The monotheist religions, for instance, all maintain that their writings have a historical foundation.[22] For the ancient Greeks it did not matter whether their divine legends were true or not, but for the Christians the historical accuracy of the tales in the holy scriptures, not just their moral truth or narrative power, becomes more salient.

The mythical narratives remain important and are not abandoned in the new religions. On the contrary, now they actually become even more important, since they also need to be true. The truth claims make it easier for the Abrahamic religions to legitimise their message in a time of more reason-based thinking. With this demand for truth, religion will, however, as we shall see, start to dig its own grave. A problem with the reading of the Bible is that the Old Testament came to exercise its influence from the perspective of the Greek translation. The Jewish rabbi, professor and author Jonathan Sacks sheds light on how the inner dimensions of the human that the Hebrew texts have spoken of are turned into concrete occurrences in the *logos*-influenced Greek-language version.[23] This fusion of Greek and Jewish thinking will later constitute the foundation for the Western symbol world during the Middle Ages.

The apostle Paul is decisive for the creation of Christianity. Paul is a Jew and a Roman citizen who converted to the new religion of Christianity. He tries to spread the Christian message in Greece, which during this time is part of the Roman Empire, where the influence of *logos* is great. With Paul, the Jewish tradition and the Christian message meet reason-governed Greek culture; hence Christianity's ambiguity towards reason and myth begins. In the end it is reason that will decide which writings will be included in the New Testament and how the Hebrew texts are to be translated. The start of the Gospel of John is a classic example of this through its introductory text: 'In the beginning was *Logos*, and *Logos* was with God, and *Logos* was God'. In English translations, *logos* is usually translated by 'the word', but 'reason' or 'consciousness' are actually more correct translations.

A few hundred years after Paul had unified Christianity with *logos*, more of antiquity's doctrines are taken up by Christianity. This happens when the Roman citizen and Church Father Augustine around 400 CE attempts to integrate Plato's world of ideas with Christianity. This coalescence has a major influence on the doctrine of the Catholic Church during the following centuries. Plato argued that evil is merely the absence of good, and that there is a 'genuine reality', a world of ideas that is unalterable and true beyond time and space. Augustine thus argues that God is transcendent, beyond the physical world, and that the world is inherently good since it is created by God. The body is created by God and not evil in and of itself, but Augustine still regards bodily love as lower than spiritual love. Matter is lower, further from God, than spirit. For the Catholic Church, the separation between the two Greek concepts of *agape*, love for all fellow humans, and *eros*, romantic love, becomes crucial. Augustine also emphasises a free will that allows the human being to choose between turning towards God or the world. Dualism thus takes a firm place in Christian thinking. This and many other strains of thought and concepts of antiquity are then included in the doctrines of the Catholic Church.

THE PHILOSOPHY OF THE CATHOLIC CHURCH

We thus arrive in the era that in the West is called the Middle Ages. The Roman Empire's decline is a fact, but its religion and written language live on into the Middle Ages and become the most important symbolic systems in Europe over the thousand years that follow. The preserved Greek and Roman writings will inspire later societies and even constitute the foundation for the later scientific revolution.

After the fall of the Roman Empire there has arisen a new Western European cultural sphere with a common symbolic language, held together by the Roman Catholic Church and Latin written language. Otherwise the continent is divided into a host of more or less independent states, large and small, and a multitude of varying languages and cultures. In contrast to China, whose cultural and institutional unification survives the fall of the Han dynasty, Western Europe remains divided after the fall of Rome. But on the ruins of the Roman Empire there arises a meme fusion of various Jewish, Greek, Latin and Germanic elements. This mixture will later prove an explosive cocktail for further development.

It is important to stress that religion does not stand in opposition to reason. Rationality plays a decisive role in both Christianity and Islam. As such, the great intellectual project of the Middle Ages, known as scholasticism, is not just an irrational enterprise that science would later turn against, but rather a decisive step forward towards the reason-based, rational thought perspective that characterises our scientific thinking today. The theological discussions of the times are actually an attempt to find a more reason-based foundation for religion.

In the thirteenth century, the theologian and philosopher Thomas Aquinas attempts to combine the newly rediscovered empirical philosophy of Aristotle with Catholic doctrine.[24] Aristotle's philosophy, which had been forgotten in Europe, returns via Aquinas, who acquired it from the Islamic culture in Spain. Initially, Aquinas encounters major resistance within the Church and is accused of heresy. But later, his integration of Aristotle's philosophy enjoys a near-total victory and becomes the Catholic Church's official philosophy.

In Aquinas' integration of Greek philosophy and Christianity, Aristotle's *telos* becomes God's intention that exists in all parts of creation. God's purpose in creation can therefore be inferred from two sources: in the Bible's narratives, and in creation itself by interpreting its *telos*.[25] Aquinas also argues that God has given humans *logos*, reasoning, so that we may understand *telos*. All parts of creation have been given a *telos*, but only humans have received *logos*. Hence, there is according to Aquinas no contradiction between reason and the Bible (and if there appears to be a contradiction we have either not understood God's *telos* or failed to interpret the Bible correctly). This line of thought becomes the basis of what has been known as *natural law* within Catholicism. It states that since God has given all things a *telos*, God's intention and will can be interpreted through observing creation. How something is created provides guidance for how we should relate to it, and from there we can arrive at a suitable course of action. We can, according to the Church, draw conclusions about how things *ought* to be from observing how God's creation *is*: if plants start to grow in the spring, then it is because God wants it so. And if night is followed by day, then that is equally the way it ought to be because it is the will of God. However, this kind of thinking can also be applied to social and political matters: if kings and popes rule, and peasants obey, then it is because God intended society to work that way. The natural law of the church is thus as much an ontological thought system as it is a political means to support the dominant social order.

Natural law has long been part of the Christian thought tradition and we can still find it, for instance, in the Church's sexual morals that consider sexual activities not intended for procreation in violation with the natural law of God, who created sex with the purpose of making children. Yet deriving an *ought* from an *is* has been proved to be an argumentative fallacy, known as the 'naturalistic fallacy', which was first articulated by David Hume as the 'is–ought problem'.[26] This is, however, a line of reasoning that is surprisingly common even today. People may argue that homosexuality is wrong because the purpose of sex is to produce babies, or that humans should not refrain from eating meat because we are evolutionarily adapted to this kind of food. It is often used to defend male dominance: that because men are physically stronger than women, then they should also be in charge. That such arguments are still heard today, despite the fact that it has been solidly established as an invalid way of arguing, may partly have to do with the firmness with

The seven virtues – Fortitude, Temperance, Prudence, Justice, Faith, Hope, Charity – helps us reflect over our inner world. Here illustrated as statues on the Basilica of St Thérèse in Lisieux, France. Wikimedia Commons.

which Aquinas' reasoning was established in our symbol world through the Church.

The ambition to unite faith and reason thus had unfortunate consequences for our way of reasoning that persist to this day, but it was also an important step forward. Religion asks us to reconsider our actions, usually by making us think about whether they are in accordance with the ethical guidelines of religious doctrine, yet it also prompts us to take a step back and inquire into what we are doing and why. Religion makes us more conscious. It helps us develop a richer inner world from which we can imagine alternative objectives in life. From this we become capable of shouldering more responsibility for our actions, and, in a sense, become freer. We are asked to *choose*, not merely obey. As such we become (perhaps rather unintended by the religious authorities) capable of questioning the morals to guide our actions.

In the aftermath of the Axial Age the human being thus becomes a more reflecting creature. We are now in a more tangible way conscious of the fact that we are conscious, and can think about the fact that we are thinking and want to control our will. The human being starts to ask questions about itself and the world: is there a purpose? Why do I act the way I do? How should I act? We start to reflect upon ourselves and existence to a far greater degree than before, and thus can be said to attain a new understanding about what it means to be human.

The religious thought perspective is a leap in fantasy where we can imagine a conceived world, a hypothetical world that we cannot experience with our senses. While the objective of the religious authorities who cultivated these abilities in us may have been to make us conform rather than question, the consequences of this development are probably more in line with the initial intentions of the 'righteous rebels' who pioneered the religious thought perspective during the Axial Age. With our newly won cognitive capacities to transcend and reflect, we can imagine that the world could be different from how it is now. Christianity actually mentions a potential God's realm as a better world, that there might be an *ought* that is better than our *is*. The religious thought perspective thereby provides us with the capacity to reflect upon visions of a more morally evolved world, and how to create it. A hidden door in the old religious thought perspective is thus discovered, and on the other side we are greeted by a new perspective to be unravelled by rationality.

Chapter 5

THE AGE OF SCIENCE AND FREE TRADE

With the ever-growing complexity and commercialisation of society during the early modern period, the old Axial myths gradually begin to show their deficiencies. In a world where several competing symbol worlds intermingle, all with equally universal claims to the one and only truth, it becomes painfully obvious that they are contradicting each other. But not only that. Under closer scrutiny they are even revealed to be rather self-contradictory in and of themselves. Their universality does not appear as universal as before. The conceptual limitations of the religious thought perspective start to show, driving thinkers to question whether more universal principles exist; furthermore, whether the only way to determine the ultimate truth is to subject it to evidence-based inquiry. Rationality thus comes to characterise the following era.

Rationality was initially a means to untangle the many conceptual contradictions of inherited religious dogma, but it quickly spills over into scientific discourse. No longer is tradition to be sufficiently relied upon. If the authorities are no longer gods, as established by the Axial traditions, but merely the gods' representatives on Earth, who are then to interpret the ultimate will of the divine other than our own God-given souls, the one domain where all humans are supposedly equal? Myth has to be subjected to evidence, and the means to do so are the rational faculties of our soul. The universality of the old moral religions has to be exchanged for a more functional universality where all people can verify the truths. No longer does it suffice merely being told what is true and right: humans have to think for themselves. Eventually, this thought perspective will sound a death knell to all mythologies.

In the wealthy northern Italian city states of the fifteenth century, during what later came to be called the Renaissance, trade has grown and given rise to a privileged class of city dwellers who seek to lift themselves above the prevailing religious thought perspective. Within a small elite of secular artists, authors and statesmen, the Roman past is rediscovered, admired and interpreted in a new light with focus on the individual and reason. In their interpretation of antiquity, they emphasise how the human being, not God, was considered central before Christianity. This is increasingly seen as a long-lost virtue of a golden age that the thinkers and artists of the Renaissance find important to bring back. This gives the Renaissance its particular humanistic characteristics, which will shape European culture in the centuries to come. Humanism is also a distinct feature of the rational thought perspective: If the secrets of the world are to be unravelled by the rationality of the human mind, then it also follows that the human being itself, rather than religious dogma and God, should be at the centre of our attention. Perhaps the people of the Renaissance sought affirmation of their own intuitive understanding of a rational, individualistic and humanistic thought perspective that had come to resonate with the urban, cosmopolitan and highly commercialised life in Florence and Venice at this time.

From here on the rational thought perspective spreads like ripples on a pond. We begin to reflect upon the era's widespread corruption and hypocrisy within the Church in the light of antiquity's achievements, and consequently start to explore whether there are other, higher ideals we can strive towards.

TODAY'S MARKET INSTRUMENTS ARE FORMED

European cities grow considerably during the later Middle Ages, bringing about an economic and cultural upswing. The market is broadened and ideas spread more rapidly across a steadily larger area. The northern Italian city states benefit from their strategic trade position, and Venice becomes Europe's largest financial centre. Here, several of the market's instruments as we know them to this day are created along with many of the structures that come to characterise the global market later on. The late Middle Ages' particular conditions, as well as historical accidents and individual political decisions, give birth to many of the financial instruments and structures that we today take for granted and regard as near-given forces of nature.[1]

In this blossoming mercantile environment, the demand to borrow money is high, but it is partly suppressed by the Church, which prohibits the charging of interest on loans. Profiteering from interest is regarded as usury, and as early as the twelfth century the Pope explicitly bans such activities. The Church deliberately attempts to hold back market developments, a concern that is more or less built into the Christian symbol world, exemplified in Christ's anger towards the peddlers in the temple and Christianity's generally negative attitudes towards the rich. The rulers of the age are, however, aware that their power hinges on the money they can mobilise. Without money it is difficult to recruit soldiers, and without soldiers it is impossible to win wars. There is, however, a way to circumvent the ban, in that the Jewish religion allows for interest if you lend money to non-Jews. As a result, the Jews, with the approval of the Christian rulers, attain permission to establish themselves as money lenders. Moreover, the Jews are forbidden to work within many other areas. As such, the financial sector becomes a means of subsistence and financial activities start to emerge around the Jewish communities in Europe, which to a certain extent are beyond the control of the Church. In the new economy there are now merchants and bankers who engage in money lending, but they still have a lowly reputation in contrast to landowners[2] – this will, however, change in the following centuries. In spite of the Church's resistance, spiralling usury rates are nothing new. Money lenders occasionally charge interest of around 20 per cent a month (!),[3] but with the blessing of the state, greater security and a more institutionalised financial sector, the rents become much lower, which then fosters further economic development.

The financial sector also receives new tools, including a new calculation system. Advanced monetary calculations are difficult to conduct with Roman numeration, but trade with the Islamic world introduces the superior Arabic number system (which in turn was invented in India several hundred years previously), which simplifies matters considerably. The introduction of the Arabic numeration system revolutionises our financial instruments. Now it becomes much easier to make calculations – for example percentages for calculations of interest, or converting money into another country's currency – that were very difficult in Roman numerals without the zero. Once again, we see how trade generates a favourable exchange of memes between cultures and symbol worlds, and thereby strengthens continued development towards higher complexity.

The merchants in the cities grow consistently stronger. The Medici family in Florence will during the fourteenth century and several centuries onwards dominate the European markets, and through their growing wealth, culture and politics as well. The Medici family finds ingenious ways to circumvent the Church's prohibition through creative bookkeeping, developing a highly profitable banking system. From the ill-reputed Jewish money lenders around the city, the ever more powerful bank is created (which is named after the benches they operate from). In Venice, new financial instruments are introduced that still remain to this day. One such is the promissory note. The promissory note entails an agreement that a large sum of money that has been received can be paid back later, in another location and in another currency. Hence, we do not have to transport large sums of money, which dramatically facilitates the efficiency of trade.

Money is a medium of exchange and a store of value, but it can also be used as a measure of account.[4] All of these have been properties of money since its invention, but new methods of taking advantage of the information provided by the latter will now revolutionise how humans organise themselves by giving rise to the economic system we call capitalism. As a measure, or unit, of account, money can be used to represent the values of products, services and assets, and measure the relative value of a service or product in relation to someone's labour or property. The same function can also with great accuracy provide information about incomes and expenses. As such, it can be used to assess profits, losses and liabilities, and hence function as a means to monitor economic performance and to predict future profitability.[5] Exact measurements of profits can be used to provide well-informed estimates about where an economic surplus should be directed to maximise the economic efficiency of production and distribution. Investing profits in order to generate even greater profits is the central feature of capitalism. However, for this revolutionising use of money to become possible, a new 'ancillary metatechnology of capitalism,' in the words of Robert Wright, has to be invented: double-entry bookkeeping.[6]

Double-entry bookkeeping is invented in another northern Italian city state, Genoa. It is a form of accounting, which by making the inflow and outflow of trade extremely clear, makes it possible to analyse the balance of trade with a much greater accuracy and better overview than other accounting methods.[7] As such, it can with great precision be used to determine whether something is likely to generate profit. Both Max Weber and the German economist and sociologist Werner Sombart have considered the invention of double-entry bookkeeping foundational for capitalism.[8] Sombart has argued that capital as a category did not even exist before this invention since the very concept is derived from the way double-entry bookkeeping allows us to see capital and its profits in numerical values in accounting books.[9] Hence, the notion of capital, and the understanding that it can generate profits, only becomes visible to us as it starts to appear on sheets of paper in double-entry bookkeeping accounts. Only then can we begin to properly manage the risks of capital investments and make exact measurements of its profits. So in the same way that money was 'written into existence' when we began to make debt recordings on clay tablets, the symbol tool of profit is written into existence when we begin to account for our incomes and expenses in accounting books.

With this development money starts to do entirely new things. Profits can only become visible to us in the realm of written symbols. From sheets of paper the logic and social power of money reveals itself so as to become available for deliberate manipulation and exploitation. With the ability to read and write, to make precise calculations, paired with a society in which the written word has legal power and economic exchanges are measured in monetary values, we can thus begin to manage our economic behaviour in an exceedingly more efficient manner than before. 'Contracts and records are a capitalist tool,'[10] it has been argued, and so is literacy. When the age-old tool of money is subjected to rational measures of calculating economic relations, it thus opens up entirely new ways for society to organise itself. With double-entry bookkeeping we can become capitalists, and thus begin to organise society in accordance with the iron-hard logic of profit. Thus started the development of the collective imaginary we now call 'the market'.

During the fifteenth and sixteenth centuries, the northern Italian city states are constantly at war with each other. This tough competition causes an evolutionary arms race where only the most skilful survive. This brings along a string of innovations, not just in weapon technology, but in finance as well. The expenses of war, which are invariably greater than the states' yearly income, force governments to take out loans. Large debts are not sustainable in the long run, however, and it becomes increasingly difficult to acquire capital by other means. In Florence, this problem is allayed by borrowing money from the city's own inhabitants. In case of war, which tends to be the rule rather than the exception, the citizens are made liable to lend out some of their assets, whereupon they receive an IOU that is transferable. Hence the bond sees the light of day.[11]

Those who need the money can sell their bond, which then gives birth to the bond market. Greater risk, for example in times of war when entire nations can fall, entails a lower bond price, but also a greater chance of profit in case the war turns out favourably to the issuer of the bond. From the sixteenth century, enormous fortunes are thus created on the bond market, and since money equals power, the wealthy families who dominate the financial markets can also influence politics. In Florence it is now the rich Medici family that holds sway politically. For the first time in Europe's history, the landed nobility gives way to a new commercial elite. And it is now apparent that an efficient management of the bond market, and not just success on the battlefield alone, determines the fate of nations.

The Market Creates Corporate Spirits

In seventeenth-century Venice another powerful meme appears in this new collective imaginary: the company as a legal person. This will later develop into today's limited company. Previously, merchants organised trade expeditions as personal partnerships. The investment, risk and profit were all shared, and all partners took full responsibility for the joint business. But now a completely new organisation is invented as the partnership is converted into a company that is a 'legal person'. This means that a company can enter into agreements as though it was a living human being, while no physical persons bear the responsibility for the agreement. The company also provides the prerequisites for future developments with shares for investors, and thereby the means of financing that will enable larger projects by entrepreneurs and businessmen.

In the development of our collective imaginary the company is a completely new occurrence. We have now invented a 'creature' that can have a will and intentions of its own and enter into binding legal agreements, but where the will and the intentions are separated responsibility-wise from the people who have originally formed the company and who ultimately control it. Just as with our ancestors' belief in freely floating wills in the form of spirits, the human being has now invented real spirits – freely floating wills and intentions disconnected from physical persons. Initially, how these companies can act and function are regulated in agreements between its owners. Later on, the dominant forms of companies and their operational remits are legislated by the state. Influence and rights for the various stakeholders in the company as lenders and partners are, however, regulated rather arbitrarily in various laws: The laws often favour the owners of capital at the cost of other stakeholders, for instance, and lenders have the right to use compulsory liquidation to dissolve companies that do not honour their interest payments. This may appear to us as obvious and a near natural given fact of life, but if we think about it, it becomes clear that it does not need to be this way. That capital owners to this day still have primacy over other stakeholders is merely a historical coincidence that emerged from the particular conditions of Renaissance Italy.

Later, companies acquire rights that only physical persons previously had. In this way, for instance during the early twentieth century in the United States, companies get the right of free speech and political lobbying. These freely floating spirits thus steadily start resembling humans in their rights and freedoms to act. However, the difference between them and us is that they are immortal, lack emotions and often have considerably larger financial muscles. Suddenly the most powerful actors on the world stage are no longer individual humans, but these newly invented company spirits. Yet again we should keep in mind that many of the laws that pertain to companies, and that we today take for granted as inviolable rights, are the result of historical and often arbitrary decisions made in another age and under other societal circumstances.

THE REFORMATION AND THE LEAP INTO THE EARLY MODERN PERIOD

One of the most important technological inventions during this time, which will lead to a revolution in the development of new thoughts, is the printing press. Printing was, however, not entirely new. In East Asia there had been experiments with moveable types several centuries before the printing press appeared in Europe, but this was extremely costly because of the large number of characters in East Asian written languages, which meant that the technique never caught on there – another fateful coincidence of history that would later increase the gap between the East and the West. The Latin alphabet with its far fewer characters is thus much better suited for this revolutionising invention. Around 1440, Johannes Gutenberg starts using moveable metal types that can easily be assembled into words and sentences. This efficient technology spreads rapidly across Europe and results in a large number of cheap books being mass-produced. To begin with, these are mostly in Latin and with religious content, but soon thereafter on many other topics and in vernacular languages as well, which over time will facilitate a revolution in thought. Access to cheap books results in even more minds being interconnected, across geographical boundaries and over time, which creates good conditions for the spread and cross-pollination of memes.

In the wake of the Renaissance there is growing criticism of the Church. The Catholic Church is at this time a rather corrupt worldly power. But it still believes in reason, *logos*. So when the Church tries to use reason to justify its actions, which are evidently in conflict with the message of the Bible, many react accordingly. The decadent lifestyle of the Renaissance popes and the fleecing of the population enrages many of the Church's subjects.[12]

The first prominent challenger is Jan Hus in Bohemia during the early fifteenth century, but it is the German monk Martin Luther who in the early sixteenth century succeeds in spreading the criticism, largely by utilising the newly invented printing press. Initially he attempts to reform the Church, but instead he causes a schism which gives rise to the Protestant faith, dividing the Christian West into two different symbol worlds. Among other things, Luther attacks the Catholic Church's sale of letters of indulgences. He also throws out all philosophical reasoning and returns to a fundamentalist, literal interpretation of the Bible. Another decisive part of the Reformation project is the German translation of the Bible, which Luther devotes himself to during his flight from the Catholic Church which has now outlawed him. The translation will also influence other translations, e.g. Gustav I of Sweden's Bible and the English King James' Bible. In Luther's Protestant doctrine there is no longer any advanced model of our consciousness and its potential for development. Luther throws out *logos*, or reason, and returns to a more concrete interpretation of the Bible. Luther's view can be exemplified by what he has written himself, such as 'Reason is the Devil's worst whore' and 'Reason should be destroyed in all Christians'.[13] Luther succeeds in clearing away a lot of the old animist residuals from Christianity, such as magical beliefs in icons and saints, but reason is also thrown out. What remains is a mixture of innovative thinking and fundamentalism that will become the foundation of the Protestant faith.

* * *

At the beginning of the early modern period there is a rich and diverse environment of different competing symbol worlds in Western Europe, which receives nourishment from its Christian inheritance, its wealthy easterly neighbours – both Muslims and the Byzantine Christians – its Graeco-Roman past, and now two different interpretations of Christianity. Moreover, the European continent is characterised by a large number of competing states that all strive for power and wealth, which on the whole constitutes a fruitful hotbed for the development of new cultural and technological memes.

In the wake of the Reformation, the Thirty Years' War rages during the first half of the seventeenth century. It is principally a religious war, at least initially. Luther's teachings are adopted by a number of rulers who break their bonds with papal Rome, causing considerable conflict with the Catholic Church, which retaliates accordingly. In the end, neither side can claim total victory in a war that has become more about political power than religion. In the peace accords in Westphalia in 1648 it is proclaimed that every state has the right to decide which religion to embrace. The idea of a unified holy empire is thus abandoned in favour of a system of independent nation-states. This is the foundation for our modern principle of sovereignty – that no state has the right to interfere in another state's internal affairs – which will apply up until today.

An important factor for Western Europe's dynamic developments, which will later lead to a new thought perspective, is the peculiar balance of power that prevails in Europe wherein no one has a secure monopoly on either worldly or spiritual power. Before the Reformation there are three groups fighting for power: the Church, kings and the nobility. After the Reformation there are five: the Catholic and the Protestant Churches, kings, nobility and the new mercantile bourgeoisie. This creates an even stronger dynamic between many competing symbol worlds where no one holds the upper hand. In time, this peculiar dynamic will lead to the Scientific Revolution, democracy and our modern market-oriented world.

THE SCIENTIFIC REVOLUTION AND THE BIRTH OF A NEW THOUGHT PERSPECTIVE

Following the Reformation, the rational ethos that was born in the wealthy and highly commercialised city-states of northern Italy during the Renaissance gradually spreads to the rest of Europe, in particular its western parts, which become predominant when trade moves to the Atlantic after the European discovery of the Americas. As maritime trade across the Atlantic and to the Far East increases, Western societies grow more commercialised, with unprecedented wealth beginning to accumulate in the rapidly growing trading centres where goods, people and information from all around the world circulate and greatly intermingle. Along with the 'informational catalysator' of the printing press, this produces a particularly well-adapted environment for memes to interact, cross-pollinate and develop into entirely new symbolic inventions. And since Europe, contrary the larger empires to the east, is divided into a number of smaller competing states, the evolutionary pressures to innovate and adopt new memes are accordingly much greater here. All of this provides additional fuel for the rational thought perspective to develop further and more rapidly. And since the Reformation has already showed us that we can challenge even the highest religious authorities, there is little to stop us from further questioning all that we have been told to believe but have no solid evidence of. As such, it is not surprising that the Scientific Revolution takes place in this part of the world.

But what is science exactly? We might say that it is a method, the so-called natural scientific method, that entails the systematic collection of data through observations, measurements and experiments, in combination with the design and trial of hypotheses. The ambition is to let reality speak for itself, to give support, as a scientist, to a theory when its predictions are confirmed by observations and reject the theory when it does not comply with the facts. This is also called rationalism and is a completely new way of viewing the world that appeared during the early modern period – the foundation of a thought perspective that will eventually replace that of religion. Science also contains a completely new symbolic language, the first truly universal language, based on mathematics, logic and generally recognised measurements and units. Therefore it is possible, if we learn this language and its symbols, to exchange knowledge and research results with others across cultures who also know the language of science.

One of the greatest weaknesses of science, however, is that it cannot explain our inner experience, subjectivity, for the simple reason that only the individual itself has access to the inner experience of truth and that others thereby cannot verify this. But what science lacks in explanatory power for the inner dimensions it compensates for through explaining the external in nature – and it does so in a much more sophisticated and effective way than any other previous symbol system. The explanatory power of science will prove so strong that it will change life on Earth fundamentally. In just a few centuries, culture and society will develop to higher levels of complexity than the previous 6,000 years of civilisation combined. However, the Scientific Revolution, as it is spoken of in history books, should more accurately be described as an evolution. The development of science stretches far back and has its origin in the Axial traditions' ideal of reason, universality and the search for higher principles. The human being has always sought answers to its questions about the world, but this search has not been particularly methodical so far. With the scientific method we now have a tool to overcome the many limitations and failures of religion.

Astronomy is one of the earliest disciplines to be based upon observations and mathematical calculations (as in the advanced geometries seen in Ancient Egypt and Babylon), even if it is initially more of a tool for astrology and a contribution to mythology than science in a modern sense. The Greeks were the first to make distinctions between myth and the physical reality that they studied more systematically. The method was uncertain and speculative, but they had good knowledge of geometry, mathematics and logic – which they were some of the first to introduce. During the European Middle Ages, intellectual life mostly revolved around theological issues, but in these issues the Axial Age's reason-based thinking was also applied. In the Islamic world there were also thinkers who were engaged in the major philosophical issues, but neither there nor in Europe is it yet possible to trace any serious attempts towards modern scientific thinking.

The first attempt at something we would term science is made during the sixteenth century by the astronomer Nicolaus Copernicus, who studies the movements of the planets and realises through mathematical calculations that the Earth revolves around the Sun. The Sun is the centre of this cycle, not Earth. Thereby we see the birth of the heliocentric worldview, after the Greek word for sun (*helios*), a view that will challenge the existing geocentrism that has prevailed since antiquity. This conclusion leads to severe misgivings about both Aristotle's physics and the Bible's worldview. Copernicus is, however, politically cautious, only permitting the publication of his conclusions after his death in 1543. As a further precaution he also proclaims his conclusions to be a mere mathematical model rather than a statement about reality. Copernicus' works therefore do not challenge the doctrines of the Church to the same extent that his successors will do. The philosopher and astronomer Giordano Bruno champions Copernicus' theories and is burnt at the stake for this by the Catholic Inquisition in 1600.[14] Clearly it is still a very dangerous endeavour to challenge the Church at this time.

During the end of the sixteenth century, the Italian scientist Galileo Galilei starts to take an interest in experimental physics and tries out various hypotheses vis-à-vis reality, for example concerning falling objects. He is convinced that the laws of nature can be expressed mathematically. At the start of the seventeenth century, technology has progressed so far that there are optical instruments to enlarge things we want to study more closely. Galilei sees the promise of this new technology at an early stage. In 1610 he directs his telescope towards the heavens and looks deeper into space than anyone has ever done before. In a short period of time he makes a string of important discoveries. He observes that Jupiter has moons that orbit the planet, which proves that celestial bodies can have other celestial bodies around them without being in the centre of the Universe. There is agreement that the Moon revolves around Earth, but now this is no longer a sufficient argument for seeing Earth as the centre of the Universe. The Church's last argument for the geocentric worldview thus collapses. The Church long tries to save its worldview. When Galilei invites representatives of the Church to see the moons with their own eyes, they refuse. Galilei manages to avoid execution for heresy by renouncing his theory, but several of his colleagues are not as fortunate.

In 1609 the astronomer Johannes Kepler formulates mathematical laws for the planets' orbits around the Sun. This confirms Copernicus' heliocentric worldview and Galilei's belief that the laws of nature can be expressed in mathematical terms. Copernicus' and Galilei's discoveries entail a major revision of the human being's view of itself and its place in the world, something that takes a long time to gain acceptance. The human being is displaced from the centre of the world to the periphery. We are still God's creatures, but no longer find ourselves in the centre of Creation. The human being can no longer be as certain of its chosenness and special status in the world.

Reason and Empiricism

In 1620 the English statesman Francis Bacon publishes a work on the scientific method, *Novum Organum* (the New Instrument of Science). Bacon emphasises the significance of systematic observations and experiments in contrast to pure speculation and philosophical interpretations of religious texts.[15] The theories on systematic observation come to have major influence in natural philosophical circles. Bacon also maintains that science will lead to material benefits for humanity. He is thus one of the first to formulate the idea of progress – one of the cornerstones of the rational thought perspective.

In the seventeenth century, the prominent French philosopher René Descartes emphasises the significance of reason and also doubt, its critical concomitant. He is aware that insights and theories must be tested vis-à-vis reality, but argues that empirical observations are not sufficient. He maintains that we must also use reason and doubt to gain insights about reality. Systematically he subjects existence to philosophical doubt and finally concludes that the only thing he cannot doubt is that he is thinking: '*Cogito ergo sum*', I think, therefore I am.[16] As Descartes champions reason as the most important avenue for understanding reality, the focus also shifts from God as the primary authority on truth to the human being itself. As we become liberated from believing in a divinely revealed truth, and with a more reason-based self-consciousness, the ground is laid for the ensuing period of enlightenment and modernity. Meanwhile, Descartes also creates the divide that comes to separate the continental, more inwardly oriented philosophy that he himself represents, and the Anglo-Saxon, more empirically based philosophy with Francis Bacon as its main standard-bearer. Descartes also repudiates the thought that there is an intrinsic objective, *telos*, in nature. He argues that nature contains neither any divine essence, nor any natural telos, but he also distinguishes between which principles apply to nature and which apply to the human being. Human consciousness has objectives, meaning and a will in a way that does not exist in material reality, which means that the human being's consciousness is governed by other laws than those of nature. With this reasoning, Descartes resumes the dualism of the Axial Age. This mind-body dualism has characterised Western thinking since then. By pointing out that different principles apply to our consciousness and the physical world, Descartes also attempts to circumvent the Church's power and supervision. In order to shield science from conflicts with the Church, Descartes suggests that science should merely devote itself to external phenomena and completely leave investigations and speculation about the inner, mental phenomena to religion.

Previously, ever since the time of Aristotle, physics had mostly revolved around various forms of causal relationships. We had asked ourselves *why* things happen. Now, physics, with the aid of mathematics, comes into focus in describing *how* things happen. Within a thirty-year period, we manage to make ground-breaking discoveries within astronomy, develop foundational theories on science and produce a large number of important empirical studies that all come to shape our scientific thinking to this day. The first scientific academy, The Royal Society, is founded in London in 1660. Shortly thereafter we get scientific periodicals and peer review papers by independent scientists. The ground is now laid for both the Enlightenment philosophers' reason project, and the technological project of the Industrial Revolution.

A few decades later, Isaac Newton formulates his laws of motion, having realised that it is the same force that makes an apple fall to the ground that also keeps the Moon in its orbit around Earth. With the aid of Newton's mathematical theory of gravitation, it is now possible to explain movements both on Earth and in space. Newton's theory of gravitation and laws of motion are presented in *Philosophiæ Naturalis Principia Mathematica* (1687), which becomes the foundation for classical physics. This is usually considered the apex of the Scientific Revolution. In this work Newton develops a new symbolic language that constitutes the basis for the mathematical understanding of nature, serving as a model for the natural sciences over the following two centuries.

These advances obviously challenge the authority of religion. As we take on the world with reason and empirical exploration, we become our own authorities on what is true instead of accepting our humble status as

God's children in Creation. The new natural philosophers, scientists we call them, argue along lines similar to Aristotle that we best attain knowledge of nature through observations and experiments. The men of the Church, however, align themselves with Plato's argument that we do not attain the most reliable knowledge of the world through the incomplete information our senses provide us, but through the reflection of pure thought – combined with God's revelations in the Bible. The Church's starting point is that which was assumed to be God's purpose, *telos*, with various parts of Creation. The scientific perspective, however, sees that things lack intrinsic meaning or purpose: the stone does not fall because it wants to fall, or has the objective of falling. It is the subject of blind forces of nature that are dependent neither upon humanity nor God, and that are most aptly studied from a purely external, objective perspective.

Much of the Church's resistance towards the new science is largely the result of science removing *telos*, i.e. the idea that meaning and objective are built into all parts of Creation by the Creator. The major problem for Christianity is not primarily that the world according to science proves to be constituted differently to biblical accounts, but that the doctrine of natural law is invalidated. If natural law is discarded, then we can no longer derive an *ought* from an *is*, which means that the Church's moral doctrine crashes to the ground. The fact that science's narratives do not comport with that of the Bible would in itself have been possible to solve. In the conflict between the Pope and Galilei, the Church would have been able to reverse its stand and say that the Bible's narratives should merely be regarded as metaphors. In a conversation with Galilei, Cardinal Baronius famously said that 'the Bible teaches us how to go to heaven, not how the heavens go'.[17] But here it is not merely a question of the correct reading of the Bible, but about the *entire* moral philosophy of Catholicism. With the invalidation of natural law, science attacks the foundation for the Church's use of reason. The entire moral system of the Catholic Church is now threatened from two directions, both from Luther and the other reformers – who want to remove *logos* – and from science – which wants to remove *telos.* As the symbolic language of the Church itself is under pressure, the Church's dominance over the conceptual world of people is severely threatened, and thereby the social imaginaries on which its power rests.

THE FINANCIAL MARKET AND BUBBLES IN A DENSIFYING GLOBAL WEB

Europeans have at the end of the nineteenth century ventured to every continent and integrated its many parts into a single world-encompassing weave. While in later years it has been an increasingly accepted anthropological and archaeological fact that human societies ever since the Stone Age have been part of greater cultural spheres or trading systems, it is only at the dawn of the modern age that we can see the emergence of the first truly global system. The human weave is stitched together and tightened by the Europeans' – from a human perspective cruel and from a historical point of view astonishing – expansion.

Amsterdam becomes Europe's financial centre in the seventeenth century as trade moves to the Atlantic and Venice loses the competition. The Venetian idea of the company is further developed in the Netherlands. The various Dutch regions join together and form one of the first multinational companies, the East India Company, which trades in spices from Asia and becomes the largest company of the age. The trip halfway around the globe is as dangerous as it is profitable. By dividing the financial risk of the merchant voyages between many parties, one could cut possible losses, as well as the risk of bankruptcy, while the profit could be shared by many. This proved to be a highly efficient way of financing travels that a large part of the Dutch population would soon take part in, including ordinary people who would otherwise not have had the means to invest in costly trade adventures. By dividing the company into smaller pieces that people can purchase for a fraction of the total costs, with promises of dividends in future profit if the ships should be successful in their risky voyage, the Dutch can now mobilise much more capital than had otherwise been possible. The shares cannot be cashed in, but they can be sold. Hereby we see the first proper stock market in Amsterdam, where the East India Company's shares are traded. It is also here that we experience the world's first financial bubble, when the price of tulip bulbs suddenly starts to increase substantially, which leads to speculation and elevated prices. Eventually it causes the stock market in Amsterdam to crash when it is realised that the price does not correspond to the real value of the commodity. As a consequence, many people are ruined.

In tandem with the Scientific Revolution, and in its spirit, a parliamentary revolution, the Glorious Revolution of 1688, has just taken place in England. Property is ensured against the king's arbitrary power, and through the emergence of parliamentarianism the merchants and burghers are accorded greater rights, with the result that better conditions are created for further mercantile developments. The rule of law and faith in the state's ability to pay back its loans also lowers interest rates, resulting in even more capital being made available. The Bank of England is founded towards the end of the seventeenth century to finance costly wars against France and receives the task of issuing banknotes for handed-in deposits, and during the eighteenth century we start using bills of a set value. In France, a banking activity patterned on English and Dutch models is created in the eighteenth century with a similar purpose: saving the national finances after costly wars. The creator behind the financial innovations in France, an Englishman named John Law, has a background as a gambler, which heavily influences the following events. Authoritarian France proves less capable of handling these financial institutions than the parliamentary governments in England and the Netherlands. Failing control mechanisms, poor comprehension of economics and the crown's urgent need for capital lead to the issuance of even more shares in colonial areas of dubious profitability. The issuance of banknotes quickly spirals out of control, a process that is fuelled by economic incompetence and old-fashioned greed. It is possible to make enormous fortunes and the word 'millionaire' enters our vocabulary for the first time, a word with a distinctive French ring. But as so many times in the historical epoch that follows, the over-optimistic bubble eventually bursts, resulting in hyperinflation, depression and a bankrupted state. It also causes starvation, eventually leading to the uprisings resulting in the French Revolution. Meanwhile France is threatened by the further economic developments that have now taken off in England. The smaller, but economically more developed United Kingdom wins the Napoleonic Wars and then becomes the dominant European empire.

Once again it becomes clear that war cannot just be won on the battlefields, but by those who best understand how to play the market – and here the British with their large merchant fleet, solid financial institutions and trusted legal systems are superior to all other nations. At the dawn of the modern age, states adhering to the rational thought perspective – accompanied by its holy trinity of parliamentary governance, rule of law and economic rationality – thus prove capable of triumphing over bigger adversaries with more despotic forms of government and less efficient economic systems. A less developed thought perspective thereby has to give way to a more complex one, now even in the field of politics.

FURTHER DEVELOPMENTS OF THE RATIONAL THOUGHT PERSPECTIVE

With the rational thought perspective it now becomes possible to imagine 'utopia'. This means that the old religious notion of a Shangri-La, a harmonious place somewhere far away, ceases to be merely a *spatial* category and instead becomes a *temporal*, and thus more abstract, category in our symbol world. A better society thus lies somewhere in the perhaps not so distant future – and, of equal importance, in this world, and not only the next. This line of thought not only revolutionises intellectual life, it also brings radical political uprisings with it. As the possibility of a this-worldly utopia becomes widely rooted in public discourse, it also inscribes itself into the social contract: if you put up with the adversities of life, you should be rewarded – not just in the afterlife, but in this one.

Accordingly, the rational thought perspective brings further questioning of political authority. We have acquired self-confidence and a will to make our own decisions through reason. In the wake of scientific discoveries there arises a secular culture of learning in France, with the great Encyclopaedia as one of its prime manifestations. French Enlightenment culture thrives among the bourgeoisie, which has grown wealthy and powerful through the growing significance of trade. Inspired by the political developments in England, cultural salons are organised in France by female *salonnières* where science, art, music and politics are freely discussed. This concept, and the entire Enlightenment idea, soon spreads to the rest of Europe. Towards the end of the eighteenth century it leads to political revolutions in the English colonies in America and shortly thereafter in France itself. During these revolutions, the idea of human rights is developed and we reawaken the Greek idea of democracy.

Even such a peripheral part of Europe as Scotland is affected. One of the Scottish Enlightenment's most luminous figures is David Hume. He formulates what will later be called Hume's Law, based on the aforementioned idea that there is no *telos* in nature, from which he concludes that an *ought* cannot be deduced from an *is*. Hume stresses the decisive distinction between *descriptive* statements (about that which *is*) and ethical, *normative* statements (about that which *ought* to be), and that we cannot possibly draw an ethical, normative conclusion from the background of a descriptive statement about how something is constituted – the previously mentioned 'naturalistic fallacy'. The problem of how we are able to know what is ethical when we lack guidance from a divine *telos* in existence leads to the development of a completely new symbolic language within moral philosophy. This would occupy philosophers and intellectuals for centuries. However, one difficulty is that we increasingly take the dominant natural-scientific symbolic language as our starting point. This, of course, merely deals with how reality *is*, not what *ought* to be, and thus cannot serve as the foundation of ethics. Hume's law sheds light on important issues, but the dominance of natural-scientific symbolic language creates a blockage vis-à-vis an idea-based development of moral philosophy. The lack of a moral philosophical symbolic language approaching the interoperable, empirical standards of science still eludes us to this day.

As a reaction against the Enlightenment's cult of reason, a countermovement known as Romanticism emerges during the first half of the nineteenth century. Philosophers, above all the German idealists, once again direct our attention inwards to explore our own subjectivity and consciousness.[18] Herder, Schiller, Goethe and Hegel, along with others, develop insightful theories about our consciousness and its development throughout life.[19] Positivism, which arises with Auguste Comte's theories in the 1830s and '40s, will, however, during the early twentieth century out-compete the idealists' philosophies on consciousness. Positivism contributes an important symbolic system that enriches and supports the natural sciences. It emphasises facts that are based on measurable sensory experiences where the role of the researcher is to find regularities in both nature and society. Through the charting of regularities, one can then predict future events. Our individual, subjective perspective is seen by positivism as more of a problem to be eliminated than a phenomenon to study. This would become a precept for science up until the present day, and it will be thoroughly questioned only a hundred years later by post-rational, or postmodern, philosophers during the twentieth century.

The rational thought perspective is also applied to biology, most prominently perhaps in relation to the mechanisms of creation. Charles Darwin's ground-breaking theory of evolution is published in 1859. Darwin understands the mechanisms of natural selection and gives an explanation as to why animals and plants look the way they do. It would then appear a natural conclusion that it also *ought* to be so. Darwin himself is aware of the distinction between *ought* and *is*, i.e. normative vis-à-vis descriptive statements. This, however, would not stop the erroneous idea of social Darwinism, the idea that the right of the mighty to dominate the weak is given by nature, which came to be a prominent and unfortunate feature of European thought. This might be seen as a 'faulty mutation', an unfortunate hybrid between the Christian doctrine of natural law and Darwin's scientific discoveries. This untenable meme is, however, out-competed after the Second World War as it becomes clear that it entails fatal consequences. Social Darwinism's own evolutionary weakness as a cultural meme – at least in Herbert Spencer's assuredly intelligently formulated, albeit vulgar version – manifests itself in untenable colonialism, slavery's ethical inexcusability and the rise and fall of Nazism.

With Darwin's theory, which first meets with heavy resistance, we once again have to revise our view of ourselves, just as with Copernicus' discovery of the Earth's emplacement. We are no longer created in the image of God, we are not God's chosen people. This severely upsets the current moral order and results in considerable resistance against Darwin's theories that has lasted to this day, not least from religious communities. We are now merely a variety of an improbably smart ape on the outskirts of the Universe. The human being is forced to rethink. We have to change our way of viewing ourselves and our self-proclaimed chosenness, our place in the world, and in Creation. In the great Cosmos, humanity is no longer a movie star in Hollywood in the glow of divine camera flashes. Now we are merely a cosmic coincidence of minuscule importance to the greater picture. One way of handling this is to gaze outwards and instead focus on the new opportunities of science and rationality. The existential issues about the purpose of humans and their place in the world are pushed aside, and focus is instead directed towards the purpose of mastering the world.

A NEW WORLD

The great insight that nature lacks *telos*, that there are no objectives and no meaning in nature, merely blind forces, exchanges religion's great question of 'why?' for science's 'how?'. It may impoverish our thinking on certain matters, but it arguably liberates thought. By placing ourselves outside the reality we are observing and approaching it unconditionally, the opportunity of understanding and mastering reality presents itself in a much clearer light. What makes natural science so revolutionising is that it only cares about what works and does not need to understand why. If *telos* does not exist, and the human being's primary quality is *logos*, then individuals might be able to create their own objectives. Armed with this conviction, and the symbol tools of the scientific method to make accurate predictions, we then embark on a path to subject the natural world to our will.

The Industrial Revolution that begins in Britain in the late eighteenth century is a result of the new rational thought perspective that is gradually taking over at this time, but initially it occurs somewhat independently of the natural sciences. Industrialisation progresses for the first century or so largely independent of scientific institutions and is pioneered by people without any formal scientific education. The engineers who build the new machines and tools of industry simply rely on trial-and-error and common sense rather than scientific theories. However, it is probably no coincidence that it is in Britain, where the new scientific thoughts are particularly widespread, that the Industrial Revolution first takes off. Apart from the sheer luck of being positioned on huge deposits of coal to be used as cheap fuel for the steam engines, and a large colonial empire from which raw material can be acquired and to where industrial products can be exported, the circumstance that the rational thought perspective has already become well-established in British culture during the eighteenth century, exemplified by its parliamentary system, mercantile policies and scientific institutions, most likely plays a critical role as well. The presence of these inherently rational phenomena indicates that Britons to a larger degree than others at the time subscribe to the rational thought perspective, and that British culture was imbued by the ethos of reason. This must have arguably, as ripples on a pond, affected a considerable number of people outside of formal scientific institutions, including those who pioneered the many ingenious inventions and rational productive measures of the Industrial Revolution.

Why Britain had progressed so far towards the rational thought perspective is difficult to answer, but it seems to have long historical roots.

This nation is after all the home of the thirteenth-century monk Roger Bacon, who was one of the earliest advocates of the scientific method and who envisioned ideas of how it would lead to self-moving carts and flying machines; Thomas More, who in his book *Utopia* imagined a harmonious society based on rational principles; Francis Bacon (no relation to the former), who has later been called the father of empiricism; and Isaac Newton, who more or less singlehandedly established the foundation of modern science. The rational thought perspective, especially in regards to objectivity, natural science and the practical appliance of these, thus had a strong position and a long tradition within British culture prior to the Industrial Revolution. I believe it is reasonable to suppose that without the apparent circumstance of a modern, scientific and secular symbolic worldview to prevail among a sufficiently large part of the population, the Industrial Revolution simply would not have occurred.

The Royal Society, the first modern scientific institution in the world, and the Bank of England, one of the first modern national banks (created largely to support overseas expansion and to protect the interests of the country's commercial elite), are both evidence of how particularly modern, and thus rational, British society is at the beginning of the eighteenth century. Britain is even one of the first societies to systematically grant temporary monopolies on inventions in the form of patenting, so as to encourage technological progress by enabling inventors to turn a profit from their inventions. As such, Britain exhibits particularly modern traits in the eighteenth century, which helps to explain why the Industrial Revolution occurred here. The intellectual, commercial and political requirements to successfully facilitate the transition from a religious, agrarian society to a rational, industrial one thereby seem to have been present in Britain prior to the Industrial Revolution.

As the first industrialised nation in the world, Britain quickly becomes the wealthiest and most powerful state on the global stage. It uses its newly won economic muscles and industrial technologies to expand its empire, which during the nineteenth century becomes the biggest the world has ever seen. British advances in industry are duly noted elsewhere and soon spread across Europe, North America and somewhat later to Japan. During the second half of the nineteenth century, technological progress shifts into a higher gear and picks up pace as science is increasingly applied to industry. Inspired by the utility of science in industry, we soon begin to apply scientific thought to ever more aspects of life. Much medical progress is thus made during the nineteenth century, causing life expectancies to increase and mortality rates to decrease, while scientific methods applied to agriculture increase food production considerably – with the result that European populations grow excessively, creating a large surplus of people to conquer and colonise a world that is becoming more European.

Our improved comprehension of science also enables us to develop more efficient methods of warfare. The invention of the steam engine can be used to propel large armed ships, and our increased knowledge about metallurgy and ballistics can be used to make deadlier and more efficient artillery pieces. Chemistry gives us dynamite, and with the invention of vaccines Europeans can now send soldiers into areas of the world where they would otherwise have died from tropical diseases. It becomes increasingly obvious that the military commanders who rely on new technologies will be victorious in battle, and that only the nations with the industrial capacities to equip their armies with all the latest gadgets will have a chance to retain their independence. During the nineteenth and early twentieth centuries, the nations that embrace science and industrialism succeed in gaining control over large parts of the world, ensuring a technological and economic head start that has endured to this day.

It is little wonder that science and the rational thought perspective succeed in out-competing religion as the dominant symbolic languages in the world. As soon as a meme can provide strong competitive advantages, as evidently demonstrated by science and industrialism, the consequence will either be that the new thought perspective is embraced or that one's culture is substantially disfavoured in the competition and risks obliteration. Accordingly, an evolutionary race has now kicked in and there is no doubt about the outcome: those who adapt to the new rules of the game will triumph, and the most important battlefield is now how well we succeed in industrialising our nations.

Life in Modern Society

During the nineteenth and twentieth centuries, the West goes from being dominated by agrarian communities, where the majority of the population live in the countryside and work as farmers, to industrial societies where most of us live in cities and work in manufacturing or service. The process is rapid and transforms society significantly. But like the transition to agriculture, the transition to industrialism is far from a one-sided blessing. As with the Agricultural Revolution, the changes from the new industrial lifestyle also bring new stresses and maladies to life. Once again, working days become longer, and with highly rationalised work patterns in the factories, work becomes even more monotonous and harder to endure. It is also dangerous to work here, since powerful and fast-moving machines can easily rip off a limb if one is not careful. Mines are also an exceptionally precarious work environment where the risk of being buried alive is a daily concern. Even though industrialism will increase the living standards of common people later on, initially it actually increases mortality and gives rise to new diseases. The lack of sunlight in the mines and factories causes vitamin D deficiencies, resulting among other things in misshapen skeletons known as the 'English disease'. The pollution from industry also deteriorates our environment, and we risk being poisoned by the air and water near factories.

People thus have good reasons to avoid the transition to life as industrial workers. So as with the transition to agriculture, industrialism is likewise driven by necessity rather than free choice – at least for the workers. While the owners of factories reap great benefits, the people who work in these dangerous and dirty environments are mainly forced to do so because they lack other means to support themselves. That large numbers of people, who had previously worked as farmers, suddenly find themselves in this situation, also has its historical roots in the peculiarities of British society in the eighteenth century. Prior to the Industrial Revolution, the British government had long pursued commercial policies that favoured foreign trade and encouraged private entrepreneurship. In this commercialised setting, landowners realised they could earn larger profits from exports of less labour-intensive products such as wool. This put a large proportion of the peasantry out of work and turned them into a large landless proletariat who had to sustain themselves from wage labour. This would later provide plentiful cheap labour for the factories. Britain's commercialisation also seems to have developed much further than in other parts of Europe and Asia, which to a greater extent than elsewhere affected traditional patterns of ownership and land control that protected peasants' access to farm land.[20] Because of the new commercial attitudes in Britain, land is increasingly seen as a source of commercial profits, and through the so-called 'enclosure acts' the traditional peasantry is largely destroyed during the sixteenth and seventeenth centuries. In England, perhaps half of all cultivable land is enclosed before the middle of the eighteenth century. As a result, the peasantry vanishes and Britain becomes the first larger society to flourish without a traditional class of peasants.[21] And since farmers have to produce for competitive markets, it causes revolutionary improvements to farming techniques that greatly enhance the output of food production.[22] Consequently, Britain can then sustain a large and rapidly growing population, while the share of the labour force occupied in farming decreases so as to turn them into urban, industrial workers.[23]

This causes enormous cultural and social changes. The old social structures in the countryside are broken up, and a new class system emerges in the growing urban centres with a widening social divide between a class of industrial workers on one side and a new elite of industrial entrepreneurs on the other. This will dramatically alter the economic relations of society. It has been argued that the steep gradients of wealth and economic mobility in industrial societies encourage innovation and competition.[24] Since entrepreneurs rely entirely on the market and are constantly at risk of being out-competed by others, and do not have any land to fall back on from where they can sustain themselves, they are constantly forced to innovate and compete to a much higher degree than the elites of the agrarian era. An unsuccessful feudal lord could always extract some resources from his lands, but if the business of an entrepreneur becomes unprofitable, he loses all his means to make a living. Similarly, since the industrial workers do not have access to any land from which they can have their basic needs met, and since they are constantly at risk of being replaced by cheaper and more skilful labour, they too are forced to compete by improving their productivity.

The threat of unemployment has therefore been argued to be far more effective in increasing labour productivity than slavery or serfdom. A feudal landowner cannot afford to let his serfs or slaves starve, and at the same time these workers have very little incentive to increase their productivity: if the lord loses his peasants to famines he loses his economic foundation, and if a peasant puts any extra effort into his work, whatever surplus he produces will simply be appropriated by his master. Accordingly, the old economic system does not stimulate worker creativity or productivity. But in capitalist industrial societies, the lack of any secure means of subsistence fosters a level of self-discipline that was difficult to accomplish in previous modes of production. Capitalism, it has been argued by David Christian, 'generates a discipline that touches the intellect, the psyche, and the bodies of wageworkers with a power unattainable through the more direct and brutal methods typical of tributary societies', and since innovation seems to be never-ending in modern society, both workers and capitalists 'find themselves on a relentless treadmill of constantly rising productivity'.[25]

As such, capitalist industrialism fosters far greater efficiency than the economic systems before it. The workers are no longer the property of their masters, as legally they are equal to those who employ them. Accordingly, the workers are free to sustain themselves in any way they feel fit. However, exactly because they are no longer the subjects of anyone else, the responsibilities that the agrarian masters were expected to fulfil towards their subjects no longer apply. In the agrarian regime, it was the feudal lords' duty to keep his population fed, employed and provided with a place to live, but none of these responsibilities are expected from a factory owner, who can fire anyone at will. Life in industrial societies is therefore considerably more insecure than in the agrarian regime, and the legal rights and freedoms of workers, amiable as they appear on paper, do not necessarily equate with better living conditions in practice.

As Friedrich Engels once wrote:

> The slave is sold once and for all; the proletarian must sell himself daily and hourly. The individual slave, property of one master, is assured an existence, however miserable it may be, because of the master's interest. The individual proletarian, property as it were of the entire bourgeois class which buys his labour only when someone has need of it, has no secure existence.[26]

So underneath all the liberal notions of exchange between free and equal citizens in capitalist societies, there still lies a deeply exploitative relationship between the ruling elite of property owners and those with no other assets than their labour. Marx repeatedly pointed out that since the workers in industrial societies, unlike peasants, do not have access to any productive property and thus no other means to sustain themselves, they are therefore forced to sell their labour to the highest bidder. To Marxists, this is considered a profoundly unjust social relationship, rooted in the unequal distribution of private property which they seek to abolish.

Opposition to the new conditions begins to take form during the nineteenth century as the new industrial working class grow increasingly better organised. In 1848 Marx and Engels publish *The Communist Manifesto* where it is proclaimed that '[i]n place of the old bourgeois society, with its classes and class antagonisms, we shall have an association in which the free development of each is the condition for the free development of all', a call for a revolution to sweep away all 'ancient and venerable prejudices and opinions' where '[a]ll that is solid melts into air, all that is holy is profaned'. After all, the manifesto concludes, '[t]he proletarians have nothing to lose but their chains. They have a world to win.'[27] As the 'spectre' of communism and the call for working men of all countries to unite begins to gain ground among workers and intellectuals during the second half of the nineteenth century, it starts to scare the ruling classes who desperately search for new meaning-creating narratives to fill the void in our shared symbol world that the demise of religion has left us – which communism, among other things, is a response to. The bourgeois elites partly succeed by spreading the idea of nationalism: a new narrative or social imaginary to bolster loyalty to the state, create mutual bonds and feelings of communion and foster a shared identity among the people who have come from the many different provinces around the country to work and cooperate in the growing and densely populated industrial cities. The attempt is largely successful, but it does not make way with the demands for social justice. Neither does it remedy the alienation or identity crisis that many experience in modern life.

The new conditions in industrial society urgently require a new symbolic language to address the dire needs of those who have ended up at the bottom of the social pyramid. As the old religious thought perspective comes tumbling down amidst the rapid changes of industrialisation and breakthroughs in science, a pressing need for a new shared symbol world gets increasingly apparent. Science takes over parts of the authority that religion previously monopolised in the agrarian era. Science enjoys major prestige and provides us with an astonishing number of answers to factual issues, but it cannot provide us with guidance – above all on moral issues – and it does not have the same cultural and identity-creating power as religion. At an early stage, Marxism lays claim to being a scientific theory on historical development and economics, but it also becomes a sort of pseudo-religion that fulfils many of the functions religion used to serve. Marxism offers new ethical guidelines, it provides a shared identity and functions as a symbol system to address the new living conditions in industrial society. But perhaps most importantly, it gives those of us who suffer the most a highly sought-after asset: hope.

A stanza in the 'Internationale' declares:

> There are no supreme saviours
> Neither God, nor Caesar, nor tribune
> Producers, let us save ourselves
> Decree the common salvation
> So that the thief expires
> So that the spirit be pulled from its prison
> Let us fan our forge ourselves
> Strike the iron while it is hot.

Standing in a large gathering of people and singing this must have provided a similar kind of mental strength, hope of salvation and feeling of communion as that of a religious faith. Nonetheless Marxism is despite its religious characteristics deeply secular and explicitly atheist. Religion is after all 'the opium of the people' according to Marxist teachings, 'the sigh of the oppressed creature, the heart of a heartless world, and the soul of soulless conditions'.[28] Neither God nor Caesar are, as the stanza declares, looked towards for salvation. Rather, it is we who shall save ourselves.

Although religion is still considered an important institution to ensure societal stability by the conservatives of the day, it is not only the Marxists who turn away from God. The rest of society also becomes more secularised. The growing bourgeoisie increasingly put their faith in science rather than God, and political leaders increasingly rely on more secular means of governance than religious ones. The church is bit by bit separated from the state during the nineteenth century as religious authorities gradually lose their grip on the public imagination. The secularisation of society is an important step towards the final victory of the rational thought perspective. It is a prerequisite for globalisation and internationalisation in a positive sense, since it better enables us to relate to people from other religious backgrounds without the prejudices and narrow-minded views of our own religious context. Yet at the same time the waning of religion leaves a void in its wake. Who will now answer existential questions? What should we base morality on? Science cannot say what is right and wrong, and a science without morals can easily lose its foothold. Moreover, science and atheism may make us more sober in our thinking, but by the same token we lose the ability to indulge ourselves in the intoxicating experiences of higher meaning and beauty that religious practices and communities can provide. So as we get exposed to the stronger truth claims of science and our religious sentiments fade, we sober up and see the world in a much bleaker, disenchanted and more mechanistic light.

The morning after religion we thus wake up hungover, pondering what we have lost. As we leave our sheltered existence of the village and move into the rapidly growing urban centres, we suddenly find ourselves as newcomers in an alien environment that ruptures our sense of self, others and the world. The social fabric of the old society on which we used to rely and where everyone knew their place is severely fractured by the rapid advancements of modern life. It is liberating. It is scary. It is beautiful. It is different.

Our old narratives do not suffice as our old collective imaginaries crumble. They are increasingly outdated and doomed to the memetic graveyard of history. The new conditions in modern society desperately call for a new symbol world in order for us to make sense of it all. While science takes over religion's role as our primary authority on truth, it cannot generate the warm feelings of communion with other people that we can experience in religious communities. Accordingly, new political ideologies take over many of the functions of religion in regards to identity and purpose. In extension of this, the welfare state eventually starts to take over the churches' function as the provider of care and protection in times of need. However, none of the new institutions of modern society seem to adequately satisfy our higher, emotional and, with a word that has now been largely forgotten, more 'spiritual' needs. The truth proclamations of science rarely come close to the divine revelations of religion in terms of beauty and invigoration of the soul. The political ideologies have difficulties in fostering enduring identities that make us feel deeply connected to the society we live in. And even if the expanding welfare state manages to drastically increase our standard of living and material security during the twentieth century, it lacks the spiritual nourishment and mental strength that religion used to give us.

So as we venture into modernity and beyond, more knowledgeable than ever, healthier and wealthier than what any of our ancestors could dream of, as we enjoy all the fruits of industrial society that would make any king or emperor of the past envious, it is as if something vital is missing. For all the blessings of the brave new world, it is as if something has been lost. As a consequence, we feel alienated, more disconnected from the world, and start to numb our existential anxieties with passing worldly pleasures to satisfy our immediate desires. However, on the peripheries of society, at distances far enough from the circles of power to be absorbed by them, but close enough to affect the prevailing power order, new 'righteous rebels' stand ready to challenge the maladies of modern society head on.

Chapter 6

THE MARKET TAKES OVER

The first decade of the twentieth century is a time of great enthusiasm in anticipation of scientific breakthroughs, new technology and growing prosperity from the global market. However, it is an enthusiasm coupled with wonder and horror at modernity's peculiar duality: great dangers and dreamlike possibilities interspersed within a hodgepodge of everyday boredom, science fiction and totalitarian utopian promises. The new industrial society provides hope of a better future, but it also creates alienation, confusion and the erosion of old traditions. On the one hand we stand before fantastic future opportunities; on the other the abyss lurks menacingly at every corner. The twentieth century might go either way, it appears.

It is also a time of accelerating globalisation propelled by growing world trade. Never before have so many parts of the world been so interconnected. Simultaneously we also experience rampant nationalism and rising global injustices. There are great migration flows with millions of poor crossing half the globe in search of a better life. Some are winners in this age's globalisation, many are losers. This includes individuals as well as entire nations. Like today, the early twentieth century is also characterised by new global power dislocations: We go from a world where the British Empire dominates the global market and the Seven Seas to an unstable multipolar geopolitical situation with new burgeoning economies such as the United States, Germany, Japan and Russia. Old empires are in a state of decay, while new challengers are waiting and ready to replace them.

The beginning of the twentieth century is a time when modernity and the rational thought perspective stand before their final breakthrough and victory parade across the world, causing old conventions, social relations and previously robust symbol worlds to undergo thorough revision. Old worlds are in decay, and as so often before in history, the transition to the new is no smooth process. Conceptions of yesteryear no longer suffice, which gives rise to new revolutionary thoughts, philosophical currents and artistic expressions. But it is also a time characterised by chauvinism, racism and the elites' stubborn defence of old privileges. These conditions throw the world into chaos and turmoil from which it is not possible to predict what will emerge next.

THE GREAT CATASTROPHES

The first half of the twentieth century is a time that severely challenges the optimism and naive technology cult that had characterised the previous decades. The sinking of the *Titanic* in 1912 represented a serious blow to humanity's faith in technological progress. After all, she was, according to engineering science, believed to be unsinkable. The next blow, however, proves to have far more sinister consequences. The outbreak of war in 1914 comes as a dark surprise for the many observers who had argued that technology and nations' mutual relations of interdependence in the new global age made great wars obsolete. With the First World War we realise that modernisation is not just a one-sided success story. The world discovers that Western civilisation may not be so civilised after all. We learn that our heralded progress is able to bring about devastation as well as blessings, and that increased global trade is no guarantee against catastrophic wars. The very same science and technologies to improve our living standards are also capable of creating new, deadly efficient killing machines such as machine guns, tanks and mustard gas.

The war that started as a strategic move to establish a new balance of power between the leading European nations was meant to be very brief, but instead it becomes a protracted slaughter that will last for four long years. Millions of young men annihilate each other with industrial state-of-the-art weapons. The war affects entire populations. Millions of spouses, fathers and sons never come back from the trenches. Many of those who survive return with mutilated bodies, and most of them with scars on their souls that never heal. A generation of Europe's youth is sacrificed and entire societies remain in collective shock for decades to come. What should have been a golden and glorious future with undreamed-of opportunities for humanity is transformed in the bloody mud of the trenches into disappointment, broken spirits and a fight for survival after the war. There is a shortage of all kinds of goods, occasional starvation and in Germany even hyperinflation. The previously so promising international labour movement has to admit its failure: The workers of the world

The 87th French regiment at Verdun, 1916. Photo: Wikimedia Commons.

proved more willing to kill each other for king and country than to fight capitalism in solidarity with international socialism. In Russia, however, there is a revolution, but Soviet communism remains a national phenomenon. The internationalisation of the world that was well on its way before the war has to give way to a situation where the nations of the world once again become more insular. The global world that took generations to build collapses in the war, and it will take two generations and yet another bloody world war to reach the same level of international trade again. The interwar period is marked by growing protectionism and nationalism that eventually result in another catastrophe.

The Western world, marked by war, now starts to lose some of its optimism about the future. From having embraced science and technology as the path to a better future, we are now compelled to question science as a project merely for the good.[1] Science has expressed itself in unexpected and unfortunate ways. After all, it did not prove a particularly reliable instrument for giving the world a firm moral footing. Doubt and confusion are prevalent among intellectuals and common people alike. We become more disillusioned, expressed, for instance, in the decadence of the 1920s and the art and literature of this decade, but it is also a time of innovative artistic expression and new philosophical insights. The moral vacuum in the wake of the old symbolic world's lost legitimacy following the war provides a new basis from which intellectuals criticise the status quo and offer new ways of looking at existence. Science, technology and the prevailing social order are critically scrutinised, and reason and the rationalist thought perspective are questioned as the only valid precepts.

The early twentieth century is also a time of new material conveniences. New consumer goods appear such as radios, cars and electrical kitchen appliances. Growing prosperity leads to fashion for common people and entertainment for the masses in the form of cinemas. Here we see the start of modern everyday life with the high levels of comfort that we know today. Technological advances that had proved so destructive in the war can also increase our material living standards considerably. In the US we see the emergence of the first consumer society. However, with the stock market crash in 1929 it will take one more generation and yet another war before this societal model's full potential becomes apparent. In the meantime, alternative and more totalitarian models are tested.

The 1930s become a decade of extreme poverty for large parts of the population in both Europe and North America. Hitler wins the election in Germany in 1933 with promises of a better future, and in the United States the economy is reformed under Franklin D. Roosevelt's New Deal during the same decade. Both create economic growth, but Nazism's model leads to catastrophe. In the Soviet Union, Stalin manages to industrialise a poor agrarian society, turning it into a modern great power and a viable competitor to the capitalist model. During the same period social democratic movements make headway in the Nordic countries; a development that in many ways resembles the reforms in the United States but goes somewhat further, offering a compromise between unregulated capitalism and authoritarian communism. The great welfare project will, however, have to wait until after the Second World War.

The war to end all wars would not be the last. The catastrophe that was not allowed to occur happens anyway when Hitler's expanding Germany invades Poland in 1939. With the Second World War the next blow is dealt to an already shaky world. Nazism builds its ideology on a profoundly erroneous racial science, combined with an equally mistaken form of social Darwinism, that justifies the mass extermination of Jews and other 'unwanted elements'. In the new war science contributes with even more efficient weapons of destruction. It is an even worse industrial slaughter than the first, and people are being murdered with scientific precision and industrial efficiency in concentration camps, terror bombings and finally with atomic bombs. The war serves as yet another trauma to trigger a collective state of shock, a disappointment in the world, humanity and progress. The remaining faith that reason and science will *guarantee* constant and unambiguous progress definitively dies with the catastrophe of the Second World War.[2]

The United Nations is established after the war with the purpose of influencing the world in a more peaceful and democratic direction. However, this development is overshadowed by a new division of the world between a capitalist West and a communist East. No one is interested in a new world war, and yet there is an arms race on both sides with enormous arsenals of nuclear weapons that can annihilate the world many times over. The hope of a better world will once again have to give way to disappointment, and a fear that we will eventually annihilate ourselves.

At the same time humanity starts to develop an increasingly complex view in terms of self-comprehension. As early as the beginning of the twentieth century, the psychoanalyst Sigmund Freud publishes his ground-breaking insights into human psychology. Freud argues that we are largely governed by unconscious desires, not at all the rational creatures the Enlightenment philosophers previously assumed. He claims that we do not have control of ourselves and that our motives are often shrouded in obscurity – even to ourselves. Naturally, Freud's theories spark protests, just as Copernicus' and Darwin's had done before. Our self-image is dealt a further blow. It is no longer sufficient to admit that we are merely animals developed by chance on the outskirts of the Universe. Now we are forced to realise that we are not even aware of the inner, mental processes that govern us. We are controlled by murky forces that we can only with great efforts of self-examination become aware of. The horrors of war, which human reason created, or at least had not been able to prevent, also contribute to our altered self-image. A new critical spirit settles after the war. This will in time lead to a completely new thought perspective that still, to this date, strives to replace the outmoded rational thought perspective.

SOCIETAL PHENOMENA OF THE TWENTIETH CENTURY

The twentieth century's expanding urbanisation is an integral part of the overall industrialisation and modernisation process. Growing urbanisation turns us into anonymous individuals amid the masses in the cities.

The social structures of rural life and the religious traditions that used to provide stability and meaning gradually dissolve. People are transfigured into separate individuals in the modern sense. We are no longer defined by who we are related to or where we live. We go from an existence with relatively narrow social contexts and a life with few but frequent contacts, to a throng of varying contexts and shifting superficial acquaintances. With the growing lack of solid footing in our local community and inherited traditions, religion loses more and more of its remaining role as truth and precept in an increasingly secularised existence.

Life in modern society gradually takes on machine-like features as it is shaped by the new methods of streamlined mass-production that make us appear as anonymous cogs in vast machinery and amidst abstruse bureaucracy. This impression of modern life is expressed in the arts, for instance by Charlie Chaplin, who illustrated the anonymity of mass production in *Modern Times*, and in Franz Kafka's novel *The Trial*, where Mr K is trapped in a modern, bureaucratic system that has morphed into the absurd.

With the burgeoning market economy our appetite for consumer goods grows accordingly. For lack of meaningful contexts, stability, shared values and optimism about the future, consumption becomes ever more important. Religion can no longer keep market forces at bay. The common values and moral order that religion used to cultivate are diluted. Old virtues such as self-restraint, moderation and thrift are no longer cherished. Instead, self-indulgence, pleasure and limitless consumerism are given free rein. Market forces can now spread to a previously unimagined extent. Political visions, however, temporarily prevent the market from taking over completely during the decades after the world wars.

New political ideas derived from the rational thought perspective attempt to resist the market through regulations and prevent it from becoming destructive. There is a lingering faith in reason despite the disappointments during the first decades of the century. Economic redistribution is systematically put into practice and we receive more extensive health care and social security, better housing and public education. Regulated working conditions, shorter working days and vacations stipulated by law are all introduced to improve the lives of workers – and to avoid revolution.

New technologies once again change our existence, but now to a degree that even benefits ordinary people. Conveniences in the home such as household appliances improve our daily existence, and radio, television and air travel interconnect the world even further. Medical progress continues to advance and the average life span increases dramatically during the twentieth century. With Alexander Fleming's discovery of antibiotics in the mid-twentieth century we can now fight infections that had previously been deadly. This is the apogee of modern society and a resounding victory for science and industrialisation.

Now the vast majority of the population lives in cities and consists primarily of salaried workers within specialised professions in industry and service. In the new consumer society with its ever-expanding division of labour and specialisation we produce fewer kinds of services and goods ourselves and start to request things on the market that were previously taken care of within the family. This creates new jobs in, for example, the food industry, child and elderly care and the ready-made garment industry. Entertainment is also managed by specialists to a higher degree than before, e.g. through cinemas, radio and television. Moreover, life also becomes increasingly complex, necessitating completely new specialised services from professionals such as car mechanics, electricians and plumbers. What is new is that progress doesn't just benefit a small elite, but the whole population, especially in the democratic, capitalist West. Thereby democracy, capitalism and consumer society prove to be an efficient meme combination, one to outcompete all other social systems. However, despite its apparent success, this societal model would not remain unchallenged.

The Cultural Revolutions of the Sixties

In the Western consumer societies during the 1960s there appears a growing criticism of the downsides of modernity and a questioning of social conventions. Even science as the highest authority on truth is put into question. A new generation rebels against their parents who could not prevent the horrors of the Second World War and whose archaic values, chauvinism and blindness to the dangers of modernity are held responsible for the very existence of life on Earth being threatened by total nuclear annihilation. At the same time, we are dealing with the most privileged generation ever: for the first time a majority of the population in the West grows up in relative affluence, with good educational opportunities and without having to worry about food. Maybe it is not so strange that parents find it so hard to understand their children at this time. But it is precisely because of such great wealth that it is now possible for young people to create an identity of their own, question the social order and thus approach a more critical and complex conception of reality.

Social reality and our culture – our collective imaginary – become ever more fluid and without a fixed centre. We have a number of alternative subjective realities to choose from. This is expressed in new movements and new religions. Drugs are used recreationally and change the perception of the world in the hippie culture of the 1960s. Rock 'n' roll breaks on through to the other side with a new culture and a message of peace and love. Gentler values and emotions are embraced, as well as a rebellious freedom from a society that is perceived as repressive and obsolete. In the Parisian student revolt of 1968 there is a belief in change and a better world for all. The new dreams are now based on theories from psychology, sociology and Marxism, which are used to rebel against the old society. The world has changed so much from the conditions that brought consumer society into existence, and a growing part of the population feel the need for a new societal order. The awareness of the world and the human being's role in it also increases. Reactions against the environmental degradation of industrial society also start to occur in the 1960s, even though it will take a couple more decades before we reach a more general environmental awareness. Yet at the start of the 1960s a seed is sown for today's environmental movements through Rachel Carson's landmark book *Silent Spring*. This is one of the earliest harbingers of the flip side of industrialisation in terms of environmental degradation and unsustainable depletion of finite resources. It will be followed in 1972 by the report of the Club of Rome, *Limits to Growth*, which for the first time expresses the environmental challenges in scientific numbers. The development that has recovered after the world wars, and seemed so promising now appears even more precarious, questioned as it is ever more frequently and radically.

Disillusionment with Socialism

During this period we also see the communist countries conduct an optimistic but naive attempt to make the rational ordering of society work once and for all. Political ideology coalesces with and legitimises itself through science. This has never been clearer than in the Leninist socialist ideology known as 'scientific socialism' (originally from Friedrich Engels' description of Marx's socialism, which is contrasted with utopian socialism). The market economy in the West thereby receives competition from socialism's financial construction: planned economy.

The thinking behind planned economy is that the best and most efficient system does not entail goods and services freely offered on a market, but rather requires centrally planned distributions; governance of what should be produced, by whom, and at what price. The idea was full of good intentions. It started from an idea of fairness and solidarity, and the notion that society has a responsibility for ensuring that all citizens get what they need. The idea was also built on the – in my view correct – insight that capitalism has major shortcomings; that it wastes human and material resources, and enriches some at the expense of others. Should we occasionally struggle to imagine other economic systems than our own, we will find in the Eastern Bloc's 'realised socialism' an indisputable example of reason and politics creating an alternative to the market. The problem, however, was that the planned economy was less efficient than a market economy. It was not able to meet people's needs as fully, and it proved that it is not possible to centrally plan and predict every single factor needed to ensure economic efficiency. People's entrepreneurial drive and need for liberty are also suffocated, whereby society loses valuable social power and innovation. In addition, new, but less efficient, black markets nevertheless appear to satisfy people's needs and desires.

The communist societies strive as much towards material progress as towards increased solidarity, proudly displaying society's accomplishments in terms of consumer goods in propaganda and political speeches. But as it becomes clear that these products are inferior to those of the West, in terms of both quantity and quality, the communist regimes gradually lose their legitimacy. The financial shortcomings of planned economics and the superior efficiency of the capitalist market is every bit as decisive in the fall of the Eastern Bloc as the demands for democracy: people long just as much for television sets, blue jeans and other consumer goods as they long for fair elections and freedom of speech.

In the socialist countries, the individual has been forced to give way to the collective as the new classless realm of happiness is planned. Here, culture is seen as a vital tool and an integral part of the socialist ideology, not just as a subjective and meaningful reality of its own. Modernist aesthetics are used to spread the message of the collective's importance, which is seen everywhere in society: in teaching, architecture and art. But the simplified and naive view of humans – happily whistling during work in highly stylised caricatures of people in shiny industrial settings – clashes with their individuality, personal needs and desire to escape a subordinated role in a dull industrial and bureaucratic society that no longer seems to serve the interests of either the individual or the collective. In the end, the communist system becomes highly unsustainable.

Insights about the socialist states' problems become more apparent during the post-war period. The art of social engineering is increasingly questioned. And the intellectuals in the West who have previously been Marxists lose faith in grandiose collectivist solutions and in socialism as a political project are henceforth thrown into ideological crisis. Their visions are fragmented even further through the humanitarian catastrophe of the cultural revolution in China, the oppression of basic human rights in communist societies and the Eastern Bloc's tangible economic difficulties. When the wall finally comes down the failure of state socialism is already abundantly clear.

The fundamental problem of communism is that it needs considerable measures of oppression in order to work. Oppression of the human being's free will to act in accordance with market forces, as well as oppression of its will to choose a non-communist government. A large part of the communist societies' resources is thereby wasted on coercive control measures to ensure the system's continuity – as well as the military ability to keep capitalist societies at bay. This proves untenable in the long run. Just as the market economy can produce a larger quantity of consumer goods, so can it produce a larger amount of ever more advanced military gadgets. To keep up, the communist countries need to spend increasing resources on the military at the expense of consumer goods. In the end, their very own populations bring down the system – and to everybody's surprise, relatively peacefully. It turned out that faith in the system had not only been lost among the general population; even within the leading circles of communist society people had stopped believing in the prospect of a planned economy to create a better future. As such, there was simply no one to defend the system.

Even if relatively few people in the West saw the state socialist countries as paragons, it nevertheless entailed the presence of two clear political balancing forces in the world. Now, however, the market has finally triumphed and the socialist ideal has lost. As such, there are no longer any living ideals to pit against the market and financial profit. The market can thereby spread without any notable challengers. No longer does the fear of revolution restrain the forces of the market from taking over completely since no viable alternative exists to legitimise a revolutionary movement.

The Victory of Neoliberalism

When there no longer exists a strong collectivist ideal in society, the market becomes the source of people's hopes. Neoliberalism, which is built on liberal ideas of freedom from the seventeenth and eighteenth centuries, becomes a powerful political ideology during the last few decades of the twentieth century. This ideological current transforms politics with its economic ideology of neoliberalism: the unapologetic defence of capitalism and the individual's extended rights and freedom *from* the state. Rights can comprise anything from various degrees of individual ownership to the possession of weapons, depending on nation and political proponents. Margaret Thatcher and Ronald Reagan are iconic examples of state leaders who advocate the neoliberal view of individual rights and a so-called 'night-watchman state' during this period. The failure of the collectivist ideal of communism gives rise to a greater emphasis on the individual, to a degree even where it challenges the very notion of there being any collective at all, as Margaret Thatcher famously put it: who is society? There is no such thing![3]

Without a collective ideal to shape our further development of society, and the declining faith in the state and in politics, the individual and its

Margaret Thatcher and Ronald Reagan are iconic examples of state leaders who advocate the neoliberal ideology. Photo: Wikimedia Commons.

self-interest are, in somewhat simplified terms, all that remain. In addition, the steady and widespread criticism of all social conventions, moralities and notions of what is better and truer that prevails in late capitalist society leaves us without a solid compass to guide our efforts towards a better society. What is better or truer is now up to the individual and its personal opinions. No more shall any authorities tell us what is good, right or true. The void that appears is thereby taken over by the idea of the individual's personal freedom, and without any commonly shared ideas to determine where to go collectively, we thus allow the market to decide for us.

The word 'freedom' becomes a key concept around the close of the century. But it is a rather limited idea of freedom. It only entails the freedom *from* government, not the freedom *to* be guaranteed any of life's necessities or even a better life in the future. The idea of the individual is also quite limited. As individuals, we are expected to behave as consumers and producers on the market, not to form meaningful communities, and most of all not to oppose the system by means of collective resistance. The freedom *from* a system of privately own property is not an option, as it is now considered something akin to a basic human right to be defended by all means. Neither is the freedom *from* exploitation by property owners considered a worthy consideration. Although the state is seen as an essentially oppressive measure by many neoliberals, its coercive measures in ensuring a lopsided distribution of property claims are rarely questioned as something in violation of the freedom of individuals.

The surge of liberal economic thinking is, however, not without its merits. In the post-war period the public sector has grown dramatically, and at the end of the 1970s it has become highly inefficient and partly caused the wheels of industry to slow down. As a consequence, living standards are stagnating and many people have become unemployed. Change is necessary, and cutbacks in the public sector and economic deregulations during the 1980s do generate growth. The initial economic success of neoliberalism thus becomes an inspiration for a dismantling of the welfare state, which in many ways is seen as controlling and oppressive.[4] Now begins the era of privatisation. The sale of state-owned companies, public institutions, schools and healthcare facilities is carried out at a brisk pace without a thorough impact assessment. Few actually investigate which public institutions benefit from being privatised and which remain inherently unfit to function on market terms. We forget that there are values that cannot be measured in money, and that there are institutions that fulfil socially important functions that cannot be left to the caprices of paying customers and profitability.

Without any academic understanding of the market outside the dominating neoliberal paradigm, it becomes difficult to criticise and manage it. The market subsumes ever greater parts of society and encounters very little resistance. The system crashes repeatedly. This is not because the market is as such a bad idea or because of greedy individuals. It is rather the result of an unregulated – or more precisely, incorrectly regulated – market.

The fundamental flaw of liberalism is its unequivocal focus on the individual at the cost of the society. What is good for the individual in the short term is often at odds with what is best for the greater whole. Overconsumption of cheap goods produced under dubious working conditions in poor countries may benefit the individual who buys them here and now, but in the long term it puts the wellbeing of society at risk, and eventually the life of the individual, when environmental degradation and poverty-derived conflicts cause disruptions that intrude into our personal lives.

We all benefit from the wellbeing of others since it reduces the risk they will behave in hostile ways towards us, and increases the chance they will develop in ways that allow for productive and mutually beneficial cooperation with ourselves later on. Many things benefit us in our daily lives that can only be achieved through collective efforts. Not everything can be obtained by free choice on the market. If we want good roads, secure neighbourhoods and functioning legal institutions, it is necessary that we collectively make binding obligations to ensure we all contribute the necessary resources to support such measures. It cannot depend on 'free choice'. Collective goods simply do not function very well on the market: paying for roads, cops and laws every time we need them is not very practical. But there are also other services, such as schools, hospitals and cultural institutions, that in practical terms can function on market terms, but arguably are better managed collectively – if for no other reason than it ensures that everyone can obtain access to these, even if they cannot pay. We all benefit from living in societies with educated, healthy people within a well-functioning collective imaginary.

For societies to be efficient and meaningful it is required that they are based on binding obligations, collectively deliberated conventions about what is expected from the individual and what the obligations of the collective towards the individual are. This is obvious if we want to retain the rule of law and avoid regressing to an anarchy of all against all. However, if we reduce our only overarching collective structure to its most minimal functions of keeping people from physically harming one another and ensuring respect for each other's property, then we simultaneously remove all the meaning- and identity-creating fuel of the collective imaginary that keeps it together in the first place. If society is viewed as nothing more than a physical place that facilitates our production and consumption patterns, and if the role of most other people is only to serve our material needs, with our primary relation to others limited to the exchange of services and products by monetary means, it may very well cease to be a society. Not only do we risk society falling apart, as it makes us more inclined towards questioning what we actually need each other for in case we do not gain any utility from those relations, we also risk our lives becoming emotionally impoverished. A life merely preoccupied with our own personal project and the acquisition of new possessions and pleasures is a poor one, much poorer than one characterised by a project larger than ourselves, where we together with others engage in the pursuit of a better future for all.

As humans we need something more than just having our material needs and desires met, we also have strong social needs. But we need more than just social clubs where people can come and go as they please. We need strong and meaningful collectives where we can feel a sense of belonging and where we can develop personally together with others. In recent years, this has sadly become a scarce asset.

AFTER MODERNISM – POSTMODERNISM

Modernity has never been without its challengers. As soon as modern society matures into its early industrial form, the critics follow. At first, these are a few individuals – intellectuals, artists and even mystics. But in time, the many springs gather and grow into a flood: the young Marx's romantic death sentence to capitalism, major philosophical schools – like existentialism and phenomenology – that seek to emphasise the spiritual and existential sides of life, and finally full-blown student revolts in Paris and on US campuses in 1968.

Art becomes more abstract and surreal from the beginning of the twentieth century and onwards. The works of Pablo Picasso, Marcel Duchamp and Salvador Dalí are usually referred to as 'modern art', but they are more 'post'-modern: opposing the conventions of modernity such as mathematically correct perspectives, realistic-looking motifs and lighting, and the emphasis of beauty rather than provocation. Art and philosophy become more concerned with the inner psychological sides of life, the nasty and brutal aspects of the human soul, and a more critical stance towards all those aspects of society and ourselves that we are reluctant to face. Building on the new insights of psychologists like Freud and Jung. Lately, mainstream culture itself has become critical of modern society, not least thanks to mass media and the internet, from which we are repeatedly warned about industrial society's destructive effects on the environment and exposed to critical voices who relentlessly question the 'hetero-normative discourse' of majority culture.

As early as the nineteenth century we see the beginnings of a new thought perspective within the arts and philosophy. These developments are further strengthened by the horrors of the world wars and the apparent shortcomings of the rational thought perspective. While the market takes over and we lose faith in both God, science and other ideals, there is simultaneously a development of what we might call 'structural doubt' and 'organised disappointment', amounting to an entirely new thought perspective that can be termed 'postmodernism'. The 'post' prefix indicates that it is the next overarching thought structure and societal current to come after modernity. But it also carries an explicit critique of modern society and thinking, and an implicit claim of being a replacement of modernity. As such, postmodernity is an emergent phenomenon in our symbol world akin to the religious and rational thought perspectives before it. So here, for the first time since the Enlightenment, we now have a credible contestant to dethrone the dominant mode of thought once again.

Doubts about the Enlightenment project, reason and science grow ever stronger during the twentieth century, but most of society, to this date, clings on to rationality and the modern project. In the 1970s and '80s, the new postmodern thought perspective makes its way into academia, primarily the humanities: enter chic rebels like Jacques Derrida, Michel Foucault and Judith Butler; exit old bigwigs like Auguste Comte and Herbert Spencer. Good old Marx is kept in high esteem, but among the leading Western thinkers his ideas are developed beyond the structural limitations of traditional Marxism and take on more 'post'-structural forms by stressing epistemological and psychological aspects to a higher degree. It is from this development in academia during the post-war period that we have the term 'postmodernism' itself. But its intellectual heritage can be traced further back in time to great thinkers such as Wittgenstein and Heidegger in the first half of the twentieth century, and arguably even all the way back to Nietzsche in the late nineteenth century. Postmodernism is, however, not a coherent, uniform and institutionalised school of thought with fixed authorities and commonly agreed-upon methodologies and research projects. It is more of an umbrella term to designate a number of thinkers and thought traditions, which may or may not self-identify as postmodern. It is also used to describe certain societal developments, of which some are influenced by postmodern thoughts, but also developments that are merely characteristic of capitalist consumer society.

Postmodernism is first of all a reaction against the perceived superficial, intellectually inadequate and soulless rationality of modernity and the many injustices modern society brings about despite its promises. Initially, modernity and its cult of rationality were criticised for not sufficiently capturing the manifold beauty of human life and for not providing meaningful spiritual experiences. This is where we meet the Romantics of the nineteenth century as mentioned in the last chapter. Only later is modernity criticised for not fostering social justice and equality and its pursuit of knowledge and progress claimed to be self-illusory and shallow. According to these critics, the modern approach has been one-dimensional and failed in its task of enlightenment and emancipation; as an alternative, a wide range of alternative perspectives are offered in science, art and philosophy. This is where we find feminism, post-colonialism, environmentalism and even new-age spiritualism.

Jean-François Lyotard wrote in 1979 that '[s]implifying to the extreme, I define postmodern as incredulity towards metanarratives'.[5] By 'metanarratives' he meant the teleological stories that guide or structure our explanations of reality,[6] the overarching commonly shared symbol worlds

Guernica, Pablo Picasso's 'postmodern' painting of the Spanish Civil War, 1937. Photo: Moleskine/Wikipedia Commons.

that keep our collective imaginaries together in large coherent weaves – or 'myths' in another word. The ferocious killing of all mythologies that began with rationalism thereby continues with postmodernity, but now including a death sentence for myths such as the nation, scientific objectivity and even gender roles. In light of the rampant ecological destruction caused by industrial society and the unequal distribution of its spoils, the modern idea of progress is likewise criticised and exposed to be just another harmful myth. But the foremost myths to have been brought to the slaughter are perhaps those from which power and authority are derived. This would change public discourse towards the end of the twentieth century.

Postmodern Society

Postmodernism has influenced politics, media and the public debate in the Western world considerably in the past thirty years, even if many people are not aware of it. There has been an ongoing discussion the last few decades about what postmodernism really is, and indeed, whether it exists at all. During the last ten years or so, the nay-sayers seem to have gained the upper hand and it has become fashionable to assert that there is no such thing as postmodernism or postmodernity. It has been common to consider it a fad, a trend of the 1980s and '90s with some very strident voices with grand ambitions, which then petered out and returned us to business-as-usual and everyday life in modern society.

Our age has accordingly been termed 'late modernity' to differentiate it from its earlier stages during the eighteenth and nineteenth centuries.[7] To a certain extent this is a fair description of the society we are currently living in, since it on the most fundamental level appears to be more of a matured version of the industrial and capitalist society that emerged at the end of the eighteenth century than an essentially different one. Despite its technological progress and many social advances, contemporary consumer society is not as different to the industrial one of the nineteenth century as the latter was to its agrarian and religious predecessor. The societal developments of the late twentieth century that the postmodern apostles considered to be as radical as the industrial and political revolutions of modernity were after all not as revolutionary, since society had not qualitatively departed from its capitalist and rational foundational structures. Profit and private property rights remained the primary organisational principles of the economy, and civil rights, division of power and other rational, universalistic ideas that were envisioned during the Enlightenment can merely be said to have reached their final fruition in the 1990s. Not yet had the world transitioned to an entirely new stage of development. However, this was before the internet.

The capitalist society we live in today is very different from the one described by Marx in the nineteenth century. It still runs on the productive engine of industrial capitalism, but there are critical differences that are getting increasingly obvious at the beginning of the twenty-first century. With the internet becoming an integral part of ever more aspects of existence, things are starting to change in ways that may reveal the contours of a very different society emerging. Information technologies, AI and robotics have progressed to a level where more and more jobs are getting automated. The most developed and affluent economies are no longer characterised by their industrial output, but rather by their ability to generate new innovations in the symbol world. This entails scientific advances on the one hand and, on the other, cultural accomplishments, for instance in the form of entertainment products such as movies, music and computer games. Such commodities are sold on the world market at very favourable exchange rates and provide the nations who possess these productive capabilities a most advantageous position on the global stage. A Korean politician once noticed that the value of the movie *Jurassic Park* was equal to about 1½ million Hyundai cars. And with significantly fewer working hours associated with the former, the production of high-end entertainment commodities accordingly constitutes a valuable asset to the nations that produce them. The most powerful industries today are not the steel mills and automobile manufacturers, but those preoccupied with developing the latest in bits and bytes and those who control the billions of virtual dollars that make the world economy go round. This does not mean that the physical products themselves are without importance, but physical reality has been subordinated to the logic of the symbolic. In the hierarchies of value, the contents of products are mostly below that of the brands themselves, and the ones who most skilfully excel in the art of advertising will win the most profitable shares of the market.

In our day and age, symbols, not manufactured goods, have thus moved to the centre of the economy; whereby the growing emphasis on innovation and knowledge has given rise to a new privileged class of creatives and made those who master the symbols most competently the new rulers of the world.

At the same time globalisation has pushed the production of industrial goods to the margins of the world economy, leaving a growing precariat behind in the old industrial heartlands of the West. (The term 'precariat', derived from the 'precarious' living conditions of this class, has gained prominence since the professor of development studies Guy Standing published his book *The Precariat* in 2011). In the most developed economies it is no longer the working class that is the most marginalised group in society, in fact, the industrial workers have largely disappeared, and instead we see a growing number of people outside the labour market who live off government handouts and occasional odd jobs. Starvation or other poverty-inflicted threats to existence are no longer a major concern in the leading capitalist societies. Today it is rather a lack of meaning and motivation, as proposed by Jürgen Habermas, and the alienation of living a life without any higher purpose that is the root of much suffering – and simultaneously, one of the greatest threats to the stability of society. The old class structure of industrial society seems to have given way to a new kind of social division, and the issues revolving around class conflicts have changed as well. Inequalities have risen dramatically in the last thirty years, but the political divisions in late modern societies seem to have less to do with income differences as it has with more cultural and value-centred ones. This has become evident by new voting patterns, most notably with how traditional working-class people have begun to support more conservatively inclined nationalist movements. Many of those who are far better off, and in Marxist terms belong to the bourgeoisie, seem more inclined towards applauding postmodern values that emphasise equality, individual rights and environmental protection. In late capitalist society, political division thus seems to revolve more around the clash between symbol worlds and meaning making than economic differences. On one side we have the highly privileged class of creative professionals, ethnic and sexual minorities and a growing group of young progressively inclined urban people who hover between the new precariat and a foothold in the creative industries; and on the other we have the traditional working-class, religious people of varying income groups, and the older power holders of wealth and privilege. This is arguably a very different society from that described by Marx.

One of the most notable differences between the new form of modernity today and that of the nineteenth century is the way in which electronic mass media and the internet has expanded and saturated our lives – to a degree where they have come to play *the* defining role in how we perceive the world. We spend a growing share of our time and attention on various forms of news, entertainment and social interactions consumed through electronic media devices. Most of the new information and cultural stimuli we receive today do not come from other people in our physical proximity. As a consequence, our values, views of reality and even the perception of ourselves are thus increasingly shaped by strangers who reach us through the media's symbol world. When we make conclusions about how the world works, and what is important to know, it tends to be derived more from experiences we have acquired from text, pictures and recorded sound than first-hand experiences in physical reality. Electronic mass media is thereby shaping our world, or more specifically, our perceptions of it – which according to the postmodern logic is what really counts at the end of the day. How we see the world ultimately decides how we shape it; and the ones who master the symbols most competently and manage to gain the attention of people accordingly get to choose how the world is seen and what is to be done with it. All of this has led to a version of modernity, a postmodern kind, where physical reality has become more subordinated to the logic of symbols and narratives. What is imagined as real has less to do with how the world appears to our senses and more with how it is conveyed to us through the symbols in the media.

The new conditions in our media-saturated reality have, despite society's capitalist foundation, begun to take on characteristics that can be described as highly postmodern. We are no longer as well-informed about the conditions and events in our nearby physical surroundings. The lives of our neighbours often remain largely unknown to us, but we tend to be up to date with even the most intimate details of celebrities we do not know in person. This has led to a very postmodern condition where our minds are filled with images of strangers that we feel we have a personal relation with, but are only acquainted with through the symbol world. These people tend to be highly successful individuals, famous movie stars, powerful politicians or accomplished scientists and intellectuals. So when we reflect upon our social world, ponder our own role in it and inevitably start to compare ourselves with all of these people in our mind, we may feel a little inadequate, not as beautiful as all the happy people in the magazines, maybe a little fat, and far from as successful as all these smart and wealthy people who enter the headlines. We may even gain a growing sense of inferiority towards our friends on Facebook who constantly put up pictures of their happy and interesting lives. This may lead us to participate in the on-going arms-race of presenting our lives as perfect and meaningful on social media – after all, what matters the most in this postmodern condition is how reality is portrayed in the world of the symbolic, not how it 'really' is – *or*, we may gain a growing understanding of the societal discourses that oppress us and alienate us. It may be because of how we look, our sexuality or gender, disabilities or simply because the values and norms that we are constantly bombarded with from mainstream society do not resonate with our own ideas of how society and culture *ought* to be.

The explosion of new media channels has greatly assisted the proliferation of postmodern ideas and made way for marginalised and previously invisible groups to make their voices heard. Postmodern thoughts and values have thereby succeeded in changing public discourse in later years, evident by the way identity politics – social justice for minorities, criticism of traditional gender roles, etc. – and environmental concerns have entered the mainstream. Postmodernism is inherently hostile towards capitalism and modern consumer society, but plain and simple anti-capitalism is, however, not a sufficiently new phenomenon to differentiate it from the rational thought perspective. Modern thinkers, such as socialists and anarchists, have since the beginnings of capitalism criticised its exploitative nature and unequal distribution of wealth. This is part of the postmodern criticism of capitalism, but in addition it claims that capitalism reinforces traditional gender roles and racism, destroys the environment and focuses too narrowly on material growth rather than psychological wellbeing and personal self-expression. These are all very postmodern criticisms that significantly depart from the older Marxist emphasis on improving the material living standard of working people and the equal distribution of wealth that prevailed among more modernist critics. The new postmodern contenders derive their criticism from an entirely different symbol world, a new thought perspective that often alienates and confuses their modernist allies in the quest against capitalism and the market.

However, the larger societal consequences of postmodernity on the systemic level still remain rather limited. Even though society has become a little greener and women and minorities have been given somewhat better rights and recognition, society still works in accordance with the principles of industrial market capitalism and consumerism. But intellectually, especially in the humanities, postmodernity has had a more or less complete breakthrough. In sociology, anthropology, history, culture studies, etc., postmodern philosophers like Gilles Deleuze, Jacques Derrida and Jean-François Lyotard, along with other critics of modern society like Jürgen Habermas and Eric Fromm, have been mandatory reading in curricula for decades. Whole new departments have even been established as a result of the postmodern influence in universities, such as gender research and post-colonial studies, which thereby have come to be completely dominated by the postmodern thought perspective. Every year large cohorts of young liberal arts students exit university campuses, armed with Foucault, Judith Butler and Co., ready to deconstruct the world and tear its oppressive discourses apart with critical theory and queer-feminism. Even in the natural and technical sciences we see an equally growing number of students who have chosen a more environmental approach to their subject and with great enthusiasm and almost religious fervour set out to create sustainable solutions to ongoing ecological crises.

However, nowhere in the world do we see a fundamentally different societal model to the capitalist one take form. The high ideals of equality, spiritual communion and environmental sustainability advocated by postmodern thinkers and activists remain far from realisation in even the most progressive societies today. Yet, postmodern thought and new societal developments have changed the game to some extent.

First of all, many of the most developed economies have become so affluent and offer their citizens such a degree of material security that they have made ever more people adhere to so-called 'post-materialist' values. This does not mean that people have become ascetics, or that they are against material acquisitions as such. On the contrary, the high material living standards have simply made them more concerned with other aspects of life than acquiring more possessions. When a growing number of people rarely have to worry about their basic needs, the share of individuals who spend more of their time on non-monetary relations accordingly goes up, evident by the activities of many middle-class people in affluent countries. Here we see an increased number of people engaged in voluntary work, activism, hobbies and artistic expressions, and even new spiritual communities. When a certain level of material wealth has been reached, people on average simply prefer to do other things than making money. Many of these highly privileged people also tend to favour equality, environmental sustainability, and personal and artistic expression over economic growth: in short, postmodern values – partly because they are privileged enough to do so.

Secondly, people are generally better educated and informed than ever, information having become extremely cheap so as to make the means of distributing knowledge and information more accessible to a larger number of people than before. This means that postmodern thought has become widely available so that even people outside of university campuses can get access to these perspectives – often in easily digestible forms, distilled from the advanced and rather inaccessible philosophies of postmodern thinkers, by media-savvy, intelligent and charismatic internet personalities. With the internet, postmodern thought spreads like never before, and those who feel oppressed, alienated or exploited by modern society are only a click away from obtaining the intellectual and spiritual ammunition that addresses their situation and makes them feel empowered or even entitled.

The free flows of information on the internet ensure that very little oppression and injustice remain unnoticed. The novel and particular mechanisms of various internet technologies also affect *how* information can affect public discourse. Suddenly we have Wikileaks using an established technology for collaborative content management, which then provides whistle-blowers with a powerful platform to expose the human-rights violations of governments, unparalleled by anything before the internet. With Facebook, people in authoritarian dictatorships suddenly became able to organise effective resistance that would otherwise have been almost impossible to achieve due to the regimes' tightly enforced bans on freedom of assembly and political opposition. Among other uprisings around the world, this gave birth to the protests known as the 'Arab Spring' in 2011. And lately, the #metoo campaign has brought the issue of sexual abuse to the forefront in a way that seems to have changed the way in which we talk about this problem, and probably even what perpetrators can get away with in the future. This only happened because of the way in which simple hashtag technology allowed for hitherto unconnected individuals to reach

each other and confirm similar experiences. The viral, fast-paced dynamic of social media can create massive exposure to a previously neglected issue so that it can no longer be ignored. The internet has truly changed how public discourse is formed, and it seems to favour the social, cultural and political agendas derived from postmodern critical thought.

However, there is something that postmodernity has not managed to address efficiently and appears completely incapable of alleviating. One of the greatest unresolved issues in our increasingly postmodern and culturally fractured age is the lack of a new commonly shared symbol world, a new metanarrative in other words. Grand collective visions that can unite the majority of the population are a scarce resource today. Thus far postmodernism has not created a new collective narrative powerful enough to curb the relentless spread of the market, which the postmodernists, partly, and rather unintentionally, have helped to unleash by refusing to propose an overarching alternative narrative.

The Failure of Postmodernism and the Need for a New Metanarrative

Postmodernity is inherently hostile towards all authorities and power structures and has as its central objective to reveal all the injustice, oppression and arbitrary narratives on which they rely. And with many of the societal developments of late modern society, especially that of the internet, it has now acquired the means to challenge those power structures. The aforementioned philosopher Lyotard once wrote that postmodernism is 'the consequence of capital and informational flows that have moved beyond political or instrumental control'.[8] This is precisely what has happened with the emergence of the internet, where larger amounts of information and capital circulate beyond governmental control, though not completely, but still to an extent unparalleled in history. Recently, the internet has even given rise to its own monetary currencies, blockchain technologies like bitcoin, which are likely to erode the states' political control of capital even further in the future.

Another circumstance to have deprived political power holders of their control on capital and information (and if we agree with Lyotard, is a postmodern development) is the fact that the market has grown explosively in size and importance in wake of the last decades of globalisation and thus become impossible for any state to control, or even regulate, in an appropriate manner. The growing wealth this development has brought about has also made many regular citizens so affluent that it has helped them escape some of the instrumental controls that would previously have limited their freedom of action. The 'authorities' do not have the same sway over people's lives as they used to. Citizens of late modern societies are often wealthy enough, have the sufficient educational level and adequate access to informational technologies so as to defy the centres of political and economic control. Even people of modest means are increasingly capable of defying those who try to control them. Since the overproduction of industrial society makes it relatively easy to have one's basic material needs met, it accordingly makes people less inclined towards doing what they are told as they are more likely to survive if they don't.

So just like the economic development of agrarian society and the emergence of new information technologies during the Axial Age allowed for challengers to arise at the margins of the centres of power, so do similar developments in late modernity generate opponents to counter the accumulation of power and wealth, the oppression and injustices, and the dated narratives of modern society today. In simple terms, writing was to the Axial Age what the internet is to the postmodern age. And just like the Axial traditions, postmodernity likewise seeks to redistribute wealth and power in accordance with new moral standards and to alter the rules of the game in which power relations play out.

Postmodernity has many similarities with the movements of the Axial Age. Postmodernism also has its 'righteous rebels' and affiliated 'churches', such as feminism, post-colonialism and environmentalism. These rebels can be said to constitute a new priesthood, also known as the rather postmodern invention of the 'intellectual', whose mission it is to discipline and correct those unfortunate enough to gravitate towards lower thought perspectives – much like the way in which priests, mullahs and other religious figures have tried to instil good moral behaviour to conform with the religious thought perspective. The postmodern apostles of today have managed to change public discourse in favour of postmodern values to a considerable degree, even despite being a minority. They have succeeded, partly in virtue of often higher levels of education, but also since their arguments conceptually beat modern and religious arguments at their own game. Postmodernists tend to be more rational and critical in their view of science, often trapping modern scientifically inclined persons in arguments and language games that leave the latter utterly confused and without any means of disentangling themselves from their own contradictions. And traditional religious people are often left in the moral gutter, embarrassingly exposed as bigots, and stripped of all ethical credibility after an encounter with a particularly zealous postmodernist.

The result of this is that many modernists and even a fair share of religious people often pretend to conform to the postmodern ideology. The more altruistic reasoning of postmodern arguments on ethics are simply conceptually superior: *quantitative*, by a more expansive circle of solidarity that includes all humans and often even animals, and *qualitative* by considering more sensitive and delicate matters. As such, many people at least want to pretend they subscribe to postmodern values – after all, no one wants to be a racist, or a sexist, and who wants to argue against the fact that the environment is important? But in reality, many in late modern society are merely paying lip service to the ethical code of postmodernity: when postmodernists have finished picking apart 'common' people's chauvinist and narrow-minded arguments, the latter usually remain just as suspicious to their strange-looking 'ethnic' neighbours, don't really care about gender equality and continue consuming without any regards to the environmental consequences. The widespread conduct of postmodernists to intellectually strong-arm their opponents – and humiliate them if they don't – has not been without its consequences. Postmodern thought has alienated a large number of people and caused a fair amount of resentment and bitterness. In later years there has arisen a growing criticism of the oppression of the so-called 'social justice warriors', the 'politically correct elite' and the 'cultural Marxists', partly facilitated by the same internet technologies that have greatly assisted postmodernity to enter the mainstream. In recent years, it has even become increasingly harder for postmodernists to efficiently counter these critics, who have learned to master the postmodern ways of dominating media discourse.

The problem is that postmodernism does not resonate with the emotions, understanding of reality, meaning making and lifestyles of people who gravitate towards other thought perspectives. To the average modern person, the discourses postmodernists talk about are simply not visible. And the structures considered oppressive by postmodernism are often seen as hard, but well-deserved rights and natural facts of life that cannot be changed. Similarly, when postmodernists pick apart sacred scriptures and point out the contradictions of religious faiths, religious people rarely feel they are done a favour as the beauty and deep-felt meaning they get from these are severely jeopardised – all while no alternative to be grasped and appreciated is offered in return.

Another related problem is postmodernism's lack of any grand narratives to be shared by people subscribing to different thought perspectives. Postmodernists simply do not realise, or want to accept, that people vary greatly in their thought patterns and meaning making, and that it can be very difficult to understand and value postmodern ideas if one is not sufficiently adjusted to these on an emotional and cognitive level. Instead, they tend to stubbornly insist on emphasising the analytic aspects that appear so painstakingly obvious to them, using their cultural and intellectual superiority to force-feed people arguments that are perceived as utterly alien and counterintuitive by those unversed in postmodern linguistic analyses.

Apparently, the postmodern thought perspective carries no method to include the perspectives of other thought perspectives, convey its insights in ways that make sense to all kinds of people, or to make differently thinking people perceive the postmodernists as friends and allies rather than adversaries. Despite the postmodern emphasis on inclusion and diversity, this thought perspective has yet to find efficient and emotionally sensitive measures to facilitate the peaceful cooperation of modern society's many different people towards a common goal. Part of the problem is the postmodern emphasis on moral relativism and anti-theses; as soon as new overarching visions are proposed, or any other larger systemic narratives about society and the human being, the postmodernists are quick to deconstruct the endeavour, picking it apart while leaving no counter-proposals in its place. They are experts at exposing the ethical shortcomings, social pathologies and dysfunctional nature of modern society, but they rarely, if ever, propose any credible solutions or alternatives to change society on a fundamental level. This has alienated a fair share of modern people to the postmodern thought perspective, to a degree where many, in defiance of the postmodern discourse they feel is oppressing them, have reacted in ways more similar to pre-modern thought and behaviour. Anger and bitterness, it seems, tend to have this effect on people. As a consequence, we see otherwise supposedly democratic and rational people turn towards bigotry, authoritarianism and jingoism. Recent political developments in Europe and North America may be an indication of this. And since postmodernism has failed to offer any alternatives with sufficiently inclusive power to counter this development, it has thus started to lose some of its previously won legitimacy in society at large. Without any adequately convincing narratives to address the emotional and psychological needs of people, which arguably are responsible for many of the latest political developments in the West, some aspects of society seem to have regressed to lower levels of development – especially in regards to ethics.

This partly has to do with postmodernism's ambivalent approach to ethics. Postmodernists are generally highly concerned with ethical issues, perhaps more than anything else, but the seemingly inherent moral relativism of postmodernism appears to obstruct the possibility of a new moral system being developed. This is further inhibited by postmodern hostility towards all grand narratives. As a result, the postmodern era has become characterised by growing fragmentation, a branching of different symbol worlds, sub-cultures and identities with a declining connection to the overall symbol world of society. One unintended consequence of excessive focus on identity politics has been that no one is allowed to voice the concern of the greater 'we' of society. If a new moral system is to be commonly shared by the majority, it requires a shared symbol world that resonates with people on different stages of thought, identities and cultural backgrounds; one where they feel comfortable and are provided with a sense of communion with the larger society they live in. This has not occurred. As such, postmodernism has not managed to outcompete and replace the current market-driven order. In a world where people have increasing difficulties relating to each other, divided by misdirected identity politics, find little in common with people who think differently and thus lack a sense of shared identity within larger society, relations can erode. Consequently, the only thing that connects us in the end, the only efficient means to manage our productive day-to-day relations with each other, is the rather emotionally unsatisfactory and culturally impoverished measure of money.

The circumstance that postmodern thought lacks a credible alternative to market-driven capitalist society has become more obvious since the end of the Cold War. Lost are the initial optimism and beliefs in a better society to combine democracy, social justice and spiritual growth that characterised the younger generations of the 1960s and '70s. Still, many of these early postmodern movements' values have successfully been adopted by mainstream society: social customs and interactions have become less stiff and formal, old moral conventions regarding sexuality have been abandoned, and it has become acceptable for young people to choose their own path in life. However, these values are entirely compatible with modern capitalist society, in fact, they have actually been fully appropriated by market forces and no longer appear as the revolutionary threats they used to. This can be explained by the fact that the values of the counterculture that were most successfully implemented in society were the exact ones that under closer scrutiny are more modern than postmodern: the freedoms of expression, individual life choices and the hedonistic indulgence in sex, drugs and new consumer friendly music tastes like rock 'n' roll are all inherently modern reactions against the last crumbling remains of the religious thought perspective. Alienated youngsters with postmodern hippie sentiments of peace and love and the French philosophers who set out to deconstruct all the mythological discourses of modern society may have helped this development take place, but the end-result was a society more modern than ever. Following the height of the counterculture movement, consumerism reached new levels of individual indulgence and ecological destruction, the market expanded greatly and took over ever more aspects of society and the new sexual freedom became just another wrapping for commodities and a means to sell us new things to make us feel 'sexy' and desirable – all to the tones of seductive popular music, reasonably priced, and widely available in well-assorted record stores, to satisfy growing consumer demand.

The postmodern ideas of gender equality mostly progressed to a level where women were given the same formal rights as men and given a position on the labour market – so very modern. But highly male-chauvinist values remained and are only waning very slowly. Women have never reached the same level of pay as men, and blatant double standards regarding women's sexuality remain present and widespread. The concern with environmental issues likewise only increased very slowly. However, the greatest disappointment with postmodernnity's first major development on the societal level was its complete failure to replace the modern capitalist consumer society and its market-driven ethos with a credible alternative. This became perfectly evident after the end of the Cold War, when the last remaining post-structuralist Marxists either gave up, died, or hid themselves in obscure university departments far far away. The flower children have long grown up, cut their long hair and long been way too preoccupied with tending their lives as common consumers and wage earners, raising families of their own, too busy to fight the power. Consequently, much of postmodernity has become increasingly prone to sarcasm and cynicism, merely mocking its opponents, but rarely proposing any alternatives to the current order. The early postmodern hippie movement, naively, but sincerely, preaching peace and love and dreaming about a gentler and more spiritually enlightened society, has thus been replaced by today's dominant postmodern currents: the satirical and deeply sarcastic comedians, the cynical intellectuals and a new upper class of creatives using postmodern lingo and art-expressions to bolster their politically correct images and to proudly flash their higher levels of cultural capital. As the initial surge of postmodern developments has come to an end and it has become clear that the system is not going to be changed, many of those who have been lucky enough to successfully transition to the new thought perspective are now using their newly gained privilege of cultural, intellectual and ethical superiority to position themselves favourably within the current system.

The Marxist-inspired postmodern intellectuals have gradually put their dreams of revolution on hold, given up on any new overarching narratives to support a new societal model (and thereby become truly postmodern in Lyotard's understanding) and begun to engage in different *minor* narratives instead, such as various minority issues, identity projects and other more particularistic social critiques. Unlike their Marxist predecessors they rarely attempt to propose any new radical visions for how society could be reorganised on the systemic level, no overarching systems of thought, and carefully seek to always reach the antithesis. This seems to be inherent in the postmodern thought perspective, a structural feature of how it organises our thought patterns. It is tempting to suggest that the reason we have seen very few proposals for how an entirely new society could be structured from postmodern thinkers, at least the more 'respectable' ones in academic institutions, is because of the disillusion and embarrassment with the counterculture movement and the apparent failure of communism. It may also simply have to do with fears of making a fool of oneself if one were to propose something as silly as an alternative to the market economy, jeopardising one's career if ever attempted. In that case it is a much safer bet to merely criticise all the things that are obviously wrong with society, adjusting a discourse here and there, and never propose something that inevitably will be criticised and exposed to have faults and errors as any grand theory is destined to contain.

The universities have become a means of subsistence for many postmodern scholars, a haven where they remain at safe enough distances from the circles of political power, but close enough to affect the general values in society. But this has not been sufficiently efficient to fundamentally change society. As such, it appears as if postmodernity, now in its mature form, has moved to a point which equals its Axial predecessor at the later stage following the initial revolutionary era of the Axial Age. The righteous postmodern rebels have made their mark in history: they shook up society with a brief youthful outburst that provided them a foothold in the world by proudly defeating the last remnants of dated religious morality, to which modern society should pay its gratitude. Thereafter they conquered the universities and the media and managed to change social discourse to a degree where most decent people had to pay lip-service to their values. But now they have become part of the very same system they initially set out to overthrow. Nowhere is a new society to be seen on the postmodern horizon.

Part of postmodernism's failure to foster a new society has, as mentioned, to do with its hostility towards all great narratives, its propensity to always reach the antithesis, and its inherent moral relativism. But with no overarching symbol worlds shared by most of society (the 'metanarratives' rejected by Lyotard) and theorists never proposing new systems to replace the old, but always pursuing the antithesis, their stern reluctance towards new moral standards to stand above the always occurring relativism on the matter, it all leads us back into the claws of the market – if for no other reason because money remains the only thing to unite us. Despite the intentions of most postmodern thinkers, the lack of a common moral and political compass has opened up the door for the market to take over. There are no longer any robust ideas or enduring ideologies that can keep the market at bay. Political endeavours have been watered down and various identity projects, criticisms of norms and special interest group issues are not sufficient to withstand the sprawl of the market. For lack of hope and vivid ideas in a greater context, everyone has to fend for themselves in trying to secure personal salvation through the offerings on the market.

* * *

We lack a commonly shared symbol world to give us a mutual understanding of each other, generate a greater sense of communal belongingness and help us focus our collective efforts efficiently towards a new vision of a better society for all. Consequently, we are living in a society without an overarching value system where financial values are prioritised before cultural ones. Postmodernity's propensity towards moral relativism and emphasis on subjectivity has led to a condition where individual opinions, no matter how poorly grounded, are considered just as valid as carefully elaborated moral standards and expert knowledge. After all, in a world where everything is relative and all depends on the subjective perspective of the individual – who can say what's better or worse anyway? Or so it may seem.

We have placed ourselves in a situation where more people are in contact with each other than ever before, but we still cannot talk to each other. The primary reason is that we have not fully realised that people cognitively function within different thought perspectives and thereby think and act very differently. This is something the postmodern thought perspective has failed to address. The world is broadly speaking divided into three main thought perspectives: the religious, the rational and the postmodern. But since there is no common symbol language that all the adherents of the different perspectives can speak, the only thing that connects us is money.

Further on in the book we shall explore whether it is possible to go beyond this postmodern condition and together succeed in co-creating a shared symbol language to improve communication between different symbol worlds and thought perspectives; a new overarching symbol world in which differently thinking people can reach each other.

How do we increase the understanding between various symbol worlds in our increasingly fragmented and complex reality? How do we manage the growing complexity of the world in a more productive and harmonious manner? And how do we succeed in getting religious, modern and post-modern people to cooperate and live together, and live well?

These and other questions will be at the centre of the following chapters of this book.

PART 2

Our Socially Constructed World

INTRODUCTION TO PART 2

We have now taken a sweeping view of history to illustrate how a developmental perspective of billions of years can help us see patterns that are often lost in conventional historiography. We saw how the evolution of the physical Universe, life and human culture has unfolded through a number of successive, often highly contingent developments that have led to higher and higher levels of complexity. At critical junctures, we could chart our entry onto the scene as a conscious animal, the story-telling ape that we are, and onwards as the collective agent of powerful purpose, the creator of collective imaginaries and transmitter of cultural and memetic forces.

We have familiarised ourselves with the four thought perspectives that have arisen during human history, the four fundamental frameworks for our interpretation and understanding of the world: *animism*, *religion*, *rationalism* and *postmodernism*. Through its symbol tools, every thought perspective becomes its own collective imaginary which is both held aloft by culture and dominates it. What is central in such an collective imaginary is an important idea that some sociologists call the imaginary's 'fundamental authority'. This fundamental idea authorises and legitimises the imaginary and functions as its anchoring foundation stone and its arbiter. The three most important such idea inventions in human history have, in my view, been: *God*, *Science* and *the Market* – ideas that we have been able to use to *efficiently* structure our existence and our symbol worlds. They have also been the foundation for, and have legitimised, the dominating thought perspectives throughout human history.

Thus, we have three *thought perspectives*, each with their own *fundamental authority*:

1. The religious thought perspective, with God as its highest fundamental authority.
2. The rational thought perspective, with science as its highest fundamental authority.
3. The postmodern thought perspective, with the market as its highest fundamental authority.

For religion, God, karma or similar ideas were not just the primary explanatory principle for occurrences in the world, but also a way to legitimise religion's dominant role in society. Those who claimed to have God on their side were also the ones who had the right to exercise power. In modern society, science was used in a similar way; hence it was no coincidence that the institutions of science were subordinate to the state and often were formed as part of governments' attempts to legitimise themselves. In relation to large parts of the population it was not so much a case of their critical relation to science's methods or results being decisive, but rather a reference to the scientific institutions that decided whether a certain act was right or wrong. This, however, started to erode as a greater part of the population attained a more critical level of awareness.

With postmodernism's victory within both academia and popular culture, science and the rational thought perspective increasingly started to lose their legitimacy as pillars of society. But with postmodernism's inherent tendency to fight and critically explore all authorities, the unintended consequence was that when there were no higher authorities, the ethical legitimacy was handed over to the power of the market.

In Part 2 we will explore where this civilisational trajectory into contemporary 'late modernity' leaves us today, while demonstrating how our memetic systems of symbols have arrived at arguably rather suboptimal equilibria. The victories of professional doubt, leading to ubiquitous cynicism, threaten to abandon our imaginaries to the market alone. At severe risk of absconding from our responsibilities to enhance fairness, and forge meaning, we risk sleepwalking into a neoliberal world devoid of those concepts, all for the sake of efficiency.

I hope the reader will discover just how contingent our sense of selves is, and even how contingent the market is. Instead of taking their solidity as articles of faith, we can deploy the lessons learned in Part 1 to question the roots of these systems and redirect ourselves towards new dawns.

With this picture of a socially constructed, subconsciously qualified, interconnected and evolving self, we can more soberly address our shortcomings in decision- and meaning-making faculties. Furthermore, by extending these systemic insights to the world at large, we can both surrender some of our excessive expectations of command and control and also learn to manage and regulate our role in 'self-eco-organisation' far more effectively: with needed restraint and wisdom.

A crucial element of Part 2's analysis is the social construction of our reality. It is pivotal to appreciate the contingency and malleability of the aforementioned systemic developments, which we observe and concede include sizeable failings when uncritically arrived at with certain social norms (for example, current free-market fundamentalism). Part 2 will show that much of our current political discourse and economic activity lacks the self-reflection that we saw was so crucial at each iterative step in Part 1. Therefore, a conscious reflexivity towards our own systems, shifting the sacred subject and secularising it, removing it from its pedestal into a manipulable object, is key.

Chapter 7
THE POSTMODERN THOUGHT PERSPECTIVE

The discussion about postmodernism has been going on since the early 1980s. Among those who consider it a valid concept, it is commonly agreed that it is not just a diagnosis of our age, but also a critical mode of thought that questions many of the general assumptions of modernity and that it is a way of showing alternative routes to knowledge. In my interpretation it is even more than that; it is a whole new thought perspective, the latest of its kind.

Nietzsche once wrote that 'There are no facts in themselves. It is always necessary to begin by introducing a meaning in order that there can be a fact.'[1] Facts do not exist by themselves, there is no 'view from nowhere', as pointed out by Thomas Nagel,[2] from where we objectively can observe them. Facts always depend on the context in which they are situated, and contexts can always be put into question. This simple idea sums up what according to Callum G. Brown make up the two core principles of postmodernity, that: 1) 'reality is unrepresentable in human forms of culture', and 2) 'with an inability to represent reality, no authoritative account can exist of anything'.[3] By 'unrepresentable' Brown does not mean that we cannot create representations of reality, merely that our representations will never fully correspond with what they are portraying.

Postmodernism accordingly entails a deep scepticism about any authoritative accounts of ultimate and unquestionable truths, especially those of science, the highest authority in the modern thought perspective.

The foundation of postmodern epistemology is thus the key intellectual principle that the notion of 'truth' cannot be verified through empirical research, but that all knowledge is context dependent and therefore ultimately unreliable. It does not mean that we cannot make any meaningful accounts of reality, but what it brings to our awareness is that we need to remain highly critical to any truth claims and remember that our narratives about reality are severely limited and can never fully capture what they make representations of. First of all, because reality is too enormous and complex to be truly representable, second, because it requires subjectivity that can always be put into question, and third, because our representations of reality are limited by human signs which are not equivalent to the facts being conveyed themselves.

WHAT IS POSTMODERNISM?

Although many of us do not have a sufficient understanding of postmodernism, or have even heard about the term, most of us are familiar with postmodern expressions and elements from popular culture. Postmodern art is characterised by accepted rules being abandoned and replaced by an admixture of old and new, high and low, and a creative playfulness where more or less anything goes. It also emphasises surfaces, absurdity and the apparent lack of profound meaning in modern life, often in a dystopian way.

A good example is Andy Warhol, who shows us that fine art and popular culture are not so different from one another and that surfaces and appearances within contexts are all that really matter. His triptychs and paintings indicate that mundane and popular things such as images of canned tomato soup or Marilyn Monroe repeatedly drowned in shrieking colors can also be fine art – because there is really nothing behind the curtains, no depth or secret to reveal, nothing 'special' about the artist and his artwork. Postmodernism sees through all such illusions. There is only surface. And you can play with these surfaces in irreverent ways: Pablo Picasso (who was more postmodern than modern in a strict sense) squeezes several dimensions and multiple perspectives into the same two-dimensional frame.

In postmodernism's cynical optics there is nothing other than how they immediately appear, no deeper purpose or meaning is to be found behind the surfaces, and here the symbols are given a prominent place as the only thing our mental world consists of – beyond which there is nothing that we can acquire knowledge of. Only surface, context, absurdity, which can be seen as a criticism of the idea in earlier thought perspectives that there is a kind of inherent essence within phenomena. In early forms, this postmodern current first showed up in late nineteenth-century literature. You may remember the wizard of Oz, who, upon being revealed as a fraud, points out to Dorothy that he is not a bad man – only a bad wizard. Or Lewis Carroll's *Alice in Wonderland*, in which the stupefying dialogues reveal the absurd and contingent nature of speech and language.

Most of us have probably been exposed to postmodernism without knowing it from the films we have seen. For example, David Lynch's *Blue Velvet* (1986) where there are strange happenings that cannot be grasped by one's reason, such as a blind man who can see or an ear in the grass. There are constant shifts in pace and tone and normal reality is distorted and presented as something ambiguous and unknown. Lynch also created *Twin Peaks* (1990), which contains many of the same elements. Other examples of postmodern films are *Pulp Fiction* (1994), a story with a non-linear timeline where clichés from the gangster, drama and comedy genres are playfully mixed with surf music and pop culture to attain something unique, without actually offering anything new of its own. Another example is *Blade Runner* (1982), a dystopic futuristic vision with anthropomorphic robots and without easily recognisable villains and heroes. Dystopias that warn of technology's dark sides (i.e. modernity), rather than science fiction utopias that celebrate the conquests of science, are a common feature in postmodern films.

Postmodern architecture can be seen in the building styles in Las Vegas, as pointed out by Fredric Jameson.[4] What is striking as one moves down the Strip is a completely free blend of styles that have been adopted from various cultures and epochs. A good example is the Las Vegas hotel Aladdin, which on the outside is of Arab and on the inside English Tudor style. It is a revolt against modernism's rules and requirements for boundaries and order. Architectural modernism is stylistically pure and hierarchical while postmodernism emphasises style blends where all elements are given equal value. The postmodernists are not claiming to be offering something new. Rather, their originality consists of a creative mix of already existing elements and methods. Postmodernism is a remix culture where sampling, breaking up, and stirring are applauded. Along the Strip we can also find buildings that have become wedding chapels for quick nuptials with garish neon signs. The sign, rather than the building itself, which might as well have been a convenience store or a warehouse, is what defines its function. Symbols are more important than what they refer to in postmodern thinking. That the neon signs often are larger than the buildings they refer to thus make the city of Las Vegas particularly postmodern according to Jameson. As such, we can regard this city as a

'The Strip' in Las Vegas with neon signs bigger than the reality they represent. Photo: Highsmith/Wikimedia Commons.

society that in its postmodern state has lost the ability to handle time and history and the ability to value one thing higher than another.

However, one thing does count above everything else: money.

Modernism versus Postmodernism

A helpful way to understand postmodernism is by contrasting it with modernism. Sometimes it is easier to get a sense of something by reference to what it is not, and how it differs from something else, preferably its opposite. And in the case of postmodernism, we are fortunate to have an opposite within the concept's very name.

Postmodernism is derived from modernism. It as such is not a sudden departure from the thought perspective that preceded it, but emerged as an answer to many of the inherent flaws and contradictions of the modern, rational thought perspective. The logics and principles of postmodernism can thus be traced back to the premises that guided modern thought. With modernism as our point of departure, we can thereby identify some of the principles that came to shape postmodern thought.

On a philosophical level, modernism folds over to its own premises in a number of ways. For instance, if we have to be rational and consequential, then we must also accept rational arguments about society, science, politics and everyday life. In particular, that many of our societal relations and structures are extremely skewed and imbalanced and not as 'rational' as they could have been. From a rational point of view, we must simply admit that modern society has not created the just and harmonious conditions envisioned by the Enlightenment and that science and progress has not solely been of the good. Furthermore, if we accept that truth can only be known by intersubjective verification, which after all is the basis of objective scientific reasoning, then we must also accept that the premises of the intersubjective social context must be accounted for as well. For instance, if we accept that the truth is explored by a community of equals, then we must also include the truths and perspectives of other cultures, different classes and genders. And if we accept that we can only know what science tells us, then we must also accept that there is no 'view from nowhere' as a starting-point from where we can observe the world. We must always begin from a social context, and since this context always determines how we see the world, it also determines what we do not see.

Postmodernism is therefore more critical towards scientific results, insisting on including more variables, and can thus be said to be even more rational than traditional modern scientific thinking. It is also more secular, in a way, since it does not assume that we can obtain a god-like perspective on the world from where we can derive the ultimate truth – something that the secular and atheistic modernists, faithful believers in human rationality and scientific revelation, have had a hard time realising.

Postmodernism can thus be seen as a reaction against modernity's assumptions about the 'rational man' capable of solving all of nature's mysteries – just given enough time. It entails the shift of focus from the empirical investigation of the objective exterior, to the critical deconstruction of the, arguably mistaken, 'objective' spectator's subjective interior. And therefore, if valid, as much of a Copernican turn as modernity once claimed to be.

Ihab Hassan's Dichotomies of Modernity and Postmodernity

The discussion on modernity and postmodernity is a lengthy one that has endured for decades, filled with much disagreement, controversy and complicated and often contradicting trains of thought that may be more confusing than clarifying. As a consequence, postmodernism is still a rather mistaken concept, to a degree where many have rejected it as a meaningful term altogether. This is a shame. It has much explanatory power and can improve our understanding of the last thirty to forty years of societal and intellectual development if we get our heads around it. To alleviate this, it may prove useful to approach the matter in a rather alternative way, less analytic and more intuitive, to provide a shortcut to those of us who do not wish or have the time to engage in lengthy academic discussions. The shortcut that I believe can be useful to do just that has been provided by the literary theorist Ihab Hassan in the postface of the

1982 edition of his work *The Dismemberment of Orpheus – Toward a Postmodern Literature.* Here he has presented a list of dichotomies representing modernity and postmodernity.

Postmodernism is admittedly rather difficult to make sense of, but if we try to see it from the intuitive impressions we can obtain from Hassan's dichotomies below it might give us a clearer picture. The original list is a bit longer, but for brevity I have chosen the pairs I find most relevant and easy to grasp. It is highly advisable not just to read through the list as quickly as possible. The purpose is to give the reader an intuitive sense of postmodernism, so please take your time while looking at each pair and reflect a few minutes on your own personal impression. Different people will have different impressions, but it has been my experience that it can be a fruitful approach to present postmodernism in this way; especially in view of the historical context presented in the previous chapters of this book. So here goes, please take your time:

MODERNISM	POSTMODERNISM
Purpose	*Play*
Design	*Chance*
Hierarchy	*Anarchy*
Signified	*Signifier*
Distance	*Participation*
Creation/Totalisation	*Decreation/Deconstruction*
Synthesis	*Antithesis*
Presence	*Absence*
Centering	*Dispersal*
Genre/Boundary	*Text/Intertext*
Semantics	*Rhetoric*
Form (conjunctive, closed)	*Antiform (disjunctive, open)*
Narrative/Grande Histoire	*Anti-narrative/Petite Histoire*

Here is my interpretation of Hassan's list along with a few ideas they made me think of:

Purpose/Play. This illustrates how modernism tends to be more oriented towards the fulfilment of specific goals, such as scientific progress, economic growth, etc., that is, figuring out what we want to achieve and then seeking out the means to accomplish it. Postmodernism, on the other hand, is more concerned with the process, emphasising the journey rather than the destination. Foucault deconstructed reality largely because he could, not because he himself wanted to use it for some major political or societal project. And it has been argued that the main reason Derrida famously wrecked the whole endeavour of structuralism, by stating that signs do not refer to things but to other signs (something we'll return to later in this chapter), was simply to mess with his more modernly inclined philosophical colleagues. The structuralists had a grand philosophical project – so very modern of them – but Derrida, merely picking apart everything they wanted to accomplish, was more of a playful philosophical 'troll', it can be argued; 'the greatest troll in the history of philosophy', as humorously stated by an anonymous internet blogger.[5] Postmodern people, in contrast to the more bourgeois modernists, also tend to value self-expression, playful attitudes, and having fun more than maximising economic utility and a life in pursuit of one goal after the other. Living in the here and now and enjoying the moment are virtues to be found among post-materialist people in the affluent countries where postmodern values are most prevalent.

Design/Chance. Modernists are very much concerned with finding out how things work. There is a causal relation behind every occurrence, they believe. The ambition is then to figure out how in order for the human being to take control, so as to consciously steer developments and events in a preferred direction. But in postmodernism there is no such protagonist, things just happen, and in the chaotic world we live in there is no way to ensure that we can control the changes taking place. 'Shit just happens', as stated by a popular saying from the 1970s, illustrating the rather cynical and sarcastic postmodern attitude emerging at the time.

Hierarchy/Anarchy. Modernist thinking attempts to construct rationally sound hierarchies describing reality (id-ego-superego, tribal-traditional-modern, bureaucracy, management, evolution and so forth). Postmodernism will have none of that. All hierarchies are viewed with suspicion. Not only are arbitrary dominator hierarchies zealously rejected, such as whites above blacks and men above women, every hierarchy that entails someone being above others is equally frowned upon. Holders of political and economic power are critically scrutinised, but so are those assumed to be authorities on knowledge, notwithstanding their intellectual and institutional merits, which are rejected as well. Children are considered autonomous individuals and equals to adults, and even animals are often considered having the same rights as humans.

Signified/Signifier. This is an obvious reference to Ferdinand de Saussure, who distinguished between the 'signified' (that which we point to when we speak) and the 'signifier' (the pointing itself, e.g. a word or phrase).[6] Modernism focuses on the signified, attempting to see the essence of reality, whereas postmodernism is happy to merely study how reality is (inescapably) indicated in our symbolic Universe. So where modernism focuses on objects, postmodernism focuses on the discourse (collections of norms, assumptions, etc.).

Distance/Participation. Modernism studies reality from the vantage point of an 'external observer', the aforementioned 'view from nowhere', by Nagel proclaimed to be a mere illusion. Postmodernism, however, insists that we are always and already part of the studied phenomenon through our own personal perspective and narrative. On a societal level, modernism is characterised by distant institutions that control and interfere in our lives. This is something that postmodernists are very critical of. Instead they emphasise the participation of individuals to take control of their own life, personally seizing control of the institutions that govern and not only via representatives. Alternatively, they argue for abandoning them altogether by creating more participatory ways of fulfilling the functions hitherto provided by modern society's distant control mechanisms.

Creation and Totalisation/Decreation and Deconstruction. Modernism tries to build up solid knowledge about the world where each new insight is a part of a larger puzzle. Each part of this totality is thereafter used to create and control the world. This is rejected by postmodernism, which seeks to prove that things are never what they seem, that we can always find new perspectives by revealing what appeared to us as rational and sound is less so under closer scrutiny. Modernism is characterised by great social and political projects, postmodernism by problematising all such endeavours. And intellectually, modernism seeks to erect grand, total explanation models while postmodernism wants to tear apart the very same narratives – all while offering very few alternatives to replace what has been deconstructed. This is very much related to the next dichotomy.

Synthesis/Antithesis. Modernism strives towards a synthesis, the combination of the best knowledge and facts into something better and more correct. Postmodernism strives towards an antithesis, disproving the current knowledge and/or state of affairs. So whereas modernism, as mentioned above, is preoccupied with the design and creation of grand totalisation attempts to accomplish a number of pre-given purposes, postmodernism merely seeks to deconstruct these, often in a playful and anarchic manner. To the modernist, the goal is to reach a workable solution to a given problem by figuring out a way to synthesise the existing knowledge and experiences. To the postmodernist, simply proving that the modernist is wrong is often considered a job well done. The antithesis is where their reasoning ends, the conclusion that every analytic inquiry should reach in order to be complete.

Presence/Absence. Modernism studies that which is present, the apparent empirical reality that can be observed and measured. Postmodernism studies that which is not: the excluded, the implicit and the invisible. That includes the unheard voices in science and society, the many things we do not talk about, and the things we do not literally say but still imply without thinking about it when we speak. Modernism is preoccupied with explaining all the things that are, postmodernism, on the other hand, is more concerned with questioning all the things that are not, critically asking why things could not be in another way and what the absence of one thing implies to those that are present.

Centering/Dispersal. Modernism seeks the core of things, the centre of events, of political power, of knowledge. Postmodernism looks at the relations between all things, showing that centres, cores and essences are not solid at all, that they are fleeting and transient. On a political and economic level, modern society is characterised by the centralisation of power, wealth and knowledge. The centralisation of various functions in large rationalised institutions is used by modern societies to accomplish their goals in the most effective ways possible. This is something postmodernism is extremely critical of. Postmodernists seek to disperse power and wealth equally among as many as possible, and knowledge and information is sought to be made freely available to all.

Genre and Boundary/Text and Intertext. Modernism has clear categories in its understanding of reality: physics is not geography, for instance, Carl von Linné categorised the plants hierarchically, and so forth. The Enlightenment's great Encyclopaedia project is a noticeable example of modernism's ambition to differentiate things from each other, categorising them – putting things into boxes, so to speak – and seeing knowledge as something that can be put into an ordered checklist. Postmodernism views all such categories as narratives, forms of text that can and will refer to one another, something the modernists have a hard time realising because they often mistake the categories that only exist in their heads for reality. Postmodernists are also critical towards the modern project of categorisation as such – putting labels on things is by definition a bad thing, they believe – which is something they consider reductionist and incapable of capturing the truth of how the world really works. The modern obsession with clearly defined boundaries neglects how things interact with each other across borders, they claim, borders that are often rather arbitrarily conceived, imaginations that do not exist in the real world and easily could be conceived differently.

Semantics/Rhetoric. Modernism focuses on what is said, on the meaning and content of the spoken or written word. Postmodernism is more interested in *how* things are said and written. So whereas modernists derive their conclusions from what they believe the words *signify*, the postmodernists look at the words themselves, the *signifier*, how they are conveyed, and what the speaker or writer of the words, often unconsciously, may imply beyond what can be concluded by a more literal interpretation. Whereas modernists tend to be more concerned with the factual contents of speech and writing, what is immediately *present* in the words, postmodernists are more interested in what can be derived from the way they are conveyed, all the things that can be 'read between the lines'; that which is *absent* from the sentences themselves but can be revealed in a wider and often hitherto hidden context.

Form (conjunctive, closed)/Antiform (disjunctive, open). Modernism looks at entities in the world connected to one another in a coherent system. By contrast, postmodernism believes that there are only fragments and shards of reality, formless structures that will never add up to a coherent whole. The postmodern view of reality is therefore more open-ended and less prone to make final conclusions than modernism. Modernism wants to show how the world is made of coherently connected combinations of things, all making up a systematised whole. Postmodernism wants to point out all the inconsistencies that prove otherwise, everything that reveals that the asserted system is not whole after all.

Narrative and *Grande Histoire*/Anti-narrative and *Petite Histoire*. Modernism strives towards a grand narrative describing reality as a story of progress, a purposely designed total synthesis of all knowledge categorised accordingly in a hierarchical manner. And if that description of modernity's great narrating project did not include enough of the abovementioned key concepts, it can even be added that this is also a highly centering endeavour: creating one big overarching narrative – a metanarrative – to guide all others; much in the same manner that modernism has sought to create centralised institutions to govern most of society's functions. The grand narratives of modernism are those such as liberalism, communism and not least the highly elevated ideas of science and progress. Postmodernism does not accept any grand narratives (remember Lyotard's definition of postmodernism as 'incredulity towards metanarratives'). On the contrary, it emphasises the small narratives, usually considered the only valid ones since the world is so complex and chaotic that it is only realistic to expect that minor narratives can be more true than false. So whereas modernists cherish the all-explaining systems of thought, theories to provide answers about all the big questions of how the world works, in the postmodern thought perspective, detail is king and comprehensive systems are abandoned in favour of subjective observations and critical assessments. Modernists love explanations and grand totalising systemic narratives about the world. Postmodernists are highly allergic to any such attempts and rather compulsively seek to pick them apart by pointing out that they are merely narratives, and, as such, cannot be asserted to say anything about how the world really works. Once again, among postmodernists, the antithesis is the foremost goal of inquiry, and wrecking any metanarrative has higher priority than suggesting alternative ones.

* * *

With this brief interpretation of Hassan's dichotomies I hope the reader has gained a somewhat clearer idea of the differences between modernism, and thereby the rational thought perspective, and postmodernism, which I believe is a corresponding overarching thought perspective – one that poses a serious challenge to the modern mode of thought which has dominated our thinking for the past 200 years.

The world is, as mentioned in Part 1, still predominantly modern. The rational thought perspective still dominates most of the world's power structures today while only a minority of the world's population in the most affluent countries subscribe to the postmodern thought perspective. However, there is one area of contemporary society where postmodernism has had an almost complete breakthrough: in the humanities, the social and cultural sciences in academia, which I wish to briefly account for in the following.

POSTMODERNISM IN ACADEMIA

The starting point of postmodern analysis is that what we experience as fact and truth in many cases is shaped by our culture and might actually be different from another perspective, that our language contains hidden assumptions that we rarely reflect upon but still influence our thinking and behaviour, and that people live in separate conceptual worlds and always have done so.[7]

The most prominent analytic innovations to have emerged from this sort of reasoning – the new postmodern symbol tools to help us discover these previously hidden aspects – have been methods such as discourse analysis and deconstruction. These rely heavily on many of the new insights in linguistics that appeared during the early twentieth century and contributed to a renewed and more critical awareness of language, how it shapes our worldviews, and the observer's role in the construction of perceived reality.[8] The increased awareness about linguistic constructions, meaning-creating narratives, discourses, and a greater emphasis on the subjective have widened our field of vision and enabled us to more effectively make reality's complexity more discernible.

A discourse is a collection of norms, assumptions and conventions, the overall context or symbol world in which statements are made. This is often hidden from view and considered near nature-given and self-evident by the people within it. Discourse analysis has occasionally been depicted as the ability to capture and expose 'what has been taken for granted', as well as what is concealed by being commonly perceived as self-evidently true. It is a method to address and scrutinise norms and empirical material and view them from different perspectives. Discourse analysis has helped reveal hitherto unnoticed power relations that sometimes require deconstruction to be fully grasped. There is no clear definition of the term 'deconstruction', and it has even been argued that it is not even a method,[9] but it can be seen as a way to critically examine the relationship between text and meaning and separate the two from each other, expose hidden assumptions and contradictions in the way language is used and pick apart unintended and often unconscious implications of this.

By deconstructing discourses and subjecting them to critical analysis we can sometimes discover power relations that we were not aware of. Subjecting language to critical assessment can expose hidden assumptions contained in our language which influence our thinking and behaviour. Our language can be revealed to contain structures that distribute power, provide authority to some, while contributing to the oppression of others. Language creates narratives that constitute discourses, language games with specific perspectives that need to be picked apart and critically scrutinised in order to be fully realised.[10] For instance, our language contains many concepts which are often defined through their opposites: 'We' is usually considered right and normal and is automatically defined against the 'other', who is different from us. Taken against man, woman automatically becomes other, taken against Western civilisation, the rest of the world thereby becomes other, and against heterosexuality, homosexuality becomes the other. Terms like these would often not make much sense without their perceived opposites: For someone to be considered 'developed' or 'civilised', others need be 'underdeveloped' or 'uncivilised', and for something to be 'normal' something else needs to be 'abnormal'. Postmodernism wants to clarify such often unconscious ways of thinking which deconstruction serves as an important tool to unravel.

However, postmodernism, as an intellectual discipline, is not so much a method to generate new knowledge as it is a way of understanding *how* we gain knowledge from the world and how symbols and signs are used to accomplish that. Postmodern methodology in academia largely revolves around how we communicate knowledge, how it is experienced by individuals, and how they in this process construct their identity and reflect it back into society.

No coherent postmodern school of theory currently exists, and no one uses all and only postmodern perspectives, theories and methods. As Callum Brown puts it, the way scholars go about postmodern theories and methods is more like 'cherry picking', merely using the approaches they find suitable for their research while ignoring the rest. No one is therefore 'being' postmodern all the time, but all postmodern scholars are aware of certain critical perspectives, tend to be suspicious of the authority and hierarchy behind empiricism, and view the idea of modernity and progress as self-illusory and ultimately a myth.[11]

The Rise of Postmodernism in Academia

The historian Patrick Manning has described the differences between modernism and postmodernism in his account of the transition to postmodern thinking and methodology in the field of cultural history. He argues that the approach towards explaining cultural and societal change in the past used to be more positivistic, focusing mainly on delineating 'the elements of culture, the impact of various factors on culture, or the determinants of cultural change.' That is, before the postmodern turn, the main focus was to identify the variables believed to cause change and thereafter analyse them, to some extent, in isolation of other factors, much like the way natural scientists attempt to isolate different physical objects and forces so as to better analyse them. But this approach is seen as highly inadequate by postmodern critics when studying social and cultural matters since our social reality is so complex and since it is primarily shaped by the intricate interaction of large numbers of variables that rarely cause changes in isolation of one another. Accordingly, the reductionist method tends to miss the bigger picture; and since many crucial conclusions about society and culture are to be derived from that which is not present, things hidden from immediate observation, the positivist method is not as applicable to social science as it is to natural science. Instead, the postmodern approach focuses on relationships and discourses, not objects and structures, indeterminacy, not cause and effect; and where modernism seeks to locate causality, postmodernism tries to identify contingency.[12] The postmodern approach to scientific inquiry is therefore vastly different to that which dominates the natural sciences, which thus far had served as an inspiration in the humanities until the postmodern turn.

An important postmodern insight is that it is not merely our *knowledge* of the world that is socially constructed, but also many important aspects of *reality* itself. In 1966, the sociologists Peter Berger and Thomas Luckmann published their ground-breaking book *The Social Construction of Reality*. The great insight here was that many aspects of the world that we naively perceive as given by nature once and for all often are social constructions unconsciously created by humans. The theory contributed to a deepened understanding of culture by putting forth that the human being is shaped into a social creature by its society and then reproduces this society anew and that even if we acknowledge that society is a product of human actions, it is often perceived as an objective reality by the people who live in it. Along with discourse analysis and deconstruction, the idea of social constructions and how they are formed and shape our thinking and behaviour came to be an integral part of postmodern methodology in academia in the years to come.

Throughout the 1970s and '80s, a growing number of scholars agreed that economic and quantitative societal factors, those most applicable to systematic objective research, were not adequate to explain how society works. We also had to consider the importance of culture and language and how they construct the individual's perception of reality. This change of thought gave rise to one of the most influential developments of post-modernism in academia known as 'the linguistic and cultural turn'. It largely revolved around a critique of the assumption that acquisition of objective knowledge was possible through systematic research, and that such conduct, given enough time, could reveal how not only nature worked but also human societies. Prior to the linguistic and cultural turn, it was assumed (even if a material criterion of truth was never agreed upon) that there were certain formal standards, anchored in the logic of scientific inquiry, which also applied to the examination of humans and their societies. This was increasingly questioned after the end of the Second World War, when critics within the field of philosophy of language pointed out that modern science saw language as an unproblematic vehicle for the transmission of meaningful knowledge. How language transfers knowledge was seldom reflected upon by conventional scholars, social scientists included. With the intellectual current known as 'structuralism' during the 1950s and '60s, the referential function of language was thus put in question, and it was argued, as first discovered by Ferdinand de Saussure in the early twentieth century, that modern science had failed to differentiate between the signified and the signifier (what a word refers to and the word itself respectively).

Structuralism was highly influential in sociology, anthropology and linguistics, and its central tenet was that the elements of human culture and society, previously analysed in isolation to each other by positivist methods, needed to be understood by their relations to a larger, overarching structure or system. Only by uncovering the underlying structures behind that which humans do, think and perceive can we unravel the relations and laws to govern society, they believed. The structuralists were thereby no anti-modernists. Their project was well aligned with the modern ambition of identifying the structures and regularities that were supposed to govern the world. They simply used alternative methods that would later be associated with more postmodern approaches, such as hermeneutics, phenomenology and semantics. In this way they shifted the focus in social science towards more intersubjective methods, a characteristic of postmodernism. But the overall goal was rather modernist: to obtain objective accounts of reality. However, this would prove a rather difficult ambition given their object of investigation being primarily text and not physically observable phenomena. The structuralist project was accordingly shot down in 1969 by Derrida, who in a famous passage wrote that 'there is no such thing as outside-of-the-text..'[13] That is, he pointed out the impossibility of deriving any objective conclusions from the interpretation of text since signs inevitably only refer to other signs, which can only be explained by reference to other signs yet again ad infinitum. Accordingly, we can never conclude to have obtained an objective fact from studying a text since any such attempt can only be performed by creating new text; a text referring to another text, never the facts in and of themselves. This insight, which is very hard to convincingly argue against, consequently caused the structuralist school of thought to wane in favour among academics. To replace it, another current of thought emerged known as 'post-structuralism'.

Post-structuralism rejected the claim that knowledge could be firmly founded on phenomenology and accounts of systematic structures and that the interpretation of text could reveal facts beyond the text itself. Instead the text should be used to show *how* knowledge is created, how humans gain knowledge about the world, and what the intentions of the author were when writing the text, intended and unintended – but preferably the latter. However, the full consequence of exclusively concerning oneself with the text itself was taken by Michel Foucault, who wanted to eliminate the author as an active factor all together. Thereby human intentionality, as a meaningful element, was rendered irrelevant in the interpretation of a text. After all, we only have the text itself to base our conclusions on. What went on in the author's head, the subjective perspective of the writer, will always remain utterly beyond our reach as we only have access to their words. The text had to be liberated from its author, so to speak.[14]

So following Nietzsche's death sentence to God, now even the author was proclaimed dead as well. This led to an increased occupation with discourses as forms in which interpersonal communication is performed.

Discourses are ultimately made of signs lumped together in our language, so in order to reveal the social construction of the sign and the meaning of language, Foucault urged a new 'linguistic turn' to address this previously neglected aspect of reality. It was no longer just about the thoughts of certain authors, but instead about the reconstruction of discourse based on fragmentary sources. The goal was 'to embed the time in the discourse',[15] to understand the intentions of the text's author in accordance with the culture and age of origin. The new method entailed a problematisation of the observer's language, function and role. The observer's situated context now became subject to analysis and was considered decisive of how the person perceives reality. The neutrality and objectivity of scientific researchers were thereby put into question, and with that the idea that modern science was culturally unbiased and free of prejudice. Postmodern thinkers revealed that scientists, like everyone else, were products of their time and culture and that their depictions of factual matters were shaped accordingly. Historiographical investigations revealed that scientists and other thinkers from different cultures and times, albeit using the same methods, reached different results, often conforming with the norms and views of the culture and time they lived in. Many of these discourses had appeared so self-evident and natural at the time that the observer had been unaware of them. But from the perspective of the present, it was often clear that they had been highly influenced by outdated religious and cultural norms which sometimes handicapped their reasoning. This brought new awareness to whether contemporary scientists and researchers could claim to be entirely neutral and objective, and if they too were unaware of culturally determined discourses that polluted their reasoning. It thus seemed as if no one could claim to be unaffected by the current discourses of the context they were situated in. After all, why should modern humans not be as prejudiced and blind to their own cultural context as their ancestors? It was thereby justified that discourses were an important object of investigation and that efforts were needed to unravel the many hidden norms and assumptions in modern society that affected our understanding of reality.

Discourse analysis gave us a new and more critical awareness of the culture we live in. It made us see it from a distance so that we could better question many of the norms and perspectives previously considered natural and self-evident, and it helped us reveal hitherto unnoticed aspects of our thinking and behaviour so that we could better understand why we reason and act as we do. But discourse analysis was also a revolutionary method for academics since it implied that the sign itself has an ability to convey meaning, that signs are key building blocks in the construction of our perceived 'reality', which reiterated that signs do not enable the reconstruction or imitation of reality. This insight helped us understand that when we use signs to make representations of reality we are merely making representations of it, nothing more. What we try to convey with our use of speech and writing is not the same as the things they are supposed to signify. Derrida's proclamation that there is nothing outside of the text was a keen reminder that signs only refer to other signs, that we, in other words, should not mistake the map of the world for the world itself. This is something that has been well-known to philosophers for centuries, with the famous 'thing-in-itself' (*Ding an sich*)[16] being just out of range of our certainty, as famously pointed out by Kant in the late eighteenth century. However, modern scientists had long neglected this crucial insight and had come to behave as if their models and theories were equivalent to the things they tried to explain.

* * *

The crucial postmodern insight is that representation cannot be complete, that we cannot replicate the entire complexity of relations between things, and even when we try, the signs used are just signs, not the facts they refer to. Only through signs, words and symbols can states of affairs be represented, and as such our explanations about reality remain limited to what our language is currently capable of conveying and our personal interpretations of those symbols. No one can therefore claim to be in a position from where a fully objective interpretation can be made. The representations can only be examined by putting the structured signs into culturally influenced narratives, which do not exist in or resemble objective reality itself. 'Reality' is therefore demonstrably unreconstructable.[17]

However, this should not stop us from making any representations of reality. After all, putting signs together to form narratives about how we believe the world works can be very useful (notwithstanding that what is considered 'useful' is culturally determined and open for debate). The postmodern insight that reality is unreconstructable should merely serve, I believe, as a reminder that we should be careful and critical about how we portray it. Yet, this reasonable down-to-earth assessment of what postmodern thought should help us with did not prevent it from being used to relativise our perception of reality to a degree that went beyond the critical and insightful, and into the more absurd and philosophically ostentatious.

The Demise of Postmodernism

Philosophers have always taken their reasoning to the extreme, venturing into speculative and otherworldly areas of inquiry too far from any meaningful intellectual or societal concerns to be more than a curiosum and a philosophical parlour game. But with the postmodern thought perspective, philosophical reason reached new heights of absurdity and pretentiousness. As a consequence, the authority and trustworthiness of philosophers began to fade as the popularity of postmodernism in philosophy and academia grew larger.

One of the most famous discussions to bring the relevance of philosophical inquiry into question took place at the beginning of the twentieth century and involved two of philosophy's greatest thinkers:

Ludwig Wittgenstein and Bertrand Russell, discussing the presence of a rhinoceros in a room. I am not going to elaborate the discussion in greater detail here, it suffices to say that Wittgenstein tried to use clever semantic tricks and arguments about our inability to make valid objective statements to convince the more empirically minded Russell that he could not conclude whether there was a rhinoceros in the room or not. Just to be clear, there was no rhinoceros in the small room in Cambridge where the heated debate took place – at least not in any conventional meaning – but Russell had difficulties making strong enough arguments to counter Wittgenstein's claim that it could not be proven.

The discussion showed that proving the presence of an object is a much harder task than convincingly questioning the ability to do so – especially if the sceptic is armed with the right argumentative tools. The sceptical approach to knowledge advocated by Wittgenstein showed the argumentative strength that would later come to characterise postmodernism. But it also revealed an underlying weakness to this kind of thinking, namely the lack of any alternative routes to knowledge. Wittgenstein was just as incapable of proving the whereabouts of the rhino as Russell, but at least the latter's assessment that the room was devoid of any such creatures remained the most plausible one.

Not only does this event clearly illustrate the presence of postmodern thought in action early on in the twentieth century, it also reveals the danger of postmodernism rendering itself irrelevant by turning towards the flatulent and bizarre; using its argumentative power to merely mock its modernist opponents and flaunt its rhetorical superiority. The circumstance that a genius (who wrote one of the earliest designs of a jet engine in his past life) started a discussion like this, and another (who figured out why mathematics works in the first place) found it important enough to spend time on such seemingly ridiculous matters – time that could be used to make other valuable discoveries – may not have been enough to make such postmodernly inclined discussions considered devoid of any substantial usefulness in society. But the fact that the whereabouts of a rhinoceros in a small room in Cambridge in 1911 is still being discussed by people today certainly makes postmodern philosophy more likely of being seen as irrelevant by the general public.

With the Scientific Revolution and the Enlightenment, philosophers and academics gained prominence and public recognition by making intellectual discourse a vital ingredient in our development of a better society. With the postmodern turn in academia, this would soon start to wane as it became increasingly questionable whether cutting-edge thinking in philosophy would offer any relevant and meaningful ideas to how society could be improved.

The philosophical discussion on invisible rhinos suggests how messy things can get when postmodernism eliminates its connection to empirical reasoning and established scientific inquiry. If we insist that we cannot prove something as fundamental as a big animal in a room, and that this is important to discuss, it obviously asks the question why we should bother with philosophy in the first place. And if we carry out further inquiry about the nature of the world, but reject empirical reason as a valid method to do so, it is not difficult to predict that things can easily slide into the obscure.

Discourse analysis and deconstruction became increasingly popular among scholars and students within the human sciences during the 1980s and '90s, and as empirical truths were questioned and the ties to established scientific methods were loosened, much progress was made in uncovering previously invisible aspects of social reality. New important topics were brought to the agenda: It was shown that science was not as objective and free of prejudice as commonly believed, systematic discrimination was discovered to remain widespread in supposedly equal and democratic societies, and racist and misogynist discourses that clearly contradicted the values modern society adhered to were exposed as rampant. These remain important accomplishments we should thank the postmodernists for. However, as many postmodernists within academia lost their foothold in empirical facts, and in their anarchistic rejection of all authorities refused to acknowledge any standards of acceptable academic conduct, much of postmodern inquiry soon became a hotbed of pseudoscience and pretentious intellectual swashbucklers, ripe with academic dishonesty and lazy interpretations of scientific scholarship camouflaged by fancy rhetoric.

Einstein's discovery of relativity, for instance, would often be misused by postmodern thinkers to support their claim that 'everything is relative'. The realisation that our knowledge is relative, that facts are relative to our assumptions about what is real, was thus falsely believed to have support by modern physics. In this way, not only our perceptions of social reality were seen as relative to the observer, even physical reality itself was seen as relative. And if right and wrong were relative to the cultural context in which ethical statements are made, ethics as such was claimed to be entirely relative as well. True and false, right and wrong, all were just a matter of subjective perspective, the postmodernists claimed. This is somewhat true; however, to then conclude that nothing can be more or less true or false, that everything is just as right or wrong as something else, is an erroneous conviction which follows from neither the insight that knowledge is relative, nor the theory of relativity. Unfortunately, such beliefs became widespread among many postmodernists during the 1980s and '90s.

But the theory of relativity does not say that everything, in physics, is relative. In fact, a better name for Einstein's theory would have been the 'theory of the absolute', since the theory starts from the very proven fact that the speed of light, in contrast to all other physical movement, *is not* relative to the movement of the observer or their perspective, but is *absolute*. The German description that Einstein himself initially gave the theory was actually the *Invariantentheorie*, derived from the discovery that the speed of light does not vary. The theory proved that no matter how fast an object moves in space, the speed of the light it emits remains the same. But for some reason another great physicist, Max Planck, came to call the theory 'the theory of relativity',[18] and it was by this – somewhat confusing – name that the theory became generally known. If one should at all intersperse the physical perspective into postmodernism (which I believe one should *not* do) we can thus declare that the theory of relativity proves that there *are* – in any case physical – absolute and universal quantities and laws. But as it happened, the theory came to be misinterpreted and was used to support the claim that the entire world is relative. If not even physics has fixed values that we can trust, then, in accordance with this particularly mistaken branch of postmodern thought, it must imply that there can be nothing in the world that we may hold to be fixed or absolute. It is tempting to suggest that a belief like this would make people overcautious about their claims about reality, but instead the exact contrary seemed to happen. Rather than limiting what could be said about the world, the relativisation of all knowledge and scepticism of empirical reasoning opened the floodgate for an unprecedented amount of poorly researched and unfounded scholarship. The notion that everything is relative thus did not come to mean that everything depends on something else, but more that 'everything goes' – especially if it complies with the scholar's political ideology.

Consequently, postmodern thought tended towards the absurd and the presumptuous, and without firm and systematised rejections of the less substantiated sorts of reasoning within the postmodern sphere of academia, it became harder to differentiate between the more valuable contributions and the more nonsensical. Without any standards or authorities to determine what was true and false, just about anything could be proclaimed as yet another breakthrough in academic thinking. Who was there to say it wasn't? The critics of postmodernism would therefore have abundant material to ridicule and compromise the whole endeavour. As the absurdity peaked around the mid-1990s, university faculties were increasingly criticised for wasting funds on pseudoscience, societally irrelevant inquires and academic dishonesty. Postmodernism as a valid academic approach thus gradually lost its public and academic favour, which forced university authorities to shape up and more critically scrutinise their employees' and students' activities. It is probably from this circumstance that postmodernism by many is considered a fad of the 1980s and '90s that eventually petered out. This did not mean that academics ceased being postmodern, however: fewer simply self-identified as postmodern in the following years.

Nonetheless, that postmodernism waned in prominence is not only due to pedantic discussions about rhinos and mistaken conceptions of relativity, but to some extent also because of a particular event known as the Sokal affair. The Sokal affair was a hoax designed by the physicist Alan Sokal against the leading postmodern journal *Social Text* in 1996.[19] Sokal dispatched a veritably nonsensical article for publication just to test whether it might still be admitted if the article contained postmodern lingo that merely 'sounded good' and comported with the editor's ideological views. In the article, titled 'Transgressing the Boundaries: Towards a Transformative Hermeneutics of Quantum Gravity', Sokal argued that quantum gravity is a 'social and linguistic construct' with 'progressive political implications', and that the 'morphogenetic field' (a debunked new-agey physical theory developed by Rupert Sheldrake) could be a cutting-edge theory of quantum gravity. Sokal proposed that the concept of 'an external world whose properties are independent of any individual human being' was 'dogma imposed by the long post-Enlightenment hegemony over the Western intellectual outlook', and concluded that because scientific research is 'inherently theory-laden and self-referential', it 'cannot assert a privileged epistemological status with respect to counterhegemonic narratives emanating from dissident or marginalized communities' and that therefore a 'liberatory science' and an 'emancipatory mathematics', spurning 'the elite caste canon of "high science"', needed to be established for a 'postmodern science [to] provide powerful intellectual support for the progressive political project'.[20] The journal accepted the intellectually absurd article for publication without having submitted it for review by other researchers, which otherwise is custom by scientific journals. The same day the article was published, Sokal had another article published that revealed the hoax and the nonsensical reasoning along with a critique of the academic postmodernists and the political Left. It thereby shed light on a flagrant ignorance and paucity of critique in the foggy reasoning within the postmodern sphere of academia. Today we would probably have called Sokal a troll, a modernist troll who effectively trolled a number of postmodernists into revealing their own inadequacy.

The Sokal affair was widely noted within intellectual circles, and the postmodern critique of science and the absurd rejection of rational and empirical reasoning gradually waned during the late 1990s as measures were taken to subject postmodern academics to the same scientific standards as others. The extreme relativisation of all truths thus became unfashionable, but even if postmodernism as a concept lost favour it did not mean that intellectual life became any less postmodern. Postmodernism was after all not a rejection of scientific rationality, but rather an extension of it.[21] As Derrida once proclaimed: 'The revolution against reason can be made only within it', the method to undermine reason would still be reason itself.[22] Accordingly, postmodern thought, following its initial first decades of anarchistic and highly anti-hierarchical attitudes, was subjected to new standards of valid reasoning, commonly agreed-upon methodology, and thereby became firmly established within existing academic institutions. In the same way that the 'righteous rebels' of the Axial Age eventually established themselves within the very same structures they had once sought to overthrow, the postmodern academics likewise became part of the scientific institutions they rebelled against and wanted to tear apart. A few concessions were made to accommodate the postmodernists in academia: discourse analysis and deconstruction became accepted methods of inquiry, and new departments such as gender research and post-colonial studies were established. But they remained subject to modernist standards of scientific reasoning and methods to institutionalise knowledge. The postmodern scholars agreed to make their investigations more evidence-based, and their wild ambitions of a more anarchistic approach to science were toned down in favour of staying within academia.

After all, it turned out to be very difficult to achieve the grand ambitions of postmodernism. The dubious practicality of the postmodern approach to knowledge is perhaps its greatest weakness: Resisting rationality with nothing more than rationality itself, deconstructing language with the use of language, and criticising metaphysics without any new metaphysical tools to replace the ones used for the very same criticism seem very difficult at best, impossible at most. Deconstructing every metanarrative without attempting to build new ones on their ruins likewise made the, largely implicit, postmodern ambition of being a new metanarrative to replace modernism an implausible endeavour.

What postmodernism primarily achieved was that it questioned our naive belief about the Enlightenment's project that, given enough time, and with a lot of carefully conducted systematic research in accordance with the scientific method, eventually, it will provide us with the ultimate truth about the world. Its great accomplishment was thus a change of our epistemology. Our answers to what we can know about the world, what we can proclaim as true and right, are essentially what differentiates the postmodern from the modern worldview. The world itself, and how we go about it, remain more or less the same as before. What postmodernism provides to academic discourses is thus a precautionary principle and a greater humility towards our claims of truth, not so much an entirely new way of making scientific sense of the world.

THE POSTMODERN SECRET

Despite its fall from grace in academia it is not without reasons that postmodernism has been and remains extremely influential here and elsewhere. One reason is its new insights about our understanding of how humans acquire knowledge about the world. Discourse analysis and deconstruction have proved very effective analytic tools to shed light on this. Another reason is, of course, the many topics postmodern thought has brought to the intellectual and political agenda, such as racial and gender equality, criticism of norms and the unfortunate consequences of technological progress and economic growth. A main reason why this has made postmodernism so influential, perhaps more than the analytic methods themselves, is that they can empower people who feel oppressed by modern society. Armed with postmodern ideas, previously marginalised groups can make their voices heard, and thus be able to more effectively criticise modern society. This, however, is not all. A secret to postmodernism's success, one that is rarely talked about, is the argumentative power that can be obtained from it. Not only has the postmodern thought perspective empowered modernity's adversaries by virtue of new ideologies to address various minority issues, it has also made people feel empowered by providing them the means to win the argument. Despite being a minority, and despite not having any clear alternatives to replace modern society, postmodernists have tended to come out on top in discussions with their modernist opponents – much to the annoyance of the latter.

But what is it exactly that makes the postmodernists, at least the more skilful of them, capable of gaining the upper hand in discussions with the advocates of modern mainstream society? When listening to such discussions, it is often apparent that modernists are ethically on thin ice compared to the postmodernists. It is usually the former who have to excuse themselves or explain why the things they have said have been misunderstood or taken out of context, that they did not mean what they said, and that they in fact adhere to the ethical principles of the postmodernists (even though they often only talk about how they are against racism, gender inequality, and similar things when confronted by claims that they aren't). But ethics is not the only argumentative advantage of postmodernism. Postmodernists also have a secret ace up their sleeve on an analytic level. This often manifests itself in the way they manage to entangle modernists and others in semantic language games the latter cannot escape from without losing the argument. But what actually goes on when this happens? It is not only because postmodernists tend to have greater knowledge about gender, racial and environmental issues.

One of the foremost insights of postmodernism is, as mentioned, that signs always refer to other signs and that signs are context dependent. Remember the way Nietzsche asserted that 'there are no facts in themselves.

It is always necessary to begin by introducing a meaning in order that there can be a fact', and that there is no 'view from nowhere', as stated by Nagel; that our perception of reality is determined by our own private and cultural context. So when postmodernists win discussions on factual matters, it is often not just by questioning the facts themselves but rather by questioning the context the facts are situated within. For instance, if someone defends the accomplishments of technological progress, the postmodernist is quick to put the cultural context that determines what is considered good and desirable into question; and if someone argues that a certain scientific result is valid, the postmodernist can point out that it is only so in accordance with pre-given standards of what is seen as true in the first place. The validity of such assumptions about what is good and true are often difficult to establish without reference to a higher, overarching context – contexts that are often invisible to the defendant of modern notions of progress and science. And even if the person to have landed in a contextual and semantic language game with a postmodernist is well acquainted with such contexts, and competently can discuss facts and truth-claims on the higher level, the postmodernist can always point towards yet another context and thus reach the satisfaction of arriving at an antithesis where it must be conceded that we do not know what is really true or good from the perspective of this higher context. Eventually, we always reach philosophical bedrock, and at this point we can only make assumptions about reality that cannot be proven.

Contexts within Contexts within Contexts

Everything we say and think can be questioned since it is located within a context, a context which finds itself within yet another context, within another context ad infinitum. In a very simplified way this sums up the postmodern approach to reasoning about reality. And because postmodernists usually are only concerned with the antithesis, merely criticising statements for depending on unproven contexts and rarely suggest counterproposals, they can thereby end up on top of the discussion and walk away victorious. However, the reason for this is actually somewhat culturally determined. In our current intellectual discourse, it is considered sufficient to merely reach the antithesis, and it is seen as fully acceptable that a refusal of a thesis should not be followed by a superior one to win the argument. It is simply OK to just refer to a context on a higher level of abstraction without discussing the validity of the facts on the lower level. The reason for this is probably the circumstance that most of us are unaware of what is *actually* going on here: that higher-level contexts can always be pointed out, and by doing so the facts in question can always be revealed to rest on unfounded assumptions. However, and this is important to keep in mind, that does not mean that the statements on the lower level context automatically need to be rendered invalid overall. They can still contain truth values worthy of consideration, but this is often forgotten when confronted with a higher-level context.

Pointing out that scientific research is merely based on human-made conventions of what is correct, culturally determined principles that could be different does not exclude that we can use them to accurately predict future outcomes. That gravity is just a theory developed by white males does not negate the fact that we can send a man to the moon using that theory – or a woman if we desire – and the circumstance that contemporary economics is based on models that hardly resemble the reality they seek to describe, and in addition are shaped by capitalist notions of efficiency and exploitative structures of division of labour, does not exclude that lowering the interest rate and establishing international trade agreements can increase employment. With a postmodern awareness of contexts, we can always question that our current understanding of reality is based on assumptions that we are yet to prove. However, this does not mean that we cannot make truth claims about the world and treat them as valid within a given context. That Einstein's theory of relativity proved that Newtonian physics was not entirely accurate does not mean that we cannot use Newton's equations to predict the trajectory of a cannon ball. The equations are still 'true' in the sense that they can accurately describe the motions of physical objects on Earth. In a similar way, our day-to-day experiences of physical occurrences as they appear to us should not be rejected as false just because they depend on the essentially unproven assumption that we are provided accurate information about our surroundings through our senses: within the context of sensory experiences as a source of truth, visual information of an open door is simply proven valid by a subsequent experience of walking through it. This is not invalidated by reference to physical space as an illusion or the concept of the door as merely a social construction that only resides in our mind. Philosophically inclined postmodernists may have a bit of fun by questioning physical reality and our assumptions about it, but even they need to walk through doors once in a while.

Postmodernists can tease their less philosophically schooled peers by pointing out how unaware they are about their assumptions of reality, how most people do not see that many of the values and customs they consider natural are just culturally determined conventions, and what most people consider logical and evidence of factual states of affairs are only so in relation to assumptions they have not considered that they have no proof of. Yet, many such arguments can easily be rejected by referring, if correct, to how the statement corresponds with the truth criteria within a given context. That a scientific result is correct can be demonstrated by showing how it fulfils the criteria of the scientific method and established conventions within a given field of inquiry. The notion that science is just a social construction and that all knowledge is uncertain can simply be rejected as irrelevant to the issue in question since those are merely circumstances that we need to accept but still should not stop further scientific inquiry. Similarly, that one's reasoning on societal matters may be Eurocentric can in a similar manner be rejected as insufficient in itself of rendering one's thoughts invalid. We are always situated within a certain cultural context, using a specific language, and rarely adequately acquainted with foreign cultures or languages. But that does not mean that there cannot be any truth to what we say, that the specifics still should be discussed within the given and often limited cultural context where we are currently situated. English speakers who do not speak Chinese can still make valid truth-claims about China, and being male does not automatically exclude one from making correct assessments about females.

Postmodernists love to point out that our understanding is limited by contexts we are insufficiently acquainted with or unaware of, asserting this as the end of the discussion. But this can effectively be countered by questioning the assumption why the presence of higher-level contexts should refrain us from pursuing the matter in question on the lower level; why statements demonstrated to be in accordance with truth criteria on the lower level should be considered invalid by mere reference to those on the higher level. However, this is rarely asserted by modernists when confronted by the postmodernists, and when it is, often not accepted by the postmodernists themselves. Still, it is currently accepted that theology, for instance, can be discussed within the context of the religious thought perspective. Despite the ways in which religion often contradicts the higher context of science and rational thought, modernists and postmodernists are often willing to accept that the work conducted by theologists can be true or false within the context of religious discourse. But the same courtesy is rarely seen when modernism and postmodernism clash today – a situation not entirely dissimilar to that when the remorseless battle between religion and rationality was at its height prior to the modern breakthrough.

Modernism's unwillingness to accept the higher-level contexts referred to by the postmodernists, and reluctance towards insisting on discussing the matter in question in accordance with the lower level, may once again have to do with modernism's stubborn notions of totality, claims of having reached the ultimate synthesis – a conceptually impossible endeavour – and refusal to acknowledge that only a 'proto-synthesis' is conceptually possible. A proto-synthesis is a provisional synthesis of the best currently existing knowledge, always prone to future revisions and eventually complete rejection when a sufficient understanding on a higher-level context has been achieved – but still valid for further inquiry within the context in which the matter is stated. But many modernists seem utterly incapable of seeing their understanding of reality as incomplete. Not that they claim to know all there is – science is after all considered work in process – but when out-of-reach contexts are put into question, modernists often compromise their rational reasoning and react in heedless ways against the perceived evil that just exposed their entire thought perspective as inadequate. When modernists are exposed to notions about their view of reality being biased and shaped by their culture or gender, that social constructions and discourses (which requires a postmodern perspective to be visible and fully grasped) are shown to determine their opinions and values, and when it is asserted that scientific objectivity is impossible and unconscious factors determine our behaviour, they often react with bitterness and resentment while resorting to sub-par argumentation.

As a consequence, discussions often grind to a halt. And instead of acknowledging the objections of the postmodernists, while insisting on their participation in the discussion within the context in which the facts are stated, the modernists usually depart from the conversation embittered and confused by the annoying approach of the postmodernists. The latter often derive considerable enjoyment from this, but it is arguably not the best approach to promote new insights or to improve the mutual understanding between modernists and postmodernists.

The Importance of Thinking 'Both/And'

Part of the animosity towards postmodernism that seems widespread today can be explained by the human being's need for universalism, to create order and posit the world within a whole – something the postmodernists are masters of disrupting (albeit the postmodernists have the very same need themselves; they simply find consolation in principles and orders on a higher level of abstraction than most other people). For many, this constant questioning, which yields no answers, can be rather repetitive and tiresome, which makes up another source of conflict and resentment between modernists and postmodernists, even on a personal level. When thought perspectives clash it is not just a question of 'you have your opinion and I have mine', but an ontological battle with hurt souls and devastated worldviews in its wake. Modernists strive to encompass the world within a cohesive system. This is how they create order in their worldview and obtain psychological wholeness. The postmodernists in turn strive to reveal the inconsistencies of the system, pointing out that it only exists within just another system. This is how they achieve order and wholeness. To the postmodernist, any undeconstructed grand narrative is a nuisance that has to be made away with in order to achieve peace of mind. To the modernist, the deconstruction of their narratives is a source of emotional suffering that can only be alleviated by piecing it back together again. Currently, no widely available measures exist to alleviate this conflict, and the result is that people live in separate ontological bubbles with very little understanding of different-thinking people.

Both camps, modernists and postmodernists, are, however, correct in their own ways. It would be unfair to declare either of them more correct than the other. There do exist systems, structures that can be empirically analysed and from where valid truth claims can be derived, as proposed by the modernists. But the thing is that all conceivable systems are merely 'sliding' systems. As in semantics (where we can see that the meaning of words and concepts are constantly changing, sliding from one meaning to another depending on time and context), the systems in which truth claims are made are sliding as well. Many postmodernists do not really deny that there is truth in itself, but rather insist that truth and meaning are context-dependent, that every context is part of an even larger and more complexly assembled context and so on in all eternity. The modern project's ambition to reach a final destination of truth is therefore pointless – but the creation of new knowledge need not be.

Starting from the total context is an impossibility, both in principle and in practice. Every meaning-making truth is limited by its own context, but the number of possible contexts remains unlimited. There is always yet another context. This is what I mean by saying that the truth 'slides': Every time we try to cement reality and say 'now we have framed everything within a greater context', it turns out that our new context depends upon another. But even if the system slides, this does not entail that truth does not exist or that we cannot focus on a context and explain something from its own premises. In order to have a meaningful conversation about truth and falsehood, right and wrong, we must then admit that there is truth and knowledge although these, of course, only apply within certain given confines – if we don't, we might end up in the 'postmodern trap': the inability to have any meaningful conversations since we constantly claim that 'everything depends on the context'.

By deconstructing the discourse (revealing that a context finds itself within an even more complex, more overarching context) postmodernists can deconstruct anything to which they object, and, like a child incessantly asking 'why', obviate the possibility of any meaningful dialogue. If we are able to show that everything is context-dependent through discourse analysis and deconstruction, others will find it hard to argue that their claims are universal truths. But this postmodern insight does not, as mentioned, constitute an obstacle to discussing certain facts within a certain context and in accordance with its own truth criteria. The conversation is only made possible when both parties in the conversation agree to the rules of the discussion and do not divert it by pointing out an overarching context without sufficient justification for why that is relevant to the topic in question – which can be rather difficult if one of the parties is so postmodern that they merely seek to reach an antithesis, i.e. exclusively wants to point out how something *is not*, instead of taking on the difficult task of explaining how something actually *is*.

We must submit to the postmodern insight that what appear to be self-evident facts within a certain context, only do so in relation to a not so self-evident overarching context; that facts do not exist independently from the context in which they are stated. Modernists who do not understand postmodern thinking tend to be provoked by this, in their eyes, uncomfortable notion, and often throw out the baby with the bathwater by dismissing postmodern thought altogether. They usually fail to see that the postmodernists have actually made substantive contributions to philosophy, culture and science. Here it is important to think 'both/and': *both* postmodernist relativism and antithesis *and* modernist totalism and synthesis. But the modernists fail to understand that they are on epistemologically shaky ground when they are constructing their scientific and societal truths. It is here that most modernists go astray in insisting on elevating linear relations to universal truths without questioning truth criteria or how they relate to the overarching context.

The Postmodern Fallacy

It is by attacking many of modern society's established ideas and assumptions about reality that the postmodernists have been able to score some rather cheap points during the latest half-century – without trying to explain how the world actually works. The postmodernists argue that every part of reality can be explained away through seeing the greater context. They often proclaim that various parts of reality are now dead, such as God, the subject, rationality, patriarchy – yes, even the writer is now dead (despite the fact that I'm alive and well while writing these words). The things that we hitherto thought were autonomous reveal themselves through the postmodern thought perspective as merely parts of something larger, which means that the postmodern game never ends, for there is always another discourse to deconstruct within an already deconstructed discourse. However, sooner or later it tends to end for the individual postmodern critic who either tires of this constant deconstruction or eventually finds an ideology to find comfort in (usually Marxism, feminism or other schools of thought that are critical of modern society). After all, we all need some order in our worldview to obtain psychological wholeness, most postmodernists included. Rhinos or no rhinos, eventually we need to exit the room and get on with our lives.

Contexts are boundless and we never finish unveiling them. But how these are part of new overarching systems is not postmodernism's role to explain. Many postmodernists get lost in this world of contexts within contexts. This becomes problematic when they go from thinking that one context or a particular perspective is not the only or definitive one, to opining that neither has any advantages or disadvantages vis-à-vis another. When the idea of the relativity of knowledge is erroneously transferred to the area of ethics – where relativism hardly belongs – we then have what can be seen as a postmodern variant of the naturalist fallacy (the aforementioned notion that we cannot derive an 'ought' from an 'is'). That we cannot say anything about right or wrong is arguably a fallacy, which really does not belong in postmodern philosophy that inherently is highly concerned with ethical matters. So with a paraphrase of the naturalist fallacy, we can say that some postmodern thinkers tend to wrongly derive an 'it-doesn't-matter' from an 'it-depends'. That it depends on the context is an important insight. That it then does not matter is a fallacy as erroneous as the notion that science can give us answers to ethical questions. We cannot base ethics solely on empirical investigation, but it would be dangerous to make that stop us from pursuing ethical answers.

THE LIMITATIONS OF POSTMODERNISM

Postmodernism's, largely implicit, view of its own pluralistic relativism as the only acceptable worldview contains some pretty obvious inherent incongruities. For instance: all truth is culturally situated, except postmodernism's own, which is true for all cultures; there are no transcendent truths, except its own pronouncements, which transcend specific contexts; all hierarchies or value rankings are oppressive and marginalising, except its own value ranking, which is superior to the alternatives; and there are no universal truths, except its own pluralism, which is universally true for all peoples. These are, in my opinion, the cracks in postmodernism's armour that will be the point of departure for the next thought perspective to replace it.

Postmodernism can be criticised for placing cultural perspectives above all others and thus for being more interested in *the representation* of reality than in reality itself – as in the example of Las Vegas, where the signpost is larger and more important that the premises it boasts of. To constantly reduce everything to social constructions, and in the name of relativism even refuse to decide what is most true, reasonable or even useful, naturally becomes a rather twisted excess. Postmodernism can also be criticised for its inadequate explanatory power. By exclusively focusing on conceptual worlds, merely illuminating and visualising rather than explaining, there is a risk that the result will be that nothing is explained. The 'why' (perhaps the most important question within the humanities) is thus replaced by the less incisive 'what' and 'how'.

Postmodern theory can be accused of undermining faith in science through its perception that there is no reality outside language and that all knowledge is value-based, subjective and uncertain. But when the boundary between fact and opinion is eradicated by philosophers, it provides a fertile ground for 'fake news', which can then flourish on social media. There is also a risk that researchers under the influence of postmodernism become uninterested in explaining concrete reality. Instead of trying to explain material inequality and analysing economic conditions, the focus shifts towards merely exposing race, class and gender discourses and social constructions of poverty at the expense of figuring out how to actually alleviate these ills.

A large part of the postmodern project has been devoted to the resistance of all hierarchies and value scales, but ultimately the old hierarchies have merely been replaced by postmodernism's own. Implicit in this is that pluralism stands above absolutism, diversity over homogeneity, anarchy above regulations, and liberation above conventions. As such, a new value scale has snuck in.

In its extreme form, moral relativism not only states that the way others perceive the world *can* be just as valid as one's own, but that *all* ways of perceiving the world *necessarily* are equally valid. 'I see the world in one way, you may see the world in another way, but both are always equally true', the postmodern logic goes. But if all perspectives are correct there is no way of determining what should be considered better or worse. Hence, there can be no absolute values. All rankings of values, so-called value hierarchies, fall. The only correct way of viewing the world will then be the perspective of pluralist moral relativism. Since nothing according to moral relativism can be valued more highly than anything else, the question of whether we shall produce pornography or theatre, liquor or medicine, merely becomes a matter of individual consumer preferences and an issue for the market to decide. It is not even possible to value one form of governance as better than another. There is no way to determine what is right or wrong, better or worse. Gandhi or Hitler, Shakespeare or reality television, it is just a question of personal opinion and taste. Everything is relative.

Moral relativism has helped bring about the pluralist society we have today. But pluralism can unfortunately become a powerful magnet for narcissism. By breaking down every form of overarching, cohesive culture, a culture which we all share and take responsibility for, the result can be that in the end it is just I and my own ego that take centre stage – an emphasis on the individual at the expense of the community. Without fixed values, ideals dissolve into subjective preferences and the interests of minority groups. It removes any shared ideals to guide our thinking, acting and collective ambitions. Moral relativism thus paves the way for the market's dominance in our cultural sphere since that is all that remains to coordinate our collective activities.

If we relativise everything, we end up with no fixed point, no overarching perspective from which to view the world. By attacking all metanarratives (except the metanarrative of the relativism of everything) we end up with a worldview in pieces without any cohesive narrative into which our observations, thoughts and experiences can be woven. Such an incoherent, fragmented view of the world can cause a sense of disorientation, a world where we as individuals do not feel we fit in anywhere. Ultimately, this may result in a rather alienated human condition. The consequence of a totally deconstructed reality, without any attempts to build a new, better metanarrative, may thus be the opposite of the human liberation most postmodernists desire.

* * *

Today we seem to have approached a postmodern condition like the one described in this chapter and the last, a condition in which faith in all objective truths and shared values has been severely eroded. It has liberated us from obsolete ideologies and religions, but in the void to have emerged, many have lost the guidance and comforting social context that the narratives of yesteryear used to provide. Reality has become fluid, unpredictable, and all boundaries have been loosened. Some find empowerment and freedom in this, but many feel deprived of a steady anchoring in existence and a source of meaning and motivation.

The postmodern human is both rootless and restless. Life is constantly in a state of flux with shifting roles. This has liberated the individual, but also weakened the collective as life has become an individual project where we continuously have to create our own identity and reality. Each and every person is the maker of their own happiness and no one should submit themselves to the opinions of others, but at the same time our shared culture and symbol world has been impoverished and reduced to the only common symbol language that we all share: money.

As an unintended consequence, the postmodern thought perspective has thereby opened the way for the market to become our highest authority. In a world where no authorities are considered valid for all, the market forces are all that remain.

Chapter 8

THE MARKET: THE POSTMODERN ERA'S HIGHEST AUTHORITY

We will in this chapter take a closer look at the market. We do this because the market is the most dominating aspect of our current collective imaginary. It has even started to dominate all the other important fictions of our current imaginary, like the nation-state and democracy. The market seems to surround us as water surrounds fish. It has come to be our enveloping social reality and therefore often rather hard to spot. Consequently, instead of us controlling it, we and our society are controlled by it. The ambition of this chapter is thus to convey the insight that we cannot let the market become our new god and that we instead start seeing it as the incomplete human creation it is.

Over the last half century, the market has stealthily become the dominant ideology of the world thanks to the value vacuum of our time and the lack of any other shared narratives. The market has taken the role as our primary authority, with a language of its own that permeates most aspects of our society and culture. It has managed to become so dominant through functioning as a watered-down compromise between the rational exaggerated faith in the human being's (i.e. the consumer's) reason and autonomy and the postmodern age's denial of absolute values.

We often take the market for granted as though it were an inevitable force of nature, and only rarely do we manage to see or analyse it clearly.

The market is an incredibly efficient tool and can serve us well, but this does not apply always and everywhere. We live with an image of, and a faith in, the market that does not comport very well with what actually happens in reality.

THE MUSINGS OF AN INVESTMENT BANKER

As a former banker and financier, I have used the market as my personal gateway to many of the questions posed in this book. I have had many years of experience with the market, of how we make money and create value. I have long been working in the 'engine room' of the world economy, so to speak, where I have observed the market and got an understanding of how it works and why it sometimes does not work so well.

All entrepreneurs must understand *their market*, but a banking entrepreneur must understand *the market* in itself. Without any product of their own, bankers need to get the market to deliver profit from the market itself. In its purest form this is called *market arbitrage*. Hence, in some way the market is both the investment banker's product *and* laboratory. The investment banker experiments both *in*, *on* and *with* the market, and the better one understands it, the more money one earns.

An investment banker quickly realises that money is a commodity. And like all other commodities, it has a price. It takes time to digest that even money has a price, that *money costs money*, what we call 'interest'. Through interest, one can get the market *in itself* to deliver profit without having any real commodity to sell. This is the principle behind most financial instruments. When other entrepreneurs produce innovations to earn money *in* the market, the banker must understand the market so well that he can earn money *on* the market. As an investment banker you are one of the few who have a licence to twist and turn the market to create profit directly from it – without producing anything!

As a banker I could not help but feel a little bit like a high priest: a member of a small, select group allowed to step behind the curtain and into the most sacrosanct area of our current society, into the market itself. But it also made me question what money really is, made me see it as a language and the most vital component in a vast self-organising system.

THE MONEY LANGUAGE

Language and symbols in different forms have been the means of communication that during much of history have coordinated our collective actions. In the Stone Age, primitive forms of language, such as sounds and gestures, could coordinate the social relations of twenty to thirty individuals in small bands. With the emergence of more advanced language, we could effectively hold together upwards of 150 people in tribes. And with symbolic language, humans became capable of creating narratives and social imaginaries that could shape millions of individuals into religious and national communities. In our globalised civilisation today, the language of money coordinates the daily activities of more than seven billion people. We may not understand each other's vernacular languages, and we often have great difficulties understanding foreign cultures. But even in the most remote village in the Amazonas or Siberia, most understand the uncompromising and unambiguous language of cold hard cash. Money talks, and the market is a language most of us speak and understand today.

With the language of money we have attained an unprecedented level of global coordination. It may be a meagre and one-dimensional language, but it is highly efficient. To obtain this efficiency, however, we have sacrificed much meaning, cultural value and nuance in our communication by replacing many complicated aspects of value with a number: the price. In many regards this number is rather arbitrary: it does not tell what is better or worse, what is economically or socially most sustainable, or what is really most valuable to humans. But the price unambiguously tells us what an individual, here and now, is willing to exchange a given service or product for. Most of our social reality has been subjected to this principle, and it this that above all coordinates most of our daily activities in the market-driven society we live in today. Much of reality is thus ranked by, and reduced to, its market price.

But the market is not just a mechanism to coordinate our productive activities. It is also a power structure to determine who is entitled to what. Money is power; not just something that characterises powerful people, but what makes them powerful to begin with (whether it is the size of their personal bank accounts or how much they have at their disposal through private or governmental organisations). When the full potential of the market was finally realised during the early modern period, and when it became evident that wars were won with money, organised violence as the primary means of societal cohesion and management was gradually subjugated to the logic of profit and economic utility. Since then, money and the market have come to be the most important means of power to control society. Moreover, the market is a *smart* power structure. It is efficient and it is difficult to see through. A means of control becomes more powerful when most cannot see that it controls them, and thus cannot question it.

THE MARKET AS A SELF-ORGANISING SYSTEM

What is it that makes the market so efficient at coordinating our productive actions and distributing resources? The answer is that the market is a complex self-organising system. It is efficient because the billions of daily transactions that make up the world economy are coordinated by the collective brain power of everyone who participates in it rather than a limited number of authorities who would not be able to obtain a complete overview of everything that is produced and consumed. Letting individuals use their personal judgement to calculate maximum utility in accordance with the logics and principles of the market is far more efficient than making it a task for centrally governed control mechanisms. Fewer resources are thereby used to control the market, and more calculation resources are made available to sustain and optimise it. It does not, however, ensure that resources are distributed equally, or even that resources are distributed rationally where they are most needed. But it does optimise the degree to which products and services are produced and distributed to those willing to pay the highest price.

When markets are allowed to function freely, when people are free to decide the price of their commodities and customers are free to decide from whom they wish to buy, money functions as a language that in a most effective and frictionless way tells the system what shall be produced, in which quantity, and to whom it shall be distributed. And it does so rather automatically, with no one to carry the overwhelming burden of organising it all. The system organises itself towards maximum economic efficiency though the participation of each and every individual merely seeking optimal utility for themselves.

During the eighteenth and nineteenth centuries, science and philosophy became increasingly interested in understanding the market. At this time it became clear to philosophers and social researchers – there were still no economists – that the market had come to be a significant societal force. The research area that began studying the market's societal effects was called political economy. The eighteenth-century philosopher Adam Smith, who has been called the father of economics, presented the idea of 'the invisible hand',[1] which we today would call a theory of self-organisation. According to Smith, economic life is governed by an invisible force, almost a law of nature, which ensures maximum utility if allowed to roam free. Governments should therefore not intervene in economic affairs if the invisible hand is to yield greatest possible economic efficiency. Accordingly, many of the economic models that emerged in the nineteenth century were based on Smith's ideas. As I have described in my book *The Market Myth,* our view of the market is tinged by the economists' simplified models that appeared during this period. However, it is important to realise that the simplified economic theory, which still dominates within academy today, was born out of deep disunity. The 'classic standard economic model', which it came to be called, arose after a major academic battle at the end of the nineteenth century. In historical accounts it goes under its German name *Metodenstreit*, the 'method dispute'. Physics was held in particularly high regard at the time, so accordingly the researchers' ambition was – as in physics – to build mathematical models of the economic system. Inspired by Newton's mathematical formulae for the forces of nature, they wanted to create formulae for the invisible hand. But instead of using empirical, evidence-based investigations as their point of departure, they started from a belief in the invisible hand and made a number of strongly simplified and rather unrealistic assumptions that were needed to make this mathematical ambition succeed.

The rational thought perspective's exaggerated belief in the human being's reason and autonomy contributed to an intellectual defence of a very simplified model of human action. But some political economists considered this model insufficient in providing a fair view of the market. They were not prepared to sacrifice the more complicated, subjective, human factors for elegant mathematical formulae. This led to a thinking about the market which bifurcated into two scientific paths: those who wanted to build mathematical models established modern *economics*, and those who did not want to make such crude simplifications would belong to the new field of *sociology*. Unfortunately, the high status of natural science resulted in the economists' view of the market gaining the strongest position and thereby coming to enjoy the greatest dissemination during the twentieth century. However, contemporary economic research shows that their approach was so denuded that it is often downright erroneous.[2] It may produce correct results on paper, but it is highly questionable how well it works in reality. The economists were perfectly aware of the limitations of their models,[3] that we should not mistake the map for the world, yet we would later come to confuse their method for reality.

* * *

The limitations of our economic models became very clear to me after having gone from theoretical physics in Uppsala to studying economics at Stockholm University in the 1980s. When I asked my professor when we would

The early economists knew what they wanted: a model of Adam Smith's 'invisible hand', which could be expressed with Newtonian calculus.[4] *Illustration: Charlie Norrman.*

try to adapt our abstract formulae to real-world economics, he just replied that at the department of economics we do not do this. It was simply too difficult, he added. No studies on real economic conditions or experiments were published at the time. It would take another twenty years, until the birth of 'behavioural economics' with psychologically grounded studies of the real market and real-world consumers and decision-makers.[5] This new psychological approach is still in its cradle and lacks a broad-based dissemination in society, but it is arguably a promising approach if we want to gain a more comprehensive understanding of how the economy really works.

In the following I will provide a brief outline of a few insights that can potentially give us a better understanding of economics and the market.

THE ECONOMISTS' UNREALISTIC ASSUMPTIONS

As mentioned, the economists knew what they wanted: a mathematical model of Adam Smith's belief in the invisible hand. To achieve this, they had to make the simplified assumptions that were required, even if they knew they were unrealistic. These assumptions are largely based on eliminating human subjectivity and other complicating factors from the model of the market. The economists needed to assume a number of hypothetical ideal prerequisites in order to make their model work, such as:

- **Rational consumers with pre-given preferences:** Consumers are predictable, completely rational, and fully conscious in their decisions. Their actions are based on self-interest, they remain fully aware of what they want to buy or not, and they do not change their preferences. All market actors, including producers, simply act completely rationally in all situations.
- **Individual goods:** Utilities traded on the market are assumed to be of a rather simple kind that are easy to handle as individual goods in accordance with the principle of private ownership. Collective or common utilities, such as the environment, security measures or culture, do not belong to this type.
- **Perfect competition:** The market offers goods and services from various manufacturers that compete in terms of price and quality, and on equal terms. If one is discontented with the price or quality, there are always easily accessible alternatives available elsewhere on the market and there are no monopolies.
- **Perfect information:** Consumers have access to all information about commodities and potential alternatives. They are also assumed to have the necessary know-how and time to evaluate all information.

The economists were also compelled to assume that both supply and demand are given beforehand. All parties are knowledgeable about what will be available on the market and what consumers want. The consumers' firm, unalterable preferences, 'utility functions', mean that they will not be influenced by various factors such as new information or advertising. The consumer is assumed to maximise their utility, given these fixed utility functions, and companies are assumed only to be interested in maximising their profits. This model, with idealised, highly unrealistic assumptions, is called 'the perfect market'.[6] But this is a very unfortunate choice of words. It leads us to believe that it represents a desirable and attainable ideal condition. The perfect market is merely perfect because it fits into the mathematical formulae, nothing else. A better name would thus have been 'the economists' assumed market'. If so, fewer people would probably have confused the model with reality.

The crux is that the market that the models describe does not exist in reality. In reality we know, for example, that advertising works, which means that we as consumers do not have given preferences. Our needs and wishes are the results of our culture, social norms and expectations, and of the marketing strategies of producers. The human being is not perfectly rational, neither as consumer or decision-maker, and competition is far from perfect in most parts of the market. Another problem with our current models is that we are forced to assume that the market always remains close to equilibrium, that supply and demand balance each other out. Today, however, we know that complex, self-organising systems never find themselves close to equilibrium. One of the things that characterises complexity is, after all, that it remains far from equilibrium. In a fully equalised market, there would be no profits to be made. The free market as we know it is full of relations far-from equilibrium to yield highly unequalised profits.

The perfect market does not exist in reality, and, as we shall see, it does not behave particularly well – not even in theory. The perfect market lives its life on the desktops of theorists and is built on certain notions of efficiency. If the theory's ideal prerequisites are fulfilled, the standard economic model predicts efficiency in the sense of profit. This is not, however, the same as the outcome, even in theory, being desirable in other respects. It is important to understand that economic efficiency in terms of profit is the only thing the model promises. No other inherent values are accounted for. It does not claim that the results are fair or ecologically sustainable, not even under the most perfect circumstances. Although it often turns out that way, the model does not even guarantee satisfied customers or suppliers.

POPULAR VIEW OF THE MARKET

That the standard economic model can give us a simplified view of efficiency within the economy is in itself not a problem. We need simple models to make sense of complex phenomena. The great problem arose when an erroneous view of the model took hold in popular belief and we forgot that the model presumes certain unrealistic assumptions in order to be valid.

In popular belief there is thus a conception of the market's abilities that far exceeds what the economic theories ever intended; an erroneous view of the simplified market models that came to characterise much of our thinking and even made its way into political thought during the twentieth century. It is often believed that the market is fair and able to accommodate not just our individual needs but also our common needs and utilities, and that it generates positive long-term effects. But all of this is wrong and all serious contemporary economists are aware of this. And yet, the popular misconception persists. Unfortunately, this has had major implications. It governs both the general public's and our politicians' perception of the market. We have started to believe more in a naive image of the model than actual reality. Even if seldom expressed, certain unrealistic assumptions about the market have thus made their way into our understanding such as the beliefs:

- that it is **fair**; that everybody gets what they deserve according to their economic abilities;
- that it favours **long-term development**; that market forces inevitably generate social, economic and technological progress;
- that it creates **diversity**; that if the market is allowed to roam freely,

it will ensure the largest number of different products and services desired;

- that it considers **everyone's interests**; that everyone's needs and desires are treated as equally important:
- that it is possible to apply it for **all types of utilities**; that all kinds of products and services can be made available on market terms and that it is best if done so.

In the following we shall look more closely at each of these common misconceptions.

That the Market Is Fair

Not even in theory does the market provide fairness. The distribution of resources that is considered efficient by economists has nothing to do with fairness. Fairness is quite simply irrelevant to the market. No form of fairness, no matter how we choose to define it (everyone gets what they deserve, everyone gets what they need, and so on) is a mechanism we can ascribe to the market. Quite the contrary. Economic theory shows that the market tends to fortify existing injustices and that market players are not treated equally.

We like to search for human causes behind events, we want the injustices in the world to be the result of greedy people's actions. To be sure, as an investment banker I have seen lots of greedy people – not least in the financial world. I am, however, still prepared to agree with Adam Smith that moderate greed works as the driving force of the market. However, the great problem is not the greed of individuals, but the maximisation principle we have built into the market itself: that much becomes more and little becomes less, that rich becomes richer and poor often becomes poorer. This is a greed in the market's way of functioning that, partly due to the political influence of capital-heavy special interests, has been built into the system: if a market player is particularly efficient, the system makes sure to reward that by providing the means to expand that actor's activities further. If one is good at making profits, more money becomes available for further growth, and with that the ability to outcompete or swallow less efficient competitors. If someone is less efficient, on the other hand, the market makes sure to limit that person or organisation's activities and ultimately subordinate them to those that are more efficient.

As such, the market does not ensure that resources are allocated to those who need them the most: this is not our current idea of economic efficiency. Rather, the efficiency it ensures is that those most capable of generating profit will experience a positive feedback loop to expand their activities while those less capable will be subordinated and limited in action by the former. In this way, the market ensures that the most profitable agents come to dominate the economy at large while the less so are pushed to the periphery.

The market is therefore good at what it does, namely yielding economic efficiency in terms of profitability, but we like to believe that it is capable of doing more than this. The market can create a large number of economic resources, but the degree to which it manages to redistribute these as rationally as possible remain dubious. The market is uniquely good at baking the cake, but not at dividing it.

That the Market Favours Long-term Development

A certain short-sightedness seems to be built into the market through the mechanism of interest. The short-sightedness of interest can be said to hinge on the insight of our own mortality and the old behavioural-scientific truth that no organism likes to wait for its reward.

For instance, consider the following thought experiment:

'How much do you want a year from now to lend me £1,000 today? £1,010? Oh no, that's way too little ... £1,050 then? Not quite enough. How about £1,100 then? OK, we have a deal, you might agree.'

As such, the price of the loan is 10% interest. But if I pay it back in ten tears? Ten years is a significant chunk of one's life. But what about fifty years? Or 100 years? Why would anyone give up money for 100 years, even if you ended up with more in the end? Very few would agree to this because they obviously would be dead by then.

Our personal mortality entails that money has greater value for us today than in the far future. Interest is a sort of compensation for the decreasing value over time. This is the foundation for interest and thus the relative short-sightedness of the market. If we had an expected life-span of twenty years, market interest would most likely be much higher; if humans could live for centuries, yearly interests would probably be much lower.

This may sound quite reasonable. After all, we are all going to die and thus have good reasons to be impatient. So where lies the problem of a market that rewards quick results? The way I see it, it is unfortunate that the market sets a *general* market interest rate that applies to all projects. Today we only have *one* market interest rate, and at a level that promotes quick business success. But societies need different interest rates for 100-year-long infrastructure projects than the rate that private citizens need for car-loans and mortgages or the rate that works for entrepreneurs who seek a quick profit a few years down the line. Societies, which (hopefully) do not collapse in a few years, must be able to plan and carry out projects with a very long investment horizon. A major bridge or new railroad tracks have a life-span of more than a hundred years. Such projects can be very profitable for society in the long term, but with high market interest it often becomes rather unmanageable financially.

Private consumption, long-term investments in privately owned assets such as cars or houses and public investments in infrastructure are examples of three areas that arguably should be handled with different interest rates. Today's system however only has room for one interest rate. It simplifies and makes matters more efficient, but in many cases also extremely skewed.

Future generations are not market actors who can influence today's choices, just as they have no representation in legislation. If they had something to say, we might have seen a completely different market structure than that of today. Under such a scenario, long-term and sustainable solutions may not have been undermined by today's short-sighted market interests.

That the Market Creates Diversity

In many cases the market increases the supply of different kinds of services and products, but it sometimes also has the opposite effect when the supply is limited by what provides the best revenue. In central Prague, for instance, supply is limited to crystal wares and cheap t-shirts, Mediterranean tourist destinations are totally dominated by soft drinks, sweets and sunscreen, and on Italian television there seems to be nothing but quiz shows with half-naked women on Friday nights since that is currently what yields the best advertising revenue for the TV channels. But does this mean that the citizens of Prague wear nothing but t-shirts with images of the Charles Bridge, or that Italians only want to see trifling TV entertainment with scantily clad women? No of course not, but here the market has simply yielded less diverse outcomes.

What is supplied does not necessarily reflect all demands, simply what is most profitable. What we actually desire, or what we most urgently need, are not guaranteed. Sometimes, certain market conditions lead to homogenisation rather than diversity, and often the result of too narrow a focus on profit leads to cultural impoverishment. Cultural assets may be difficult to measure in economic utility, but they nonetheless remain something we consider important and enriching.

That the Market Takes Everybody's Interests into Consideration

The language of the market is money, and the entrance ticket to the market is money. Money talks, but if you have no money you have no voice. As far as the market is concerned, a poor person might as well be dead. The inflow of money is the market's only information channel. The market ignores everyone without financial resources, and since neither the people of the future nor the poor have money, the market is not fed information about their preferences and thereby no considerations are made in regards to their interests.

The market pays no consideration to the environment or limited natural resources either since they are not part of the profit model. Profit is created by exploiting natural resources, maximally: every drop of oil must be extracted from the ground, and waste must be dumped in the cheapest possible way. All this as long as the consumers do not actively choose to pay for more sustainable, and costly, manufacturing methods. The same conditions apply to labour. Profit is often created by exploiting an underpaid work force in environmentally hazardous locations since this is the cheapest option. No consideration is given to these people, as long as no one with money requests this.

Through the market we use natural resources and labour to satisfy human needs. In this process there are always revenues and expenses: We spend certain resources in order to obtain others, and if spent wisely we should end up with higher utility than we started out with. But profits and loss are only measured in terms of profitability to the producer. Environmental losses are, as mentioned, not accounted for, but neither are the actual losses and benefits for the consumer. If a transaction is good or bad to the consumer, whether it makes the person more or less happy, or whether it causes more harm than benefit, is entirely irrelevant. The degree to which the market produces things of high utility to humans is of no concern as long as it makes profits. For instance, when a patent for a medication expires and the medication becomes available at low cost to those who previously could not afford to pay, which may save lives, the lives saved will not enter the calculus, only the revenue loss of the pharmaceutical company. No consideration is taken to this in our present economic societal calculi. But this is quite strange, really, since it means that we do not measure the most important aspects to determine economic efficiency: how we consume our finite natural resources and how well we satisfy human needs.

Considering ecological sustainability, and thus future generations' chances of having as good a life as we have had, along with the actual benefits the extraction of these finite resources can provide to human lives, should be a self-evident part of our economic thinking, and determine what will be considered loss and profit. Bewilderingly, it isn't.

That It Is Possible to Use the Market for All Types of Utilities

The standard economic model assumes products and services that are easy to define and measure, that can be privately owned and that are used up when consumed. This applies to many of the products that were scarce in early-industrial society, such as coal and steel, bread and potatoes, and so on, which explains why the industrial age produced an economic model revolving around such commodities. But there are a host of utilities that do not meet these requirements. There are areas that quite simply cannot be subsumed into the market without the system capsizing completely.

Market thinking turns downright alarming when applied to many of society's shared functions, the collective goods that cannot be reduced to simple consumer commodities. With the recent decades' surge of privatisations, an increasing number of society's collective interests have been brought to the market, such as water and electricity utilities, railways, telephone services and so on. Some of these have worked well on the market, others arguably not so much. We have got cheaper telephony, but train tickets have not become more affordable. The punctuality of public transportation has not improved either. The competition among providers of such services forces everyone on the production side to keep costs at a minimum. Privately owned service providers are usually more inclined towards cutting expenses than publicly owned. After all, the former has a profit motive, the latter does not. But in some cases, this leads to very disastrous consequences. In the case of train operators, it has resulted in inadequate maintenance of rails since rail maintenance yields no profit in the short term. At stake are passengers' lives and health, something that is hard to measure here and now and likely to be neglected when competition threatens the profitability of private investors.

Privatisations in health services, education and elderly care, which to varying degrees have swept the world in the past couple of decades, have also seen their share of unfortunate consequences. In certain countries, people have been denied life-important health care because they have not fulfilled complicated legalities in their health insurances, legal details that privately owned insurance companies have employed armies of expensive lawyers to investigate so that care can be denied and profits thereby maximised. Students have been burdened with ever-increasing fees and loans, subjecting them to a life of servitude, as a result of private universities and loan-givers seeking to maximise profits as well. In my home country of Sweden, the absurd and unforeseen consequences of school privatisations in recent years have led to a number of bankruptcies, with the result that schools have closed and children have been without basic education in their local community. Schools have even competed in guaranteeing high grades and offering more 'fun' and less demanding curriculums. The end-result has been a growing distrust in the grade system and pupils finishing school with poor skills in basic math, writing and reading. In many countries, the privatisation of elderly care has led to abandoned seniors, put to bed at five o'clock, often without diaper change, showered once a month and rarely offered walks outside – all in the name of increased efficiency and profitability. And being able to talk with someone, basic care in the form of someone who actually *cares*, is of course not part of this new concept of efficient care. The compassion and human contact, which is just as important in the care we show our fellow humans, has thus become an occasional event to occur between the more schedule-adapted work-tasks of an increasingly time-pressured staff. If profit is the main goal and the results of labour have to fit into economic calculi, less measurable tasks such as listening and consolation are likely to be rationalised away. The result is a level of service that may appear efficient on paper, but in terms of what we consider good care is below what anyone would wish for their loved-ones or themselves.

And still we cannot simply disavow ourselves and blame the market or the owners when they are merely doing their job. There is no reason to remonstrate over the market in itself. If we hand over health care to the market, it will do its job and produce services in a cost-efficient manner: as cheaply as possible with as large a profit as possible to its owners – it's business, so why would they do otherwise? Yet, we become livid when the profit-maximising companies weigh urine-drenched diapers in retirement homes to maximise the use of the diapers' capacity in order to produce care at the lowest possible cost in order to pay maximal dividends to the owners. But this is precisely how the market works, it has done exactly what it is good at. If money has been saved on higher-capacity diapers, or if staff have been cut to limit the amount of unnecessary chit-chat, the market strategy has been efficient and succeeded well in the only manner in which market success can be measured: maximising profit.

THE LIMITATIONS OF THE MARKET

If we make health insurance a private responsibility between independent market players, what sense does it make to be morally outraged about care denial when customers fail to properly investigate the legal terms of the service they have purchased? And if medication is made a market commodity like any other, it should not come as a surprise that certain medications are sold at higher prices than most can afford. If demand exceeds supply, or if a company has a patent, why should we expect them to sell their commodities at anything lower than what is most profitable? Similarly, if the goal of our education institutions is to yield profit, why should we expect them to request a lower price for their services than what they can get away with? As long as students purchase these services, why should we question the quality of their education? After all, if the students are not satisfied, they can always, as good consumers, switch to another supplier. With the privatisation of the school system, we should not be surprised either to see schools competing for customers by offering them higher grades and less demanding topics. Once again, the market has merely done its job. The customer is always right, so why should they not shop around for the best offers, and why should the market not attempt to accommodate their wishes? And if we make schools and other services subject to market terms, why are we then surprised that they close down when their businesses turn unprofitable? That is, after all, the whole point of the market: ensuring maximum profitability and making way with what does not comply with this principle.

However, the better the market succeeds, the more livid we become over news reports that expose the unfortunate results of things that the market is ill-suited to accommodate. This does not mean that privatisation is only negative, we just need to more closely evaluate what privatisation can accomplish and what it cannot. The market is superbly efficient and good at what it is supposed to do, but it is not a universal institution for everything that needs to become more efficient. The market is efficient, in terms of profit, but it is blind to whatever cannot be expressed in money, and a blind efficiency is every bit as sinister as it sounds.

The market is good at producing an abundance of consumer goods and selling it as cheaply as possible. This is because products and services that are easily defined and consumed fit perfectly into the logics of rational consumer behaviour. If we want to have pins, give the assignment to the market. There is no better way to efficiently produce pins. The market will ensure that the cheapest iron ore is purchased, that the most cost-efficient manufacturers are hired, and that we will have an abundance of cheaply made pins available. But the fact that the market works well for pins does not mean that it works well for everything. If we take the example of elderly care above, food and cleaning are aspects that can be expected and have proved to benefit from privatisation. If a retiree is unsatisfied with the quality or price of the food (or the staff realises that is the case), another supplier of food can be found to deliver a better and more affordable product. And if those who clean the retirement home are too sloppy or require too high wages, the managers can find someone else. Food and cleaning are aspects that can benefit from privatisation since their contents are easily defined and measured, and thus makes it simpler to weigh quality vis-à-vis costs. But when it comes to the quality and efficiency of the care itself, then we are dealing with a service that is not as easily measured and thus is not as well adapted to market terms as food and cleaning; good and compassionate care is hard to quantify. Inserting it into rational utility-optimising calculi is nearly impossible. Expecting it to reveal itself as profits on the bottom line is never going to happen. To expect people who are senile, or too weak to protest, to behave like rational consumers and find another supplier of care if they are not satisfied is not very realistic, especially if they do not have concerned enough relatives with the necessary financial means to request another service provider.

The problem is not that politicians seek to improve efficiency through privatisations. After all, funds are limited, and if they succeed, there will be more resources for other things. No, the problem is that privatisations have been used rather uncritically without any understanding about when the market can be used and when it is not appropriate. Instead of carefully investigating what functions benefit from market conditions – what exactly it is that the market does and why those mechanisms would improve a given service – privatisations have become an ideologically determined measure, considered a good in itself, that without any consideration to the wider implications, and with a poor understanding of the market in the first place, has been imposed on anything its devoted advocates have mustered political support for.

But certain functions are quite simply not possible to privatise. The service of caring for a human being is too complex for the market to handle as a commodity. This 'commodity' has too much content regarding the human being's *inner, subjective dimensions* for it to be packageable and tendered administratively on the market, which primarily operates within the outer, objective dimension, where everything is measurable and calculable. But the degree of empathy and compassion in health and elderly care is too difficult to measure objectively. How many times a day someone's diaper is changed, or how often someone is taken out for a walk can easily be measured. But whether the diaper change is performed with respect and kindness, or the degree to which a strolling partner is a good and friendly companion, is not as easy to measure. The quality of such work must be evaluated by other standards than financial ones. This is already a difficult task. Determining the degree of empathy in one's staff requires careful observation and individual evaluation that cannot be obtained from an

Excel sheet. But in a setting that prioritises economic efficiency and profitability, and a care sector characterised by constant rationalising pressures to perform, the emphasis on compassion is likely to be under-prioritised in the end.

It is simply not possible to tender healthcare services with 'at least one hour of empathy per day'. Not because the companies do not understand that empathy is important, but because the supplier who nevertheless budgets for the invisible cost of empathy is likely to lose out to companies who neglect this aspect. 'Cruelty there is none in this,' the Swedish author Viktor Rydberg once wrote about the effects of capitalism, 'merely arithmetic.'[7]

Multidimensional human values are difficult to reduce to the market's unidimensional value-world solely measured by price. According to the market's idea of value, services must be 'procured' by the individual healthcare consumer, who then should make their own valuation. But often, such a valuation is only possible afterwards when the service has already been 'consumed'. The only way the market can function in this regard is if the hospital or retirement home resembles the hotel business. There must be real competition between service providers, and the consumers must be in a position to switch suppliers if they are not satisfied. If a customer is not satisfied, they can promptly check out and go across the street to another hotel. However, personally I barely have the energy to do this as a healthy businessman after an Atlantic flight. Expecting an old, sick person to do this with regard to elderly care, assuming there are even any alternatives, is not very realistic. This would be too large a responsibility to place on the consumer. If the consumer cannot handle the procurement process themselves, for instance if they lack time, knowledge or strength, the service should not even be offered through the market. Sometimes we simply need to be able to rely on being well taken care of, without needing to use the threat of changing suppliers. In itself, this has value for the customer. It can be compared to how we trust that a qualified electrician will not make dangerous installations or that a bank will pay back deposited money. The market cannot offer these guarantees by itself. Only legislators can create the prerequisites for the market to do so. If that is not possible, we should find other means than the market to offer the service in question.

THE MARKET AS OUR SERVANT – NOT OUR MASTER

The market is an efficient, albeit blind, piece of machinery. But it is always we humans who must make the final assessment regarding the desired consequences and end-results. Without competent analysis, the market's efficiency can yield unexpected and ultimately undesired results. We can never excuse the negative effects of the market and just refer to those as the unfortunate, but fair, will of the market forces. If things do not work on the market, it is not the will of God. It is our responsibility to change it for the better. The market is simply a tool to obtain certain goals, and when it does not, we need to find another one that works.

Economic efficiency is an important value which ought to be coveted, but it is also the only value that automatically results from the market. Other human values such as dignity, fairness, sustainability and empathy must be consciously built into the market.

The market has expanded into domain after domain of our society and culture, hand in hand with the postmodern worldview that made its entrance during the latter part of the twentieth century. First of all, the postmodern thought perspective has been used to *legitimise* the market, even though this has not the intention. When the grand ideologies fell to the wayside, very little remained to believe in. Postmodernism's value vacuum did not contribute in setting up new overarching goals for society, hence the field was left open for the market. The market succeeded in proliferating itself for lack of a yardstick or any official value compass. Postmodern moral relativism thus became a perfect background for the market's newly gained dominance.

Efficiency has been an extremely important value throughout human history. But postmodernism's moral relativism has allowed the market's efficiency to spread at the expense of other values. Efficiency, such as the ability to produce great amounts of material riches, have been necessary for survival and to create tolerable lives. But in the West today we have attained such a high level of material welfare that we must ask ourselves whether it might be time to let other values matter just as much. GDP has doubled over the last thirty years, but it is questionable whether this is proportional to how much better we are feeling; whether the actual utility for the individual also has doubled?

The Threat to the Secularised Market Society

Western society is currently threatened from several corners: from the outside in the form of religious fundamentalism and burgeoning authoritarian superpowers in Asia, from the inside in the form of xenophobia and fascist tendencies. Still I do not see these as the greatest threats to the secular liberal market society, but rather the failure of the market society in symbiosis with postmodernism to create meaning; hence triggering the threat of inner, social dissolution. If the market stands alone we will experience a great number of negative consequences from the cultural and existential emptiness that it causes and that postmodernism does not seem to be able to handle.

Societies have been created around shared principles and values and have survived revolutions and catastrophes by adapting to new conditions. The secular market society that the Western World has created, and that has given us unprecedented liberties and affluence, is the product of the toil of many generations. I basically see this as a good society; a society that has liberated the individual from feudalism's harsh social confines, one that has fed a growing humanity, and a society that produces culture, science and charitability at an unprecedented level. I definitely do not belong to the postmodern choir that insist that nothing has fundamentally changed or that everything is getting worse. Things have improved. We live longer than ever, we are eradicating disease after disease, and we generally live better and more meaningful lives than ever before.

Previously, free capitalism was considered threatened by the socialist states. Today it is rather the Islamic world that is cast as the threat to our way of life. But Islamism is hardly a threat to our society in spite of terror attacks from radical Islamist groups and the terrible human tragedy they cause. The greatest threat to the market society is rather its own inability to create meaning and value. As early as 1945, Karl Popper described the market's inability to generate credible meaning and value systems in *The Open Society and Its Enemies.* Where earlier societies' main problem was a lack of food and material assets, in the affluent societies today, the lack of *meaning* and *motivation*, pointed out by Habermas, is one of the greatest challenges of our time.[8] The market has not succeeded in creating an integrated meaning structure. Rather, the reverse seems to have occurred as the market is in the process of breaking down the meaning structures that already exist.

The idea of the responsible citizen has been subjected and reduced to the market's logic and thereby demoted to a passive consumer where political participation has been replaced by political 'shopping' of various producers of 'political commodities'. And in the religious domain meaning has been reduced to a product directed at the individual's personal needs rather than a social meaning-making context to be part of. Many things have now been subject to market adaptation, and as such lost deeper values, meaning and content.

We need a deeper social context to feel that we are actually part of something meaningful. Without it, society disintegrates into a bunch of individuals that only associate as economic agents. A society cannot solely consist of consumers and producers. The market-liberal world view is impoverished, unidimensional and void of meaning in any greater sense. Alienation, which the young Marx wrote about, is a serious threat to our wellbeing, our sense of meaning and context. If individuals cannot find meaning in their life, they will deaden their existential anxiety with distractions such as vapid entertainment, alcohol, drugs and unfettered consumerism – or even self-harming behaviour or misdirected violence.

* * *

The revolt against stale, conservative thought systems during the post-war years was necessary. And so were the economic liberalisations during the end of the last century. We needed to 'tear things down to get air and light', as August Strindberg once wrote.[9] But as individuals in the society that has now emerged, we are left in a vacuum between political correctness and neoliberal emptiness.

Postmodernism's moral relativism has meant that the market has not received significant resistance and that economic efficiency has been able to spread at the expense of other human values. In our postmodern world the market has become our new fundamental authority – a secular God.

But nor should we throw away the market. We must move on and as humanity take the awkward responsibility of creating new shared values with greater consciousness and insight, but still continue to use the market as the capable tool that it is. We must give up our naive popular belief in the market and become better at deciding what needs and utilities it is suitable for. We need to become better at seeing through the market, to see it for what it is.

Chapter 9

CULTURE AND OUR COLLECTIVE IMAGINARY

What is culture? Culture can be seen as that which has been 'cultivated' or simply created by humans, in contrast to occurrences in nature which have emerged irrespective of human activities. Often, the term is used in a much narrower sense to refer to artefacts and occurrences in the arts. In this book, however, the concept is used more broadly to refer to our collective subjectivity, the interior perspective of society if you will; the many ideas, norms and symbols that make up a society, but cannot be observed objectively. A culture is all the immaterial phenomena that exist between subjects and make up a greater whole, the intersubjective dimension of society.

We saw in Chapter Two how our shared symbol worlds – our collective imaginaries – are ultimately held together by the narratives that carry our intersubjectivity. It was through the stories we shared around the camp fire and various rituals we performed that our otherwise random and chaotic collective imaginary was given the structure and meaning that the social world needs in order for us to survive and thrive as a group. It is the same today. We need narratives, cultural expressions and shared ideas to create context, meaning and common objectives.

In the corporate world, which I am quite familiar with, we talk a lot about corporate culture. I have in this book consistently used the term societal culture to show that I am referring to something broader than art, literature and theatre when I use the word culture. So just as the term 'corporate culture' does not (only) revolve around the cultural expressions and experiences that the company sponsors, or the works of art to decorate the walls in office corridors, neither does societal culture (only) revolve around the art that hangs on the walls in museums, but rather the culture that 'hangs on the walls' of society itself.

In the corporate sector there is a broad, practical understanding of the significance and possibilities of culture, perhaps even more so than among academics or politicians. There is an understanding of its significance in marketing and lobbying to influence our values and societal norms. Practical knowledge about how to shape society's values and norms, consumer behaviour and political decision-makers so as to serve the interests of corporate interests has been widely available to companies for decades. But above all, many corporate leaders understand the significance of the inner culture to the success of an organisation. In modern management literature there are many who argue that the most important task for the management of a company is to establish the right culture in the organisation. With a well-honed company culture, everything else tends to fall into place. So what if the same applied to society's culture?

CULTURE AS A BEARER OF OUR COLLECTIVE SUBJECTIVITY

When we experience reality and orient ourselves in everyday life, we always – unless we are newborns – start from the culture we are part of. Every moment of our lives is born from culture. It shapes our very emotions and most intimate experiences and even follows us into our dreams. Even if we to a large extent share emotions and perceptions with other animals, our experience of sensory impressions is shaped and coloured by our culture and its symbols, meanings and sentiments. One way of phrasing this is that *culture bears our subjectivity.*

On the one hand our subjective reality is always inaccessible to others. We cannot in any real sense feel with others' hands, see with their eyes, or hear each other's thoughts. But on the other hand, all these experiences adhere to a meaning-creating structure that is highly impersonal; an overarching contextual framework of meaning that has been co-created by other people who have lived before us and is continuously recreated and further developed by people in our surroundings and others in our cultural sphere that we never meet. This constructed world of mutual meaning, shared norms and symbols and truth criteria makes up 'the inside' of our society, the intersubjective domain of our social reality. As such, culture also bears our *collective subjectivity*. But how can anything as personal as our subjectivity be collective? Illustrating how we can fail to achieve intersubjective understanding might help explain this circumstance.

Imagine that you travelled back to the Middle Ages and tried to explain a concept such as 'corporation' to the people who lived back then. Where would you start? 'It is a registered organisation that is treated as a legal entity' you could explain. Yet no one understands. You could then go on to say that 'it is a value-creating association with the purpose of generating profit for its owners, and that it can be owned by a number of different shareholders who can freely sell their parts on the stock market'. Still, no one understands what you are talking about. The more you try, the more you entangle yourself in references to the modern, industrial society's way of thinking and functioning. You could go on to explain that 'corporations make services and/or products to be sold on the free market, that the owners, depending on the size of their share, can vote on who should be on the board of directors, who in turn decide who shall be CEO and whether profits shall be reinvested or paid out to the shareholders, while the employees who do the actual work only have a legal right to their wage no matter how profitable or unprofitable the company is … All of this relies on voluntary agreements between wage earners, managers and owners; professional and impersonal relations that are shaped by a number of legal regulations.' However, none of this, despite how detailed you try to explain what a corporation is, can be understood in a medieval context. They may understand that it is a group of people who work together, but the notion of the 'free-floating spirit' in our social world that is the essence of the company would probably be entirely lost on a medieval person.

A reason why it is so difficult to explain things out of someone else's contextual framework is because signs can only refer to other signs, as pointed out by Derrida. All the signs we have available to describe the meaning of the term 'corporation' refer to yet other signs just as incomprehensible to our medieval ancestors as the very concept we are trying to explain. Everything we say and do is permeated by subtle impressions, sentiments and associations that require prolonged exposure to modern society with its cities, factories and offices. You might be able to convey a vague image, but hardly a complete understanding. The idea of the company is something that you and I have a common, subjective experience of because we share a fairly similar symbolic language and are both exposed to the social imaginary of the company and its effects on our lives. Without this shared intersubjective symbol world, the chance of understanding what we are talking about is very slim.

But let us imagine that a person from the future is trying to reach us with a concept or experience that exists in their society and that can only be understood in a wider context that we have not been acquainted with. Now we, the people of the twenty-first century, would come off as stuck in the dark ages, utterly incapable of understanding what is self-evident to someone from the future. If they tried to explain a concept referring to an advanced productive system of organisation that is just as free of money, profit motives, legal agreements and professional roles as the modern corporation is free of military means, religious motives, feudal privileges and social castes, we would probably not be able to understand what they talked about.

Our contemporary corporation is nothing but a symbol to refer to a number of complex relations, principles and mechanisms that we see as a coherent whole; a social imaginary needed to make sense of how we organise production in modern societies. We can point to the factories and offices, labour processes, exchanges of goods and various documents about what is going on and who owns what. But the company itself only exists in our imagination, a sort of fiction. It requires a shared cultural context to be fully comprehended. If the people from the future were to explain an even more advanced way of organising production by reference to a corresponding social imaginary of their time, with even more complex relations and mechanisms, this would probably be as incomprehensible to us as that of the corporation to our medieval ancestors. We are prisoners of our time and culture, and symbols and imaginary entities referring to a large number of interconnected phenomena that do not resemble anything we have had a personal experience of are almost impossible to grasp.

What we can understand and imagine, how we see ourselves and others and what we think and do are severely limited by our cultural context. Our culture can change, however, it does develop over time, as history has taught us. But we only have the symbol tools we have obtained from others, very few of us singlehandedly invent new ones. And if we do, whatever advances we make always depend on what is currently available in our shared cultural tool kit. It is therefore of utmost importance that we start to investigate this phenomenon thoroughly, that we see culture as something more than music, theatre and visual art but as a fundament for humanity and our society – and ponder whether we could refashion and shape it in a more preferable direction.

THE THREE DOMAINS OF REALITY

Philosophers sometimes speak, albeit in different terms, of what can be boiled down to what I have chosen to call the three domains of reality: the *physical*, the *mental* and the *social*. Being able to recognise and distinguish the three domains is, I would argue, crucial to navigating between the most fundamental perspectives of reality.

Descartes argued that the only thing we humans can be completely sure of is our own mental world. Everything else might be a mental illusion. He wanted to start from scratch, be free from earlier theories and questioned whether both the *rational thoughts* of reason and the *empirical reflections* of the senses make it possible to attain definite knowledge. Descartes' starting point was *radical* and *sceptical*, and his reasoning *logical*. He argued that the human being has freedom in their mental world and that it clearly differs from the physical. This is also known as the 'dualist' worldview. The physical environment and our mental reality are thus two completely different worlds or domains. However, he missed out one crucial world that is neither.

Karl Popper is best known for his philosophy of science. He famously argued that scientific theories must be falsifiable, that it does not suffice that they are verifiable. Theories cannot be regarded as true in any absolute sense, he claimed, the theories that endure have simply not yet been proven to be false. This was Popper's great contribution to epistemology. Popper's great contribution to *ontology*, how reality is disposed, is less known. Popper argued that the world is best understood, not dualistically, as with Descartes, but as consisting of *three* different realities, with fundamentally different properties. Aside from the *physical* (objective material) domain, which Popper termed World 1, W1 for short, and the *mental* (subjective mental), W2, there is a *social reality*, an *intersubjective cultural* world, W3, that we humans construct together but nevertheless cannot be measured objectively.[1]

Yet, one can argue that things in the socially constructed domain of reality simultaneously are located in the physical domain. Money, for instance, indeed consists of physical objects, be they coins and notes or electrons in a computer system. Popper was aware of this, and used the example of books to show why the social reality in some instances is more central to particular phenomena than the physical reality. Books are physical objects all right, concrete objects that we can observe and measure with our senses. However, they are also collections of words and ideas that only make sense in the mental domain of reality. Objectively they are nothing but paper with ink on them, but this is hardly the most relevant aspect. When we talk about a book we rarely define it by the weight of its paper and the amount of ink on its pages, but rather by its symbolic content, which only appears in the mental domain. The symbols, however, can only be perceived as meaningful by their connection to the social domain. Without a cultural context to give meaning to the signs on a book's pages, they cannot be perceived by the mind, the mental domain of reality, as words and sentences, but only appear as row upon row of random letters – or, if the reader has no knowledge of the alphabet, simply as strange figures. Books are therefore to be seen as a phenomenon primarily within our social domain of reality. This is further revealed when we talk about a specific book. The Bible, for example, exists in numerous editions in several languages, but when we say that all these books are one and the same we are referring to something other than a particular physical book. We refer to an entity that only exists in our intersubjective, social domain of reality.

The idea of three different domains of reality has been a recurring theme in philosophy. Plato, for instance, reckoned that there were three major ideas: the *true*, the *beautiful* and the *just*. The 'true' corresponds to the objective, physical domain, W1, in the way that truths need to be objectively valid irrespective of personal opinions and cultural conventions. The 'beautiful' corresponds to the subjective, mental domain, W2, since beauty – as the saying goes – 'is in the eye of the beholder'; that is, aesthetic qualities can only be perceived subjectively. And finally, the 'just', which corresponds to the intersubjective, social or cultural domain of reality, W3, since ethical statements refer to matters *between* subjects; intersubjectively valid principles, that can be derived neither from objective facts nor subjective opinions alone. Immanuel Kant also builds his philosophy around these three different domains of reality or perspectives in his three major critiques. In the *Critique of Pure Reason*, he studies the way in which the human mind acquires knowledge about the world, basically how we create objective truths (this is the one with the '*Ding an sich*'), W1. His second critique, the *Critique of Practical Reason*, is concerned with ethics (the one with the famous categorical imperative), W3. And in his third and last critique, the *Critique of Judgement*, he investigates the human mind's capacity for aesthetics and teleology; subjective aspects that correspond with the mental domain of Popper's W2. In contemporary philosophy, Jürgen Habermas, who is regarded by many as the greatest philosopher of our time, similarly argues that language consists of three different truth criteria that we inevitably relate to when we speak: 'With every speech act,' he argues, 'the speaker relates to something in the objective world [W1], something in a common social world [W3], and something in their subjective world [W2].'[2] As you may have noticed even without my brackets, Habermas refers to the very same domains proposed by Popper. Habermas argues that each of these contains its own distinct truths that cannot be reduced to each other. Validity claims should be subjected to their own type of evidence and thereby be controlled for their actual validity. Speech acts relating to the objective world claim to be propositional truths, objective state of affairs that require empirical evidence to be validated. This is distinctly different from the validity claim of those speech acts relating to the social world that refer to normative rightness, which are validated if they correspond with 'legitimately regulated interpersonal relationships'. Claims of moral truths need to be intersubjectively verified in other words. This again is profoundly different from the validity criterium of the subjective world, which can only be verified by reference to the attributed truthfulness of a subjective experience – the perceived sincerity of a person to make a claim regarding a subjective, mental experience.

The different sorts of truths within each of these domains, and the circumstance that none of these can be reduced to or deduced from another, also explain the error of the naturalistic fallacy that Hume pointed out: that an *ought* (the Just, W3) cannot be derived from an *is* (the True, W1). The reason for this is that we are dealing with two very different speech acts, belonging to two distinctly different domains of reality that must be judged on their own premises, in accordance with their own specific validity criteria, and you cannot lightly apply conclusions from one to the other.

In the history of philosophy, the reduction of one of the three domains to one of the others has often been the source of many of the most famous and hotly contested quarrels. In the past, these battles revolved around whether W1 or W2 is the ultimate reality, debates concerning the futile objective to establish once and for all which of these should be considered subordinate to the other. Here, the philosophical discussion that first comes to mind is the squabble between the *rationalists*, who followed the example of Descartes and emphasised W2, and the *empiricists*, who saw W1 as the ultimate source of knowledge just like John Locke. This conflict was precisely what Kant tried to solve in his critical works. Sometimes, however, the debates have not been as explicit as the former, but merely relied on different perspectives derived from one of these domains. For example, the century-long debate of the 'problem of universals' that tried to solve whether the properties of an entity exist in a separate, mental reality, or whether they only exist in the entity itself. This confusion was derived from an inadequate differentiation between W1 and W2 and a failure to see the ways in which our language within W3 determines how we perceive properties. The conflict between the Enlightenment philosophers (W1) and the romanticists (W2) that followed is another well-known example of two philosophical camps emphasising the perspective of one domain over the other. The schisms between psychiatry (W1) and psychology (W2), or positivism (W1) and phenomenologists (W2), are likewise derived from this one-perspectival bias. Recently, the fiercest battles have been fought between W1 and W3, usually with modernists emphasising empirical evidence on one side and postmodernists emphasising cultural and hermeneutic approaches on the other. Often, these debates revolve around the classic 'nature' (W1) versus 'nurture' (W3) dilemma, whether human behaviour is determined by our genes or our environment. This either/or fallacy could adequately be resolved if people learned about the three domains of reality, thinking both/and instead, and thereby got the means to create better explanatory models.

Popper's three worlds thus seem to have a very solid basis in philosophy. Accordingly, we should try to view reality from each of these three perspectives, learn how to properly differentiate matters and identify in which domain they belong, and emphasise all three equally. Here is a short description of each domain:

1. **The physical domain (W1):** The objective, physical domain consists of material objects, such as stars and planets, rocks and liquids, and plants and animals, but also of forces such as motion, light and gravity, and other natural phenomena that we cannot experience directly with our senses, but which exist all the same, such as radiation, magnetic fields and quantum dynamics. In short, everything that can be described as propositional truths with reference to objective states of affairs.
2. **The mental domain (W2):** The subjective, mental domain consists of psychological phenomena such as impulses, emotions and thoughts. It even consists of what we perceive as objective, sensory impressions of vision, sound, touch and taste. Joy and pain, warm and cold, the beauty of a poem and the feeling of love, even our decisions and perception of self, belong to this inner subjective domain of reality. All are statements that can be attributed to the sincere truthfulness of a subjective experience. This reality cannot be reduced to purely physical matters. If you feel love for someone, a skilful researcher can surely find out what happens in your brain, but never explain why you love that very person. In the same way the mental domain of reality cannot be reduced to the physical one, it cannot be reduced to the social one either. It is not possible to explain love merely as a cultural construction that we are socialised into with the purpose of organising the continued reproduction of society. The emotion of love can emerge, often rather inconveniently, in spite of what society tells us is correct love.
3. **The social domain (W3):** This is our socially constructed world, the domain of reality that harbours our culture and its intersubjective products of human thinking such as language, mathematics and theories, along with various social imaginaries such as laws,

religions and communal identities. Cultural expressions like music, poetry and art, as well as technological achievements in the form of buildings, machines and economic systems, can also be said to belong the social domain. Material human-made artefacts obviously have properties that belong to the physical domain, but they are only meaningful in relation to the social and mental. Tools or artworks are not defined by their physical properties such as weight and material composition, but from the purpose they are experienced to have in the mental domain, which once again derives their meaning from the social. When we talk about hammers or paintings, we do not refer to the iron or paint in a particular object, but to the categories that exist in our social domain. These rely on legitimately regulated interpersonal relationships, meaning that when we use language to make truth claims about the world, the words need to correspond to the current social conventions in order to be considered valid. In the mental domain of an individual, the word 'hammer' might be a meaningful way of describing a piece of cloth with paint on it. But if that does not correspond with what is currently considered a legitimate way of using the word by others, then it will violate the intersubjective validity criterion of W3. Occurrences and entities in the social domain cannot be reduced to their physical constituents just as little as they can be reduced to the personal, mental experiences of these. W3 is a separate world of symbols, the domain from which we can obtain the symbol tools to articulate meaningful narratives about both our physical and mental world, and convey these to others as well as ourselves. Our private world of thoughts may be full of words our inner voice constantly puts into meaning-creating sentences, but the words themselves are derived from our social world, which shows how intimately connected our minds are to this domain of reality. W3 is the domain of all those things that derive their meaning from the relation between subjects, viz. 'inter'-'subjective'.

It may appear rather self-explanatory and banal when the three domains are presented like this. Physical objects are obviously something different from our subjective experience, and symbols clearly only make sense in relation to a cultural context. However, this seemingly has not been very self-evident throughout most of human history. Metaphysical notions of spirits and gods were long considered part of the physical world, and social conditions were likewise seen as given by God or nature, between which there was no difference. In the past, there was no difference between religion, science and society either, individuals were defined by their position within a community, and personal speculations and cultural conventions were seen as just as valid sources of knowledge as empirical evidence. Certain symbols were even considered to have magical abilities in the physical world, and the physical world itself was seen as enchanted with spirits whose secrets could be unravelled by studying the dreams and visions of prophets in holy scriptures. Only in modern times have such ideas been abandoned in favour of approaches that more clearly separate the different aspects from each other, subjecting them to evidence in accordance to the validity criteria within whatever domain of reality they belong.

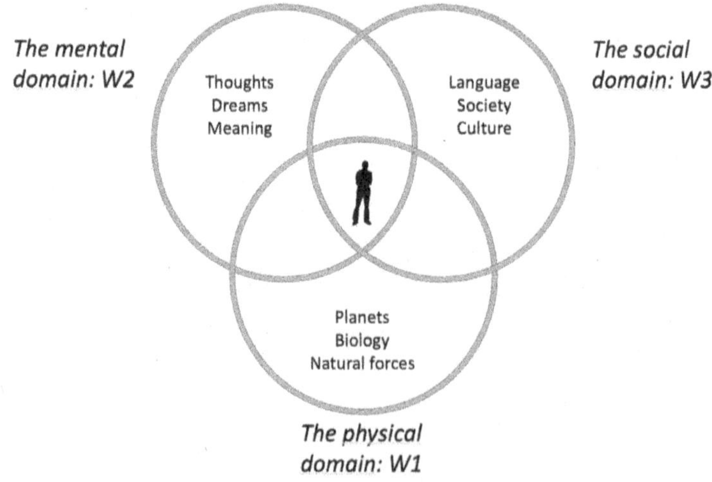

Karl Popper's three worlds/domains.

Differentiating between physical, mental and social phenomena is a relatively modern phenomenon. Max Weber, commonly seen as one of the founding fathers of sociology, argued that the hallmark of modernity was the differentiation between Plato's three major ideas. Truth had to be separated from religious and political interference. Neither moral conventions nor personal preferences should have any validity within science. Beauty likewise had to be separated from outside interference. Everyone should be free to have their own perspectives, personal preferences and beliefs of what was beautiful to them, with neither religious nor political authorities telling people what to believe and say. The Just was equally separated by the modern project. Justice should be transferred to the public, who themselves were to collectively decide which principles they thought as fair and morally respectable, rather than arbitrary rulers and religious authorities, which independent courts then should ensure were upheld in society. This was far from self-evident before the modern turn, and still remains a contested issue in many parts of the world today.

In a way, the separation of the three ideas resembles the equally modern separation of powers envisioned by Montesquieu, the legal foundation of every modern state. However, just as the separation of powers is far from something we should take for granted, suggested by the presence of dictatorships and struggling developing nations, the idea that science, morals and personal preference should be kept far apart is neither something we can expect as self-evident in all situations. Even in fully modernised societies today, there are still religious sentiments that claim to have a right to interfere in individuals' personal lives and what should be considered scientific truths.

However, pre-modern institutions are not the only ones that fail or even refuse to separate the three domains. Sometimes modern people also fail to separate objective observations, moral conventions and personal preferences or tastes from each other. Injustices are often defended by reference to social conditions or biology, for example that citizenship alone is enough to defend why some people should have a right to certain benefits that others should be denied, or that men have a right to dominate women because of some biological difference. If people are personally disgusted or offended by something – a different kind of sexuality, alternative way of life or simply their visual appearance – and even though it does not harm anyone and really does not have anything to do with them, they are often quick to demand a ban on whatever it is that annoys them. Even scientific results are sometimes frowned upon when they conflict with personal beliefs or moral conventions, such as climate change, evolutionary biology, research in intelligence or developmental psychology (which we will look into in chapter 11), gender studies and other controversial topics. When modern people feel particularly outraged about an issue – whether it be a criminal individual making the headlines in the tabloid press, someone exploiting a loophole in the legislation or simply the odd behaviour of some minority – they sometimes forget the very foundational principle of the modern state, the tripartite separation of powers, and demand immediate punitive action, disregarding both parliamentary decision processes, independent courts and a rule of law that does not contradict itself.

Modern society is based on the separation of powers, the idea of the individual as a separate entity from the community (and thereby the freedom from enforced morality as long as one does not hurt others) and science as a discipline that should be allowed to pursue the truth without consideration for moral conventions, political interference and the personal opinions of others. As such, it would be tempting to suggest that modernity has been the point in history where the insight about the three domains of reality finally came to its fullest fruition. However, even though the domains may have been separated in many instances, they are yet to be properly synthesised in a way that includes the crucial insights and perspectives that can be obtained from all three.

Within modern science, the confusion between the different domains of reality and their equally different claims of validity has been a source of many fruitless debates. The centuries-old conflict between the natural sciences and the humanities is mainly derived from the fact that the former works within the exterior, objective domains of Popper's W1, and the latter primarily within the interior, subjective domains of W2 and W3. Reducing one to the other and proclaiming it to be the only valid reality is a big mistake and an endeavour doomed to failure. You can objectively observe and measure a human brain, but you cannot measure the personal experience of consciousness – dreams can't be measured, so to speak. You cannot reduce the human mind to mere atoms and expect to understand it. And even as the law of gravitation may be a social construct, gravity itself is not. The mind is the brain seen from the inside, the brain the exterior biophysical manifestation of the mind. The brain will drop to the ground just as any other physical entity under the effects of gravity, but the mind works according to other rules than those limiting physical objects.

In a similar way our culture is society seen from the inside. We can measure the flows of money that make the economy go around, and we can study the laws that make up its legal system. But we cannot use the same tools to identify the human emotions and desires that drive economic decision-making or the norms and ethical sentiments behind society's laws. For that we need to adopt a cultural approach. If we want to truly change society for the better, it does not suffice to tweak a few financial instruments or change some laws. We first need to change its culture.

But how do we change something that is not as easy to observe as these exterior surface phenomena? What are the mechanics and properties of this seemingly hidden domain of Popper's W3?

CAN WE CHANGE OUR COLLECTIVE IMAGINARY?

The limitations that apply to the physical world do not in the same way apply to the social world that we create. Material resources obviously remain limited in the physical domain of Popper's W1, but since the social or collective imaginaries that make up the social domain of W3 merely consist of non-material entities that reside in the limitless imagination of our minds, how can it be that we still seem as restricted by our social reality as our physical? If money in fact is just a social construction and so easy to create, why then is there so much poverty and inequality in the world? If human beings have created things such as money and the market, could we not just change them in a way that benefits more people than they currently do? How can we change our collective imaginaries and cultural norms that determine how these surface phenomena work? And how did we create them to begin with?

Since money is just a product of our imagination, a fiction that we collectively have created to govern our everyday games of economic transactions, we could use the example of how children play together and make up rules in their games.[3] Imagine a group of children playing together who decide to invent a new game. One of the children suggests that they divide into two groups separated by a deep canyon, symbolised by a carpet in the room. A girl says that there is a bridge across the canyon that you only may cross if the queen (the child points at herself) gives permission. 'Maybe,' says another child, 'the queen will let you cross if you give her some gold.' He points at a few pieces of Lego. 'That is gold,' he says. The children then start to address the girl as queen, giving her Legos in order to cross the carpet, while another child starts to manage the limited supply of yellow Lego bricks, which are suddenly seen as precious resources that they start trading among each other for other toys in the small new collective imaginary that the children just created. The game progresses and they start to imagine all kinds of reasons to cross the imagined canyon in order to keep the game interesting. But suddenly they are interrupted when one of the participants runs out of the room saying that she has had enough of this silly game. The other girl is just a girl and no queen she says and the collective imaginary is broken. Now the Legos have no other value again than what you can build with them.

Obviously, the games that govern our adult everyday lives are vastly more complex than the children's games, but the story has some interesting similarities with our own social world. We adults also set up rules; rules determining what are considered national boundaries, who is considered an illegal immigrant, or who has the right to decide who is allowed across the border. The rules also define the roles within the system. And with every role there come rights and obligations, just as the queen has the right and responsibility to decide who is allowed to cross the bridge. We also assign a value to certain objects, pieces of paper instead of pieces of Lego, or blips on a computer screen, and start to see them as something more. And when we start believing, collectively, in these pieces of paper being money, then they can be used for various transactions. If we do not like the current game, we can change any of the constitutive rules, like the children changed the rule that the queen should accept Legos to let them pass. Although difficult, we can replace an old institution with a new one, or one game with another as long as we all agree – or at least as long as everyone has not left to play another game. Our social reality is like the children's game, a world of conceptions and fantasies. It is a result of our collective conception and can only exist as long as a sufficiently large number of people believe in it and play the same game with the same rules. This social reality is also rather fragile: it only exists because people believe it exists. But this does not render it any less tangible or real.

However, there are many important differences between children's games and our social reality. In the game described above, the carpet serves as a canyon and the pieces of Lego as money. In our social world, we obviously cannot create a canyon by simply saying 'this is a canyon' (W1). But we can decide that certain geographic areas are national borders and that some objects shall be valid as means of monetary transaction (W3). It is also worth noting that when a child suddenly drops out, it can easily do so. For us, as members of a society, it is not quite as simple to leave. We can, of course, commit suicide or become refugees. But in the latter case we still remain participants in the game, albeit in another part of the world and with a partially different collective imaginary. Normally, however, we cannot just leave the social world. If we started to say that the queen no longer is queen, or that those pieces of paper no longer are money, we would be regarded as odd or maybe even insane. Few would care about our proclamations. Unless we accomplish the unlikely feat of a revolution, queens and money continue to have the same functions whether we like it or not. Perhaps this is why it is so easy to take our collective imaginary for granted and regard its limits in the same way as the limits of the natural world. Our collective imaginary often appears just as difficult to change as natural phenomena and tends to affect our lives just as much. But this does not mean that we cannot change it. In theory, we can as a collective decide not to regard those pieces of paper as money and – in a flash – the paper would cease to be money. And through a referendum we can likewise decide that the United Kingdom should cease being a monarchy and thus turn the Queen into a normal citizen. We do, in other words, collectively have the option of remaking our social world.

* * *

In 1967, before he became prime minister, Olof Palme was minister of transport in Sweden. The Swedish parliament had a few years earlier decided that it was time for motorists to drive on the right side of the road. The whole thing was carried out, after extensive planning, on the night before the third of September the same year. The trams in Stockholm were taken out of service and old buses were replaced by new ones with the doors on the other side. Had it occurred seventy years earlier, it would have been a simple task. In 1897, a driver only encountered few other travellers, and it hardly mattered whether they passed each other on the right or the left. But in 1967, traffic was so intense that it was necessary to have regulations for which side of the road to drive. The number of roads, cars and trams made the switch to driving on the right a major project, but one that was still possible to achieve overnight – it needed to be.

The idea to change which side of the road we should drive on emerged from speculations and prolonged debate over several years until it became the subject of political decision. And then after years of careful planning

Sometimes we make a drastic change in our collective imaginary. On 3 September 1967, Sweden changed from driving on the left side of the road to driving on the right side.

and plenty of information campaigns it suddenly – literally overnight – became a social reality that no one could reject believing in (without risking their own and others' lives). In the same way it is possible to change many of society's fundamental principles in a considerably short time span if we thoroughly investigate how they can be improved, muster the political will to change them and make the necessary preparations and careful forward-planning to implement them in a considerate manner.

Our social world is created by us, and we can change it if we decide to do so. Collectively. It was the sociologists Peter Berger and Thomas Luckmann who helped me understand this.

OUR SOCIAL REALITY

The year before the right-hand traffic diversion in Sweden, Berger and Luckmann released their ground-breaking book *The Social Construction of Reality.*[4] This book laid the ground for the school of thought that came to be known as 'social constructivism'. Their great insight was that many aspects of the social world that we naively perceive as eternally given by nature have been created by humans, often unconsciously. In other words, we often tend to mistake Popper's social World 3 for the objective World 1. The theory of social constructions contributed to a deeper understanding of culture and came to be one of the leading societal theories within postmodernism.

In *The Social Construction of Reality*, Berger and Luckmann demonstrate the following:

- Society is a product of human actions.
- Society is perceived by humans as an objective reality.
- The human being is shaped into a social creature by their society.
- The human being reproduces society.

The starting point according to Berger and Luckmann is that human beings, after they have separated themselves from their instinct-driven existence, have acquired completely new fundamental properties. These properties have given rise to a number of processes that have made us shape our world that will be presented in the following.

Habits and Externalisation

In contrast to animals, who more or less 'run on auto-pilot' based on their instincts (at least in Berger and Luckmann's simplified presentation, which indeed does not clearly define instincts or take animal species' differences and ethology – the theory of animals' behaviour – into consideration), humans can direct and use their energy in many different ways with a number of possible choices. To balance this, our activities tend to become forces of habit.

Habits help us govern our desires and impulses, which otherwise would have lacked a fixed objective, and thus function as a stabilising factor. Habits require minimal attention and reduce time spent on decision-making, which simplifies existence and frees up energy for other activities. Since we rely on habits to direct our efforts towards recurring actions we can also practise and learn specific abilities that are of use in society. Routines also make social collaboration simpler and more predictable. This paves the way for the specialisation of functions that is typical of a society and which has been decisive for its development.

Berger and Luckmann further argue that the human being creates a steady outpouring of itself through its activities. As we leave traces in the environment in the form of our habits, these spread to others who have not themselves participated in shaping them. This *externalisation* of our activities produces the social order, and thereby the stable environment that serves our survival and efficiency.[5]

Institutions and Objectivisation

Berger and Luckmann referred to those habits that have been externalised in society and secured a foothold – thereby coming to be shared by new groups of people – as 'institutions'. Other people are then schooled into these from birth, for example, in the ways adults might explain to children the roles of men and women, which gods and authorities to believe in, which customs to follow or how money functions. The institutions now exist as *social facts*, and people take them for granted since they are born into them.

Instead of viewing money as debt recordings, for instance, which the first humans to come up with the idea that these could be used as means of transactions probably did, the next generation would be more likely to have forgotten this origin and started to see the bits of metal or whatever means used in everyday transactions as having some intrinsic worth of their own. The institution has thereby been objectivised and thus exists independently of those who once gave rise to the habits. The institution is then by later generations experienced as an objective reality and more than a human product. W3 becomes W1, so to speak: not in the sense that we mistake it for natural phenomena and physical objects, but in the way that we perceive social conditions as given facts that cannot be changed. We may smile at the cute perceptions of indigenous peoples who see their rituals and spirit beliefs as objective truths they do not realise they have created themselves, but modern people are no less susceptible to beliefs in imaginary ghosts, such as nations, money and market forces.

Our behaviour, and our life, is governed by institutions that we have been born into and that might be difficult to comprehend as merely social and more or less arbitrary inventions. They create a framework for collaboration and enable us to predict each other's actions, a prerequisite for trust within society.

Internalisation and New Generations

The objectivised institutions are absorbed and internalised by new generations. It is through this process that we become social creatures that can understand other people and our common reality, according to Berger and Luckmann. It is in the form of a perceived objective world that the social institutions can be relayed to new generations, which we inherit without knowledge of their history.

An institution is relatively easy to change in its initial stage. We can change routines that no longer serve their purpose, we can still remember why we established the routines and we understand the little world we have created. All this does, however, change during the transfer to the next generation. For children, the social world that is handed to them by their parents is not fully transparent. They internalise the customs as something self-evidently objective and an integral part of existence.

Children encounter the social world as a given reality that, like nature, in certain respects cannot be immediately comprehended. As Berger and Luckmann put it: 'In early phases of socialization the child is quite incapable of distinguishing between the objectivity of natural phenomena and the objectivity of the social formations.'[6] The child perceives language as something self-evident and given and cannot understand that it is based on conventions and customs. The institutional world ossifies not just for children, but also through a mirror effect for their parents as well. Parents are affected by how their children take the constructed world for granted so that it also appears increasingly real to themselves. The greater the share of people to embrace the routines and institutions, the more they become normative injunctions, and the harder it becomes to change them. At this stage, there is a ready-made social world, a content-rich given reality that new generations encounter in a way that resembles the reality of the natural world.

For society, institutionalised action is easier to predict and control. And if the process of socialisation into the institutions is efficient, less control is needed.[7] If we are to truly understand an institution, we need to get at the historical process through which it has emerged. Most institutions have a history that most often precedes our own birth and thus is not accessible to our memory.

Legitimisation and Symbolic Universes

Institutionalisation is followed by legitimisation. Legitimisation is the process that maintains institutions and makes them firmer after the connection to their origin has been broken. If an institution has become so well established that people have come to see it as an objective fact rather than a social invention, and if they have forgotten why and how it was implemented in the first place, it becomes easier to legitimise. For instance, if people believe that money has some kind of intrinsic worth of its own, and don't just see it as a clever debt system, it then becomes easier to legitimise as a foundational pillar of society – and for governments to manipulate its use in ways that are rarely questioned. It was once necessary to write on otherwise worthless money notes that they were legal tender – 'for all debts, public and private', just to be sure that people understood. It was even thought necessary to stress that people had a legal obligation to accept paper money for transactions. That is hardly required any more. The institution of money currently has such strong legitimisation in our social world that few of us ever ponder its imaginary properties. And even if we do, the fact that this institution is so well established, that so many of us believe in it, means that we cannot deny its abilities to shape social reality.

Legitimisation contributes to make the objectification of the institutions appear more reasonable and just. Various means are used to legitimise an institution, such as laws, norms, authority figures and symbolic customs. Many of which being institutions themselves that fortify and support each other in a positive upward spiral of mutual reinforcement and increased legitimisation.

Legitimisation of an institution always entails an *explanation* and a *defence*. The explanation makes clear what role one has within the context, for instance within a social hierarchy; what designation one has and what applies in a formal sense, for example as a parent, physician, chauffeur or newlywed. The defence makes clear what applies to this role within the structure, what is right and wrong to do, think and say. A secretary, for instance, is not expected to offer any opinions on a manager's decisions, nor is a child expected to decide how long the parent can stay out at night.

The legitimisation can be divided into four levels, which can occur in parallel:[8]

- **Language concepts:** Language concepts can imply a certain behaviour or action, e.g. the designations 'cousin', 'boss' or 'salesperson', for instance, which imply a certain relationship and expected behaviour both by and to that person. The designations 'dinner party', 'conference' or 'teaching' also contain similar behavioural prescriptions. Many language concepts thus entail directives.

- **Simplified explanatory schedules:** These comprise proverbs, idioms, moral maxims, words of wisdom, legends, folk tales, etc. An explanatory schedule is a package of sentences, values and guidelines that can provide guidance for behaviour and thinking. For example, proverbs such as 'every man is the architect of his own fortune' or 'once bitten, twice shy' harbour more comprehensive messages that can be understood at a more abstract level. A moral maxim such as 'do unto others as you would have them do unto you' provides guidance for one's behaviour. The market's notion of the 'invisible hand' can also be placed in this category.
- **Explicit theories:** This pertains to elaborate theories that are developed and administered by specialists within an area, and that can provide specialisation for those who choose to study the theories. Such more detailed specialist knowledge may, for instance, be found within a particular research area or an academic discipline. The field can give rise to an internal, growing world with its own terminology and further explanations.
- **Symbolic Universe (or Collective Imaginary):** This is an all-encompassing frame of reference, as all phenomena and experiences can be said to be interpreted within this symbolic totality. It entails large symbol worlds such as a certain religion or scientific tradition that refer to other realities than those that are part of daily life experiences. Symbolic Universes (like religions) appear to be fully developed and unavoidable frames of reference that create context and meaning for existence.

On a societal level, symbolic Universes are protective vaults both in regards to the institutional order and the individual human's identity. They create order by integrating experiences from various spheres into one and the same Universe of meaning. They also provide order by saying what is more or less important.

Symbolic Universes also set the boundaries for what and who is included in the sphere of social reality. Occasionally they include animals, natural phenomena or inanimate objects. Other times, certain human individuals are excluded, for instance foreigners, people of other beliefs, other races, etc. In addition, the symbolic Universe designates certain hierarchies and categories to determine the social order, e.g. caste systems, gender roles, occupational status, etc.[9] Another term for society's symbolic Universe, its outermost frame of reference, is 'metanarrative'.

Berger and Luckmann's theories can help us understand how we socially construct and reproduce our culture, how our social world in turn shapes us into the people we are and perhaps how we can make culture and the whole of our collective imaginary an object for deliberate reflection so that we can come to shape our culture, before it in turn shapes us.

At the Burning Man festival in the Nevada desert you experience constructing and living in a completely different collective imaginary. For many it is an eye-opening and life-changing event. Photo: BLM Nevada, Wikimedia Commons.

THE THREE CRUCIAL ASPECTS OF SOCIETY AND THEIR IMPLICATIONS

There are three aspects of our socially constructed reality that are particularly important in order to understand society and its development: *efficiency*, *fairness* and *meaning*. Hence, for every fact in our social reality we might pose three questions:

- **How does the fact influence the efficiency of society?** How does it affect our capacity to survive and attain our objectives?
- **How does the fact influence fairness in society?** Who benefits from society's efficiency, and how does it relate to what we consider reasonable?
- **How does the fact influence how and the degree to which we create purpose and meaning in society?** How does it relate to the way we determine the objectives of society's efficiency, who we wish to benefit from this, who we want to have power, and the values with which it should be in accordance? In what ways does it support and direct our individual and collective meaning making? What values and actions will it promote?

The efficiency, fairness and meaning aspects each correspond to one of Popper's three worlds (although all admittedly remain highly interconnected in a number of ways). Society's efficiency largely depends on our capacity to understand the physical World 1 and to investigate how we can generate maximum utility from observable, factual affairs. As mentioned, however, we cannot derive any ethical guidance from this objective world of *is*, only what works.

The fairness aspect addresses that which *ought* to work and corresponds with the social or cultural world of World 3. Fairness is the most crucial issue within the ethics of society: who gets what? Who should be in charge of giving it to them? What are people not allowed to do? What should happen if they still do it? And who should be the ones to make all of these decisions, on which principles, and with which means and authority available to them? We can only answer these essential questions by reference to valid claims of normative rightness within World 3; and the better we understand the manifold properties and intricate mechanisms of social relations in this domain, the more justice, harmony and societal cohesion can we build into our social constructions.

However, we can neither identify nor create the meaning that both society's efficiency and power order depend on from W3, only what *ought* to be; fairness yes, but not how that should give rise to feelings of meaningfulness. To find meaning, we need to look inwards, into our own subjective world of sensations, emotions and thoughts, the W2. In here, we can investigate what feels meaningful, what we think is true, just and beautiful, all of that we ultimately perceive as good: objectives worth striving for, persons and other beings that we care about, and all the things that make life worth living. The better we understand our own mind, the more likely we are to understand others, and with that what is most important to our society, our culture and ourselves.

If we balance these three aspects with each other, and if we learn how to differentiate between Popper's three domains of reality and thoroughly investigate the intricate mechanism of each and how they interact, we will be able to develop our society and culture to a degree that substantially increases our efficiency, fairness and meaningfulness.

Currently however, it seems as if we have emphasised one aspect over the others: efficiency. Many voices are therefore urging that we start to make fairness a much greater concern. And rightly so. But I believe that we have to stress the importance of higher levels of purpose and meaning as well. This can only be achieved by a cultural and – for lack of a better term – *spiritual* development of our world. We might also refer to the latter as psychological development. This is something that once again needs to be *cultivated*, rather than implemented from above – a long-term project that will take generations of deliberate development. And even though we are dealing with a much less tangible and rather ambiguous matter compared to the usual surface phenomena we usually take as our objects for societal improvement, the gains can be all the greater if we actually succeed.

If we change how the human being perceives the world, we change the world – and this we need to do collectively.

Chapter 10

RECONSTRUCTING THE MARKET

When I decided to leave my career as a physicist and instead launched my own business in finance, I started to think about the problem of understanding human society. I began to question what money, right of ownership and the market really are, and started to realise how the social world in fundamental ways differs from that of nature and physics. In view of my new occupation as a banker, I realised that many of the things I had previously taken for granted and seen as self-evident facts, such as the market, are actually arbitrary social constructions without much anchoring in physical reality.

The market is a self-organising complex system, but in contrast to life, consciousness and other biological systems, it is a system that we have created ourselves – virtually without noticing it. We may not see the market as a god, yet by virtue of the power it wields in our personal lives, the way it structures our social reality and how we tend to ascribe it almost divine magical abilities, it has almost come to behave as one. If we do not gain a better understanding of the mechanisms of the market, if we see it as self-evident, and fail to expose the myths surrounding it, the danger is that we will actually allow it to become our new God.

The market is a socially constructed phenomenon that only exists in our shared symbol world, Popper's World 3. Only from the perspective of this domain can it be perceived in a meaningful manner. As such, it belongs to a type of phenomena to have emerged at the cultural stage of evolution that made a group of biological creatures capable of creating novel conceptions in their minds and externalising them in very tangible ways. The market is thus a cultural phenomenon that previous generations have invented. Now, however, it has been institutionalised in our symbolic Universe to a degree where it has come to appear to us as part of our objective reality. Rather than just a clever tool to organise society, it has become a social imaginary containing myths and illusions that we see as facts rather than the fictions they really are. If more of us did, we would probably be able to reconstruct it to generate higher levels of efficiency, fairness and meaning.

THE ILLUSION OF A FREE MARKET

The market is *both* a self-organising complex system *and* a social construction. Much of the confusion that prevails in the debate about the market today is derived from the failure to realise this dual aspect. In order to think more clearly about the market, both as a self-regulating and socially constructed system, it is important that we distinguish between two sorts of rules: constitutive and regulative rules.

To even function as a self-organising system, there is a need for internal rules to define the feedback mechanisms in the system, or *constitutive rules* with another word. Without such rules, self-organising systems cannot exist. The game of football, as an example, cannot exist without constitutive rules to define the objective of the game. In fact, if players did not agree on the rules that football is played by kicking around a ball on a field, that only goalkeepers can use their hands to catch the ball, and that the winning team are those who have kicked it into a goal the most times when the game ends, it simply would not be football. Similarly, if market participants did not agree about the right to own private property and that only the state can use organised violence to persecute those who violate this right, that economic transactions are to be voluntarily negotiated, and that money is used in the exchange of services and products, the market as we know it could not exist either. These basic conditions are not just certain characteristics of the market, they *are* the market. A market where no one respects non-coercive monetary transactions is just as little a market as a game where players throw around hockey pucks in a game of football.

In addition to these constitutive rules, which are necessary for even starting a game, we can regulate the system with a number of *regulative rules*. In football, these include rules such as each team consisting of eleven players, matches being played over two periods of forty-five minutes, and goals being invalid if scored by players who are offside. What characterises a regulative rule is that it could be different without violating the constitutive rules. A game played by two teams of seven players for thirty minutes without the offside rule would still be a game of football. It is the same with the market. For example, today the market is governed by a number of regulative rules, such as capital owners being the primary stakeholders in companies, copyrights lasting seventy years after the death of the copyrighted material's creator and limited natural resources being privately owned. However, as long as the basic constitutive rules are still upheld, a situation where other stakeholders, such as workers, the environment or the local community, also had legal rights regarding a company, or copyrights were much shorter, or natural resources could only be owned collectively would still be a market.

Constitutive rules define the self-organising system, regulative rules the particular ways in which it organises itself. The constitutive rules are the 'what', the regulative the 'how'. If football is defined by two teams with the objective of kicking a ball into the opponent's goal, regulative rules to determine the number of players and time of a match are obviously required. Likewise, if the market is defined by non-coercive economic transactions between individuals who can own private property protected by the state, rules to determine what should be considered private property and what should be done if anyone uses coercive means to obtain others' property are obviously required too. So, like in football where using one's hands can result in a penalty kick, stealing and robbing on the market is punished by fines or jail. Regulative rules are thus used to support the constitutive rules. But whereas the latter cannot be different without completely changing what the system is, the former remain open for variations. A hand foul could be penalised with a red card, and stealing could be punished by hanging. Whether we decide on one regulative rule or another depends on how we want the self-organising system to function.

All of this may sound rather simple and self-explanatory, but surprisingly many fail to make this differentiation when it comes to the market. Most of us have no problems differentiating between the constitutive and regulative rules in football. Few would argue against the constitutive rule that football (at least the European sort) is defined by kicking a ball around a field and into goals, not the later-added offside rule. We have different kinds of football games in the way that different regulative rules apply to football proper: street football, indoor football or a game of football in a schoolyard. They are all considered football as long as the constitutive rules are upheld. But when it comes to the market we often fail to make the distinction between these two fundamentally different types of rules. Many of the most zealous advocates of the free market, for instance, often assert that we should do away with the regulative rules all together in order to make the market function more efficiently. Here, however, they forget that the regulative rules are that which makes the market work to begin with. The ideal market, they claim, is a free market, meaning that it should be free of more or less any external regulation. However, an entirely free market, a market without any regulative rules, is just as inconceivable as free football. If we did not agree on the number of players in a football team or what the penalty should be for using one's hands, football as a game could not function. Similarly, if we did not have any regulative rules to determine what can be traded on the market and what to do when people break the rules, the market as we know it could not function either.

Just imagine what an entirely free market would look like. Without any rules to decide what could be traded, such as prohibitions on slaves, human organs and dangerous substances, for instance, or with no security regulations regarding food and medication, mechanical and electrical appliances or construction, the market would probably struggle to remain the arena of peaceful economic transactions that it is defined as today. If we wanted to create an entirely free market, what would there be to stop the sale of heroin to children, or nuclear weapons to terrorists? If supply and demand were the only sacred principles to prevail on the market, nothing would exist to prevent it from destroying itself. The absence of any regulative rules would simply make the market an increasingly dangerous place, which would lead to a lack of the very feedback processes that ensure the functionality of its constitutive rule set in the first place. So just like 'free' football would not be a game, an entirely free market would be something else than what we currently consider a market.

Even a market free from regulative rules needs constitutive rules to start functioning in a self-organising manner. Examples of such constitutive rules are property rights and the freedom of market actors to decide the price of their products and services themselves. The outcome of this self-organising process of the market, Adam Smith's 'invisible hand', therefore depends on how these constitutive rules have been formulated. A system without private property and extensive price regulations would therefore amount to a very different market than the one we currently have – as different as curling is to football – and hence produce very different outcomes.

The way Smith's invisible hand functions simply requires the presence of constitutive rules such as private property and the freedom of individuals to adjust their prices. As such, the invisible hand is not a force of nature, it is not the hand of God, but simply the way in which the system organises itself from the constitutive rules we ourselves have built into it. Contrary to the constitutive rules of non-random elimination in biology, those of the market have been created by us and can thus be changed if we desire. In nature, self-organising systems are not governed by deliberate actions and objectives. The 'laws' and regularities in physics and biology are derived from necessity, a certain logic pertaining to the iron law of existence or non-existence – to be or not to be really is the question. But with the social systems of humans, what we want them to self-organise into existence, and how, is something that we can deliberately influence.

There are always external reasons as to why social systems have emerged the way they have. They have all been created by us to fill certain functions in society. Initially, the constitutive rules were created in order to give rise to certain self-organising processes which at the time were considered desirable. Thereafter they may have become increasingly self-generating, started to live their own lives, and evolved new complexity through feedback processes with the environment in ways that were often not foreseen to begin with or even considered desirable later on. As the system organises itself towards higher complexity, the way it shapes the surrounding world in turn shapes the structure and behaviour of the system itself. In a constantly changing world, the degree to which conscious actors successfully adjust the functionality of the system determines how well it keeps generating desirable outcomes. So just like biological systems, socially constructed ones only survive if they adapt to more complex circumstances. But whereas non-random elimination among organisms ensures the continuous development of new regulative biological functions (and eventually whole new constitutive ones amounting to entirely new species) so as to cope with the increasing complexity of their surroundings, human systems require conscious choices to change how they adapt to the new circumstances. 'Non-random elimination' is, as mentioned above, a better choice of words than 'natural selection' to describe the principle of biological evolution, since no one really selects what is to survive or not. Regarding human-made systems, however, someone actually has to select the constitutive and regulative functions to ensure the continuous survival of the system. If we do not make the conscious effort to do so, if we do not select what can naturally – determined by the merciless logic of existence/non-existence – accommodate our systems' ability to self-organise patterns generating increased efficiency, justice and meaning, we will risk elimination; non-randomly that is.

Different Markets, Different Regulations

The market is a deeply political creation. Both the internal rules of companies and the external regulations on the market hinge on political decisions that were created under particular circumstances and with the purpose of serving specific interests and objectives. There are also different rules and regulations dependent on what kind of assets we are talking about, different constitutive and regulative rules to determine the functioning of different markets within the overall market economy.

The real estate market, for example, does not only consist of land, piles of wooden boards and some cement, and a number of individuals who freely engage in monetary exchanges. The real estate market consists of lots of internal and external rules and regulations that determine how such economic transactions can take place, what can be traded and to whom and what can be done with the acquired property. Besides stipulating what actually constitutes a piece of real estate, a good example of a constitutive rule on the real estate market is that buyers of property acquire very strong rights of ownership to their purchases through a title deed, the official registration of the real estate. However, that does not mean that one can necessarily do everything one desires with the newly acquired property. If I buy a building in central Stockholm I might believe that I own it – that it is mine and that I can do with it what I want. But in certain cases, there are rules that limit what a buyer can do. For instance, I cannot move into the property myself if all the flats are already rented out. In Stockholm, there are regulative rules stipulating that the tenants living in 'my' property have the right to remain as long as they wish, provided they in turn follow the rules of the lease. And if they wish to move, they can swap their flat for someone else's so that a person unknown to me moves into my building. In addition, I am not allowed to build an extension to the property unless the plans are approved by the city council. Also, if I purchase a property in the historical centre, I certainly cannot tear down the building I just bought. The real estate market thus consists of a number of rules to ensure the rights of tenants, the decisions of city planners and the preservation of collective cultural goods, rules that make this particular market different from other markets.

The book market is another good example. Suppose I go to a bookshop and buy a book. I pay and leave the shop with a book, thinking I now rightfully own it. And yet, I do not actually own the contents of the book. The book's copyrighted material is owned by the publisher or the author (or sometimes even the author's grandchildren). The publisher's and the author's mutual contract of ownership might also entail that the author cannot do whatever they want with the text after publication. Whether it is the publisher or the author who owns the contents depends upon their, often very complicated, agreements and the copyright rules applying in the country of publication. What I have paid for is merely the right to read the book, in some cases the right to copy a few quotes in my own work if I make a formal reference to the original, but not to copy the entire book and sell it or even make it freely available online. The book market thus contains a number of particular rules that have been created to safeguard the interests of authors and publishers that differ fundamentally from those of other products.

Very few commodities and services are freely exchanged on the market without any rules or regulations. It is debatable how reasonable many of these are, but the idea of an entirely free market quickly appears dubious under closer scrutiny. For instance, what would a 'free market' for real estate look like? How would this market function if there were no regulations to protect property owners from the damage to their property value caused by a neighbour constructing a noisy and polluting factory next to them, by a high-rise building depriving them of sunlight or by razing a historical landmark? Or how should the rental market work at all if the previous contracts were rendered null and void by the transition to a new owner? Similarly, what would the book market look like without copyright? Could this market exist at all without the protection of intellectual property? Different commodities simply require different rules in order to function on the market at all. Other examples that can be mentioned are medication, foodstuff or construction. What would a free market without any regulations regarding the safety of drugs, foods or electrical installations look like?

If we were to remove all rules and regulations there would be nothing left to call a market. We often take the constitutive systems of rules for granted and do not realise how arbitrary these human-made systems are and to what degree they influence how the market behaves. But we must realise that the market – in itself – not only contains a lot of rules but, in a sense, *is* a collection of rules. We should therefore ask ourselves where these rules come from and whose purpose they serve. The pivotal question is then whose rules shall control the market and whose interests shall take precedence. Those of the company? The executives? The shareholders? The employees? The consumers? The state? Future generations?

We simply need rules to protect the interests of as many as possible. An entirely free market, one without any regulations, does not entail more freedom overall. On the contrary, the freedom of one person often entails less freedom for someone else. The freedom of property owners to evict their tenants for no particular reason violates the tenants' freedom from being made homeless, and the freedom to copy and freely distribute the contents of others' books violates the freedom of authors from having their intellectual property stolen. Similarly, the freedom of manufacturers to make products anyway they like is likely to violate the consumers' freedom from bodily harm.

Removing all regulations and believing it will lead to absolute freedom is simply not feasible. We always have to consider a large number of complex variables and carefully determine how we should regulate the system in order to achieve the most benevolent end-results. It is simply naive to believe that we once and for all can make the market as free as possible and then expect that it will also be good. A free market is not a virtue in itself. Freedom, in terms of fewer regulations, does not magically equal a more ethical market. Often, quite the contrary.

The Market's Two Invisible Hands

Different rules will yield different results on the self-organised market, both in terms of the number of commodities that are produced and how they are distributed. We should therefore strive towards designing the rules so that they maximise productive efficiency while also ensuring a distribution of wealth that is perceived as fair. Once the constitutive rules are optimal, there may still be a need to introduce regulative rules, but then in such a way that the loss of efficiency that often comes with regulative rules can be kept to a minimum. Admittedly, this is not an easy task. There are no clear answers to how we reach the perfect balance between these two aspects – especially not in an ever-changing world in which yesterday's solutions become inefficient tomorrow.

In football, for example, we want the game to be dynamic and exciting, but we also need it to be considered fair. Even if the offside rule may limit the efficiency with which players can score goals, it is necessary to prevent them from breaking the game by using the same exploitative tactic over and over again. Similarly, in order to ensure that people consider the market system fair, we need certain regulations to prevent the strong from exploiting the system at the expense of the weak. If football is not seen as fair, it ceases being a game. If the market economy, which has become such an integral part of our society, is seen as too unfair, if people do not experience that it serves their interests, they will eventually rise against the system and seek to demolish it. This can have very unfortunate consequences if there are no alternatives to replace it. If we think football is unfair, we may merely refuse to play along and do something else. But if we refuse to play along with existing market rules, we may succumb to a severe case of 'game denial' (denying that there will always be a 'game' among humans regarding economic transactions given the fact that resources and opportunities remain limited. Everyone cannot get everything, which means that we need game rules to determine what we are allowed to do to acquire these finite resources). Game denial regarding the market can make the efficiency aspect disproportionally neglected in favour of equality, which can then lead to increased poverty, corruption and often violence. Soviet communism and most recently the catastrophic developments in Venezuela are sad reminders of this. As such, it is better that we seek to regulate the current market in a way that ensures the optimal balance between efficiency and fairness. To do so, it is critical that we do not see market forces as given by nature, understand that Adam Smith's invisible hand is not that of God's, but something we can alter to deliver more desirable results.

Indeed, it would assist our understanding of the market as a self-organising system if we were to expand Smith's metaphor to comprise *two* invisible hands: one that bakes the pie and one that divides it. The first hand takes care of the non-zero-sum game regarding economic efficiency, the mechanisms responsible for baking as large and beautiful a pie as possible. When it comes to this invisible hand, all of us are more or less on the same side, everyone wants a large and beautiful pie from the oven of the market. As for the other hand, we all tend to desire a larger part of the pie for ourselves. Whether we are talking about corporate lobbying activists or the political parties serving the interests of low-income groups, they all strive to influence the market in ways that distribute a larger share of the total economic output to one group or the other. The way the market constantly balances out supply and demand so as to reach an equilibrium of maximum utility, as noted by Smith, is thus only one of its self-organising mechanisms. The other is the way in which a large number of agents seek to influence who gets what. This happens in several ways, such as companies acquiring government contracts, influencing legislation in ways that benefit their particular business models, sometimes at the expense of competitors, or advocating lower corporate tax. And then there are others who seek to redistribute more resources to public welfare, increase taxes for the wealthy or limit what can be privately owned. The first self-organising principle regarding supply and demand may appear more invisible than the second, since the numerous everyday transactions of the former are that much harder to account for than the more tangible results of the latter that end up in legislation. But the political market actors, if we use that term, make up just as much a self-organising mechanism as the economic ones. Just as the system self-organises itself through the self-interest of individuals when they purchase commodities, the very same self-interest is responsible for the way political actors seek to affect the rules of the market and thereby how its produce is distributed. The latter is just as little the result of any overall planning as the former. Both are the result of numerous conscious actions with the purpose of serving people's self-interests, which then gives rise to a complex, overarching self-organising structure no one has planned.

The ways in which economic assets are produced and circulate in the system are just as complex as the many internal and external rules and regulations making up its structures – both are intimately connected, one cannot exist without the other. Demand, as mentioned in chapter 8, is not a given and independent constant. It is derived from somewhere. As is supply. So whereas the first hand manages the balance between these two, the second determines who can supply what, how much, and to whom; and in turn what the demand then might be, who is demanding it, and what then becomes the optimal balance between supply and demand that the first hand seeks to reach. The balance between these is namely just as little a pre-given constant as each of these in isolation. What the market demands and what it can supply depends just as much on its constitutive and regulative rules, as the rules themselves depend on what the self-organising political process arrives at as the currently negotiated balance, determining who exactly should supply what and to whom. In simple terms, one hand bakes the pie, another slices it into pieces of varying sizes.

Once we realise that the way the market functions is a result not merely of individual consumers' decisions, but also of joint political decisions about its rules, we can no longer hide behind the idea of a free market. It is we who must take responsibility for the outcomes in the market. Whatever it does, we allow its doing.

If we understand this, questions arise about what we want the market to do, and which rules we believe will make that happen. In the following

The two 'invisible hands' of the market. One bakes the cake and the other divides it.[1] *Illustration: Charlie Norrman.*

I will attempt to answer these questions and make a couple of suggestions as to how we could make the market produce more desirable outcomes if we changed some of its rules.

TOWARDS A BETTER MARKET

Planned economies succumbed to bureaucratic inefficiency because planning became too complex. To be able to make decisions in a planned economy, the decision-makers must have sufficient knowledge of all supply and all demand and be able to balance these out without sacrificing too much efficiency. This rapidly proved an all too complex task to handle towards the end of the twentieth century. The market economy has shown more endurance. But will the market economy too succumb because of the economy becoming too complex? Is it possible that the self-organising mechanisms of the current market model, which in the past proved capable of matching the increasing complexity of the world, will eventually fail at handling the hypercomplex society of the future?

Under favourable circumstances, the invisible hands will organise the market in a way that reaches the optimal balance between supply and demand on one hand and efficiency and fairness on the other. But there is no invisible hand (other than the lobbyists) that helps the politicians create the best rules to govern the market. How regulation is affected by the continuous flow of information provided by numerous lobbying actors demanding new rules is a self-organising system. But the political process itself is *not* self-organising. What is decided or not decided as a result of this process does not automatically guarantee that the rules reaching the best compromise between society's many different special-interest groups will be implemented. Neither does it guarantee that the system as a whole manages to successfully accommodate the increasing complexity. If we fail at making the appropriate political decisions, we will risk that the market degenerates into a lower level of functionality just like when the communist planned economy succumbed to the growing demands of handling higher levels of complexity. However, with the market system it will probably not translate into empty store shelves in the near future. Rather, the contrary seems more likely to happen: an increased surplus of products that we do not really need, and that we waste precious ecological and social resources on.

Today, however, there is no alternative system to outcompete a degenerated market like the market economy of the West outcompeted the planned economy in the East. Had planned economics been without competition from an already existing alternative, it would probably still be around –

albeit even more inefficient. Cultural evolution often requires competition to advance at a faster pace. But where is the competition to our current market model? Would we be persuaded to deal with the market's problems without competition from an already existing, better-functioning market system? Will we bother to realise – and deal with – the problems of the market before we have used up our entire social and ecological capital? We simply do not know yet, but the lack of competition may prevent us from evolving fast enough. If we do not react in time, we risk reaching a point where we have consumed all the resources needed for a soft transition to a sustainable economy – with the end-result that there won't even be any stores to contain the products that we no longer manage to produce.

In the following I will present a few examples of how we might improve upon the current market system in order to, among other things, make it more sustainable.

HOW WE CAN MAKE A DIFFERENCE

As mentioned, the market consists of a number of internal and external rules and regulations that govern what the market is allowed to do. The question is how we relate to these and what we want them to accomplish. One way of preventing the market from creating things we do not want is by introducing bans on certain goods and services. Historically however, this has often proved quite a malicious path. Prohibition often creates even greater economic incentives for those who are willing to defy the ban. Since prohibition decreases the number of people willing to supply a certain commodity, the profits to be made grow that much larger. And given the risks associated with breaking the law, those who chose to do so can demand a comparably higher price for their commodities to compensate for this, thereby increasing the profitability of the enterprise even further.

The prohibition of alcohol in the United States in the 1920s is a good example of how bad things can go when a completely unregulated, underground market emerges as a response to a national ban on a highly sought-after commodity. It created major problems in terms of organised crime, violence and gangster bosses who gained as large an economic influence as many major corporate executives. The same can be said regarding the ban on cannabis and other illegal substances today. Simply banning a product does not take away the demand. And historical and contemporary examples provide plentiful evidence that outright prohibition rarely leads to the desired outcome of limiting consumption. Instead, the market simply reorganises itself by transferring the source of supply to more dubious channels. The result is actually a freer market, one free of taxation, regulation and the protection of the state. Moreover, it entails a wider number of unfortunate side-effects such as polluted and potentially lethal products, criminalised and imprisoned consumers and economic transactions based on coercion.

A better alternative is to try to change market forces by altering rules so as to attempt to generate more preferable outcomes. Lobbying organisations have long understood that the outcome of the market is shaped by its rules, and as activists and social entrepreneurs there is no shame in acquiring inspiration from their work methods. In this regard, the lobbying activities of the financial, pharmaceutical and media industries in the US can be particularly insightful. Various lobbying organisations have long been highly successful in influencing political decision-makers in various ways, not least through endowments, in the hope of sparking congressional decisions that serve corporate special interests. And since these conspiracies rarely become known to the public, the small risk of losing goodwill among the electorate has often left politicians willing to play along.

I am, of course, not arguing that these corporate lobbying organisations are paragons or that their activities amount to fair play, merely that we could learn from those who have actually changed how the market works. It is important that we realise, as the economic power elite already has, that it is crucial to change market forces so that they will be working for whatever we want to attain. Going against the market is rarely a productive strategy. The corporate lobbying strategies have proved so successful that they should serve as inspiration for those who want to change the market for the good of humankind.

In this regard, there are a number of areas in which we could direct our lobbying efforts that I will present in the following.

What We Could Do Differently – Copyright

In the case of copyright, there is an unfortunate discrepancy between the societal value of intellectual and cultural assets and that of their market value. For instance, if the media industries in Hollywood only had ten years of copyright applying to their products, their profits would definitely be reduced – but not very much: a film earns 80 per cent of its revenue during the first five years after its theatrical release. With films freely available after ten years, the societal benefit would, on the other hand, increase significantly. A cultural profit at the consumer level would thus translate into increased societal value.

One problem, however, is that our current bookkeeping systems only measure market value through the one-sided profit in the production and distribution chains. The benefit or damage that arises outside of these is not measured. Such gains and losses are termed *positive and negative externalities* in the standard economic model, in which they are seen as merely a disturbance to the equilibrium model. If an asset becomes freely available to consumers and the producers cease making profits from it, as when a film's copyright expires and the film falls into public domain, the desktop model of the economic system will report a loss in revenue in the economy as a whole. But the gains to the public will not be accounted for anywhere in our current economic measurements. It is merely apprehended as a loss in the corporate sector. For society as a whole it is actually accounted for as a reduction in GDP. This, however, does not have anything to do with a loss in economic utility. That people profit from the cultural asset without monetary transactions – which is the only thing our current models measure – is simply considered irrelevant.

The consequence is that something that increases societal value only receives negative headlines in the reports that are issued: lower profits, lower GDP and thus an apparent deterioration of the economy. But only on paper. The fact that society has been enriched beyond what can be measured in monetary terms is not accounted for and is therefore not visible in bookkeeping. It is the same with natural assets. Neither environmental degradation nor the availability of non-commercial natural areas for recreational activities make their way onto the desks of most contemporary economists. As negative externalities, our own and future generations' *common* costs of harm to the environment will not be included in these calculi.

If we could see societal gains in a larger perspective and made the copyright period shorter, it might also lead to further added value elsewhere. Other companies, consumers and artists would gain access to material for creative reuse and further alteration much sooner. Freely mixing the cultural accomplishments of long-deceased geniuses with old and new material, copying and pasting bits and pieces of our recent cultural heritage into new contexts and altering existing masterpieces in ways that make us see them from a new perspective – which already characterises the explosion of new creativity in burgeoning internet cultures – would definitely add to the overall level of creativity in society and thereby increase these works' societal value.

There are many era-defining songs and melodies, iconic film and literature characters and fictional Universes that play as large a role in our public imagination as the works of Homer did to the ancient Greeks, but unfortunately will remain copyrighted material for a considerable time. Currently, a copyright expires seventy years after the death of its creator, and for works of corporate authorship 120 years after creation or ninety-five years after publication, whichever is earlier.[2] This, however, is likely to be extended even further due to corporate interests. The Disney corporation has successfully lobbied for an extension of the copyright period every time Mickey Mouse has been close to entering public domain. As a result, much of what has been produced during the twentieth century remains the intellectual property of large media companies or the descendants of dead artists. In terms of societal value, this is rather unfortunate.

Our shared culture does not only consist of century-old classics, the *Bildung* of our times consists just as much of more recent additions. Many of the cultural references that have made their way into our common symbol world today stem from popular culture of the last century. *Star Wars* and Mickey Mouse, Elvis and The Beatles, these are just a few examples of cultural phenomena that have become an integrated part of our culture, and thereby just as important to be acquainted with as Odysseus and Mozart. These treasures give us a shared language by enabling us to use cultural references to express what we mean. Since others know the very same symbols, characters and narratives, things that would otherwise be hard to put into a single sentence can be more easily conveyed, and with greater accuracy. If someone asks us to 'use the force' and not be tempted by 'the dark side', or if they say that a particular societal development resembles George Orwell's *1984*, those of us who know the *Bildung* of today immediately know what they mean. References like these can help us articulate complex matters in simple terms since we can make use of all the nuances and intricate meanings of these works. Unfortunately, we cannot use the fictional character of Darth Vader or use explicit references to the Ministry of Truth in our own work without risking being sued by the Disney corporation or the copyright holders of Orwell's bibliography – the latter of whom recently sued a person for printing '1984 is already here' on some t-shirts.[3] But imagine if the same applied to the works of Homer. How would Greek culture have evolved if the ancient Greeks were forced to pay royalties to the great-grandchildren of Homer every time they used the *Iliad* and the *Odyssey*? Their culture would probably have been somewhat poorer if our current copyright laws had applied back then.

But if a copyright expired after ten or twenty years, or simply after the death of its creator, independent artists of little means could use many of our most important and widely known cultural phenomena in their work without getting sued. This could bring new life to the classics and enrich experimental artworks by adding something familiar to the unfamiliar. If copyrights expired earlier, the many symbolic constructions from popular culture that have become part of our shared symbol world, in which they have come to live a life of their own, and hence at least culturally can be said to have entered public domain, could then increase their overall utility. Freely adding a clip of Humphrey Bogart kissing Ingrid Bergman from the movie *Casablanca* – arguably the most perfect kiss in cinematic history – to a music video can enhance the message of a new love song, and playing David Bowie's song 'Space Oddity' during a scene in a movie can likewise increase the emotional impact of watching the film by triggering the memories associated with listening to this song many of us have had. The reuse of culturally iconic masterpieces can enhance our experience of new artistic productions – and thereby increase their societal value – because so many of us have had powerful emotional experiences of beauty and meaning from watching classic movies like *Casablanca* or listening to the compositions of Bowie. But complicated copyright laws often decrease their societal value. Recently, an entire video game was removed from the market since its licence to continue using, among others, Bowie's 'Space Oddity' expired.[4] This not only made the world poorer in terms of one less cultural product being available, it even impacted the future profits the video game producer could have made from keeping their game on the market. It is hard to imagine that the late David Bowie, who himself showed an interest in digital games as an artform and who even appeared in one, would have objected to their continuous use of his song from 1969.

The outcome of making copyrights expire earlier would not simply be increased societal value, as companies would also be able to make more profits from using older material to add additional value to new productions. Profits in the economy as a whole would probably also increase if companies did not constantly worry about copyright infringement and if they wasted fewer resources on lawsuits regarding intellectual property.

So what could we do to improve the system? First of all, copyrights should be much shorter than they are today. Generally, they should not last long after the death of the copyrighted material's creator. Another possibility is that we make different rules depending on what kind of product we are talking about and who is producing them. Independent authors and books could enjoy longer-lasting copyrights, bigger corporations and blockbuster movies comparable shorter ones. This would protect the livelihood of intellectually significant writers and increase the societal value of having a large number of movies freely available to the public respectively. In addition, the state could charge companies for the service of protecting their intellectual property – which can be a costly endeavour to the state when big companies use the courts to prosecute people who have violated their copyrights. Instead of granting copyrights free of charge, the state could thus sell these rights for a certain amount. The first five or ten years could, for instance, be free, but if the company wished to extend their copyright for an additional ten or twenty years, they could be required to pay a fee. In this way the state could tap into the profits from the cultural productions of large corporations so as to cover the expenses of their use of the legal system. And if the company deems an extension of a copyright unprofitable, the copyrighted material's entrance into the public domain could thus make profits in term of increased societal value. The dynamic effects of such externalities could potentially be that someone managed to extract additional value from an unprofitable movie by using its contents in a way that people would enjoy more than the original.

In this way we might even be able to revive the original spirit of intellectual property rights by prioritising the purpose of encouraging the creativity and ensuring the livelihood of natural persons (musicians, authors, artists). If the creative work of individual persons enjoyed longer copyrights than that of corporations, and if only the former received this right free of charge, we would be likely to ensure the continuous productivity of creative individuals, while avoiding the impediment on further cultural development caused by large corporations' endless lawsuits against anyone who creates works with even the slightest resemblance to their copyrighted material long after their productions have been released.

On the whole, we ought to re-establish the individual as the central actor on the market. In today's market society, the individual is totally dwarfed by big corporations. In practice, and even if the same rights apply to natural as well as purely legal personhoods, the complicated laws on intellectual property and the legal difficulties regarding copyright infringement tend to favour large corporations who have the means to hire expensive and highly specialised attorneys. Individual citizens, whether they are the owners of intellectual property copied by a company or are accused of violating the copyright of a company, often do not stand a chance in these court proceedings. The costs are just too high for modestly successful writers or artists.

The purpose of copyright should not be to serve the financial interests of big corporations at the expense of private citizens. It was initially intended to encourage innovations and creativity in society at a whole. If it on the contrary inhibits creativity and the further development of others' work, and in addition has become a money machine for already highly profitable organisations, we should start lobbying for changing the rules in a way that increases the societal value of cultural assets.[5]

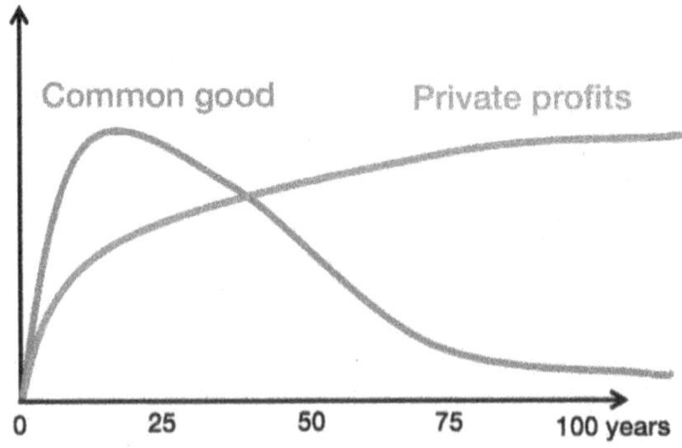

Copyright does not only stimulate new production but also blocks innovative reuse of older material. Private and common interests strive in different directions when it comes to how long a copyright should last.[6]

What We Could Do Differently – Limited Companies

The particular way our corporate laws and many internal rules in large companies are articulated may appear self-evident and logically necessary. However, they are more contingent than they initially appear. Since many companies use the same internal rules to govern their decision-making processes, it is tempting to suggest that they do so out of necessity. But on closer scrutiny, they are often shaped by rather arbitrary historical processes and tend to depend on customs and conventions rather than case-specific considerations. As shareholders, for instance, we usually have the right to exercise our influence once every year. But why exactly should this depend on how many days it takes for the Earth to do a lap around the sun? In some cases, it could actually be preferable to do this more often or make it an on-going process. Just because the merchants in Venice during the Italian Renaissance thought it was appropriate to gather to make decisions each spring does not mean that this should also be the case in all situations today.

Our corporate laws have emerged from historical coincidences and particular conditions in the past, but we are actually free to redesign them if we like. Indeed, it would probably be advantageous if we did. In the course of centuries, the legal entity of a limited company that we have today emerged from the needs of balancing the interests of governments, those of the public and that of creating financial security and incentives for investments. Sometimes one of these priorities took primacy, sometimes another. The company has evolved through a number of different societal conditions that it had to be adapted to, from the guild system of the late medieval period, over the mercantilist economy of the colonial era, to the industrial factory economy of the nineteenth century. At every era, changes were made in order to compromise between the interests of the state, civil society and capital owners. During the mercantilist age, a corporation could own slaves and employ troops to occupy large tracts of land in foreign countries. This model was then abandoned during the industrial age, when civil society's concerns with the liberty of individuals led to the abolition of slavery and the state's need for security and stability made the government take over the trading corporation's territorial possessions. Today, a corporation cannot own human beings, employ soldiers or invade foreign countries (we take that for granted, but history teaches us that it could be different), which obviously inhibits the extent of corporate interests over those of others. But it has been a long time since there have been any substantial changes to the way we legally define a company. It is basically the same construct as the one we had in the industrial age, albeit the companies we have today are much larger and sometimes even more powerful than states.

This obviously begs the question whether a more successful compromise could be reached if we re-envisioned the limited company today. Since our current society is based on democratic principles and large corporations have such unprecedented influence, should these not also be governed by democratic decision processes? And if industrial companies are responsible for the environmental destruction of our planet, would it then not be sensible to make ecological sustainability a legal requirement and a purpose-driven objective to be rewarded in the same way as financial profitability? Currently, neither of these are part of the constitutive rules pertaining to corporations; not because that is inconceivable and defeats the purpose of a limited company, but because there are yet to be any historical processes to include these aspects.

The rules and regulations pertaining to the limited company are as aforementioned to a considerable degree the result of historical processes that could have been different. An aspect that potentially could have been different if the company evolved along a slightly alternative historical path is that of the types of stakeholders with legal consideration in the rule sets of companies. If we imagine that profit-making companies had emerged earlier and thus been shaped by moral considerations of the public interest that characterised production and trade during the medieval period, it would not have been entirely impossible that other stakeholders than just capital owners would enjoy legal rights in contemporary corporate law. Since many of the principles that permeated the economy during the

Middle Ages are similar to those of the kind of social entrepreneurship that only recently has started to become influential, this could perhaps have appeared much earlier. But, as it turned out, the particular societal and economic conditions in Western Europe during the early modern period and the colonial conquests around the world led to a constitutive rule set where only shareholders have any legal rights to decide the faith of the company – that is, as long as they fulfil their duties to their creditors, who are the only stakeholders whose interests enjoy higher legal priority.

Clearly this does not always serve the interests of the public. First of all, the workers, the consumers and the local community have no say in regards to a company and thereby little opportunity to have their interests taken into consideration. What is most profitable to the owners is often at odds with the interests of other stakeholders, including those of future generations. That the legal construct of the company only prioritises the interests and rights of capital holders often leads to decisions being made that do not favour the greater good, not least when the rights of creditors stand above all other concerns. This can often have catastrophic consequences when insolvent companies, which nonetheless fulfil crucial functions in society, are forcefully closed, stripped apart and sold for a fraction of their actual value. The overall societal value of jobs, particular productive capabilities and dynamic effects of a company in a local community often outweighs that of a few impatient creditors. But the latter still enjoy greater legal consideration in our current system.

Sometimes the greater societal value becomes such a pressing issue that the state needs to intervene, even though there are no purely legal imperatives to do so, such as when the US government decided to bail out General Motors following the financial crisis in 2008. At about the same time, governments around the world did the same with the major banks – the very creditors responsible for the crisis. If the market had been allowed to organise itself in accordance with the constituent rules without any exemption in intervention into the business of those failing to meet their legal obligations – which is the whole point of having these rules to begin with – the banks would have had to obey the 'will' of the market and gone bust. After all, the whole system was designed to prioritise the interests of creditors over other concerns. In the end, however, the damage to the greater good was considered too high to be left to the self-organising mechanisms of the market, hence governments circumvented the rules that had otherwise run their course outside the banking sector. The purpose was, of course, to protect the overall interests of society and not the creditors as such. However, since the banks were not kept accountable for their poorly managed business models, the price for serving the immediate interests of the public was a further economic and political imbalance in favour of corporate interests. The disproportionate increase in the market system's priority of the interests of capital owners that occurred during the thirty years before the crisis had made the banks 'too big to fail', which then became the position of strength from which they could increase their influence even further at the expense of others. Yet if the constitutive rules had been better adapted to accommodate the explosive growth of the financial sector and managed to balance out the interests of other groups, the unfortunate exigency to bypass the rules could probably have been avoided.

It barely needs mentioning that if the outcomes of the rules are so intolerable that exceptions must be made, the rules most urgently need to be changed. It generally compromises the whole system if people are subjected to rules and very well know the consequences if things go badly, but then get special treatment in case they actually fail. What then makes them expect the rules will apply the next time – especially if no substantial changes have been made? The unbalanced emphasis on profit motives and the narrow interests of capital owners written into the legal structure of our banks and other limited companies were largely responsible for the financial crisis. But if the modern corporation had evolved more closely from the manufacturing and trading companies of the medieval guild system, and thus had come to be governed by constitutive rules that prioritised the interests of other stakeholders, we could have seen a very different historical trajectory in which crises such as the one in 2008 would have been unlikely to occur.

Another historical coincidence that could have been different is the curious case of legal personhood for companies. That such artificial entities are legally equal to that of natural persons is far from self-evident. In fact, most people tend to be surprised by this circumstance the first time they hear about it. Since it is rather counterintuitive that natural persons are not considered legally above companies, it is thus easy to imagine an alternative historical development where the rights of individuals enjoyed higher protection vis-à-vis companies. If so, this could for instance have led to a higher proportion of cases where courts ruled in favour of individual humans rather than companies. We could also imagine that the legal notion of personhood would have entailed many of the things we expect from individuals, such as good public behaviour, helping others in times of need (it is actually a criminal offence to refuse someone help if their life and safety is in danger) and the obligation to serve one's country (like that of compulsory military duty). Since companies are not as frail and mortal as we humans and generally have much larger resources at their disposal, such societal obligations could have been adapted to reflect these facts. There could thus be legal requirements for companies to spend a share of their resources on civic duties, such as the maintenance of public infrastructure in their surroundings, making their facilities available for various public activities or providing security measures in case of national emergencies. If capable, companies would thus be legally required to assist if accidents or disasters were to occur, similar to the conduct expected of individual citizens when others are in danger. We could also imagine that companies would be banned from destroying their surplus production and be legally required to donate it to the public, or that they would be obliged to participate in public hearings beyond purely legal matters where they had to listen to the interests of the public.

There is also a significant discrepancy between the legal repercussions applying to natural persons and corporate personhoods. If humans break the law they can get a prison sentence with severe personal consequences as a result. If a company breaks the law, it mainly risks financial penalties

– which can often be worth it. Even if managers can get prison sentences if they go against the law, the financial incentives of their company can be so great that they are encouraged to take the risk nevertheless – with the prospect of considerable legal assistance from expensive lawyers and support from government officials on the company's payroll in case they get caught. Since companies have far greater capabilities of circumventing the legal system than natural persons, it is not unreasonable to demand that legislation should attempt to accommodate this fact by setting higher standards for companies and imposing more severe penalties when they break the law. Fines should therefore not be the only repercussion, but also include other punitive measures such as prison sentences for owners and board members overseeing the criminal conduct of managers, revoking the owners' voting rights for a period and dismissing the current board members in favour of new ones chosen by the court, or perhaps even nationalisation with the purpose of auctioning it to the public.

Even when it does not entail any legal violations, individuals are often subject to social repercussions when they behave indecently and fail to comply with the prevailing standards of good behaviour. Given their comparably larger resources, the extent to which companies can misbehave without being penalised is therefore considerably greater. To ensure that companies do not behave in ways that are otherwise considered socially unacceptable, there could thus be institutionalised arenas to scrutinise their societally immoral, but technically legal, actions and various punitive measures to encourage changes in their behaviour. Some of these things do exist in some forms and to varying degrees, but if we were to treat corporate personhoods in ways that paralleled their power, such measures would probably be more comprehensive.

I am not advocating that we should necessarily make all of the above changes to the current system, merely that it is possible to imagine that corporate law could have been different if history had taken a different course. Some of these examples could serve as inspiration for improvements.

There are, however, some amendments that I believe could provide more efficiency and justice to the current system:

1. Other stakeholders than owners and creditors should be given legal consideration and rights in limited companies. If employees and the local community were given voting rights and representation on the board of directors, the decision-making process would be likely to serve the interests of more people. And if societal concerns were written into corporate law and better balanced in relation to that of the profit motives of creditors and shareholders, the risks of societally important facilities being dismantled or government resorting to bailouts would be smaller.
2. The introduction of other types of bottom lines beyond the purely financial, for instance a social and an environmental one. If a company has a very negative bottom line in terms of social responsibility and ecological sustainability, it should be subjected to external control and demands for change in the same way a negative financial bottom line does in relation to its creditors. If all companies were expected to present a positive social and ecological bottom line, the companies who emphasise these would not be at a competitive disadvantage in relation to those who do not.
3. Shareholders should be given greater influence and extended obligations, such as keeping the board accountable for ensuring that production is socially and environmentally sustainable, that the company upholds its ethical codex, and that the company upholds its responsibilities to the local community.
4. Limited companies' status of personhood should be restricted and made secondary to that of natural persons. Companies should still be treated as single legal entities, but this should not entail the same rights as those of individual citizens such as the right to influence politics, unrestricted freedom of expression or liberty to always do with their property as they please. Since large companies

have overwhelmingly more power than individual citizens, it can endanger our democracy if we give them the same rights. A system in which the rights of natural persons are above those of artificially conceived legal entities could balance out the disproportionate power of corporations in favour of the former.

5. Finally, we should create a number of new legal corporate forms that better encourage social entrepreneurship, sustainability and other purposes than profit alone. The current system primarily favours organisations that are either driven by profit incentives or purely devoted to charity. There is little legal consideration for those in between. But since many of the companies with the greatest prospects of fostering higher social and ecological sustainability are a kind of hybrid organisation, legislation should be adapted to better accommodate their particular needs. Many companies that strictly speaking are not non-profit organisations are still founded on other purpose-driven principles than profit and managed by decision processes, such as sociocracy and holacracy,[7] involving more stakeholders than traditional profit-driven companies. Often, they also contain alternative notions of ownership. These kinds of companies currently have very little support in legislation. Changing corporate law in ways that gave such company forms higher legal recognition and protection, made them easier to register and institutionalised their principles could assist the transition to more socially responsible and ecologically sustainable business models.

The above suggestions would increase our capacity to manage the many social and environmental challenges since they would ensure that priorities other than profit would be given consideration and that the interests of the state, civil society, the individual and capital holders became more equally balanced. It would also make society more democratic, since workers and other stakeholders would be given a voice regarding how we as a society organise production and what purposes we want it to serve. Thus far, democracy only extends as far as who we want to govern the state. While on the job as wage-earners, we still live in a dictatorship. But if we changed the constitutive rules of companies, even the productive domain of society could be made democratic.

What We Could Do Differently – Taxation

All economists agree that taxes have negative effects on the efficiency of the market. In my view, it would therefore be better to make the market outcome different at the outset. By doing so, we would also avoid the feeling of something rightfully deserved being taken from us. The reason for the existence of taxation is, of course, that the acquisition of economic assets with military means, basically robbing people, was the only way for the rulers of the past to fill the state coffers. We have merely inherited this system, and the principle is the same: if you don't pay your taxes, the state's monopoly on violence will make sure that you do. Yet if we defined the market better from the start, we would not need as extensive a redistribution system as the one we have now. Our Stone Age brains would then not make us feel robbed of something considered honestly earned. It is unwise to go against human psychology, although we may be irrational. So even if it technically does not make much difference whether we receive a large sum to begin with only to pay back a proportion later or whether we receive a smaller sum without the need for further redistribution, in psychological terms it is always preferable to aim for the latter.

Income taxation could be replaced by a system in which the state derived its revenue from property rights, for example if all natural resources were considered the shared property of every citizen. All exploitation of natural resources – anything from oil extraction to air pollution – would then incur a fee. A similar system already exists in the US state of Alaska, whose inhabitants are considered the joint owners of the state's oil resources, receiving an annual dividend accordingly.[8] A similar principle could, if the political will is available, be implemented to encompass all of our limited natural resources. Another source of revenue could be that of fees on copyrights, as previously mentioned.

As consumers we could also be charged for our use of natural resources when we purchase physical products and properties. This does in fact exist in most countries in the form of value-added tax (VAT) and yearly property taxes. The advantage of taxing people when they purchase a product is that it does not cause the same psychological penalty as income taxation. If the state derived a larger share of its revenues from VAT on physical products and to a lesser degree from income tax, it would probably make the taxation system more frictionless and thereby increase society's overall economic efficiency. It could even improve ecological sustainability and increase employment. Higher VAT would entail higher prices on physical products and lower income tax would lower the price on human labour. In this way it could become more cost-efficient to pay people to repair and renovate old products rather than to buy new ones. The environment would benefit greatly and people struggling to find manual employment in our current hi-tech information economy would get new opportunities to make a living. This development could be further encouraged by higher VAT on environmentally damaging products and lower VAT – if any – on services.

Higher property tax is another source of income that could compensate for the loss of revenue to the state if we were to abolish income tax. The advantage of taxing property is that it prevents a small number of property owners from enriching themselves at the expense of people with low incomes – who actually pay a form of tax to the owners by paying rent. Higher property tax could thus ensure that a proportion of the property owners' profits came to serve the greater good. It would also encourage productive labour rather than speculation since the gains of owning real estate would be that much lower. As a result, society would likely become more equal, with fewer people owning a disproportionately large share of all available property, while ambitious people would probably be more inclined towards using their skills and energy on more productive endeavours than speculating in real estate. Since the richest individuals primarily derive their wealth from property and not actual work, higher property tax could compensate for the relative inequality caused by lower income tax and higher VAT.

If we abolished income taxation, it could even save resources that would otherwise have been wasted on unproductive bureaucratic measures to ensure that people pay their taxes. The amount of resources available to the state, all things being equal, would, of course, be more or less the same whether adjustments were made through the market or after the market. But the psychological effects would be completely different by making people less frustrated and less inclined to work against the system. Whether the state derives its funds from the production and sale of environmentally damaging products or organic foods and services requiring little else than human muscle and brain power does not in financial terms make a difference either. But in terms of the increased societal value gained from more environmentally sustainable consumption patterns, higher equality on the property market and service jobs that would otherwise be unprofitable, the difference could be a more resilient and sustainable market system.

LET US CREATE A BETTER MARKET

It is impossible to imagine our current world without the market. The market is the primary engine of production and creativity, and its efficiency is central for our welfare and security. Every day we make political decisions that influence how the market works. These decisions should always be seen in relation to the three crucial aspects of society – efficiency, fairness and meaning – so that we may ask ourselves the following:

- **Efficiency:** are we using the market in the best conceivable way? Is the market the best tool in a particular case, or should we use a different one to better accomplish what we want to do? In simple terms, will the market be able to bake the pie?

- **Fairness:** what distributive effects will our decisions have? Who will be the winners and who will be the losers? Can we design the rules differently to create fewer losers? How will the market, given these new rules, divide the pie?
- **Meaning:** what other human values, aside from economic efficiency, do we strive for on a particular issue? Ecological and social sustainability, cultural enrichment, or perhaps existential meaning? And how do we safeguard these values? Will the pie look the way we wish when we take it out of the oven?

If our political decisions regarding the market were based on informed discussions about its efficiency at carrying on particular tasks, how to make it generate fairer outcomes and what exactly we want it to accomplish, we would be more likely to create a better-functioning market – decisions based on ideologically inclined convictions of being either for or against the market simply won't. Although I am critical of the market being allowed to penetrate parts of society where it does not belong, the secular market society still remains the best foundation from which to build a better future society in my view. Even if there is a connection between the market and neoliberal, postmodern emptiness, this does not mean it cannot be used for the good. In fact, it may be one of the most powerful tools at our disposal.

A hundred years ago it was much easier to get an overview of the market economy than it is today. In those days it was usually sufficient to think in terms of linearly conceived economic plans where the most important variables were accounted for, and further economic development was more predictable. Central planning functioned fairly well for a time, but during the twentieth century the world became too complex for this to ensure efficiency. The Soviet Union collapsed for the very reason that their linear way of economic thinking no longer worked. The world had become too complex. The market economy has worked better at coordinating this complexity, but recently there have been signs that we are no longer guaranteed that it will organise itself to produce the most desirable outcomes. The economy is growing, albeit slower than before, but new technologies, a vast and uncontrollable global financial market and burgeoning economies in the developing world have made it more difficult to create sufficiently well-considered economic policies. We also need to consider new phenomena such as climate change and the surprising insight that increased GDP does not automatically equal higher levels of satisfaction and continuous social advancement. There are truly more variables to consider in our hypercomplex global information society today than back when we could create a sufficiently accurate overview of the economy from the perspective of the industrial nation-state. As such, we need to increase our capacity to grasp and manage complexity above what we have previously been used to.

There is currently a growing chorus of voices saying that liberal democracy no longer works. For many it is clear that democracy in its present form has failed at fostering increased equality, that it no longer provides believable prospects of better opportunities for all, and that it cannot protect our natural environment from destruction. Others call for strong leaders who can take us back to a simpler world where we do not need to worry about globalisation, climate change or refugees, and where we can find comfort in traditional family life and trusted national and religious identities.

But there is no way back. We cannot rewind the clock and close our borders to the world, bring back the jobs in factories and mines and once again make economic plans along the lines of the industrial nation-state while we happily ignore the climate changes ravaging the Earth. Over fourteen billion years the complexity of our world has consistently increased and accelerated. It has always brought new challenges with it, and those who have not adapted in time have always succumbed to their inability to develop new complexity themselves.

The market as we conceive it today is a myth that worked well in the industrial age. But it remains a social construction that we largely imagine, not an objective fact that could not be different. It is important that we become aware of this fact if we are to change it to better accommodate increasing complexity. In the same way that we could not leave the religious thought perspective behind us before a sufficient number of us started seeing God as a social imaginary that we ourselves had created, a larger proportion of the population in modern society needs to see the market as a similar socially constructed myth if we are to move forwards. When we do that, we can see it as an object for manipulation, rather than blindly experiencing it as an all-encompassing reality that we do not grasp we are mentally embedded in.

Previously, society *was* a religion. Now we *have* a religion – or not. This is because we developed the ability to see it as an object rather than being embedded in it. Today, however, we still *are* a market economy. In the future, we could develop to the point where we *have* a market economy. But for this to happen, we need to see it from a mental distance, just like that of religion. Today in particular, where there are no visible alternatives to the market and market forces have come to penetrate ever more aspects of our lives and culture, this is getting increasingly difficult. That which just a few generations ago was still being debated and carefully institutionalised has now been firmly internalised in our shared symbol world to a degree that most do not remember that things could be any different. As such, it becomes harder to see the market as the arbitrary human construction it is. It has simply become a natural fact of life. It has become to us as water is to the fish.

The next and final part of this book will be devoted to how we develop our psychological capacity to become aware of the things we are currently embedded in, how we develop our society and culture to accommodate ever-increasing complexity and what a future thought perspective and new highest authority to outcompete postmodernism and the current market god could possibly look like.

PART 3

Going Beyond God, Science and The Market

INTRODUCTION TO PART 3

Now, here in Part 3, we finally arrive at creating our future. But to do so, we need to reckon with the fact that we live in a world of ever-increasing complexity, and the pace at which it becomes more complex is accelerating rapidly. The burgeoning complexity is both a danger and an opportunity: a danger, because it threatens to overwhelm our institutions and ability to make prudent decisions; an opportunity, because it is only in such testing times that we are given the means and incentives for taking substantial leaps into the future. Given the risks, it speaks to our hearts as well as our heads that we can be forerunners of a fairer, more meaningful and efficient way of doing, and becoming.

But it certainly isn't easy. As global, regional and national interconnections and interdependencies increase, the requirement for cooperation – something we cannot admirably achieve if thinking from limited perspectives, and in fragmented fashion – increases too. Complication, as a function of greater quantities of connection, and moreover complexity, as a function of more qualitatively different components, structures and networks, all raise the stakes for our civilisation. The number of moving parts is bewildering; especially as we discover that the world is more non-linear and chaotic than we anticipated just fifty years ago. Most incisively, our default patterns of thinking are less astutely rational, and more prone to bias and tribalism, than our cosy rationalist thought perspective would have liked to admit. Nonetheless, we are not doomed to micro-narrative fragmentation and intellectual Balkanisation, as postmodernism might imply.

We face innumerable interconnected crises – a 'meta-crisis' – all while we also paradoxically enjoy the highest standards of living (at least in the first world) ever seen. The disruption that characterises our quickened pace of living requires faster information processing; the quantity of informational inputs across all our systems requires magnified responsibility also. Most decisively, this does not merely quantitatively complicate our decision making, it complexly adds layers of abstract reality to manage. Thus, while our agency is often already constrained by social, cognitive and cultural deficiencies and obstacles, we are now expected to deal with voluminous tasks of varied types and degrees, all at a faster pace. The tentacles of these struggles also stretch far further, often globally, and are knotted in a Gordian fashion, ensuring even collective actors such as states or regional bodies find solutions to international security, climate change and sustainability not just elusive, but sometimes entirely daunting at their scale. Recent political developments, such as the risks of unhinged populism, arrive at just the time we need more expertise, humility and intelligence, not less. Following the lead of such simple answerers of complex questions risks us repeating, or exacerbating, the linear errors of planning – even failing to plan at all. These trends and countertrends thus all serve to cluster confusion, mental ill-health and societal stasis. Hence, we increasingly see, and feel, a loss of agency and the dangers of potential fatalism emerging. Brexit, the election of Donald Trump and insufficient action following the symbolic hope of the Paris Accords provide concrete examples of these troubling trajectories.

Part 3 then takes up the task of addressing these wicked problems, at systemic levels, and by building on the rich resources we have gathered from Part 1's history, and Part 2's theoretical and empirical appraisals of our systems.

Chapter 11

AN INCREASINGLY COMPLEX WORLD

THE rising complexity of modern society has also caused less obvious maladies than global inequality and environmental destruction which some of the more sophisticated social critics tend to point out, such as: lack of meaning, alienation and a lost sense of community, stress and anxiety, life being more complicated and confusing, increasing mental illness, and other socio-psychological issues of a high level of complexity and dependent on a multitude of reasons that do not reveal themselves easily with more linear analyses. And recently, we have seen a growing number of scholars warn us about all the new technologies that very soon will be part of our daily lives and completely change how our societies work, and even threaten our very existence, such as: artificial intelligence and robotics, nanotechnology, new advances in biotechnology, human genetic manipulation, quantum computing, autonomous drones performing a countless number of tasks (that may even include that of killing people), and a multitude of other revolutionising technologies that all have it in common that we are yet to figure out how to relate to them politically. The world is changing fast, and if we are not sufficiently foresighted and carefully consider how we shall tackle these changes, it is reasonable to predict that more things will be worse than better.

If we are to approach an answer to the question of where the increasing complexity comes from, I would like to suggest these four points:

1. Increased *technological complexity* – that we have greater knowledge and thereby a greater amount of technology, more tools, which we constantly must relate to.
2. The increasing power or efficiency in technological tools (and that they use greater energy flows). This causes the effects, the consequences, of technology to have a much wider scope, both in time and space. The consequences of our decisions thereby become harder to foresee. Think atomic bomb and climate change. We may call this an increased *consequence complexity*.
3. The increased *speed* in technological development. Great technology shifts previously occurred over several generations. The human being could more easily adapt. Now, during our lifetime, we constantly have to relate to new technological realities. Think cell phone, the internet and AI. We might call this a *dynamic complexity* – that the world changes ever faster.

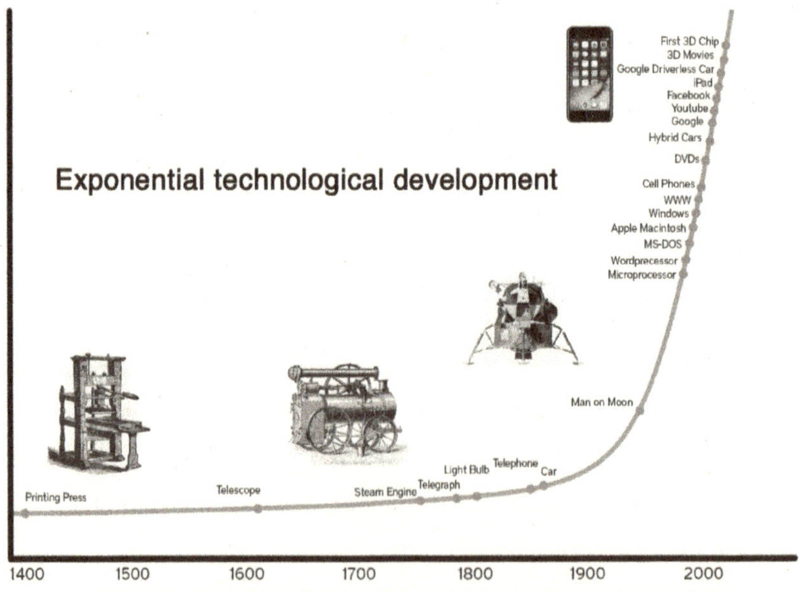

With the exponential technological development follows an exponential increase in complexity in our human world.

4. Increased *subjective complexity* – that we no longer live in a monocultural society where we easily can understand each other's inner worlds and meaning creation. In order to understand our fellow humans today we must be able to handle many different cultural perspectives – other humans' extremely varying subjective experiences of the world.

Symbolic language has enabled consciousness to interact with increasingly complex and abstract phenomena. To abstract means to 'draw something out', being able to see decisive patterns that constitute that which is most relevant, in some sense the kernel of a phenomenon. So abstraction for us in this sense moves us *closer* to reality, not further from it. When the symbolic language has advanced in complexity, people have been able to interact with themselves, each other and nature in a more trenchant way. Therein we have also been able to fulfil more of our needs. And there are now more of us. And the distances between us have been reduced. And the exchange of information has become simpler and cheaper. And suddenly we have awoken to a curious rushing, interconnected world system that is developing in a direction that we are somewhat unclear about.

MANAGING COMPLEXITY

As individual people we might find it increasingly difficult to handle the new complexity. The world becomes odd, amorphous, contradictory and deeply confusing. This has a string of various consequences. One of the clearest is that psychological health is undermined. This might be a large part of the explanation for the trend of increased anxiety, depression and a host of psychiatric diagnoses. The complexity quite simply puts steep demands on our psyches: a world that is all too multilayered and difficult to interpret makes us hesitant and our inner conceptual worlds are threatened.

It is not only we ourselves as individuals that do not manage the existing complexity. It is increasingly clear that our societal institutions have serious problems. It is convenient to interpret the increase in extreme right-wing and populist forces as an expression of the imbalance between society's complexity and our own simplicity of world view and thought perspectives. During 2016, the United Kingdom voted to leave the European Union (Brexit) through a referendum and Donald Trump was elected president of the United States on a platform of increased protectionism and reduced immigration. This might be an expression of many people creating simplified stories of reality in the lack of more complex frameworks of understanding.

LEVELS OF COMPLEXITY

We are facing problems of different complexity in our daily lives. Some problems are simpler, some more complex. The same problem can also be viewed with more or less complex thinking. For simple problems, a simple way of thinking is more efficient than a more complex way of thinking. We should not over-complexify problems. We do not have time to do that in everyday situations, and evolution has given us a presence for simple and efficient thinking. But often problems are more complex than they might first appear and we need to employ more complex ways of thinking than we perhaps usually do. Here we will focus on the specific aspect of cognitive complexity and look at what different levels of complex thinking enable us to do. The following is based on a model by Thomas Jordan and Pia Andersson from Gothenburg University that in a simple and perspicuous way ranks different levels of thinking on a scale from one to four.[1]

1. The Category Level

The category level is the most rudimentary level of cognitive complexity. Here we perceive problems and other phenomena separately without any notable reflections on their possible underlying causes. Our awareness is limited to concrete occurrences, and it is mainly these we react to, have opinions about, and want to do something about.

Let us, for example, look at the problem of city-centre vandalism. At the category level, we may become frustrated and angry about instances of vandalism. However, since we do not see the underlying causal contexts and relationships, our proposals are unlikely to alleviate or influence these underlying factors. To the extent we have any explanations at all, they mostly revolve around the character traits of the vandals, such as lacking respect, a destructive attitude, etc. Yet we do not ask ourselves why the perpetrators lack respect or why they happen to behave destructively.

Since the chains of cause and effect leading to the problem are not part of the picture, the remedies then become narrowly oriented towards direct measures to prevent the concrete occurrence. In the example of vandalism, it may revolve around physical measures such as more robust building materials, increased surveillance and deterring forms of punishment. These actions can be effective, but since they are not directed towards the underlying causes, they rarely prevent the problem from repeating itself.

It is also characteristic of this level that we do not reflect upon what undesired effects our counter-measures may possibly have in a larger perspective. Such reflections presuppose that we think in terms of more complex cause-and-effect connections, both as explanations for what has already occurred but also in terms of possible future consequences. This often results in quite near-sighted thinking: focus is limited to concrete, delimited matters and problems without closer consideration of more abstractedly conceived prerequisites and contexts.

2. The Connection Level

On the connection level we attempt to identify and analyse the underlying causal connections when exposed to a problem. On the issue of vandalism we may seek to find and understand the chains of cause and effect leading to someone vandalising. We then focus on different types of causal connections beyond the problem per se, for instance how youth gangs are formed and develop certain dynamics, how unemployment and idleness may lead to anti-social behaviour, or perhaps even the significance of absent parents in young people's lives.

To the extent that we focus on such underlying connections we not only direct our actions towards the problem itself, but also towards influencing the causes of the problem. We also try to predict the greater long-term consequences of our actions, not just in terms of what we want to attain, but also in terms of possible undesired consequences. It may revolve around the possibility that increased surveillance and harsher punishment can lead to an escalation of antagonism and stigmatisation and reinforce anti-social identities.

Another way of describing the connection level is by the term 'linear thinking', which means to focus on the direct causal chains we can observe and create counter-measures that in a straight line direct themselves towards the problem we wish to solve. This kind of one-dimensional and linear logic is good at solving problems with well-known and well-delimited variables. But it is rarely adequate when trying to comprehend and solve more complex societal problems – 'wicked' problems such as crime, drug addiction, social marginalisation, etc. – that are the result of a large number of intimately connected causal chains, cultural and psychological factors and other structural prerequisites that we cannot observe in full detail or address directly.

3. The System Level

The system level increases our ability to reflect on non-linear causal contexts and systemic properties. We now start to question and investigate how society's overall structures, discourses and other societal contexts give rise to a given problem and make it likely to persist and reappear. With systemic factors we can come to see the wider societal implications of things like political and economic power structures, cultural and religious ideas, norms and attitudes, inequality, levels of trust in a society, etc. The effects of such factors tend to influence the system as a whole, usually in ways that cannot be observed linearly.

At the system level we not only think in terms of concrete cause and effect connections, but also in terms of the systems' overarching properties. To the extent we see the systemic properties responsible for the emergence and persistence of various problems, it becomes obvious that we need to change and redesign the system itself. In regard to the issue of vandalism, it may revolve around things such as ensuring young people feel more respected and valued, strengthening their self-esteem, promoting positive role models, increasing their faith in the future or perhaps even advocating new masculinity norms that encourage prosocial behaviour.

Since many of the problems that most urgently need to be solved in modern societies tend to be of the wicked kind – social problems such as crime, drug-abuse, mental disorders, etc. rather than absolute poverty and security – that need to be viewed at least on the system level, it is no longer sufficient that most of us merely think in terms of linear connections, simple cause and effect. Many of these problems are the result of prolonged feelings of marginalisation, alienation and lack of meaning and have emerged from the way society works on a systemic level: structural and contextual conditions that only can be changed for the better if more of us develop our cognitive complexity to reach the system level of complex thought.

4. The Perspective Level

The perspective level entails not just an understanding of causality and complex systemic properties, but also that we notice that there are many different ways to perceive and interpret causal connections and properties in systems. At the perspective level we can reflect upon the properties that belong to perspectives themselves. We can perceive and reflect upon both our own as well as others' way of thinking, compare the properties of various perspectives and use the different and often contradicting views to gain a better understanding of how different perspectives interact so that we can come up with more well-considered measures.

Wicked social problems often give rise to different schools of thought advocating various sorts of action in accordance with particular perspectives. Sometimes it revolves around pure conflicts of interest and personal power struggles, but often there is simply a considerable disagreement between various camps due to cognitive investment in a particular way of thinking. From the approach of the perspective level these disagreements depend upon the various perspectives directing attention towards various types of causal connections. Every perspective is specialised in one particular type of causal connection, while other types of causal connection are not brought to the attention.

In the case of vandalism, we can see that some people emphasise causes pertaining to weakened social control and thereby unclear boundary-setting. Others focus on welfare gaps, segregation, alienation and unemployment. Yet others see vandalism as a result of a youthful search for identity through affirmation from one's peers leading to group dynamics where individuals seek to surpass one another in crossing boundaries. The perspective level's starting point is that the problem descriptions differ between different actors because they have different perspectives and thereby different types of understanding of the problems.

From this vantage point it is possible to see the differences in the various actors' perspectives as a contributing cause to the problems being handled or not handled in certain ways. How various parties view a problem is quite simply part of the explanation for the problem looking the way it does. Making the cumulative perspectives an object, not subject, of a deliberative process to find new solution thus becomes possible on the perspective level.

Opposite is an overview of the various levels of cognitive complexity:

Illustration of causal relationships	Level of thinking about causality	Common questions	Examples of strategies
	'Oops ...'	'What do we do now?'	No strategy
	1. Category level Attention to problems, but not underlying causal relationships.	'How do we avoid unwanted events?' 'What can happen and how do we need to prepare?'	Control, impediments, preparedness.
	2. Connection level Attention to causation which explains how the problems arise, but not systemic properties.	'How can we prevent that problems arise?' 'And how can we mitigate negative effects if they occur nonetheless?'	Prevention.
	3. System level Attention to the properties of the system in which the problems occur, but not the properties of the perspectives used to describe the problems and their causality.	'How can we change the system's properties so that the prerequisites for problems to occur change?'	Strategies to develop norms, social ties, well-functioning institutions, early detection, competences.
	4. Perspective level Attention to the properties of the different (own and others') perspectives used to describe the problems and their causality.	'How can we develop our ways of interpreting world and prioritise the advantages of different perspectives?'	Transformation of systems.

Four levels of thinking around causal relationships and contexts.[2]

If we use this model vis-à-vis an issue such as terrorism and take the attack on *Charlie Hebdo* in Paris in 2015 as an example, it becomes clear how an all too low complexity level is unable to handle the problem:

- At the category level, we only see things such as Islamist terrorists attacking the offices of *Charlie Hebdo*. The terrorists define themselves as Muslims and the editorial board defines itself as a satire publication. Concretely there is hence a need to protect satire against terrorism and Islam and to force Muslims to accept satire aimed at their religion. The solutions are thus likely to include more security measures and surveillance.

- At the connection level, more variables become visible. There is not just one type of Muslim, there is an Islamist ideology and a peaceful religion, there is a connection between immigration and alienation, there are socioeconomic factors, there is a lack of cultural capital that creates intolerance towards satire, there is resentment towards the West, there is too much testosterone and too little meaningful work for young men, especially if they have an immigrant background, etc. The proposed solutions are therefore greater social community efforts, more education, various integration projects, etc.
- At the system level, we can see several factors and interacting contextual connections at the same time. However, those who carry out the analysis rarely see their own perspectives. The social worker sees how social factors influence each other, but not how psychological aspects also play a role. The psychologist sees how various factors can affect the psyche of young people under certain circumstances and how, based on their age, they cannot handle their rage, but not the significance of religious sentiments. The imam sees how a specific variant of Islam destroys the search for context and meaning inherent in the religion, but does not have the necessary knowledge to understand the interplay of social and psychological factors in this. And so on. Society's reply is thereby defined by those who get the task, while no one sees the whole picture. Any of these may alleviate the problem to some extent, but the lack of coordination and mutual understanding between different perspectives can make their efforts less efficient and sometimes even futile.
- At the perspective level, we attempt to understand the personal perspective of those who react violently and harbour antagonistic feelings towards society. We wonder why a society with so much to offer still creates so much personal and collective anger and so little meaning that young men become terrorists, and accordingly attempt to find out how those factors and perspectives

are connected. Our response thus becomes a string of questions that do revolve not only around economic, social and religious issues here and now, but also as intimately connected processes over time. We then try to identify the structural developmental changes needed for young people with immigrant backgrounds to feel hope, meaning and a sense of belongingness in society. The perspective level has a deeper existential understanding of individuals and society – and the history of both. We thus attempt to combine the many informed perspectives on terrorism, religious fundamentalism, social marginalisation and security measures to find the optimal coordination between these to solve the problem.

The Key to Developing Our Ability to Handle Complexity

From the discussion above we understand that in a more and more complex world, the ability to understand the world in more complex terms becomes more and more important. The increase in outer complexity in the world will have to be met by an increase in the inner, cognitive complexity of our minds.

When we look at psychological research on children's development, it is evident we humans go through various cognitive stages of development as we mature. Earlier developmental models about our ability to handle complexity usually ended with a stage corresponding to the connection level. However, today we have good reasons to believe this isn't the final stage of cognitive complexity; that some individuals develop beyond this level during their adult life.

Typically adult cognitive development is understood in *quantitative* terms such as experiences, knowledge, specific competences or abilities and the like, with the basic assumption that the *qualitative* or *transformative* cognitive development ground to a halt after the teen years. The focus has been on the content of our consciousness rather than our consciousness's ability for scope and complexity. Below, this antiquated view of cognitive development is illustrated:

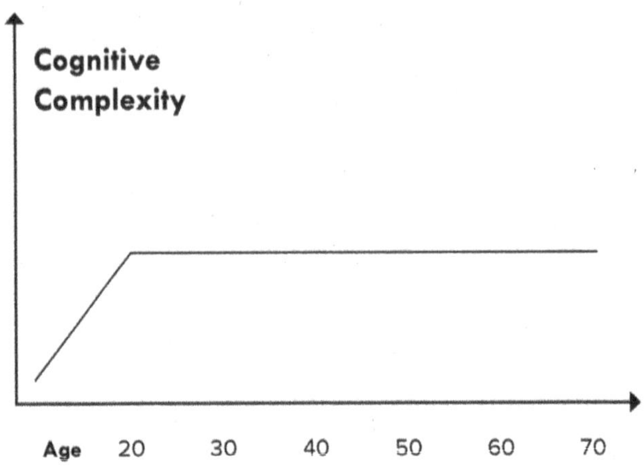

The old view of cognitive development over age.[3]

But as we shall see in the next chapter, modern developmental psychology of today has shown that we as individuals have great variation in how complex a question or reasoning we can handle at a given age.[4] It also proves that our ability to handle complexity is not fully developed at an early adult age, but the ability of our consciousness to handle complexity can continue to develop throughout life. Below, results of current empirical studies of cognitive development are schematically illustrated:

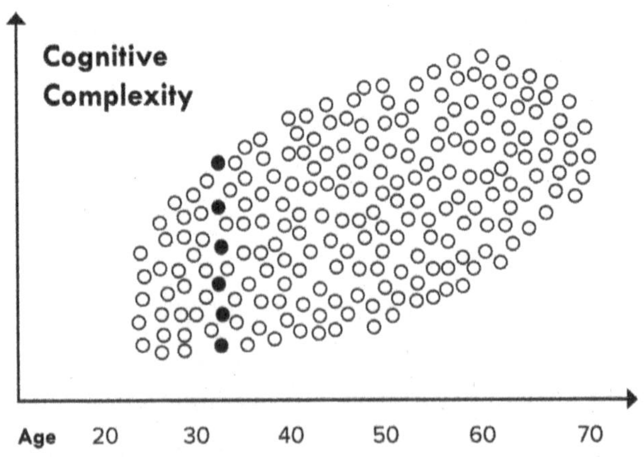

The new view of cognitive development over age.[5]

In the same way that it was necessary with a population that could function at a higher complexity level to get our modern society to work, it also seems reasonable to assume that we need a population that has the ability to act from thinking that corresponds to the world's increasing complexity in the global society of the future.

We cannot, however, expect that it will happen in and of itself. The development is rapidly complexifying, and if we do not react quickly, we risk the collapse of our political system as well as the entire biosphere. We only have our Stone Age brain to rely on, so the only solution is – once again – to reshape our symbol world in a way that favours a sustainable development. The big question then becomes how we can create the best frameworks for the development of humanity, so that as many as possible can act from the higher complexity levels needed. How can we make sure that as many as possible reach a level of personal development during the course of life that makes it possible for more people to develop an understanding and feel for the complex problems humanity stands before? The survival of democracy and of our planet depends upon this.

The insight from developmental psychology can be said to amount to a paradigm shift of thinking within the field of psychology and sociology – and may very well be the missing ingredient for an overall paradigm shift in our thinking at large.

PARADIGM SHIFTS

As a result of the increasing complexity, we have throughout history undergone a number of paradigm shifts in which we started to think differently and see the world and ourselves with new eyes. A paradigm is *how* we collectively think, rather than *what* we think. In this way a paradigm is analogous to a thought perspective, but not synonymous since it can also refer to other paradigms than the five thought perspectives presented in this book.

Paradigms are constituted by our thoughts about how the world works and how we should best go about trying to understand it. In philosophical terms, our paradigms are formed by our ontology[6] and our epistemology.[7] Paradigm shifts typically happen when both our ontology and epistemology are altered, and both of these are anchored in our symbol world. This is when our symbol world changes – for example, when a newly dominant thought perspective has prevailed, as a result of technological development or new scientific breakthroughs, such as Darwin's theory of evolution or new philosophical insights; or when someone creates great art or popular culture that makes us view the world differently.

In 1962, Thomas Kuhn published the book *The Structure of Scientific Revolutions* in which his relatively simple observation shook the natural sciences: scientific knowledge is a fractious process. Research methods are a constant struggle between researchers attempting to debunk each other's hypotheses and results; new knowledge is created through assuming that what we already know does not hold true. And yet there are basic assumptions behind all research that no one questions, for example, Newton's physics and Einstein's theory of relativity – right up until Niels Bohr and others developed quantum mechanics.

Sometimes there emerge scientific results that gainsay these basic assumptions, results that should not be possible according to prevailing scientific knowledge. Initially, these are explained away as anomalies, but when results are repeated, the consequences can no longer be ignored and the prevailing theories must be overthrown and replaced by a new, more coherent one. It was this insight with which Kuhn shook natural science: scientific knowledge is knowledge in the present moment. Knowledge is a process in constant development.

If we look at the development of the scientific paradigms that have supplanted each other throughout the ages, the historical trajectory, as we saw in Part 1, looks something like this:

1. During the Renaissance and the Enlightenment both the Bible and Aristotle are questioned, and especially by Newton the mechanistic worldview is developed.

2. With the steam engine, thermodynamics is one shift away from the mechanistic worldview.
3. Einstein develops the theory of relativity but still has a strictly causal view on cause and effect.
4. Bohr and Heisenberg discover quantum mechanics, which holds true at atom-level, where cause and effect according to our usual assumptions are disconnected from each other. Quantum ontology and therein the quantum paradigms that are developed from it break radically with ordinary human experience of the world.
5. With computers it becomes possible to find completely new patterns in data, and from there theories on complexity, networks, chaos and self-organising systems are developed. Complexity theory's explanation of emergent phenomena allows us to comprehend how life, consciousness and culture have arisen out of matter and we can start to regard ourselves as open systems instead of merely individuals.

All these scientific paradigms define not only *what* we can understand but *how*. They were and are frameworks for how we can understand our environments, and they were developed because the prevailing paradigm was no longer sufficiently explanatory.

Paradigm shifts are scarcely easy to predict, and often arrive with bombastic claims that may require equally incisive evidence. The allergens that guard against charlatanism or simple error in disciplines must, when a justified paradigm shift arrives, be combatted by insurgents who often do the thankless work of questioning fundamental principles. This is in contrast with usual scientific work, which engages well-defined research questions within the given paradigm. Rather than rocking the boat, most researchers add to it, expanding its hull and following the set course that previous revolutionary thinkers laid down. It is only once a critical mass of evidence has been reached, and it has overcome the social struggle of winning over territorially minded and rigorously defensive (for good cause) scientists, that one paradigm can usurp another.

The difficulty in doing so can, sadly, also occur because of less justifiable defensiveness. While institutional caution and extraordinary evidence for extraordinary shifts in perspective are fair, our cognitive biases and even egoistic reasons for defending an orthodoxy are not. They are, nonetheless, inescapably human. Our propensity to fit evidence to our preferred arguments, discount challenges based on how they are framed, or fail to recognise the promise of work that doesn't fall into clear disciplinary boundaries are all errors from bias. Worse still, should personal animosity or motivations surrounding self-interest intrude, people may deny new information because of motivational errors. If science is to work, ideally at least, it must aspire to standards of rationality that are not decided by the above, but rather by evidence that confirms or disconfirms formal abstraction.

Our worldview has for some time been so dominated by the rational thought perspective that it is not surprising it faces a backlash from the post-rationalist postmodern thought perspective. Similarly, we should not be shocked if the allergies of members of both camps are sparked by our all too human ability to read what we want to understand, and ascribe the motives we assume our 'antagonists' hold. We are replete with biases, and to pretend otherwise is to abscond from our responsibility to hold them in lucid view, so that they can be variously distinguished between the necessary features of our nature as embodied, perspectival agents; and the unnecessary, damaging failures of intersubjectivity that these same predispositions can become.

I believe that we are in the midst of such a paradigm shift right now, and that it is propelled by both new scientific discoveries and new philosophical insights. The overarching topic of the rest of this book is thus the potential paths on which such a paradigm shift might unfold.

TRANSITION

In a complex system, many small quantitative changes can occur over time without any notable qualitative effects on the system's fundamental properties as a whole. A society can experience prolonged economic growth without any significant changes to its governing principles, for example, and a species of animals can increase its numbers for a considerable time without any disruption to the balance of an ecosystem. But eventually the many small changes may add up and the system will not be able to adapt using the same organisational principles. This will cause a sudden disruption leading to a *phase transition* through which the system changes from one state to another, a so-called *tipping point* or *bifurcation point.* At this point the system will either break down and fragment into lower complexity; or find a new, more complex, organisational principle that allows the system to organise in a completely new way that gives the system new, emergent, properties. A quantitative change that at one point did not have

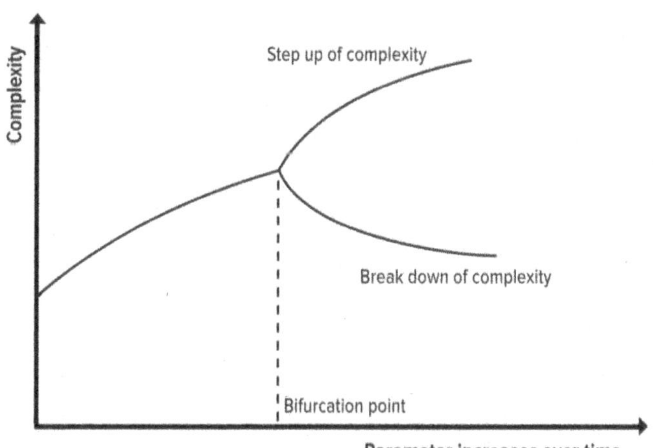

Any self-organising system that comes under pressure to transform will eventually reach a bifurcation point at which there is a possibility for a higher level of complex organisation to emerge, or the possibility of a breakdown.

any qualitative results can thus at another point suddenly alter the system's characteristics drastically. But exactly when this will happen and what the emergent properties will be can be difficult if not impossible to forecast.

How incremental changes to the temperature of water do not affect its fundamental properties of being a liquid until it reaches 0° or 100° Celsius is analogous to the sudden emergent change that can occur in a chaotic system after a longer period of steady development. Before such a tipping point occurs, the steady quantitative changes to a chaotic system do not bring about any fundamental qualitative changes. In accordance with a linear logic, a steady temperature increase simply makes the climate warmer and a rising birth-rate simply makes a population larger. Prior to a phase transition we may thus find linear approaches adequate since they can predict the relevant quantitative changes and since there are no qualitative ones that require a non-linear explanation.

A simple definition of linearity is that output is proportional to input. A linear approach will thus conclude that the outcome of an increase of 1% is 101%. There is of course no denying that, but such a method does not account for the emergent phenomena, the 'surprises', that may occur as a result of an increase of 1% at a certain stage – for instance that a temperature increase of 1° to water at 99° will change its state from a liquid into a gas. If we did not know better, a linear approach would simply make us believe that the only change to the properties of the water would that it became a little warmer. From a linear perspective alone, we have no basis to deduce a qualitative change from a quantitative since the emergent properties of a chaotic system as mentioned cannot be predicted from its components in its initial state. There is simply nothing in the properties of water that can tell us that it will boil or freeze at a certain temperature, just as little as there is anything in an individual ant that can tell us it can build anthills.

But until a chaotic system enters a phase transition, and as long as what we consider most important are the qualitative changes that occur, it may in fact appear as if it behaves linearly; that the output (outcome) is proportional to the input. Whatever dynamic qualitative effects this can have on the system as a whole, which the linear qualitative approach cannot foresee, we may account for empirically since there are yet to be any emergent surprises that have not been observed before – or we might disregard them altogether since such novelties are likely to remain minor prior to a tipping point. So even though the global climate is a complex system that every climatologist knows cannot be reduced to simple linear functions, a linear conception of climate change can appear adequate as long as the most notable effect of global warming is that the climate becomes warmer. And since we already have comprehensive empirical knowledge about the consequences of higher temperatures locally (how it influences harvest yields, flora and fauna, desertification and so on), we may feel convinced that this can compensate for the limitation that linear analyses cannot be used to deduce qualitative outcomes from quantitative observations. But doing so obviously makes us incapable of accounting for any potential emergent consequences of rising average temperatures.

An illustrative example is how the accelerating melting of the Greenland ice sheet caused by global warming in theory could lead to a sudden halt of the Gulf Stream when the steady increase of cold fresh water injected into the North Atlantic reaches a tipping point. This hypothesis could not have been derived from a linear analysis. With a linear projection we can only see how the increase in temperature is proportional with the pace the ice cap melts. Whether that will lead to a halt of the Gulf Stream is nothing such analyses can give us reason to consider. And since we have no observations about similar occurrences, we cannot use empirical methods either to prove or disprove the hypothesis – not until it is too late.

We do not know if the above hypothesis is valid or not. This can only be determined empirically, after all. But the question remains if we are willing to take the risk that it is not.

From complexity science we know that any continuous linear or exponential pattern of development will make a system unsustainable in its present form. Eventually, the balance that keeps it together will break down, which leads to a chaotic process, a phase transition, that will only end when it reaches a new equilibrium: a new and more sustainable state, with new emergent properties as a result. An understanding of complexity may not make us capable of determining exactly when this will happen, what the decisive quantitative change will be. The straw that breaks the camel's back, so to speak, cannot be determined. But if we adopt the non-linear way of thinking of complexity, it can make it abundantly clear that if we continue to add straws to an animal's back, eventually it will break.

We now know that tipping points and emergence are universal properties of chaotic systems and that phase transitions can lead to drastic and highly unpredictable changes in a short amount of time with little prior indication of what might happen. That phase transitions in chaotic systems are sudden events is another reason why the water analogy is suitable here. A water molecule does not gradually freeze, it changes its state almost instantaneously. It is either solid, or it is liquid. A similar dynamic pertains to many of the states of complex chaotic systems. A view from complexity thus serves as an urgently needed warning that we cannot expect to receive gradual indications about a potentially catastrophic development. Complexity not only highlights the analytic limitations of too linearly conceived analyses, it also marks the dangers of failing to adopt a more complex way of thinking alarmingly evident.

TOWARDS A NEW LEVEL OF SOCIETAL COMPLEXITY

As an interdisciplinary field of inquiry, the principles and methods of complexity science apply to physical and social developments alike. The same dynamics that can be accounted for in the chaotic systems in nature can thus be seen in human-made ones as well. The critical developments that bring emergent orders of qualitative complexity into being tend to occur quite abruptly rather than gradually. The same can be observed in chaotic human systems like those of societies and cultures. As such, the preoccupation with levels of complexity and stage theories that characterises much of complexity science is not just an arbitrarily conceived method of ordering gradual quantitative changes so that we can discern them more clearly. Rather, by the very nature of complexity science, the way these levels and stages are conceptualised is derived from the logics and non-arbitrary principles of qualitative emergent developments, not merely temporal ones. And from the distinct properties each stage of complexity exhibits, they need to be clearly delimitated in theory – and in practice, indeed emerge in sudden leaps and bounds.

Societal and technological progress may appear as a gradual process, though, and to an extent it certainly is. But from a longer historical perspective it becomes visible that it is often characterised by sudden change and longer periods of stability or stagnation. In evolutionary biology it is widely recognised that major biological changes do not occur through processes of steady piecemeal increases, but through sudden bursts of rapidly evolving complexity. The same dynamic seems to apply to societal development as well. When new levels of societal complexity emerge, it usually does so in accordance with the aforementioned dynamics of sudden chaotic phase transitions.

If we view the transition from a feudal, agrarian society to a democratic industrial one in a long historical perspective, it arguably appears more like a marked transformation than a gradual development. In comparison with the many centuries of largely identical, fundamental properties of society prior to this, the transition to modernity seems like an almost instantaneous event. It only took a little more than a century for this level of societal complexity to emerge, starting with the political revolutions in America and France and the industrial one in Britain at the end of the eighteenth century and ending with the fully industrial societies and universal suffrage in the West at the beginning of the twentieth. This emergent phenomenon can be seen as the result of a long historical process stretching back to the Middle Ages, or even further, as many historians have done. And in a way they are right. But the many incremental changes only added up and reached a critical tipping point that completely changed the fundamental properties of our society during the aforementioned shorter period.

I admit it can be hard to see how the so-called 'long nineteenth century' is a critical chaotic state transition given the seemingly just as turbulent centuries both before and after this period. However, the kinds of emergent chaos we are looking for here are not to be found in the perpetual political conflicts and social uprisings that characterise most historical periods. It is to be found in the qualitative changes to the fundamental properties of societal systems. The societies that emerged as modern at the beginning of the twentieth century are vastly different to anything that had existed before – and in terms of their properties, largely identical both to those they would have a century later and to those of other societies anywhere else in the following period. Although economic growth has been staggering since the early twentieth century, the fundamental qualitative properties of our current society – market economy, parliamentary institutions, rule of law, etc. – are arguably more or less the same. Our society has changed, but it does not differ as much from that of 100 years ago as that of the early twentieth century differs from the late eighteenth century.

Our society has changed dramatically in terms of economic growth, technological progress, population increase and so on during the past 100 years, but the changes that have occurred may only be as different as water at 1° Celsius is from that at 99°. The temperature of water can have significantly different effects on a human body, but the fundamental property of water itself is still the same. It remains a liquid. Similarly, our current society still remains a rationalist, market-liberal democracy. These are its most fundamental properties. Given the many quantitative changes since the early twentieth century such as the ones mentioned above, our society certainly has widely different effects on its inhabitants today. But in itself, it basically behaves in accordance with the same overarching principles and self-organising dynamics as a century ago.

However, this may not last very long. For all we know, we might be at a state of 99° and stand before a tipping point at which everything solid melts into air.

It has happened before.

Chapter 12

THE EVOLVING MIND

Let us turn inward for a moment. Close your eyes and clasp your hands and stop for a moment to observe how your hands *feel.* You might notice that the sensations in your hands make up wide inner landscapes of perception. Is there warmth, pressure, smoothness, moisture, a certain pleasure? Can you feel the contrast between the touched and the untouched? Between the hand and the finger tips?

Then try to answer what it means *that* you feel something. How do you actually recognise these perceptions? What is *feeling* in *itself,* as it so self-evidently appears before your inner horizon? We have now begun to observe our *perception.* We can go on and investigate the rest of our body, how everything feels within us. Maybe there is something deep down in our stomach that we did not notice before we closed our eyes, some emotional need or issue that needs attention. The more time we spend focusing on our inner landscape, the more emotions and thoughts we can become aware of, and the better we will understand them. As we mature, most of us have probably experienced that we get better at relating to ourselves, that we improve our understanding of our *self,* who we are as persons, and thereby come to understand others and the world around us much better. That which previously lay silent in the background, what remained outside the scope of our self-perception when we were younger, can become an object in our awareness that we can relate to. We often refer to such experiences as personal growth, learning experiences that gave us new wisdom or simply 'growing up'. But sometimes the term 'psychological development' is a better description. When we say we have grown as persons, we often do not mean that we have merely acquired more knowledge, but rather that we have obtained new perspectives and attitudes towards life. This may entail that we have come to see the world and ourselves from a 'higher' perspective and that our mind has developed to become a more sophisticated piece of machinery.

When we turn our gaze inwards and reflect upon our experiences, thoughts and emotions, we can take these subjective aspects as objects for investigation and thereby alter how they interfere in our lives. This exploration of our inner world has been the bedrock of mysticism, spirituality and religion for millennia. The creation of institutions to cultivate the human soul's capacity for self-reflection became a highly prioritised societal concern during the Axial Age; not only in order to serve individuals' personal needs and desires, but also as a crucial means to ensure the wellbeing of society itself. That it is possible, with a more contemporary phrasing, to create support structures to help develop desirable traits in our psyches, that we can increase our consciousness and thereby foster better-functioning societies, has been known for thousands of years. Today, however, this insight seems to have been largely forgotten as our focus has more or less entirely shifted towards the development of aspects in the exterior world. 'Progress', as the term is commonly used today, mostly revolves around the development of new technologies and societal structures. But to accommodate the changes we make to our exterior world, we need a corresponding development of our interior. If we are to manage the increasing complexity of the world, we need to develop the complexity of our minds as well.

In this chapter I will introduce the idea of the mind as an evolving entity. With the help of the growing research fields in *transformative learning* and *developmental psychology*, I wish to show that adult humans can develop their cognitive capacities throughout life, and why it is not only possible that the average level of psychological development can be higher than it is today, but that it is also critical that we achieve this.

TRANSFORMATIVE LEARNING

There is plentiful empirical support indicating that humans – under favourable conditions – can develop their ability to perceive and interpret increasingly complex phenomena and contexts in fundamentally new ways.[1] But what exactly is meant by this? And what is it that needs to happen in order for this transformative development to materialise?

Our inner representation of the world and ourselves – the remarkable, ever-present world map we navigate by – must be experienced as coherent and meaningful if we are to remain psychologically functional and navigate our exterior world successfully. Our mind is a meaning-creating machine that constantly attempts to make sense of what we experience. Our mind's capacity for meaning-creation can be developed throughout life, not just in its *content* but also in its *structure*. It is not merely *what* we know that can be developed, but also *how* we know.

Some thinkers talk of 'horizontal' versus 'vertical' development, which also can be described as 'in-breadth' vs 'in-depth' development. Horizontal development represents *what* we know and *what* we can do: the *breadth* of our knowledge and skills. Vertical development represents *how* we know, *how* we arrange our knowledge and experiences and *how* we tie these into meaningful and cohesive wholes. This development usually occurs in larger steps – transformations – rather than the piecemeal acquisitions of new bits of knowledge that characterise horizontal development, and is therefore sometimes referred to as 'transformative learning'. The term 'vertical' implies that we develop 'deeper' and 'higher' modes of cognition, the capacity to perceive and make sense of aspects that previously remained out of reach before the transformation since they were too 'deep' or of too 'high' a complexity. *What* we know may remain the same, but *how* we know, how we interpret this knowledge, will have increased in nuance and sophistication.

How our consciousness *knows* also influences how our consciousness *experiences*. Our experiences of the world, and thereby our emotions vis-à-vis the world – and eventually our actions – are influenced just as much by *how* our consciousness knows as *what* we know. The function in our consciousness that 'knows' and 'experiences' is commonly referred to as the *subject* by philosophers and psychologists. Our subject is that within us that *contains* our experiences, the objects of our subjective mind. The subject is also what we might call the 'self'. That which we know about or experience is referred to as an *object* of our consciousness. We cannot experience our subject ourselves. We merely *are* our subject. If we could experience our subject, as some might claim, it would not be our subject, but an object of our consciousness. What we perceive as objects and what constitutes our self can thus change throughout life. By gaining transformative learning experiences we can make objects out of what previously remained subject and thereby change what constitutes the self. In this sense, transformative psychological development is the development of our experiencing subject or *ego*-development. In other words it is *the development of consciousness itself.*[2]

Philosophers (and others) long believed that our inner experience of the world was an accurate depiction of an objective, external reality. This view is called 'naive realism' by some: that we believe we are experiencing the world as it is. In the Western philosophical tradition it was Kant who in 1781 in his work *Critique of Pure Reason* first pointed out that it is our consciousness that *creates* our experience of the world. Kant went as far as to claim that we really cannot know anything about external reality, about things in themselves (the famous *Ding an sich*). This view is called 'absolute idealism': that the only source of knowledge we can gain access to is the experience that our consciousness creates, that all we can know about the world is how our subject or self perceives it.

Generations of German philosophers following Kant took an interest in how this subject works, how it creates our experiences and how it creates meaning from these. In Part 1 we briefly talked about Herder, Schiller, Goethe and Hegel. They all asked the question: Is the subject – our apparatus of interpretation – constant, given by nature, or can it evolve? And if so, what is it that makes *how* we experience evolve? How can we foster such transformative learning? In the German-speaking world during the nineteenth century, these philosophers began to refer to the process through which our subject (our 'consciousness') is formed and transformed by our surrounding societal culture and life experiences as *Bildung*,[3] which means 'to form' or 'to become'. *Bildung* has often later been used to refer to the ideal of having sufficient knowledge about high culture, literature, music, philosophy and so on considered canonical. But initially this term was meant to denote kinds of mental traits that went beyond mere horizontal acquisitions of knowledge. As kings and nobles gradually lost political control in Europe during the nineteenth century and the people then had to take over the responsibility of governing themselves, it was believed they needed more than just knowledge about how society works in order to behave as responsible and ethical citizens. They also needed a certain amount of *Bildung* – sensibilities, values and ways of thinking – that, contrary to formal education, required what we today would call transformative learning experiences. Thus *Bildung*, it was claimed, could not be taught in the conventional meaning of the word; it had to be 'cultivated'. To achieve this, it was believed that 'destabilising' cultural experiences played a vital role to give new perspectives on life and in that way push development forward. The preoccupation with fine art, classical music and literature was therefore not meant as something to be learned in order to appear cultured or to entertain one's guests at dinner parties, but as a means to expand our horizons and develop consciousness in ways considered to meet the complexity of modern society. These ideas became particularly widespread and influential in the Nordic countries and came to shape how these societies developed during the twentieth century. How the idea of life-long transformative learning, the emphasis on aspects beyond formal skills in the education system and the ambition to raise consciousness levels and awareness in the general population became salient in the Nordic countries is a topic that I, in collaboration with Lene Andersen, have written about in detail in our book *The Nordic Secret.*[4]

Psychology was not established as a separate academic discipline of its own prior to the twentieth century, so academic thinking regarding consciousness occurred within philosophy instead. What is interesting to note, however, is that what the eighteenth- and nineteenth-century philosophers arrived at concerning the development of the self matches very well with what developmental psychologists have been able to confirm during the last thirty years of research. But for various reasons these original insights were later overshadowed by positivism's focus on the objectively measurable that dominated much of twentieth-century science. It was only at the end of the century that psychological science began to seriously take an interest in *how* we experience and create meaning.

Interestingly, the first modern 'psychologist' who came to look more systematically at psychological development was no clinical psychologist, but a biologist and early systems theorist named Jean Piaget.

OUR MIND AS A SELF-ORGANISING SYSTEM

That our consciousness in fundamental ways can evolve throughout life can be hard to digest with our present rather static view of the adult mind: Homo economicus. Even if most in the West has now accepted the theory of evolution, and thereby that life and the human being have arisen through the development of self-organising complex systems, many still feel dizzy at the thought that our individual consciousnesses could also be complex systems under constant development.[5]

But why is this so difficult to digest? Perhaps the hardest part of buying into the theory that truly transforming psychological development is possible in adult age might be that we thereby also have to admit that our own sense of reality – our feelings, and experience of being, indeed, our entire way of thinking – might be inadequate, that we might be 'underdeveloped'. We have to admit that we really 'have not understood' the world, that we invariably find ourselves on a little island in a greater sea of possible perspectives, that we may have all too superficial, flattened or in other ways limited perspectives. As such, it may not only be a difficult idea to wrap one's head around, it can likewise be a rather painful realisation that others may be more psychologically developed than ourselves. For *if* our consciousness really can develop throughout adult life, then it also becomes apparent that we ourselves may not be the most developed sentient beings on Earth. Accepting the insights and findings of developmental psychology is therefore tantamount to undermining one's own self-conception – 'cutting off the branch one is sitting on', if you will – from which our psychological wholeness is derived and therefore a line of thought most of us seek to avoid.

It is, however, precisely in this way the biologist, systems thinker and developmental psychologist Piaget in the middle of the twentieth century started to understand and describe the development of the human mind or consciousness. This view has been further developed by many, among others the Harvard professor in psychology Robert Kegan who has integrated Piaget's systems thinking with Lev Vygotskij's insights about the supporting significance of our symbolic worlds.[6] Kegan sees Piaget's contribution to developmental psychology as fundamental. Albert Einstein, too, brought attention to Piaget's unique idea about the evolving mind. Einstein got to know Piaget in Zürich, where both of them lived during the First World War, and later came to call Piaget's central insight 'so simple that only a genius could have thought of it'.[7] So what then is this insight?

Piaget's great contribution to psychology is fundamentally a systems perspective on our consciousness, seeing our individual consciousness as a complex self-organising system that constantly absorbs energy and information from the environment to increase its own complexity. This is a view that recently has been confirmed by neuroscience. In what is sometimes called the second-wave cognitive science, the metaphor of the brain as our hardware and our mind as the software is abandoned in favour of an understanding of our mind as a self-organising system where there can be no distinction between hardware and software. All is one co-evolving process and where before we might have been talking about the possibility of our consciousness evolving, it is becoming more and more clear that it is not that our consciousness in evolving, but rather that this constant interaction with the environment and the resulting adaptation process is the ground of our consciousness. Without this development, there would be no mind. Our mind *is* this self-organising developmental process.[8] And as in all self-organising developmental processes there are more or less marked phase transitions.[9]

Piaget observed already at the middle of last century that children in clearly delineated stages exchange their entire way of thinking for another mode, and that the lines of reasoning they employed in various cognitive experiments followed a clear pattern that was possible to connect to various ages. He demonstrated with great clarity that most children of a certain age made the same cognitive missteps and advances. His experiments showed, for example, that it is rare for a five-year-old to understand that juice in a low, wide glass still constitutes the same amount as a tall, narrow glass (with the same volume). Not even if the child is watching while juice is poured into it! The child insists that there is more juice in the tall, narrow glass, because it simply *looks* as though there is more. After the age of seven most children have reached the next stage and thereby internalised the insight that their own sensory perceptions are not the same as reality. The structure in the child's thinking has thus taken a developmental step. The child has learned to treat its own sensory impressions as an *object*, as something that one can reason around and relate to.

We see in Piaget an interplay between the individual organism and its environment, a perspective that is clearly rooted in biological systems thinking. In the study of mice and humans, the same fundamental principles apply: the organism recreates the environment in its mind, but this recreation can, through participation in the same environment, be recreated itself by yet higher functions of cognition.

Piaget's model contained four stages, but more of them have since been identified and proven by other researchers (most clearly in the mathematical psychologist Michael Commons' general theory of development 'The

Model of Hierarchical Complexity').[10] Without going deeper into Piaget's theory, we can emphasise one of the crucial consequences of this insight: if consciousness is indeed this constant developmental process, is there any reason to believe that when we have celebrated our twentieth birthday we have reached the highest possible stage of thinking? Have we reached our outermost limit of thinking? Wouldn't it be odd if that were the case?

This suggests the following questions: in what respects might adult humans reason in ways that in relation to other adults correspond to those of a five-year-old vis-à-vis an older child? In what respects do we insist on confusing our own identifications and experiences with reality? In what ways are we failing to detach our perspectives from what we are observing so that we get mired in mirages and a flattening worldview? Are there apparent connections and self-insights that we are systematically missing? Is there anything which is invisible to us today that we can objectify in order to relate to it in new ways? Are we really as adults as mature and rational as we want to believe?

Here we are moving away from the everyday apprehension of knowledge and education and are putting ourselves in a developmental perspective. It is not about absorbing any particular new knowledge, but about reorganising our thinking and inviting ourselves to embrace new, breakneck leaps in the transformative development of our consciousness. There are many diverse families of research on such development, but let us now concentrate on an aspect that we all encounter throughout life: the self.

THE SELF'S LONG JOURNEY THROUGH LIFE

Who am 'I' really? Or *what* am I? The self is something that arises in the encounter between humans, something that we learn to relate to through interaction with others. We *reflect* ourselves in each other and create narratives and identities from our many interactions in daily life. What constitutes one's self today can come to be an object of one's consciousness tomorrow. The self has, of course, not disappeared – it has instead been reborn on a new, more extensive and more embracing level. This circumstance has elegantly been put into words by Tomas Tranströmer:

> Within me I carry my earlier faces,
> as a tree that has its growth rings.
> It is the sum of them that is 'I'.
> The mirror merely sees my latest face,
> I can feel all of my previous ones.
>
> – Tomas Tranströmer, *Memories Look at Me*, 1993[11]

When we are infants we do not have an apprehension of such a self. We do not know our name, and according to research consensus we do not even clearly separate ourselves from things in our environment. Things just happen: hunger happens, fatigue happens, discomfort happens, mum's breast happens (if we're lucky), warm milk happens. Eventually during our childhood we learn that I am 'I', that I have a name, an identity, particular personal qualities, that other people cannot see and hear everything that I see and hear – and at best, that everything in the world does not revolve around me after all.

But the body, the emotions and the sensory impressions obviously do not disappear. There are only new, *emergent*, layers built on top of our previous self. These new layers, like Russian dolls, encase the previous ones. Here I am sitting, organising my sensory impressions and movements in order to write a book. Yet at every moment something is insisting on emerging: the overgrown baby that I am at some level, with hunger, fatigue, impatience – and maybe other things that are related to inner insecurity and yearnings, hope or despair. New layers of the self enable us to catch a glimpse of the earlier ones instead of merely *being* them.

The self is thus a kind of pattern, a structure that arises in consciousness, and this pattern continues its development through life. This particular aspect of our lifelong maturation is sometimes called *ego-development*. In his book *The Evolving Self*, Kegan proposes six stages of ego-development from the 0th to the 5th order of self. He also maintains that there is a particular dynamic in the development of the self, a logic that explains why the various stages of self-apprehension must arise in a particular order. In a later book he speaks about six 'orders of consciousness'.[12]

Kegan's stages, or selves, can, as a suggestion, and without violating the theory, also be termed layers. The word 'layer', I believe, gives a more illuminating image of this ego development. As new layers of development are formed, the earlier ones remain within us and keep influencing our thinking to some extent. So instead of using the word 'stage', which brings forth the image of a ladder that we gradually climb while losing contact with the lower steps, seeing this development in terms of the formation of layers better illustrates how we always carry around the earlier ones. This can remind us that our consciousness, from one time to another and in various situations, acts from older as well as newer layers; something that Kegan is careful to point out. The formation of a new layer does not mean that our subject has made its home there. It merely means that we under favourable conditions have the possibility of experiencing and acting from the new, more complex possibilities this layer provides. On a bad day we may interpret things in less complex terms and act from lower layers.

OUR LAYERS OF EXTENDED CONSCIOUSNESS

There have been many thinkers who have observed that our consciousness – under favourable circumstances – even in adulthood, can continue to develop. The presentation below follows to a large extent the psychologist and researcher Kristina Elfhag's insights into Kegan's theories.[13] It also deserves to be pointed out that I do not claim the specific layers below are the only ones or the most correct way of ordering ego-development. Around this there is still much ongoing research. My foremost ambition is merely to show that transformative development *can* occur throughout life, that we should replace our static view of the adult consciousness as a ready-made machine in favour of a dynamic view of consciousness as a process under constant development, and that this development can be facilitated or impeded by the environment.

The Formation of Layers 1 and 2

As infants we are not conscious of a self, and we are not separated from our perceptions, reflexes and movements either. In the experiencing core of our consciousness we merely *are*. We have not developed any structure in our consciousness from which we can perceive our sensory impressions or emotions. We are completely governed by our instincts and completely dependent on our care-givers. However, we are slowly starting to become aware of a world around us that is detached from ourselves, a world we can start to relate to with an emerging perception of a self.

This first layer of a more complex consciousness, which will encase our consciousness' core of direct sensory impressions, emotions and instincts, begins to form at birth, or even earlier, and is often well developed at some point between two and six years of age. With this layer, an awareness of our bodily functions, emotions and actions is created. There are structures formed in our consciousness from which we can perceive and form opinions about some of the mental and bodily processes that we previously were completely embedded in, subjective experiences that we once were one with, but have now become objects in our consciousness. It is here, for instance, that we can start potty training. Until a child has developed an awareness of its bodily functions, it is meaningless to try potty training.

Usually after six years of age a second layer in cognitive complexity will form. With this layer, structures allowing us to see our own sensory perceptions from a mental distance start to develop. This also gives us the possibility to understand that others see the world from other vantage points, that everyone does not have the same sensory impressions as oneself.

Thus far the development is largely determined by our biology. We can assume that most of the early Homo sapiens that we studied in Part 1 developed this second layer. This layer was necessary for our survival on

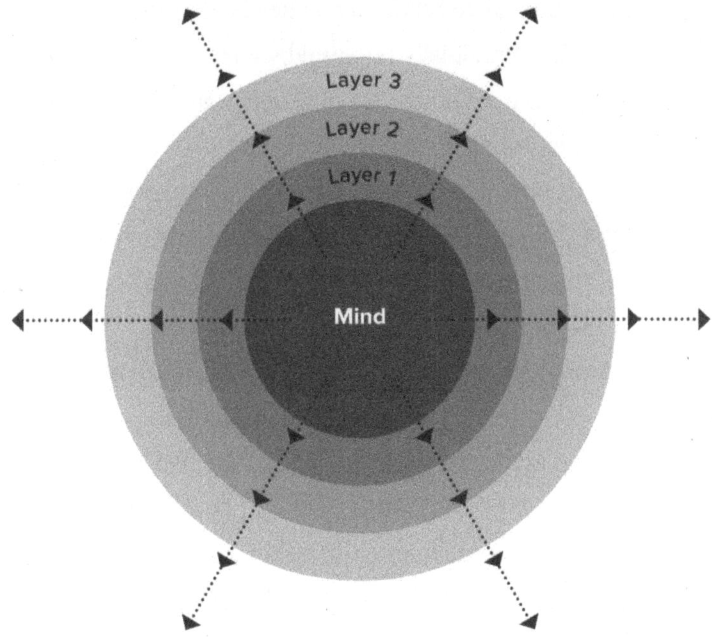

Expansion of our consciousness through increased awareness. Kegan's layers 1 to 3 of our mind are formed.

the savannah. We had to be able to distinguish our sensory impressions from reality, for example during the hunt. We also saw how important it was for our survival to develop an understanding of what is going on in the consciousness of others, a theory of mind to understand neighbours and enemies. However, very few humans today remain over their entire lives within this 'Stone Age consciousness', where our needs and immediate desires still own us. This level of consciousness – an *instrumental mind* – is in many ways insufficient for our society today. And if we do not evolve further, there is a considerable risk that we get problems in life, for instance, by ending up in prison.

The Formation of Layer 3

If things progress smoothly, we will have a well-developed second layer before we enter our teenage years. Most of us develop mental capacities in our teens that enable us to relate to our needs, desires and wills from a mental distance. What previously remained subject becomes object – and with that, the ability to manipulate the new object in our consciousness.

A few years ago, when I was the leader at one of the Foundation Ekskäret's youth camps, I heard a conversation between a fifteen-year-old girl and a youth leader. The girl said she constantly felt stressed and torn between all the things she wanted to do and could do: meet friends, hang out on social media, do sports, etc. The somewhat older leader said a few wise words that made her stop and think. Evidently she was mature enough to take a considerable step in her development, for she answered, somewhat surprised by her new insight: 'Now I see that I really don't *have* to do everything I *want* to do.' Thus far her wishes, desires and needs had 'owned' her, which had caused her considerable stress. But with this step in her transformative learning she came to regard her own will as an 'object' for reflection. For the first time she could liberate herself from her 'will' and thereby gain greater control over her life, an *increased freedom* to act in ways that had previously not been possible for her.

With the formation of the third layer during our youth we also begin to see the significance of being part of a larger group. Not merely as a means for personal gain, but because we seek shared values and want to be part of a greater togetherness. What others think of us also becomes more important. Our sense of self-worth becomes dependent on what others think. We want to fit in, and we internalise our surrounding society's culture and values. When this layer is fully developed we become part of our culture and society, and we are expected to have the ability to control our immediate inclinations. We adhere to laws and social conventions not just because we want to avoid punishment, but because it feels right to follow our group's norms and values. This process, where we internalise our environment's culture and values, is sometimes referred to as 'socialisation'. Accordingly, Kegan calls this layer 'the *socialized mind*'.[14]

That we have formed this third layer of consciousness, however, does not mean that we always act from this more complex layer of thinking. If we become stressed or fearful we will often act from earlier layers or even from our instinctive core. This has obvious evolutionary roots: those of our ancestors on the savannah who stopped and started to reflect upon their emotions and will when attacked by a lion probably did not survive. When exposed to dangers it is usually better to just react from lower-level instincts than from the time-consuming reflections on our immediate will. The problem, however, is that the same pattern of reactions governs us even today when we, for example in our work, feel challenged or worried and therefore cannot bring ourselves to act from our highest layer of consciousness. Scared and stressed humans rarely behave in accordance with their highest potential.

The third layer's socialised self turns our desires and needs into an object for our consciousness while the mutual relations and agreements in everyday life become subjects. I *am* a responsible parent, a wise teacher, a party animal, and so on. One's needs are then shaped around these roles: I want to have a safe Volvo car *because* I am a responsible parent, a Porsche *because* I am a playboy. We shape our relations and personality to accommodate society's expectations, attempt to fit into the role our culture has given us and act accordingly. Usually we do so rather unconsciously. We are aware of what is expected from us, but rarely ponder why that is and why we want to fit in.

In this layer of consciousness our values and norms, our ideology, or our religion function as the filter through which we view and relate to the world. We have acquired these from our culture, our friends or our family, and they have become an integrated part of who we consider ourselves to be. These filters own us, we do not own them. They are templates through which we create meaning and understand the world. But if these are challenged we cannot reflexively relate to what is happening and may become confused or even feel violated. Critical refection on social norms is a cognitive capacity that requires yet another layer of psychological complexity.

The Formation of Layer 4

Many, but not all (less than half of the population in the West according to some research),[15] develop a fourth layer later in life. If this occurs, it is often in the middle of life in connection with some kind of crisis or other major disruption. We might then start questioning our life ambitions and values. We may ask ourselves whether our life objectives and values really are our own, or if they may be those of our parents, our colleagues or quite simply what our culture expects of us. In exceptional cases it occurs as early as during our late teens, but then the right form of support and challenges are often required from our environment.

With the formation of the fourth layer we start questioning society's norms and become less dependent on what others think of us. With our own reason and logical thinking we begin to find our own inner compass. In a traditional society this can be expressed by questioning religion. We may find that our religion or culture does not represent what we deep down stand for. We may become engaged in the rights of homosexuals and gender equality and summon the courage to question moral strictures that we find outmoded, even if this would entail being stigmatised. In a more secular society we may question what are considered the accepted truths (e.g. political correctness, scientific authority, etc.). We challenge social boundaries that we cannot venture outside without running the risk of being called into question by our society. We may become 'righteous rebels'.

We also gain the ability to relate more freely and openly to our values. We can take our own values as objects of reflection and may not feel as threatened if someone challenges them. We are not, as previously, completely identified with them. Our values no longer own us. Instead, we acquire the ability to own them and reflect upon them as something outside of our self.

Layer 4 thus revolves around being able to perceive social norms, ideologies, religions, morals and other abstractions as objects that we can actively choose among. Through these choices we become authors of our own selves for the first time. We become *self-authoring*, in Kegan's words.

Nonetheless we cannot yet perceive our own need for autonomy, our own emancipation process or personal self-realisation project as an object since we are too heavily embedded in this.

Bildungsroman is a term that is sometimes used for novels about a person's maturing from being unconsciously embedded in their culture and context to becoming able to liberate themselves from these confines and take their environment's values, expectations and requirements as objects of independent reflection. Good examples of such novels about personal transformation are Goethe's *Wilhelm Meisters Lehrjahre* and *Faust.* A more contemporary example is J. K. Rowling's *Harry Potter.*

Even though a large share of the population in the West at some point in their lives initiate the formation of Layer 4, there are studies indicating that less than half of all adults have the ability to act consistently from this stage of cognition. The following layer is even rarer.

The Formation of Layer 5

A small part of the population experiences the formation of a fifth layer later in life, often after the age of fifty according to Kegan. Here we begin taking our own autonomy as an object of reflection and develop what Kegan calls a *self-transforming* mind. We are no longer as dependent on maintaining our individuality and sticking stubbornly to our own inner compass. Increasingly we orient ourselves towards the group and society, though this time not as a socialised part of our culture but with a playful questioning of our individuality and society's norms. If the self-evident objective had previously been to find ourselves and build our identity and our self, we can now enable ourselves to make this process an object of reflection and thereby start letting go of the identification with our own self-realisation project. Hence, we can begin to surpass – transcend – our self. This enables us to much more freely choose our perspective on ourselves and our environment. We can relate more openly to several perspectives, perspectives that we earlier, in our quest for authenticity, might have considered contradictory and irreconcilable. Paradoxes become something that we can appreciate and learn from, not necessarily something to avoid or try to dissolve. Reasoning with formal logic is thus complemented with what can be termed 'dialectical logic':[16] It is no longer a question of either/or *or* both/and, but of *both* either/or *and* both/and at once.

Now we can choose whether we want to be autonomous or not. And we can become better at relating to our thoughts and behavioural patterns, emotional 'hang-ups' and passions and frustrations as objects. We also develop an ability to see how events and relations influence our emotions, and how we respond to these in turn influences events and relations in a constant interplay without beginning or end. This interplay between ourselves, our emotions, our autonomy, our cultural context, how we choose to act from this, the environment's reactions to our actions, and how these in turn influence us, becomes something we can take as object of reflection.

When the fifth layer has been formed, the self assumes increasingly abstract, detached and more universally applicable forms. We see that our self-perception is not directly tied to ourselves as bodies and persons. Instead, social contexts and creation processes – including *other* people's completely different perspectives and levels of psychological development – become subsumed into what we identify with the most. Even our values are now regarded as something that are under constant reconstruction and development. The inner convictions that the previous layer frenetically defends as its most sacred treasures now instead become something to tinker with, replace and further develop.

Once again, however, I need to point out that the previous layers remain within us. They can be activated and may become governing if we are threatened or put under considerable stress. If we risk losing our sense of who we are we may revert to thinking and acting in accordance with Layer 2. Moreover, we can, on good or bad days, shift between the various layers. A heavy migraine or a caustic divorce can make it harder to see oneself as part of a dancing interplay with the environment. But on a carefree morning when we are working with the project of our dreams it is easier to embrace a more abstract self-conception.

It is a very small part of the population – studies indicate it may be around 1%[17] – that consistently acts from the fifth layer. This may not sound a lot, but 1% does after all represent many millions of people worldwide. However, the problem is that these people are often not in contact with each other and often feel isolated and poorly understood by their society. Our culture assumes that we all function in accordance with the earlier layers, so whenever someone makes arguments derived from the fifth layer of complexity, their thoughts are often misunderstood or ignored – with the sad consequence that society fails to learn from the useful wisdoms of these people.

* * *

The table on the next page sums up how we, through the formation of new layers of cognitive complexity, can take new parts of our self, our subject, as an object of reflection and how they relate to the complexity levels described in the previous chapter.

In the rest of this chapter and the following I will refer to these layers simply as Kegan 0 to 5.

What then is the pattern that unites these developmental layers or phases of transformative learning? In fact, I have mentioned it already: an object–subject dynamic. Every new layer makes the previous one an object, something that we can relate to and manipulate from a previously unobtained distance. This developmental dynamic has been observed by many of psychology's most notable thinkers and has been given many different names. George H. Mead argued that the self consisted of an 'I' and a 'me', where 'I' corresponds to the subject and 'me' corresponds to the object.[18] Freud's motto 'where id was, there ego shall be'[19] speaks the same language. C. G. Jung talked about incorporating various parts of the unconscious, the so-called 'shadow',[20] which can also be seen as a sort of developmental process making previous subjects into objects. The developmental psychologist Erik Erikson, who claimed that individuals can

Layer	Subject ('I')	New inner object	Complexity
0th Layer Symbiotic Mind	Reflexes, sensations and own movements		
1st Layer Impulsive Mind	Impulses and perception	Reflexes, sensations and own movements	Concrete experiences
2nd Layer Instrumental Mind	Desires, enduring objective and own needs	Impulses and perception	Categories
3rd Layer Socialised Mind	Mutual relations and agreements	Desires, enduring objective and own needs	Connections
4th Layer Self-authoring Mind	Ideology, values and a unique identity in relation to others	Mutual relations and agreements	Systems
5th Layer Self-transforming Mind	The general interaction that develops both own and other identities	Ideology, values and a unique identity in relation to others	Paradigms

Subject, object and complexity for Layer 0 to 5.[21]

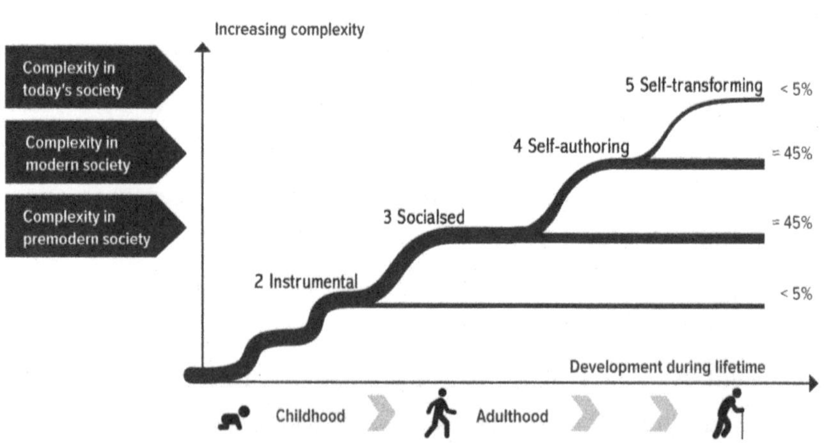

Development of complexity of mind during life in today's Western society. Adapted from Elfhag (2019).[22]

develop ethically throughout life, equally argued that the later phases in life were built on the development of earlier ones. While one can hardly equate these theories with each other, they address the same overall issue: that the self can incorporate new parts of itself and thereby transform itself into a higher-functioning subject, a more conscious individual.

THE DIFFERENT ASPECTS OF OUR EGO DEVELOPMENT

Every new layer creates some kind of structural reorganisation of our consciousness that comprises many different aspects of how we perceive and relate to ourselves and the world. This entails, for instance, that:

- we can participate in and relate to more complex relations;
- our meaning-creation and our interpretation of the world become more nuanced and sophisticated;
- we can assume more perspectives on a formulated problem;
- we become increasingly adept at understanding others' thoughts and emotions;
- we gain an increased ability to include more sentient beings in our circle of empathy;
- our way of reasoning around moral dilemmas thereby becomes more consistent and universal;
- and what we value most in life changes to accommodate these new insights, and thereby increases the likelihood of our behaviour being more prudent, reasonable and considerate.

With every layer we thus become more complex thinkers, capable of grasping more perspectives and aspects of the world, and arguably even somewhat better-behaving – as claimed by Erik Erikson. All of these are necessary to manage an increasingly complex society and the many different, often contradicting perspectives of its inhabitants. However, that we can develop ethically is perhaps the most important point. That transformative learning can increase our ethical reasoning, that more developed individuals may behave more ethically, and that they can be more empathic is perhaps the most contested issue within the field of psychological development. But given that psychological development can basically be summed up as an increase in our awareness, this ought to include ethical aspects as well. For instance, when we become aware of aspects of our mind that once remained hidden to ourselves, it is reasonable to claim that that should improve our understanding of other's perspectives that once were similar to our own. This arguably increases the likelihood of becoming more empathic towards them, which thereby helps develop our ethical reasoning. The idea that psychological development goes hand-in-hand with ethical development is therefore not as far-fetched as it may sound to begin with. It does not, however, mean that highly developed individuals always behave more ethically, that a person who acts stably on Kegan 5 cannot be a scoundrel and a delinquent, or that a less developed person cannot behave more ethically than a more developed one. But the scope of one's capacity to see the perspective of others, the level of sophistication and consistency in one's ethical reasoning, and thereby the odds of behaving accordingly, may arguably be higher in a more mature individual than a less mature one.

However, ethics, or empathy or compassion, is just one aspect that can be developed throughout life. According to Thomas Jordan there are five others: complexity awareness, contextual awareness, relational awareness, self-insight and perspectival awareness.[23]

Compassion, Empathy

Empathy entails compassion for, and understanding of, other humans. Empathy can only be developed once we have separated ourselves from the world and realise that other people have their own experiences, i.e. when we have left the egocentric perspective of the child. Through socialisation processes we develop the capacity to 'feel with' others that belong to our closest circle. But this is not to say that empathy is fully developed at this stage. Empathy can be developed throughout our lives, deepened and extended to encompass more people, even those who are strangers. The extension of our empathy is then not limited by group belonging. The greater the togetherness we feel, the greater a part of the world can be included into our circle of solidarity. All of humanity, and sometimes even all sentient beings, can come to be contained in our capacity for empathy. We also become more involved in and touched by world events at further distances from ourselves.

The capacity for empathy requires that we set ourselves aside and develop insights and emotional involvement about others' inner states. With empathy, we bridge the distance to other subjects. Instead of seeing them as objects, they become subjects – as a benign reversal of the subject-to-object development – of equal consideration to ourselves.

It should be added that *real* empathy consists of both emotional engagement *and* cognitive understanding. If only the latter is present (as in psychopaths), it does not constitute what is here meant by empathy. If the opposite is the case, the experienced compassion can be seen as a kind of empathy, but a severely handicapped kind that inhibits the person's ethical reasoning in general and one that largely relies on the intensity of the feelings of compassion which can vary from moment to moment and thereby results in less reasonable behaviour. A well-developed sense of empathy can generate deep-felt emotions of compassion towards others *and* an accurate understanding of what they feel and why.

The capacity to feel compassion towards others and understand their perspectives obviously has great significance in a society. And since ever-increasing complexity has made our mutual welfare and survival reliant on the cooperation between billions of people both within and across national borders, with more diverse and vastly different perspectives than ever before, the demands for our empathic capacity to include more individuals into our sphere of solidarity and understand alien perspectives have never been greater. In our hypercomplex global society it does not suffice to merely feel compassion with those in our closest proximity or to only understand the perspectives of people with whom we share the same culture. In order to manage an increasingly complex world we need to ensure that more people develop the empathic capacities required of a truly global citizen.

Complexity Awareness

Complexity awareness is the capacity to make analytically sound inferences. A higher complexity awareness can manage more variables simultaneously, make more inferences from these and better coordinate these into systems, systems within systems and so forth. The kind of cognitive complexity we are talking about here is sometimes referred to as 'vertical complexity'. 'Horizontal complexity' is that of intelligence, or IQ, which merely determines the speed of our analytic thinking. Vertical complexity, on the other hand, is about *how* our analytic thinking works.

Complexity awareness revolves around *expecting* that there are circumstances, underlying causal connections and system properties, which *might* be relevant to see and understand in order to carry out a task successfully. A low degree of complexity awareness entails that one does not reflect as much upon more abstractedly perceived possible causes and consequences, but rather takes a stand and acts based on what is tangibly evident. A high degree of complexity awareness generally leads to a more investigating and reflecting approach where one is well aware that there probably exists a host of relevant circumstances, causal contexts and possible consequences that one remains ignorant of.

To grasp and handle the world's complexity, we need to develop a corresponding cognitive complexity. Managing the increasing complexity of our society obviously requires that we obtain more knowledge and specialise in highly advanced occupations. But knowledge and skills are not the same as cognitive complexity. Performing highly complex tasks requires a corresponding degree of cognitive complexity, but cognitive complexity in itself is not something one can be taught. According to Michael Commons, complexity is an inherited trait just like intelligence. However, in the same way average IQ increased during the twentieth century as living conditions improved, complexity likewise seems to be a cognitive capacity that can increase under favourable conditions, as shown by a famous experiment where a parrot, after much training by very patient instructors, became capable of performing tasks one complexity stage above what is usually observed in nature (from stage 5 to 6 on the MHC scale).[24]

Although contested, I believe it is plausible that complexity awareness in humans can be increased as well. Intelligence may be genetically determined, but nutrition and intellectual stimulation in people's upbringing have proved crucial factors determining whether they reach their highest potential. Similar factors, and others yet to be identified by research, may likewise determine whether we reach our highest level of complexity awareness. The question of whether our level of complexity awareness is innate (which the research of Commons suggests) or not, is thus secondary to that of how we reach our highest potential. In my own personal experience, I have known people who all of a sudden started to perform tasks on higher levels of complexity than earlier in their lives. In these cases, new challenges and changes in their environment seemed to function as a kind of scaffolding from which they obtained the necessary means to support their cognitive development towards higher complexity awareness. They may have had some kind of innate ability to think more complexly, but it seems to have been external factors that made them achieve this level of thought.

Thus people may come to think more complexly under the right conditions. We do not know exactly what is required, but since the ever-increasing complexity of the world demands that more of us think more complexly more often, it is paramount that we figure out how we can support this. In the industrial age it sufficed to think in terms of formal logic and linear causality to make the machines and bureaucracies of modern society work. But in our current chaotic and hypercomplex globalised information society – a civilisation on the brink of an ecological disaster – we need more people with highly complex analytic abilities, such as thinking in terms of chaos theory, self-organising systems, multi-perspectivity and developmental non-linear logic.

Contextual Awareness

Contextual awareness is the ability to survey the wider context that tasks and events are situated within: the kinds of properties that prevail in a wider context, the processes of change going on there, what the interactions looks like, i.e. how actions might possibly influence the wider context, and how the context in turn influences these. The more contexts we become aware of and the better we understand them in depth, the more likely we are to develop a sense of responsibility for the greater whole since we then better realise how it is all connected. Improving our capacity for contextual awareness can also complement our complexity awareness by increasing our understanding of the wider contexts in which complex matters are situated.

In a wider context there is, of course, society or culture. We can therefore also speak of a greater *societal consciousness*. Being able to see our societal and cultural contexts as objects for reflection also means that we can treat them as the kinds of social imaginaries they are. A higher contextual awareness can thereby make us see the social constructions that previously remained part of our subject from an outside perspective so that we better manage to analyse and alter them. This also gives us the opportunity to distance and liberate ourselves from the societal and cultural contexts we were once embedded within.

Our hypercomplex human civilisation requires that we increase our awareness and understanding of the many subtle, and to ourselves often culturally alien, contexts that have come to play a greater role in our lives. In the industrial age it was sufficient to know the contexts of society's primary productive and political relations and one's national culture. Today, however, we need to understand a high number of less tangible societal contexts, such as gender norms, identity creation processes, social dynamics, etc., as well as a host of foreign cultures and religions. Even ecological and technological contexts must be considered if we want to get a remotely accurate map of the current world and if we want to navigate it successfully.

Relational Awareness

This aspect revolves around the awareness of other people, groups and social matters that exist in relation to one another, ourselves and other people. Our relational awareness can help us figure out who others are, what their interests and intentions might be, how they reason and why they act the way they do, how they experience encounters with ourselves, see the situation, and what they might expect from us. Our relational awareness is intimately connected with our empathic capacity to see the perspectives of others. It largely depends on this capacity, but relational awareness is different in the way it determines how well we interpret the information provided by our empathic capacity and how we strategise about social relations.

Another word for 'relational awareness' is 'social intelligence'. And like the previous aspects, this can also be more or less developed. A low level of relational awareness makes it hard to manage high numbers of social relations, understand the roles of others and determine what others want and think about us. People who have a low level of relational awareness often cannot differentiate their own role in a group from that of others. They often fail to see that a social relation does not necessarily mean the same to others as it does to themselves, that people can experience the same relationship differently, and that people might want different things from the relation. As a result, low relational awareness often leads to mismanaged relationships, misunderstandings and anger and bitterness. A high degree of relational awareness makes it possible to perceive our own perspective on social relations and role within them from a distance.

Once again, by making what previously remained subject an object for our consciousness, it becomes possible to investigate it and thereby make better choices. If we more clearly see our role within a relation, how it differs from others' and what is expected from this kind of role, the chances of improving our relations with others will increase. And if we understand how others think and see us, we get a more accurate image of the social dynamics we are situated within, which can help us change how we are perceived and thereby improve our relations and status within the group. This not only serves our own interests, but can also benefit the group. A high level of relational awareness can make us better at figuring out ways to merge the interests of different persons and how to cooperate with others.

It is hardly necessary to mention that relational awareness is very important and that high levels of this aspect can make societies better functioning. A well-developed relational awareness is more important than ever since a growing number of occupations require that people are good at cooperating and managing complex social relations. Improving peoples' social intelligence should therefore be just as important in our educational system as learning more formal skills. The increasing complexity of our ever more well-connected society requires that we become just as competent at analysing people and relations as we are at analysing symbols.

Self-insight

Self-insight is the awareness of how our self functions on a psychological level. This entails the ability to feel and understand what is happening within ourselves, what we feel and think and why, thus understanding why we behave the way we do. We can thereby better evaluate what we need to be happy, what we need to avoid and what we should do to make our behaviour more beneficial to ourselves and others. By making our desires, feelings and thoughts an object for investigation, rather than merely *being* our desires, feelings and thoughts – subject becoming object once again – it becomes easier to change ourselves and approach life in a more appropriate manner. The more aspects of our psyche we become aware of – the deeper we venture into the dark corners of our own mind – the more emotional and psychological issues we can resolve, and thereby we obtain more opportunities in life. Developing our capacity for self-insight can give us more freedom – literally speaking: freedom from things that torment our soul, freedom to do things we did not know we were capable of.

Developing our empathic capacities, ability to handle high complexity, awareness of contexts and understanding of social relations is unlikely to occur if we do not simultaneously improve our self-insight. If we do not understand ourselves, we cannot understand the world.

Perspectival Awareness

From greater self-insight we gain an improved capacity to see our own perspective from a distance, which thereby increases our perspectival awareness accordingly, which then expands our capacity to see others' perspectives. Perspectival awareness is the capacity to understand that others have different perspectives than oneself, why the same phenomenon can be viewed in different ways, and how our own perspective is just one among many and therefore not necessarily the most correct one. The more aspects of our own perspective we become aware of, the better we understand why we view the world the way we do, and the better we can become at understanding the perspectives of others. With a high level of perspectival awareness we can even hold several contradictory perspectives in our mind simultaneously, and thereby develop the sophistication, diverseness and scope of our general perspective on the world.

To make our personal perspective an object for our consciousness to investigate is perhaps the most difficult cognitive task we can perform. And no matter how aware we become of certain aspects of our perspective we will always remain subjects who see the world from a certain vantage point that we do not notice. Yet, if we take the time to scrutinise our mind and how it sees the world, it becomes possible to make objects out of what currently constitutes our subject. Philosophy, meditation techniques and time spent contemplating existence can help us get there. If we succeed, our view of the world can become richer, more nuanced and encompass more of the Universe – literally speaking: those who have obtained more perspectives when they die will have contained more aspects of the Universe within their mind.

As with all of the abovementioned psychological aspects, the development of our capacity for perspectival awareness is important if we are to cope with an increasingly complex world. The society we live in already contains a higher number of different perspectives than we currently are able to handle. This is not going to be lower in the future. Our world is a multiperspectival Universe consisting of billions of humans with varying degrees of psychological development in all of the aspects that have been mentioned here. To navigate this world, we therefore need to develop our capacity to understand these perspectives – all while keeping in mind that our own may be inadequate and erroneous, in need of further development. If we do so, we might develop in ways we had not foreseen.

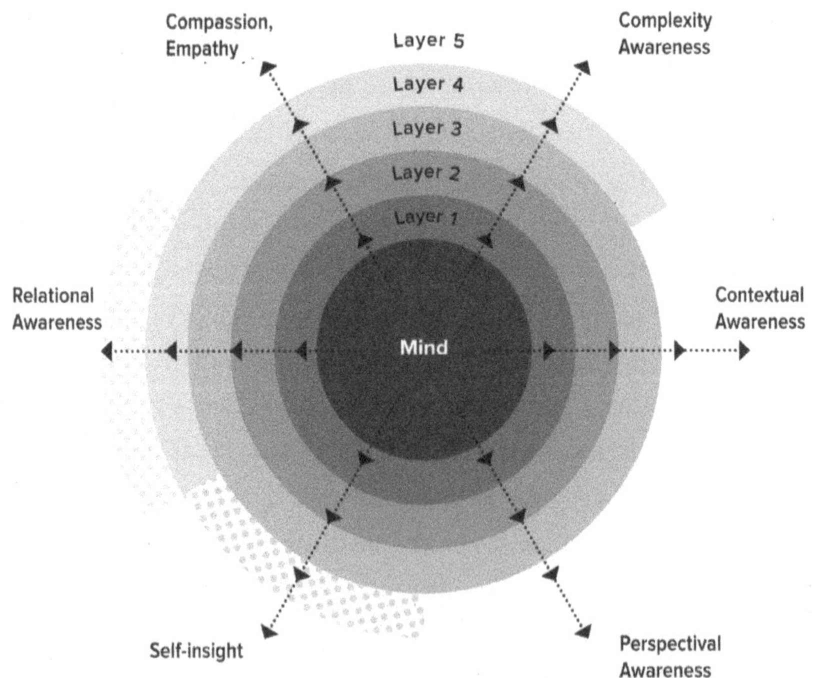

Our ego-development can be at very different stages for different dimension of development.

Transformative Skills

We can use these different aspects of ego-development described above to find a more intuitive way to approach and describe this whole field of inner development. We can see each of these developmental dimensions as describing fundamental aspects of our personality that can be developed as skills. We could then be talking about our lifelong need to develop our capacity for compassion, complex sense making, perspective taking, self-knowledge, etc. We could then again use the language of transformative learning that we started this chapter with. These capacities or skills that cannot be developed through traditional education, but require the deeper psychological development of transformative learning and could then be called *transformative skills*. Arguing for the need to develop transformative skills is probably easier in today's world than speaking about the more abstract need for ego-development.

THE ETHICAL IMPLICATIONS OF PSYCHOLOGICAL DEVELOPMENT

Developing our cognitive complexity is not virtuous in and of itself, but since the complexity of the world around us continues to increase, we risk ending up with a majority of the adult population being out-complexed by their surroundings if they do not obtain the transformative learning experiences required to develop the higher layers of cognition. A society without the necessary support structures to further the personal growth of its inhabitants is destined to have an average level of psychological development that does not correspond with the complexity of the world. If too few of us understand and can competently manage current complexity, any collective efforts to solve the many issues it brings forth will be doomed to fail and eventually lead to disaster. It is therefore a moral imperative that we make the effort to ensure that as many as possible get the opportunity to develop their cognition.

Unfortunately, the insight that adult humans can develop psychologically, and that it is crucial that we find out how if we are to handle the many challenges of an increasingly complex world, has not yet secured a foothold within broader circles in academia and even less in the general public. This is not without its reasons. For one, it is a new and relatively complicated topic, which probably limits its general dissemination. Most self-help books usually revolve around personal growth in a single superficial area (such as self-esteem, professional accomplishments or a successful love-life), and wider societal implications are almost always entirely neglected. Narrow self-interest and one-dimensional approaches still dominate the issue of psychological development in popular literature and public discourse. As regards the academic world, psychiatry and psychology have primarily focused on pathologies (the things that go wrong in our psychological development and make us sick) rather than how the healthy mind can develop in adult age. The assumption that the purpose of modern psychiatry and psychology is only to treat mental diseases and emotional difficulties, rather than to serve as a support structure for psychological growth in healthy adults, is probably the underlying reason.

A further, and no less significant, reason might be the hierarchical aspect of psychological development. The word 'development' implies the presence of hierarchies where some things are considered more or less developed than others. Whether we talk about layers, phases or stages, and whether we differentiate them from each other in terms of depth or complexity, earlier or later, higher or lower, the conclusion is the same: namely that there are psychological hierarchies among human beings. But the postmodern influence has programmed us into shying away from all sorts of hierarchies where something can be considered better or higher than something else – especially when it comes to humans. That one individual should be considered more developed than another is simply a no-go in our current postmodern discourse since it appears to conflict with the ideal of equality among humans. However, this tenacious resistance is largely derived from the misunderstanding that higher equals better, that the level of development determines a human's value. Once again we have an erroneous inference of an 'is' from an 'ought'. The observation that someone is more developed is a descriptive fact, an 'is' within Popper's W1, to then derive a normative statement from this, an 'ought' belonging within W3, is simply an argumentative error as false as it is ethically deplorable. Higher psychological development in an individual does not mean the person should be seen as more important than others. Being less developed simply does not make anyone less worthy of ethical consideration. On the contrary. Since the joy and suffering of all, ethically speaking, are equally important, the circumstance that low psychological development can make it harder to navigate in our complex world ought to increase our consideration and care towards those less developmentally fortunate among us.

It is interesting to note, however, that we rarely derive normative statements about the value of children from their obviously lower levels of cognition vis-à-vis adults. Despite most of us agreeing on the fact that children are less developed than adults, they are still considered just as valuable members of society as everyone else. Yet when it is claimed that the same differences exist between adults, the fear that the less developed should automatically be seen as second-class citizens tends to make people dismissive of the notion of hierarchical stages of psychological development all together. However, as argued throughout, understanding that there are developmental differences between adult humans can actually help us create a more equal society. Our needs and desires often depend on our level of psychological development, so if we better understand the values and way of thinking of people on different stages of development it could help us make their lives better. That someone is currently at a stage in life that makes them value material security and belongingness within a religious community does not make them less worthy of consideration than someone in the middle of their personal emancipatory self-realisation project. In fact, obtaining the former is necessary for the latter. So learning about psychological development can help remind us that the needs we ourselves may have had satisfied earlier in life and forgotten all about still remain relevant to others.

The layers of cognition that are formed as we develop throughout life do not constitute our essence. They are merely more or less floating expressions of where we presently are in life. Our level of cognition is not who we are, and having developed highly complex layers certainly does not make us better persons per se. We shift between different layers depending upon the situation, where we are in our life, our stress and energy level, and a host of other factors. Fear and anxiety can make us behave from more primitive layers, while positive emotions and fortunate conditions can make us act from our highest potential and sometimes even help us develop new more complex layers. Being highly developed also means that we contain all the earlier layers, which thereby can make us more understanding and tolerant towards those who have not progressed as far as ourselves – even if the feelings are not mutual and our higher cognition makes us appear odd or outright immoral to them.

Learning about psychological development should serve the ambition of seeing our fellow human beings and their perspectives in more tolerant ways. If we understand that every stage of psychological development is necessary, that we must pass through all the preceding layers before the later and higher ones can be formed, it can make us less inclined towards condemning others for their developmental shortcomings and make it easier to cope with our own. If the opinions of others appear morally detestable to us, knowing about psychological development can help us realise that they probably lack a certain perspective that they can obtain under fortunate conditions later on – rather than that they have some kind of immoral and static essence making them an inherently bad person. When we realise that all layers build on each other, that all of them are needed on the path forward and that we cannot skip any when we are forming our wider, greater self, then it is no longer a question of any being inherently better or worse – only that some of them are better suited for certain purposes than others.

HOW CAN WE SUPPORT PSYCHOLOGICAL DEVELOPMENT?

We have evolved from a society where most of us functioned in accordance with Kegan 2, driven by our immediate instincts and desires with little means to control them; through a society where the great moral religions provided us with the necessary symbol tools to help us curb our will so that the majority of us began acting from Kegan 3; to a modern society with widely available education where many of us are able to critically scrutinise our inherited norms and values in accordance with Kegan 4. Developing our society further so that more of us reach Kegan 5 should therefore not only be considered possible. Given the aforementioned capacities of this layer and the way in which they can address the current crises of our increasingly complex world, it is also a moral imperative. A greater share of the population who sees and truly understands the manifold perspectives of others, who derive knowledge and wisdom from the seemingly paradoxical nature of the world, and who do not identify with their autonomous self and put their private project of self-realisation at the centre of existence is urgently needed.

In order for transformative learning experiences to take place and foster increased psychological development, the individual needs both a certain level of perceived security, materially as well as emotionally, and exposure to reasonably demanding challenges.[25] We need a solid foundation of security to start from so that we do not regress to earlier and more primitive reaction patterns and defensive survival mechanisms. But we also need a fair number of life challenges that we feel we can overcome so that we are spurred to move forward and develop novel cognitive tools to tackle the new problems we encounter.

Growing up in a loving family and with good schooling can provide us with the sense of security we need in order to develop beyond the most basic layers of cognition. And as we venture into adult life with all the obligations and challenges that that entails, the environments we become part of in our studies, work life and other social contexts can serve as more or less favourable support structures for our personal development. If we feel secure and confident within these while we are simultaneously exposed to stimulating challenges, we become more likely to experience a healthy and prolonged development. Besides obtaining new knowledge, education or similar learning experiences can make us more independent, more responsible and better at handling more complex issues. If we are lucky to get a job that encourages us to think for ourselves, and maybe even provides us opportunities to learn new things, we may not only acquire new technical skills, but grow as persons as well. If our work only consists of repetitive tasks, if we feel that it does not allow us to reach our highest potential, and if we feel disconnected from what we are doing and do not have any influence on our work situation, it may hinder our development.

Yet, good opportunities are not the only thing to spur psychological development; challenges also play a critical role, even if we initially may feel overburdened by them. Sometimes it is the hardest challenges in life that make us grow the most, but only if we make it to the other side without breaking apart. Elfhag has described how various difficulties and crises can compel us to re-orient ourselves and our perspective throughout life.[26] Within the field of transformative learning, there has also been much research describing how confrontations with seemingly unsolvable paradoxes and exposure to disconcerting perspectives can function as catalysts for our transformation. Throughout our life journey we are often put through great stress and severe crises, pain and hurtful emotions that may challenge our very existence and view of ourselves: growing up and suddenly having to take responsibility for ourselves, heartbreak and sorrow, disease, loss of loved ones, ageing and so on. Such experiences may paralyse us or make us regress to a survivalist mode of living, but they can also serve as learning experiences that provide us with a wider perspective on the world and ourselves. Successful transformation through such crises is more likely to occur if we have access to support structures that help us make sense of our experiences. Loving family members, a loyal lover or spouse, or trusted friends who understand us can help us through such difficulties. Sometimes even professional guidance can function as a support structure to facilitate a personal transformation through a crisis. Culture, not least literature, can also play an important role here. It can provide us with a language to articulate what we feel by providing us access to others' experiences that we can use to mirror our own in order to obtain greater clarity and present us with inspiring narratives to guide us through life's many difficulties and challenges. A culture richly endowed with wisdom traditions and artistic expressions that address the difficult and upsetting things in life is consequently more likely to produce individuals who overcome crises and turn them into valuable learning experiences.

Culture and society as a whole can thus play an important role in promoting our development. Generally, affluent societies tend to generate higher levels of psychological development than poorer ones. This partly has to do with higher social security, better education and more stimulating work opportunities. But these may not be the only factors. Even though psychological development is a relatively new field and much still remains in uncharted territory, there has been research indicating how we might facilitate increased transformative learning on the societal level:[27]

- We know that people who have had access to therapy and other kinds of professional help have been more likely to turn periods of personal crisis into transformative learning experiences. Accordingly, ensuring that such services are available to everyone who needs them ought to be highly prioritised.
- Institutional measures to provide comprehensive personal support in the form of well-informed and listening professional guidance, for instance in schools and other education institutions, social services, hospitals, etc., have proved beneficial for increased personal growth. Expanding their availability, and improving the

quality of the existing services as well as offering ordinary people additional assistance from a form of professional life-coaches could therefore be a political strategy worth pursuing.

- It has been proved that children and youngsters who have had access to education that emphasises other aspects than formal skills, and which encouraged critical thinking, self-expression and creativity have reached higher levels of cognition as adults. The educational methods that most efficiently facilitate our continuous psychological development, supported by empirical evidence, should therefore be implemented in the entire education system. In addition, we could establish a new research field investigating how education influences our development, with the purpose of creating new methods to further it.
- We also know that higher levels of trust and love in our relationships are beneficial to our development. We should therefore investigate if there are policies that can increase the average quality of people's relations, how we as a society can ensure that more people become able to establish healthy relations to others: find trusted friends, a loving spouse, a functional family life, and forge good relations with their colleagues. On a general level, societies and communities characterised by higher amounts of trust likewise seem to further the psychological development of their inhabitants. We should therefore learn from these examples and see if there are things we could adopt in our own society to this end.
- People who from an early age and throughout their lives have been exposed to a considerable amount of art and other cultural experiences also tend to be more developed than those who have not. Opportunities to express oneself artistically or musically have likewise proven highly beneficial. Political measures to support society's cultural life, fine art as well as popular culture, should therefore get a higher priority, and we should investigate how culture can be used to stimulate further transformative learning.

- There are even investigations indicating that the privilege to engage in other activities than work during adult life can help people reach higher levels of development. Increasing the amount of spare time and encouraging people to take time off from work in order to devote themselves to interests that may further their personal growth should therefore become a political concern. If every citizen got at least one year of leave during their work lives, with governmental support, the average level of development would probably increase.
- And there is plentiful evidence showing that various contemplation techniques, meditation and subtle body exercises (yoga or tai-chi, for example), besides higher well-being, can contribute to increased self-control, inner self-awareness and empathy. As such, these ancient and well-tested methods remain some of the most efficient ways to increase our psychological development. If they became more widely available and were politically encouraged, for instance by making meditation and body exercises part of our schools' and workplaces' daily activities, it could lead to some of the most far-reaching positive developments for our society and culture.

These are just a few examples of things we know are capable of promoting our psychological development. How exactly they can generate transformative learning, and how we best make use of them, remain open for further research. But we do know that we can support the development of the human mind. It would therefore be foolish not to make it a societal concern. Learning about the many new insights that a growing number of researchers within the field of psychological development have brought forth, and making transformative learning a highly prioritised societal concern, may very well provide the solutions we need for the countless issues we currently appear hopelessly incapable of handling with our existing thought tools – if for no other reason than because there do not appear to be any better alternatives.

If not psychological development, then what is the missing piece to the puzzle, what else could there be that we have not tested yet? I am open for suggestions, but until a more convincing alternative becomes apparent I will continue to claim that psychological development remains the most promising solution.

Chapter 13

THE METAMODERN THOUGHT PERSPECTIVE

Increasing our level of psychological ego-development is crucial if we are to understand and manage our complex world, but we also need access to more complex symbol tools to go along with these higher cognitive capacities. Eventually we will also need to co-create a new collective imaginary that is capable of supporting our constantly complexifying world. We need a new overarching framework of symbols – a new thought perspective – to get the most out of our cognitive complexity and to help us all to develop our minds further. We need both more individuals with the cognitive and emotional ability to handle higher amounts of complexity *and* a corresponding cultural context from which we can obtain the necessary symbol tools to manage and conceptually order this higher complexity.

In the first half of this chapter I will focus on cognitive complexity and present some examples of what different levels of complexity can enable us to do. In the second half I will present a proposal for a new thought perspective to follow postmodernism, an overarching symbol-kit that I have termed the 'metamodern thought perspective'.

POLITICS AT VARIOUS COMPLEXITY LEVELS

We will now return to the complexity levels we have discussed in the two previous chapters:

1. The Category Level
2. The Connection Level
3. The System Level
4. The Perspective Level

The system and perspective levels are far more effective at handling many of our most difficult and wicked complex social problems. Today, however, a very large part of societal and political life remains characterised by far too linear ways of thinking that is characteristic of the connection level.

The simplest definition of a non-linear system is that its result (output) is not proportional to that which is fed into the system (input). In principle, everything that belongs to society and its development is non-linear, but in different ways. And yet we humans have a stubborn habit of thinking all too linearly around societal issues, overlooking things such as exponentiality, unforeseen risks, chaos, developmental qualitative leaps, dissemination and cross-fertilisation of knowledge, and so forth. The concept of non-linearity is a good, but rough-hewn, protection against such linear thinking. It pushes us to revaluate our thinking, reconsider whether there is something we have missed, things we cannot fully predict or factors that remain hidden from view. It is a reminder that if our analysis is too linearly conceived, then it is likely to be insufficient to guide our actions. We need to keep in mind that the world is a highly complex and chaotic place. If we do not sufficiently consider this and let ourselves be blinded by our own ingenuity at devising linear causal analyses and plans of action, we are likely to fail at solving complex tasks in the real world.

Linear ways of thinking that are common today are those such as:

- That the job market revolves around giving people jobs.
- That education revolves around giving people the competencies required for them to be able to participate in the job market.

- That people's competences increase through longer education.
- That the society of the future is more of the same of that which we have today.
- That the decisive environmental issue is a reduction of emissions.
- That poor psychological health in society is primarily contravened through more resources for psychiatric treatment.
- That public health is primarily improved through more resources for health care.
- That crime is primarily fought through more resources for crime fighting.
- That social problems are primarily ameliorated through more resources for social services.
- That injustices are primarily prevented through a redistribution of economic resources.
- That society becomes gender equal through courses in gender equality.
- That gender equality is about a 50/50 distribution between women and men in all spheres of life.
- That culture is primarily enriched through financial support to art, music and theatre.
- That economic growth in itself improves human beings' living standards through gradual progress.
- That the government and parliament will solve society's decisive problems.
- That development occurs through free competition on the market.
- That people are first and foremost individuals with specific interests.
- That society constitutes the sum of all individuals.
- That technological development eventually solves all of our problems.

Even if some of these linear thoughts can be justified in certain situations, none of them can sufficiently address the fundamental issues we are placed before today. Accordingly, this sort of thinking must be complemented with a more holistic non-linear way of thinking that can handle issues like the above more effectively. The critical problem of linear thinking is that the interrelated, systemic and evolutionary properties of reality make our world develop and behave in non-linear and emergent ways and thus cannot be predicted or fully be accounted for through linear reasoning. Attempting to identify linear cause and effect chains rarely leads us to the source of complex societal problems. Measures derived from linear analysis thus tend to be directed in a straight line against the symptom itself, which can sometimes mitigate the problem for a while, but less often manages to provide a sustainable solution. Often a linear approach to a non-linear problem is counterproductive and such an approach and understanding can even be a part of the original problem.

Let us take an example of different levels of complexity thinking in action. Contemporary politics has great difficulties in handling the challenges of multicultural society since politics has not managed to integrate the astonishing diversity of perspectives, identities and norms that prevail in our current society. In other words, there is a lack of complexity in our thinking corresponding to that of our multicultural reality today. In practice, there are currently at least three political ways to tackle the challenges of multiculturalism:

1. Maintaining one ethnic identity at the cost of other identities (to flatten or reduce diversity). To build walls. Primarily to be found in nationalist movements. This thinking corresponds to the category level.
2. Relying on the job market to adjust cultural disagreements (more or less disregarding cultural diversity all together). The mainstream conception of most political parties, from the more traditional branches of the Labour and Democratic parties in the UK and US respectively, their social-liberal equivalents elsewhere, to the majority of most moderate conservatives and libertarians. This thinking corresponds to the connection level.

3. Affirming diversity in all its forms (opining that all cultural communities are equally good, but in spite of this still consider the presence of more different cultures better than fewer). This is typical of the more progressive branches within the Labour and Democratic parties, far-Left parties elsewhere, green parties and feminists. This thinking corresponds to the system level.

However, none of the above manages to fully meet the multicultural society's challenges: The ethnocentric approach of the nationalists cannot successfully integrate people who refuse to be assimilated into the majority culture, the mainstream economic approach cannot alleviate the cultural misunderstandings and conflicts that nevertheless occur even if people have jobs, and neither can the diversity approach, which even fails to qualify why any kind of diversity is necessarily a good thing.

A method to more effectively manage the greater complexity of multicultural society would instead sincerely attempt to see and fully understand all of the many different perspectives that make up a society, majorities and minorities alike, on their own terms, and in a way that explores their many varying realities while carefully considering the multitude of different interests, frustrations and needs – optimally, without judgement or moralisation, but still recognise that all individuals and cultures have the possibility – and need – to grow and mature. This level of complex thought hence gives rise to entirely new political questions that are seldom conceived of on the lower levels, such as:

- What challenges do those Muslims who have a literal interpretation of their religion encounter when they attempt to live in accordance with their faith and traditions in a secular society?
- How can their lives be made easier in ways that do not conflict with the rest of society?
- Is it a conflict between Christianity and Islam that creates problems, or is it more specifically a conflict between religion and atheism/

secularism? Or perhaps even a conflict between the religious and modern thought perspectives that creates problems in the encounter between native modern Westerners and immigrants from the Middle East? Or all three?

- What competences and types of understanding do Muslims need in order for their needs to be satisfied with the least possible disagreements as a result?
- What adaptations are reasonable to demand from Muslims and majority society respectively?
- How can these adaptations be facilitated?
- And if we see the same issue from the opposing perspective, questions may arise such as: what challenges face the part of the population that is seeing the country they have been part of building radically changed by migrant populations? Is it reasonable to demand that all traditions and norms be adapted to a multicultural reality? How do we best accommodate the wishes and desires of different cultures to make them live peacefully together and develop together?

As you see, these questions are less judgemental or moralising than both the ethnocentric and diversity approach. Neither a single culture nor diversity in of itself are valued higher than the other, and the questions do not suggest that anyone should subordinate themselves or conform to a particular view considered the morally superior one. It is a more pragmatic approach, and it does not close its eyes in anticipation of the problems solving themselves given enough time and economic progress, as the mainstream stance suggests.

Posing these types of questions meets our complex reality at a corresponding level of inquiry so as to cultivate novel approaches that can foster a well-functioning society at today's societal complexity level. A politics carried out from such a viewpoint has a greater potential to change people's lives for the better – but also requires considerably deeper knowledge of people's everyday lives and realities.

This kind of thinking promotes a new level of political questions that take people's various experienced realities and their mutual relations into greater consideration. No matter how much people deviate in terms of culture and worldview, or psychological development for that matter, all should be able to express themselves freely and without judgement and feel at home in society – it's simply ethically untenable to ask for less.

When thinking on a higher complexity level we are not limited to a single perspective but can attempt to create space and opportunity for further development to occur within the diversity of the existing (and possibly future) perspectives. As seen above, we can thereby ask questions that are more likely to handle problems that today appear insoluble.

As we have seen, the level of our thinking's complexity can affect our political prioritisations and solutions. Below I have sketched a few examples of how this can manifest itself on the meta-level, how the different levels can give rise to very different overall approaches to politics:

1. **Politics of interest** (the category level): a particular group's specific interest or worldview is defended.
2. **Politics of reconciliation** (the connection level): various interests are weighed together and integrated pragmatically.
3. **Politics of ideas** (the system level): there is an attempt to establish a particular idea of the human being and society, with measures sought to disseminate ideas and norms considered superior.
4. **Politics of emergence** (the perspective level): particular consideration is taken to how the ideas, norms and identities that govern society come into being, with this emergence made the kernel of politics.

We can, however, also add a level that lies above the perspective level, one I have chosen to call *the complexity level*:

5. **Complexity politics:** Deliberate measures to create prerequisites for a multitude of emergences of apprehensions of reality; the development and mutual relationship of these are made the kernel of politics.

Political questions can be posed from every complexity level. Now, as an example, in the area of gender and racial equality:

1. **The category level:** how can the interests of women, ethnic minorities and homosexuals be defended?
2. **The connection level:** how can the interests of women, ethnic minorities and homosexuals be reconciled vis-à-vis those of men, whites and heterosexuals?
3. **The system level:** how can multicultural and feminist values come to permeate society?
4. **The perspective level:** how can well-functioning values of gender and racial equality and acceptance of alternative life-ways emerge spontaneously in various societal groups?
5. **The complexity level:** how can better prerequisites be created for healthy and mutual beneficial relationships between genders and ethnicities, positive gender, cultural and sexual identities, and feelings of security, self-confidence and freedom in everybody's life?

The first three questions are characterised by linear thinking (to various extents). It is the first three questions that historically have dominated politics of gender and racial equality. Initially, from the beginning of the twentieth century and onwards, women's and men's interests were pitted against each other. This has in our time evolved towards the third issue, where discrimination has been regarded as an unfortunate part of society that can be replaced with superior values of equality. The less complex questions are potentially more oppressive than the more complex ones. Note how the last two questions do not create as much antagonism. They take a stand for everyone, regardless of where they are in society. The fourth question handles spontaneous emergence of various experiences from which the first three questions become meaningful. The last question handles the greatest complexity since it looks to the prerequisites for the diversity of emergence and how these can be developed in interaction with each other.

Almost all current political organisations start from one of the three lower complexity levels. The result is that major parts of the population are forced to comply and subordinate themselves to a certain amount of compulsory adaptation. It hardly needs to be explained how this poses certain problems: forcing people to comply to new norms obviously fosters resistance since people generally do not like being told what to do and think, which in the end makes the politics in question more likely to fail.

As such, it is time for politics to build on the two higher complexity levels. This requires changes in our political culture, in the political system, and in society at large. We thus need to ask new political questions such as:

- How are the many diverse perspectives and ideas that determine people's actions created?
- And how can we coordinate and further develop these perspectives in ways that are not perceived as oppressive?
- What do different kinds of people really need to feel that their lives are meaningful and full of joy?
- How are the desires and needs that shape economic life created?
- And how can we reshape them in ways that are more socially and environmentally sustainable?
- How can people's sense of self-worth be developed and how does this development influence the political debate in society as a whole?
- And how can we further the psychological and emotional development of the average citizen to a degree that makes them more competent at managing and relating to our increasingly complex world?

These questions may seem rather obvious when put in a list like this, nothing controversial really, but they do remain out of the ordinary in our common political discourse today. This is very unfortunate, because we need to ask questions like these if we are to solve the current crises. We need to develop our way of doing politics, and our way of thinking.

This is *the* great challenge of our age, and something demanding the utmost of our cognitive capacities. If we want to change the way we think about society and politics today, it will require that we are willing to make sacrifices, personal and societal, and that we put great efforts into the difficult task of coordinating a multitude of perspectives alien to ourselves, developing the necessary complexity and perspectival awareness to do so. However, it has been done before. Humanity has, as we have seen in this book, always managed to eventually advance to a higher and more complex thought perspective.

In the following we will take a look at what this next thought perspective to replace postmodernism could look like, and what it might do.

TO COMBINE THOUGHT PERSPECTIVES

If we obtain an increased awareness of perspectives, not only do we become aware of the postmodern insight that it is possible to see the world from various perspectives and that none of these contain the ultimate truth, we also become aware of the different perspectives' advantages and the strength of coalescing them in new ways.

There are many thinkers who have identified this way of thinking as a higher level of thought and considered it something that can be seen as a paradigm change, a transition to a new and more complex way of seeing the world. As this new way of seeing the world will include many aspects of previous paradigms and also be self-conscious of this fact, I think it is misleading to call it just a paradigm shift. It is a shift in some ways beyond how we previously have been thinking about paradigms. It is a shift to a new 'meta-paradigm' or in my language to a new thought perspective.

Several name suggestions for this new meta-paradigm or thought perspective are currently in circulation: post-postmodern,[1] TEAL,[2] integral,[3] post-secular,[4] [5] reconstructing postmodernism[6] and metamodern[7] to name just a few. The school of thought I find closest to my own reasoning (also the most recent) is the one known as metamodernism, which is therefore a term I will use in the following. However, the term itself and the context in which it is currently used are unimportant here. Each of the aforementioned schools of thought differ on a number of issues, but they all have a common core that revolves around integrating our previous perspectives at a more complex, higher level.

The more perspectives from which we view the world, and the better-developed these perspectives are, the more knowledge and understanding they can provide. In theory, there are innumerable perspectives from which to view our world. Here, however, I will merely attempt to show the advantages of integrating the three dominant thought perspectives in recent human history: religion, rationality and postmodernism.

To truly understand and appreciate, and thereby successfully integrate, the different thought perspectives, a deep understanding of evolution on various levels and in different aspects is required. Evolution should be seen as not only a theory that helps us explain biological change, but as a principle and a universal force that permeates all aspects of the world: from the formation of increasingly complex physical matter, to ever more advanced life forms, to the cultural development of higher complexity in human societies, and the evolution and complexification of our individual minds during our lifetime. With this evolutionary awareness, we can see how religion, science and today's postmodernism emerged out of necessity, that they each addressed the limitation of previous thinking and the dire needs of their times, and that they each contain vital components and insights to be considered important advances that have ensured the continuous progress of humanity. In addition, although we often fail to recognise this, these advances should not only be seen in opposition to one another. At each stage of development, psychologically as well as societally, we include the most important breakthroughs from the former stage. So just as we as individuals include the basic motor skills and ego comprehension we obtained at earlier stages of development when we move on to more complex stages, as societies we likewise include the many contributions achieved on earlier stages when we advance towards newer, more complex ones.

Below is a brief presentation of each of the most recent thought perspective's most important contributions to a metamodern integration. When we look at these contributions, we will have to keep in mind that – as we have seen in Part 1 of this book – the core insights of each of these perspectives were human achievements on a perspective (or higher) level. When these perspectives were communicated to, and adopted by, larger segments of the population, they had – by necessity – to be communicated on a connection (or lower) level of complexity. Many of the historical aspects of each thought system that we might today react negatively to – be it religious dogma, or scientific and postmodern fundamentalism – are lower-level manifestations of these thought systems. In a metamodern integration, it is the higher-level understandings we are looking for and *we are particularly interested in what we can learn from the interactions of the higher-level principles of these perspectives.* This has never before been considered in human history.

* * *

The religious thought perspective made us aware of the world of subjectivity, World 2 in Popper's terminology: not just as that of merely being in the world, but as a distinct category separate from the rest of existence. This was a developmental advance that made us capable of treating what had previously been subject as object. Prior to this, our subjectivity used to own us instead of us owning it. Since we did not have any tools to treat it from a mental distance, we could not see it and thus not influence it. This changed with the religious thought perspective. It is its most important contribution, one that still benefits us today. Although many modern people do not adhere to a specific religion, we still rely on many of the religious thought perspective's symbol tools and innovations when we interpret the world in terms of objectives and meaning. It has contributed with profound wisdom on the human being's existential experience of itself, of our inner world, and our being in the world. With religion, we obtained a higher awareness of 'meaning', and thus the ability to treat it as an object that we could improve and refine.

The rational thought perspective helped us see the objective, physical domain of reality, World 1 according to Popper, as a separate category. With rational, logical reasoning, ingenious scientific symbol tools and a clearly defined notion of objectivity, we can approach the physical world independently of subjective opinions, cultural norms and prejudices in a way that gives us great power to reshape our material prerequisites for a good life. Earlier, our understanding of the physical world was limited by a lack of differentiation between the objective world on one hand and our subjective and intersubjective perspectives on the other. This separation was the greatest single contribution of the rational thought perspective. With rationality and science, we also obtained a higher awareness of 'efficiency', and thereby the means to treat it as an object for deliberate and calculated manipulation so as to increase human utility.

The postmodern thought perspective gave us an increased awareness of the intersubjective, socially constructed, collective imaginary, Popper's World 3, along with the means to see it as a separate category that is neither subjective nor objective. By treating our collective imaginary as a distinct overarching entity functioning in accordance with different rules than those of personal experiences and physical occurrences, it has made us realise that we live within a socially constructed world saturated with power and narratives. Prior to the postmodern turn, the lack of any clearly defined and sufficient theoretical understanding of our intersubjective reality made us blind to the many ways it affects our thinking and behaviour. So just as religion helped us approach our subjectivity as an object for investigation, the postmodern thought perspective helped us obtain a similar mental distance to our culture and its many social imaginaries. This was the major contribution of postmodernism and yet another developmental advance. What previously remained subject, and hence hidden from view, became a new object for our consciousness so that we could disembed ourselves from its chains and subordinate it to our examination and agency. This has contributed a more critical perspective on factual claims, normative matters and societal conditions. Plus, it has provided us with methodological approaches to analyse our culture, society and inter-human power relations. With postmodernism, we obtained a higher awareness of 'fairness', and with that the capacity to steer society in a more equal and benevolent direction.

Each thought perspective has thus, by making what previously remained subject an object for our consciousness, brought significant qualitative changes in terms of new aspects being made available for manipulation: Religion's awareness of *subjectivity* gave us new means to create *meaning*, rationality's awareness of *objectivity* gave us increased *efficiency*, and postmodernism's awareness of *intersubjectivity* has made us more capable of making society *fairer*.

This, of course, raises the question of what the next thought perspective will bring to our awareness and what it will make us capable of. I do not claim to have the final answer, but if the prominent feature of this next thought perspective is the awareness and capacity to synthetise all of the preceding perspectives, as pointed out by the aforementioned schools of thought, it is tempting to propose that it will bring a new awareness to the time dimension of all of the above developments. More specifically, the evolutionary perspective on change and the crucial insight that development occurs in stages of increasing complexity – on the *universal level*, the *collective level* and the *personal level*. With this perspective we can become aware of our own significance in this evolutionary process, both as individuals and collective, and how we are deeply connected with and depend on all the earlier stages of development we carry within us, stretching back even before the emergence of life. We then start to comprehend that we are no longer merely a result of arbitrary evolutionary processes, but have reached a stage in the evolution of the Universe where we consciously influence the evolution process itself. Once again, what previously was subject becomes object, and thus available for reflection and agency. Whether we are aware of it or not, humanity has become the primary agent on the developmental edge of complexity evolving on Earth, and as far as we know, possibly also in the Universe. If we fail to realise this, and if we refuse to make evolution an object of mutual responsibility, we risk that society breaks down under the weight of complexity and evolution moves us in a direction where no humans want to live.

AN INTRODUCTION TO THE METAMODERN THOUGHT PERSPECTIVE

Where should we begin if we are to imagine a new and more complex thought perspective? If we look at the most recent paradigm transition, we see that modernity's faith in science developed into a critical questioning of all knowledge and factual claims. What could the next step be then? An ongoing description of reality that is more than just an antithesis, but subject to constant recreation and with open questions built into it, perhaps? Instead of choosing between modernism's totalisation of creation and postmodernism's deconstruction, we could aspire towards *reconstruction*, i.e. putting together the many criticised and deconstructed parts of reality into new entireties. And instead of choosing between the dubious claims of modernity's, largely mythological, grand narratives and postmodernism's emphasis on different interpretations, smaller narratives and thereby a fractured historical consciousness, the new perspective could attempt to coordinate the many interpretations and smaller narratives into an overarching narrative, a so-called 'metanarrative': the conscious creation of overarching, partially fictive narratives.

Modernity's celebration of technological progress and its large societal improvement projects became subject to postmodernism's suspicion towards all such grand narratives. Where modernity put faith in human rationality and praised its capacity to recreate nature, postmodernism pointed out that reason had failed humanity and that we were not as rational as we once thought. According to postmodernism, modernity's rationality has brought us to destroy the biosphere, alienated us and stumped our personal growth. What could be next? Could we perhaps redefine progress, create a new definition that includes social and ecological sustainability and gives the inner dimensions of life a more central role? Instead of choosing between seeing nature as a source of exploitation or humanity as a destructive force violating Mother Earth, could we perhaps start asking what the unique role of humanity in the ecosystems of nature could become? Could we see human civilisation as a continuation of an evolutionary process deeply and intimately connected to that of nature?

Modern science's preoccupation with objects, observable and measurable matters of fact, was replaced in the postmodern human sciences by an increased emphasis on symbols, discourses and states of affairs derived from the interpretation of text and other symbol-based recreations of reality. What would be at the centre of attention in the next thought perspective? Is there an approach that does not force us to choose between objects and symbols, but includes both of these? What about making the notion of 'pattern' the centre of attention, seeing what deep-seated patterns there are in order to consciously create new symbols from these, so as to recreate society's objective reality? This would entail a view of the world and human development in terms of 'self-organising chaos', i.e. that reality is indeed not interconnected in a cohesive entirety as modernism claims, but that we still can see how patterns are created from various, independent, interacting processes. Do we need to choose between modernism's striving towards objective truths and postmodernism's emphasis on subjective and intersubjective perspectives? How could we reap the best parts of these two approaches to knowledge? Could we begin to think in a manner that better balances the inner and outer aspects of reality, looks at how they are connected and co-creates a description of reality that is more holistic?

Modernism sees human nature as fixed, whereas postmodernism sees the human being as a social construction. Could the next step be to see the human being as a social, psychological, biological and technological development process? Modernism has always seen the human as an individual that creates itself, postmodernism that relations create the individual, that we as persons are created by structures beyond our reach. A new view of the person to include both of these insights could be that of the 'dividual',[8] i.e. seeing the individual as somewhat 'divisible' in that it can always absorb new ideas and properties in interaction with the environment, but still remains relatively autonomous in this process. This would free us from having to choose between an internal or external perspective and give us the possibility to retain a more nuanced view, a 'transpersonal perspective', i.e. that the individual is created by the collective while the collective at the same time is created by a number of individuals. The task thus becomes how to investigate and account for this reciprocal creation process, a process of a highly developmental nature.

Modern society relies on a meritocratic social order, a society where the thrift and ingenuity of the individual should be rewarded and those with the best qualifications should be given the responsibility to govern. Postmodernists have challenged this view by showing that it has led to inequality and marginalisation, with minority voices being excluded. Instead, postmodernism advocates a multicultural order where the weak are included. But do we need to choose between majority and minorities? Could we not instead look to the prerequisites for a multitude of diverse psychological and cultural forms and developmental levels to be working in concert? What is the best alternative to modernism's hierarchies and postmodernism's anarchy, a synthesis that is not just an in-the-middle compromise? The notion of 'holarchy',[9] that is, the ambition to create justice and democratically based hierarchies that are not arbitrary, could be a solution to this dilemma that we could expect to see as an integral part of the next thought perspective. Most importantly, perhaps, the next thought perspective would start to ask how modern, postmodern and traditional pre-modern people can live together peacefully, how we can bridge the growing gulf between people adhering to and thinking in accordance with different thought perspectives, and how we can make them cooperate productively towards the goal of a better future for our children.

A Continuation of Ihab Hassan's Dichotomies

How does the above introduction to what the next thought perspective (what I have termed metamodernism) might entail fit into a larger framework? Once again it may be hard to wrap one's head around an entire thought perspective in a few paragraphs – especially one that is yet to manifest itself – so let us approach the matter in a more intuitive way. Remember Ihab Hassan's dichotomies between modernism and postmodernism in chapter 7? In the following I will attempt to further develop Hassan's table by adding a comparable metamodern term to follow from the existing pairs. I have added a short comment to accompany each of my proposals. But since a few words admittedly remain rather insufficient, and since I have merely used my intuition to make the syntheses below, I advise you to approach it in the same reflective manner as in chapter 7. Maybe you will resonate with my thinking, maybe you will not get me at all, or maybe you will disagree and perhaps have much better suggestions yourself. The most important thing is that you stop for a moment and reflect upon these concepts. Here goes:

Modernism	Postmodernism	Metamodernism	My Comments on Metamodernism
Purpose	*Play*	*Playful purpose*	*Metamodernism has a specific purpose, but, accepting the postmodern critique, it can only state its quest for truth in provisional, playful terms.*

Modernism	Postmodernism	Metamodernism	My Comments on Metamodernism
Design	*Chance*	Self-organisation/ autopoeisis	*Metamodernism studies how remarkably unlikely events and processes happen despite the odds. How many factors come together and self-organise into new, more complex orders.*
Hierarchy	*Anarchy*	*Holarchy*	*Holarchy entails that all parts of reality are hierarchically ordered according to their level of complexity, but they are also interdependent parts of a whole.*
Signified	*Signifier*	*Significance*	*All self-organising regimes process information from the exterior world, thereby creating meaning and knowledge. Indeed, meaning and knowledge exist only through this processing of information.*
Distance	*Participation*	*Co-creation*	*When we study reality, interact with it, or conceptualise it, we also create reality. A part of this creation process is that we ourselves are changed and reorganised as a result of the interaction.*
Creation/ Totalisation	*Decreation/ Deconstruction*	*Transformation*	*Metamodernism studies how deep transformation occurs and how it is part of a greater picture of many past great transformations.*

Modernism	Postmodernism	Metamodernism	My Comments on Metamodernism
Synthesis	*Antithesis*	*Proto-Synthesis*	*Metamodernism attempts to construct an overview of knowledge in a larger context, but admits that the synthesis it produces can never be final or absolute.*
Presence	*Absence*	*Emergence*	*How things come into being is the focus of metamodernism, how they emerge through interactions with one another, and how they go from being absent to being present.*
Centering	*Dispersal*	*Dissipation*	*Like a whirlpool with a centre but no solidity or consistency, the dissipative structure has a centre, but only one that is always on the move, always changing. It can be kept intact only by dispersing its surroundings.*
Genre/ Boundary	*Text/ Intertext*	*Complexity*	*Metamodernism works with different disciplines that are distinct but in complex relationship with one another. It is by seeing these complex relationships that one can note common patterns.*
Semantics	*Rhetoric*	*Mythos Creation*	*Metamodernism is concerned with creating a meaningful myth for our time. The message is stated in mythic form, not to be taken as a truth.*

Modernism	Postmodernism	Metamodernism	My Comments on Metamodernism
Origin/ Cause	Difference/ Trace	Differentiation-Integration	Differentiation and integration are two sides of the same coin – differentiating between phenomena and concepts, and then putting them together, integrating them, into more meaningful wholes.
Form (conjunctive closed)	Antiform (disjunctive, open)	Pattern (provisionally conjunctive)	The world consists not of form but of partially interconnected patterns. These are, however, far from only disjunctive and discontinuous – indeed each pattern connects to its environment continuously, and must do so to sustain its existence.
Narrative/ Grande Histoire	Anti-narrative/ Petite Histoire	Metanarrative	Metamodernism strives towards the most comprehensive narrative presently available, but does so through the study of both large and minuscule phenomena.

This list may seem somewhat overwhelming. There is a lot to absorb in quite a concentrated format. The intention is, however, not to make the reader analyse every single point, but rather to get a taste of what the new thought perspective could entail.

* * *

I believe both modernism and postmodernism lack something of the human being's naive yearning to feel at home in reality, to feel a deep, inherent meaning in existence. There is something simple, human and moving that has been lost in having the human being rendered a mundane and jaded city dweller with a professional identity and ironic armour around its soul. The metamodern thought perspective takes the human being's – and the entire biosphere's and reality's – development as a project with certain spiritual, existential undertones. You make yourself vulnerable. You allow yourself to say: here is something I believe in, something I feel for and yearn for.

Even though I know that my story about reality and my endeavour will seem maladjusted and banal for the people of the future, I want to use an image of the human being's historical development in order to create a meaningful story. This is the significance of the protosynthesis: we synthesise the modern idea of progress with postmodern critical thinking and the naive forthrightness of religion, while we fully admit that the new synthesis by necessity remains a shaky construction. This opens up new avenues from which we can create progress, new social and political movements – along with a renewed and strengthened sense of faith and hope. One might talk about well-informed naivety, or pragmatic idealism – or maybe even enchanted realism.

The next thought perspective should emphasise that we accept both/and. We should not settle for postmodern distance and antitheses. But neither should we lose ourselves in the details of narrow fields of inquiry and propose theses with little consideration to how they connect to the rest of the world. It is both/and, and neither/nor. Neither should we capitulate in the face of our own inadequacy and distance ourselves from the world with an armour of smug irony and well-articulated criticism. Nor should we applaud our own ingenuity and delude ourselves into believing that our limited scope of inquiry has captured the ultimate truth about the world. Only then can we *both* create a healthy ironic distance between our own small existence and the world while laughing at our imagined self-importance *and* participate in the co-development of a better world with the sincerely felt experience that we have something valuable to offer. Hence, we must dare to stand for something. Knowing that we are highly inadequate beings, we must have the courage to say what kind of society we actually desire – even if we risk making fools of ourselves. Criticism and antithesis are not enough; we must allow ourselves and others to dream if we want to be active co-creators of our shared social reality and collective imaginary.

The metamodern thought perspective is, of course, merely an intellectual tool. But it is fashioned to meet deep-seated needs for meaning – to see possibilities for the human being's and society's development and to live with a faith in progress that is connected to a certain developmental course. This course is among other things oriented towards facilitating psychological development throughout life. This also means that we once again start to accept hierarchies – or rather holarchies – which affirm that certain perspectives are more complex, nuanced, compassionate and inclusive than others. We no longer want to abolish *all* hierarchies, but rather to make sure that the best and most sustainable modes of thinking are rewarded. The postmodern stance that any perspective is as valuable as any other is simply not tenable in the long turn. We need to make a choice. It is not always both/and, sometimes it is actually either/or – and we must risk that we can be wrong.

We know that the modern project and industrial society are not sustainable in the long run. But we also know that the postmodern criticism of modern society does not create sufficiently pervasive visions and political programmes for a sustainable, global society. It is good that we now know what the problems are, that we have a well-informed critique of all the things that make the current societal model unsustainable, unjust and oppressive. Still, we cannot continue to safely hide behind this criticism. If our criticism is to have any notable effect, we need to make ourselves vulnerable and propose a new societal model. We might be wrong and our ideas might risk making us the laughing stock of our peers. But if we do not cultivate the audaciousness to suggest new ideas that significantly depart from our current way of thinking, we will not have any viable paths to move us away from the abyss that we are currently approaching.

We need to experiment, leave our comfort zone and allow ourselves and others to play and think in ways that we are yet to competently master. If we allow others to make themselves vulnerable, if we accept others making suggestions that might be utopian and implausible, instead of giving in to the temptation of ridicule and rejecting everything they say with a well-articulated antithesis, then perhaps others will show us the same courtesy. If we make our intellectual discourse more forgiving, less competitive, and attempt to interpret our discussion partners' arguments as benignly as possible – and thereby change our debate culture – then perhaps we could co-develop a new thought perspective to alleviate the apparent shortcomings of modernism and postmodernism.

Creating a new way of thinking is a very difficult task. We will all initially be severely inhibited by our old ways of thinking and lack sufficient competences since we are venturing into unknown waters and therefore cannot rely on others' teachings to guide our reasoning. We will make mistakes. Yet, if we accept the risks and support each other in this endeavour, we can together develop a new thought perspective that will eventually make us more capable of solving the current crises of the world.

I believe the point of departure for this new thought perspective is seeing nature (or the Universe), society and our minds as an interconnected self-organising whole – a whole that is also deeply contradictory and diverse – in which we also see ourselves as active and conscious participants in the evolution of society and culture – in the world *we* create.

Evolutionary Awareness

Another important aspect of a metamodern thought perspective is what we can call evolutionary awareness. This represents our awareness of the evolutionary nature of change over time and becomes exceedingly apparent when we develop the capacity to profoundly grasp a timespan that extends all the way back to the creation of the Universe. The greater our capacity to see and understand the evolutionary context of our lives and our society, the longer the stretches of time we can comprehend, and the better we understand the overarching principles and mechanisms fostering change.

This, however, is not the same as merely understanding the theory of biological evolution or being knowledgeable about astronomy. To truly be aware of evolution and the 14 billion years of change it has shaped, we need to have a sense of the proportions of these vast stretches of time that is derived from more than just what the numbers can tell us and an understanding of evolution that goes beyond that of natural selection in the biological world. We need to intuitively fathom the perplexing nature of time, change and infinity as an existential, fundamental condition. We need to produce vivid mental images that capture the wonder and astounding complexity of the Universe's propensity towards spontaneous creation of emergent phenomena. We need to grasp, not only analytically, that evolution is a self-organising principle that applies to all change, to see all entities and occurrences in the world in terms of evolutionary change and how they are intimately connected to the processes that began with the birth of the Universe billions of years ago.

Obtaining an evolutionary awareness requires a highly developed capacity to handle complexity and contexts over time. Sadly, very few do this competently. Most people only see the particular developmental changes in organisms and technology and often have an all too abstract and fuzzy conception of time when dealing with billions of years. This is probably because this kind of thinking is not encouraged by the current linear-deterministic and reductionist approach that dominates the modern, rational thought perspective. This is very unfortunate. Just as our increasingly complex world requires that we start thinking more complexly, the ever-quickening pace at which complexity increases accordingly prompts that we expand our awareness of the overarching context of developmental change over time. In the past, when change was much slower than today, we could afford to neglect this time aspect. We could allow embedding ourselves in our time and age since little development was expected in a person's life. Not today, when change is so fast that we cannot assume the world-system will organically regulate itself and in time spawn the necessary countermeasures to avoid potential catastrophes. There simply is not enough time to tackle the problems as they come. We need to think ahead. The changes in technology and climatic conditions are too dangerous and occur too rapidly to be left to the world-system's own self-organising devices. Our world is under constant development and organises itself in new ways without any deliberate planning. But we have no guarantee that the current path it is moving towards is the most preferable one.

The somewhat blind and unintentional evolution of human civilisation has served us well in the past. However, every increase in societal complexity has always put new demands on our cognitive complexity and prompted us to become aware of new and more elusive contexts to accommodate the developments taking place. Now, the context that most urgently needs our attention as we once again approach a new level of complexity is arguably that of change over time itself: the developmental context that most of us still remain snugly embedded within. Instead of just *being* in the time – instead of time being a *subject* that we merely exist within while developmental change just happens – we should attempt to increase our contextual awareness of time so that we can treat evolution as an *object* for reflection and thereby take responsibility for where we want it to go, as our civilisational *becoming*.

Individuation and Integration

In the following I will show a couple of examples of how this developmental both/and perspective can make us see society and ourselves in ways that render us capable of solving problems we currently remain inept at approaching in an adequate manner.

Development is not linear, even though it follows certain evolutionary principles that can be described in rather simple terms. Human development is full of contradictions and paradoxes that can be difficult to grasp. What appears as a failure may be a crucial step forward, and things that seem to contradict each other may in fact complement each other. Here I would like to exemplify how the metamodern thought perspective can bridge the tension between different thought perspectives. The notion of individuation-integration is crucial if we want to understand societal development from this new perspective.

Individuals develop in many ways: psycho-motorically, aesthetically, morally, emotionally, sexually, intellectually and so on. One of the most important ways of developing humans' individuality is, as we have discussed, through the human being's sense of 'I' traveling through various stages of perception about itself and its place in the world. The individual finds itself again and again in ever wider layers in an ever greater and deeper I: in infancy, from identifying with all sensory perceptions to identifying oneself with the body and its needs; in adolescence, to identifying with the inner voice of one's thoughts; in adult life, to identifying oneself with the roles that the thought creates; to identifying with the processes that create these roles; in very few highly developed persons, to identifying with the consciousness behind these processes; to identifying with the consciousness that is in us all; to identifying with existence itself and becoming – and maybe further in ways that are not known yet. At every stage the individual becomes more unique, finds deeper ways to express its eccentricities and individuality. This process of developing the self towards deeper identification and stronger individuality is called 'individuation'.

At every stage of psychological development, the human being needs greater depth. We need to find deeper ways to express ourselves, to share our joy and sorrows, to share our gifts. To develop healthily we need to be properly integrated at the new level. The more individual and specialised we become, the greater the gift we have to bestow on our fellow humans and other living beings, and the deeper the loneliness and alienation we experience if we do not find a context in which our individuality can be expressed. The longer the individuation process progresses, the more complex and deep are the contexts needed in order for our individuality to be allowed to flower. The alienation that many people experience today in work and personal life can to a significant extent be seen as an expression of their individuality being deepened beyond the roles and work tasks that society offers. Our free-spirited, liberal society has yielded many unique seekers with very special insights, properties and gifts, yet most often we do not succeed in creating social contexts where people really get the chance to live out their highest potential. When people become trapped in bureaucratic systems and social contexts where they are expected to act, think and work from all too limited modes of thinking, they may abandon their yearning to live out their full potential. Personal growth can then soon be followed by a dull and meaningless existence if the level of psychological development is not accompanied by a corresponding degree of development in one's surroundings.

A person may long to express their love for the world through a job that uses their deepest insights about life – but instead life comes to revolve around meeting deadlines they have no personal interest in fulfilling other than to pay the mortgage on their house. And so life crawls on. It becomes colourless, meaningless, desolate. It may be hard to see how common this alienation really is. It arises as soon as we are (or feel as though we are) the only person who sees something, large or small, and no one understands us or wants to listen. Or when we quite simply do not fit in, do not feel at home in our everyday environment – at school, at work, or in society at large – or when we experience distance from our loved ones and do not quite know why. Occasionally we even notice deep alienation towards reality in its entirety. We wonder what our place is in it. But we are not alone in feeling this way – most people today experience this at some point in their lives. In this there is great possibility for change. There need to be contexts created that allow for personal development throughout life, but this must also be complemented with suitable arenas for people's newly acquired insights and skills to come to good use. If we develop ourselves, if we become wiser and more empathic, but there is nowhere for us to use our newly won wisdom and compassion, we are more likely to become depressed, alienated and frustrated with life. When we develop as individuals, we need to be integrated anew in a context that corresponds with the level of our new individuality.

While individuation without integration creates shattered dreams, betrayed expectations and a desperate sense of loneliness, integration without corresponding individuation creates oppression. If we are squeezed into a context without personal inner development (or spontaneous sense of self and reality) corresponding with the context that we are expected to take part in, we become oppressed. Children that are expected to sit and concentrate from the age of six for a large part of the day, when this actually requires the mind of an adult, are exposed to oppression of sorts. People who do not experience compassion for each other, but are forced to help each other through feelings of guilt and shame, are oppressed. People who feel compelled to adopt values in order to avoid exclusion are oppressed. People who do not love their partner and hold back their real needs because of social pressure are oppressed. All contexts where people are squeezed into a structure against their will constitute integration without corresponding individuation and are expressions of various forms of oppression. This oppression is always a violation of some kind, sometimes crude and apparent, other times subtle and hard to pinpoint.

Let us look, in a somewhat simplified way, at how these two sides are connected with today's political landscape. The political Left often talks, thinks and acts from an awareness of this kind of alienation and seeks to alleviate it by integrating the individual in a deeper context. However, they often fail to see the risks that might accompany an increased integration. Neither does the Left emphasise that individuation must be supported by political means, such as schooling and lifelong cultivation and development. Communism is a particularly unfortunate example of this one-sidedness. Citizens were forced to be in solidarity with each other and share everything equally. But without a corresponding degree of psychological development to ensure these feelings and inclinations would emerge spontaneously in their psyches, the system proved highly unsustainable.

Libertarians tend to defend the individual against the potential oppression that increased integration can result in, often emphasising freedom of choice. However, they are to a much lesser degree conscious of the tragedy of alienation and tend to advocate a flatter, more superficial society where people's aspirations and relations are reduced to individual interests and transactions of various kinds. Neoliberal thinkers believe that these transactions are sufficient in order to organise society's most important functions, but the wicked social problems in modern societies suggest that this is highly inadequate.

Social conservatism and nationalism, on the other hand, react against alienation and want to reintegrate the individual in old, crumbling communities, but do not see the need for integration at new, higher-complexity levels. They simply insist on reintegrating everyone into old national or religious communities while they ignore that not everyone identifies with these and that they would feel oppressed if they were integrated into them. A new kind of imagined community to replace the nation-state or a given religion rarely occurs to conservatives. Conservatism of various kinds follows political lines that leave certain people alienated and lonely (those who do not have the possibility of expressing themselves in society) and others oppressed (those who are integrated against their experienced will).

Ecologists and greens often want to reintegrate the human being in a broader context: nature's. Here, too, however, there is a lack of sensitivity for people being at various stages of individuation and that their experienced need of identification varies substantially. If people do not feel any belongingness with nature, or do not feel they are part of the great ecosystems of the natural world, or simply do not care about environmental sustainability, forcing upon them a societal model that emphasises sustainability and limits their consumption level will be experienced as deeply oppressive.

The complete picture of individuation and integration must be taken into consideration and translated into politics. Everyone, as far as it is possible, should have the right to feel part of a community that corresponds with their level of individuality, i.e. social contexts that resonate with the values and emotional needs of communion of different individuals. When people feel they are members of a community that neither oppresses nor alienates them they will not only be happier but also bring greater and more relevant benefits to others.

Instead of, as religion, seeing meaning creation as God-given or the like, we can see the human being's creation of meaning and of a world of symbols as an invariably impossible and half-finished construction – a protosynthesis, to use a word from the list I introduced above. Whatever we do, some people will feel alienated or oppressed – but this can occur to very varying extents. Pluralistic democratic societies tend to provide better opportunities for more people to liberate themselves from suffocating social contexts and to find meaningful communion with like-minded people than totalitarian and conservative religious societies. However, if we increase our understanding of individuation and integration and make it part of our political thinking, the degree of alienation and oppression could most likely be even further decreased. What is needed is an active, conscious societal effort to create better prerequisites for people's lives to be meaningful – an effort supported by scientifically acquired knowledge and postmodern sensitivity, since every new context requires new forms of thinking and feeling.

The metamodern thought perspective recognises that the human being and its society are created in constant interaction with each other and that there is a developmental direction in this process. This development runs towards a higher complexity, which also places greater demands on people to think, feel and cooperate in order for society to function and for people to thrive. The metamodern thought perspective coordinates various approaches towards the human being's inner depth (from religion) with their behaviour and organism (from science) and its culturally fixed situation (from postmodernism). The result is a new image of the human being, society and reality.

Thinking in this both/and fashion opens up a new analysis of the individual human being and its development, driving us to think 'transpersonally', which can help us solve the problems that are currently out of our reach. This I will try to explain in the last section of this chapter.

Transpersonal Development

The individual is created by the collective, and the collective is ultimately just a collection of individuals. It is not meaningful to choose a side in the debate on whether the interests of the individual are to be put first or whether the community and solidarity should be our highest priority. A common solution to this problem has recently been to emphasise the network, where relationships between people and how these relationships affect each other are considered to accommodate both the individual and the collective. The problem with the network approach, however, is that it reduces the importance of the individual's own inner experience and that it does not succeed in capturing the collective realities in a sufficiently clear way. The advocates of the network approach sometimes use the metaphor of an organism to describe society. But the organism is not a good way to understand society because an organism has an individual consciousness of some kind that a society does not. The organism itself is also more important than all its individual cells or body parts. Instead, society exists for all its members, not the other way around.

Hence society cannot be reduced to its individuals. Society cannot be reduced to its collective structures. Society is not a network. Society is not an organism.

What is society, then? It is all of these and none of them. Society is a wide variety of, often very different, experienced realities – which are inextricably linked to each other. Society is a *transpersonal* whole of partly interrelated, partly independent parts.

The deeper the level from which society is analysed, the clearer its transpersonal nature appears. Take social problems in a family for instance:

> The children are unruly and unfocused in school. The children are unruly because Mom and Dad are fighting and do not pay them full loving attention. The reason that Mom and Dad are fighting is that they experience a lot of anger and disappointment. The reason they experience a lot of anger and disappointment is that they feel their lives

> have not become what they wish and that they lack control to change their situations. The reason they experience this is that they have been counteracted in their lives and never managed to build up good self-esteem and positive relations to life. Their actions are shaped by emotions and thoughts about which they are not aware. The thoughts and feelings come to a large extent from the relations they experience in the social order in general. The social order in general is due to the fact that many other people feel the same as them. Those who represent the social order make their decisions in accordance with how society already works. They do not put enough effort into improving children's opportunities because they do not know how. The children are unruly.

And so on. It is not possible to judge whether the individuals or the collective structures or the network of relationships are responsible. These are just different sides of the same reality. The 'social problems' in a family are just a surface, a way among many to describe a part of human suffering in reality. The deeper into the experiences of the problem we go, and the more we see the interaction of these experiences with other parts of reality, the closer we will be to effectively addressing the problem.

What is the core of the complex problem above? Is it the individual's own responsibility, or maybe its own experience? Is it the collective structures? Is it the network of relations? Or is it the 'organism' of society as a whole? The problem has no core, no simple cause. There is no single person to blame, no collective structure that explains everyone's inner experiences, no single imbalance in the network, no disease in the community body. There are different consciousnesses partly separated from one another and at the same time inextricably linked. By understanding their experiences and how these experiences are created and influence each other, we can begin to see the overall picture. For example:

> The children are unruly. The children are unruly because Mom and Dad are fighting and do not pay them full loving attention. Mom and

> Dad work together to face their anger and disappointment, noticing when these feelings appear. The reason they work with their feelings is that they feel they can increase control over their lives and alleviate what caused them pain and anxiety. Their actions are shaped by the thoughts and feelings they gradually become more aware of. The ability to discover and relate to their thoughts and feelings is a result of methods to do so being common knowledge in society. This change in society is due to the fact that many people experienced similar concerns and that good knowledge about managing one's emotions eventually became widely available. Those who represent the social order are interested in and support these changes. Political measures have therefore been made to ensure that children get increased emotional support in preschool. The children's unruliness soon changes in favour of creativity and a desire to learn.

What looked like a Gordian knot from the other perspectives can, when a transpersonal perspective was applied, thus be resolved. By going deep into the personal experiences and perspectives of each of the involved parties we could handle greater complexity because we made it a problem neither of the individual nor of the collective. The problem could then be solved without identifying the exact solution to the first mentioned problem. This is because the 'problem', i.e. that the children are unruly, was only a surface phenomenon, an expression of a deeper, transpersonal social reality that was located deep inside the consciousness of many different people and in the way these consciousnesses affected each other.

The above was just one out of many ways a transpersonal perspective can handle greater psychological depth and societal complexity, and thinking transpersonally is just one out of many new modes of thought we can expect to see from the metamodern thought perspective. It shows the effectiveness of thinking both/and and either/or (and sometimes even neither/nor), of including both objective, subjective and intersubjective aspects (W1, W2 and W3), developmental psychology and non-linear thinking.

I hope to have demonstrated that it is perhaps even a way of breaching the gridlock of our current postmodern obsession with the antithesis. If more people develop this way of thinking and learn how to competently master some of these new symbol tools, rather than settling for the antithesis, there might be more who feel confident enough to make proposals to really change society.

However, for that to happen, we will first need to create the prerequisites for a far more conscious society, which will be the topic of the next chapter.

Chapter 14

THE MEANDERING PATH TOWARDS A MORE CONSCIOUS SOCIETY

There has never been so much *unnecessary* suffering in the world as today. By 'unnecessary' I mean things that we currently actually have the material means and knowledge to do something about – but that still are not addressed successfully. Much of the suffering that existed two hundred years ago was caused by insufficient knowledge and a lack of resources. In comparison to today, food was scarce, industrial production inefficient, many diseases were not treatable, and populations were growing faster than productivity. As such, it was impossible to ensure an acceptable living standard for all. But today we actually have the technological possibilities and material resources to adequately satisfy the basic material needs of every human on Earth.

Hence it is not because of insufficient *efficiency* that this has not already been achieved, but rather a lack of *fairness*. The reason that we are so far from doing this, I believe, is because of an additional deficiency relating to the third aspect of this trio (presented in chapter 9): *purpose and meaning*.

The lack of purpose and meaning in many peoples' lives is responsible for a fair share of our currently unresolved societal problems. Our market society has left many of us in a postmodern 'value vacuum' that makes life feel empty and devoid of substantial meaning-creating structures to fuel deep-felt motivation. In turn, our further personal growth is inhibited, which makes it less likely that we reach the level of consciousness in our society and culture required so that the project of creating a fairer and more sustainable society becomes meaningful to more of us. To alleviate this ill, we need to develop our culture and our collective imaginary. We need to cultivate a more conscious society. In this chapter, we examine what this means in theory and practice.

CAN A SOCIETY BECOME MORE CONSCIOUS?

But can we, our society and our culture become more conscious than today? Can we, as a collective, become more complexly thinking, more empathetic and wiser than we currently are? Or, to approach the issue from the reverse direction: is it reasonable to assume that we and our society have reached the highest stage of consciousness possible? As humanity has progressed for millennia, from animism, through the religions of the Axial Age, to the Enlightenment and the modern industrial state, have we now arrived at the last stage of societal development? Are the democratic market society, the postmodern critique and science working silently in the background, ensuring economic growth and a new gadget to amuse us every now and then the pinnacle of human evolution? Have we reached 'the end of history'?

I do not believe we have reached the end, that all we can expect is more of the same, a couple of new technologies here, a little economic growth there. I believe it is possible – and urgently necessary – to create an entirely different and vastly better society where we take human well-being to a level that is considered utopian today. For that to happen we cannot only rely on the market to do the job for us. Neither is it a matter of merely piecemeal adjustments to our existing institutions and legislation. If we wish to make society better adapted to the increasing complexity of the world, it is paramount that we start thinking about our cultural evolution, that we ask ourselves how we can collectively reach a higher level of consciousness.

A culture with its collective imaginary is not an immutable entity with a fixed essence. If we look at history from a long-term perspective, we see that cultures can develop and over time advance to handle higher levels of complexity, that they can expand their circle of belonging to include more individuals, and that they can come to wiser and more sensitive decisions that take new aspects into consideration that previously were not accounted for. In short, that human culture has become more conscious. Despite the questionable behaviour of many modern governments, we must admit they generally behave more consciously than the Vikings or Genghis Khan. We usually think twice before we let our instinct-driven inclinations for aggression and immediate self-gratification guide our political decisions, we are less inclined to accept superstition and unfounded personal opinions regarding societal matters, and overall our societies adhere to and function in accordance with fairer, more inclusive, values than before.

Now the question that needs to be posed to the world's rapidly ageing populations is: As we as individuals have a lifelong capacity to evolve in our ability to perceive and handle complexity, what would a positive, nourishing social environment look like – one that supports transformative learning and the emergence of higher mental complexity, and perhaps even inner wisdom? Contemporary developmental psychology has handed us a few clues: social security, sufficiently large challenges, ample support in learning, a high degree of acceptance of failure, a healthy diet, a lot of exercise and physical contact, practice in social and emotional intelligence, existential conversations, meditation, gaining access to more social arenas in which to move in parallel – but here we are starting to digress beyond the purpose of this book. Let us merely sum up by saying that we have many clues today, but that we are at the start of this voyage of knowledge and that skilful researchers and others must unveil the unifying pattern and put it in the service of human development.

However, what we all can do is to start asking the right questions: How can people be supported in their inner and cognitive development?

And why in the world is this not already a highly prioritised political and social objective?

But what indeed does a 'more conscious society' mean? The answer lies on at least three levels, closely related to each other: development on the personal level and the collective level, and the latter can be divided into cultural and structural development. Let us look closer at these three, one by one.

More Conscious Individuals

As individuals, we can be more or less embedded in, and more or less detached from, our understanding of ourselves and of our environment. We might in other words have 'props ' in our inner landscapes that are more or less taken for granted – assumptions, perspectives and perceptions that we cannot bring ourselves to question, that simply exist and that shape our comprehension of whom we are and how our world works.

Inner Disembedding – we become more and more transparent to ourselves

The inner landscape that we take for granted, as we saw in Chapter 12, becomes a sort of grid through which our entire experience of reality is filtered and interpreted. Maybe even filtering isn't the most appropriate metaphor, it is merely an editing medium. With Kant and the social constructionists we can say that our perspectives in some sense are co-creators. For we never get to see anything beyond our own perspective.

Here I once again want to return to Robert Kegan's model of the evolution of consciousness: the subject becomes an object and a new subject is born. This can occur in many different ways. We may for instance habitually assume that we 'are' our thoughts. One day we may discover that the thoughts occasionally fall silent for long periods and that the inner monologue appears to take place rather compulsively and most often beyond our 'own volition'. Suddenly we understand that we 'are' not the inner stream of thoughts. We thereby also understand that there ought to be a more general, underlying, in some sense greater 'self' than we have previously realised – otherwise my 'self' could of course not hear the thoughts and direct them and every so often lose control over them. This 'self' can then suddenly take responsibility for reshuffling the stream of thoughts. Maybe we will notice that the stream of thoughts often has a short-term character and does not shy away from denial, repression and self-delusion. In a sense our degree of freedom has increased. The self has awakened to some degree – matured, grown.

On another occasion we may notice that the mute, peculiar pain in the chest that comes and goes can be seen for what it is: a reaction in part of our core, which is precisely a subtle, albeit strong sensation in the chest. We suddenly understand that we can avoid reacting so strongly to this emotion, thus being controlled by it to a lesser degree. Maybe we might even develop an ability to venture into such difficult emotions – however unappealing this may be – and see how they are transformed into sharp pain, into fear and partly into relief and a vibrating warmth.

We might use the word 'disembedding', meaning that something which had previously been embedded is unveiled, so to say, is opened up and becomes visible. It is a curious thing, but in a sense we live embedded in ourselves and in the world. As we find new layers of reality to relate to – and at best even can bestow well-functioning words upon – this embedding is unfolded. It is a little bit like unfolding a crumpled piece of paper.

What I am anecdotally trying to describe here is what one might call 'inner' development (inner 'disembedding'). Here it is the self that attains new levels of psychological maturity and self-realisation, thereby becoming more conscious of inner aspects that we have previously been unaware of. Thus, an increased consciousness.

At best this also might lead to increased understanding of people in our environment. We can learn to recognise others' inner state and thought patterns and become conscious of these. Here we might also speak of an increased level of consciousness. The very reason that psychology is possible is that people in our environment occasionally see our core more clearly than we do ourselves. This is most apparent for those who have had children and who have noticed how they have become ferocious and all but uncooperative after nine o'clock in the evening. If you ask them if they are tired, you will be briskly reprimanded. But as soon as you have put them to bed, they go out like a light.

Correspondingly, society can be more or less rich in people who can see through their own smokescreens of thoughts, roles in society, self-aggrandising personal stories, frustrated background emotions and prejudices. Further, society can be rich or poor in terms of accurate but respectful and well-meaning interpretations of people's inner lives.

A more complex self is also more prone to be reflected in more complex phenomena: the future of humanity, all sentient beings, the development of consciousness and perception themselves, the balance of the biosphere, the labyrinths and potential of language, and so forth. It is precisely that sort of identification that is necessary in order for people to piece together complex life stories, own narratives, in which they participate in influencing the world in those areas that are most urgent for the world system as a whole. This is yet another example of increased consciousness.

Outer 'disembedding' – our collective imaginary becomes more and more transperent

Correspondingly, the individual can evolve in her relationship to the world around her. We can increasingly become capable of questioning the 'ultimate authority' on which our worldview is based. We have in this book seen how the human being has gone from an animist to a religious to a scientific to a postmodern thought perspective.

One way of comprehending this progression is as an increasing degree of *secularisation*. With such a view the word 'secular' naturally receives another meaning than we usually attach to it. Most often, one argues that the secular society is that which is characterised by the scientific thought perspective, which has been contrasted with the religious (and/or the animist) perspective. But one can also see secularity as a graded scale:

the divine highest principle expels the spirits (but these can live on as superstition and folk belief in creatures of the forest and so on), science expels the divine and degrades it into a private matter (and the spirits disappear), postmodernism expels the uncritical faith in progress and science's monopoly on the truth. One can also view this book as part of a similar expulsion project: the complex thought perspective expels postmodernism's faith in culture's and contexts' truth monopoly, and indicates how inner development and progress can be created through consciously designing our society. Every step is more secular than the preceding one. Every step is more conscious of the human being's real role and responsibility in the world. The more we realise that we are not in the hands of God, science or the market, the more conscious we also become of the important role that we humans play in this development.

Every thought perspective must be able to fell the preceding one on its own premises in order to be regarded as genuine progress. I will not go further into this, but merely emphasise that even here that which is taken for granted becomes a new detached object that we become conscious of when it is 'disembedded'.

God becomes a theological object, and then 'religion' becomes an object of the science of religion, rather than ultimate reality. Thereafter science becomes an object of the sociology of knowledge: one describes how discourses and paradigms emerge in particular communities, bound by social norms, methodological inventions and also power struggles. Thereafter postmodernism becomes an object: a thought perspective amid others, a developmental step that follows the same basic dynamics as the earlier ones. And this is, of course, a little ironic, since postmodernism generally does not believe in historical stories of developmental steps.

What I am getting at here is that we as individuals in varying degree can detach ourselves from these thought structures, thereby becoming more conscious of them. Actually, they all coexist in today's 'modern' society: some of us go to fortune tellers and invoke spirits, some believe that Jesus is our sole saviour and that an almighty God with a capital G has had everything we need to know written down in a book, some believe that we live in Newton's Universe which ultimately is a kind of machine, some believe that we live in various arbitrary cultural constructions, and then there are those – myself included – who believe that we live in the Universe's (or rather reality's) kaleidoscopic development of perspectives of itself. All these diverse people walk the same streets, eat at the same tables, give each other Christmas presents and talk with all and sundry. But what a mixture; what a blessed hotchpotch!

Here we see that inner and outer 'disembedding' can – and do – interact and support each other, creating ever-increasing inner and outer 'transparency'.[1] We can develop to more clearly see through what initially appears to us as an opaque self and an opaque society.

But this development is not without problems. How good are we at reflecting on our own perspective, and discussing those of others? When should we just respect the perspectives of others and when do we have a moral obligation to try to broaden others' perspective? It is for instance not enough either to invoke spirits or to pray to God to solve the climate crisis. Nor is it sufficient – which may be more surprising – to only study the climate crisis as a meteorological and atmospheric-chemical phenomenon. And it is not even sufficient to deconstruct and criticise the discourses, power relations and uses of language that stand in the way of our ability to address the climate crisis. One must instead, in accordance with the metamodern thought perspective, consider how one communicates with developmental levels and all the other thought perspectives, and coordinate this multifaceted communication with both scientific, developmental psychological and sociological understanding of how one can create realistic solutions.

But all this requires an inner, emotional and existential maturity, and an ability to take others' perspectives. For the question is after all not merely how we can broaden our thought perspectives. The even more crucial question is how well we can empathise with, and understand, others.

Some 'wise' people, for example in animist cultures, may have evolved considerably in their inner 'disembedding', and less so in the outer ditto.

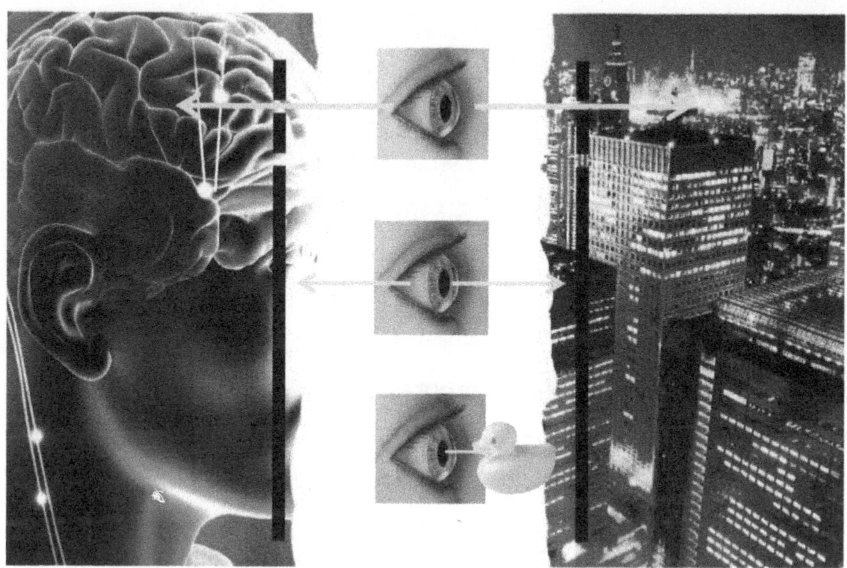

To see deeper into ourselves and into society. The picture illustrates how we with increased awareness can see behind the surface to get a deeper understanding of ourselves and of society. The middle eye represents the self-authoring mind using the rationalistic thought perspective for sense making.

Young intellectuals in today's society might have the opposite profile. For a more complete profile of the more conscious individual, both these sides – and their mutual interplay – should be viewed as decisive.

More Conscious Cultures

As for cultural development, this can be studied both at meso- (between) and macrolevel. The mesolevel within sociology usually pertains to such structures that exist both at organisation and institution levels. This is for understandable reasons an area into which I have delved extensively, as I have been part of launching and running several companies and organisations. In recent years, academic sociology has also to a greater extent begun to emphasise the importance of the mesolevel for society. When we seek answers as to why a certain country has certain social or economic characteristics, it is often the institutions and their mechanisms that offer the firmest explanations. Previously, one tended to search for explanations of a historical kind, about modern society as a whole, about cultures and national characters. But it is often the way the organisations are constructed that provides the clearest image of what happens in society.

There is of course a rich and growing literature, primarily within the 'softer' parts of business administration, emphasising that organisations do have not only formal structures, but also cultures of their own, for better or worse. This insight has over the last few decades often assumed slightly ridiculous expressions when corporate managements have produced values and value-systems for their companies. These are naturally more often experienced as awkward and seldom as identity-creating. One most often tends to forget them.

But is it possible to do something to create a 'higher consciousness' that permeates the organisation? Unarguably, many interesting clues have started to appear. First of all, one can create a cosy environment with different types of meeting rooms: the official, the reflective, the creative and playful, and so on. If one wants to work with values, one can recruit qualified consultants who take the employees' own values as a point of departure. When one launches a company, one can apportion decision powers and create democratic structures. One can have a room for mindfulness and let some simple training be part of work hours – an increasing trend providing an increasing number of yoga teachers with work opportunities. One can structure how meetings are held so that speaker time is apportioned, which has proven to even out the gender balance and raise the collective intelligence. One can set aside time that is free from conversations, email and cell phones: so-called 'workfulness'. One can create a clear structure for how complaints are lodged and how conflicts are moderated. One can create IT systems that support holistic thinking and help establish contacts, horizontally and vertically, across the organisation – as a way to avoid drainpipe-thinking organisations. One can preserve, reinterpret, and use one's cultural heritage – songs, dance, literature and great stories – in meetings, communication and in the operative discussions. And one can endeavour to create a rich network of various organisations whose competences and experiences can support each other; create an ecosystem. To sum up, one can create a corporate culture that consciously and intentionally supports the inner development of all members of the organisation. Robert Kegan calls such an organisation a DDO: Deliberately Developmental Organisation.[2]

It is, of course, easier to influence culture at an organisational level than at a societal level, a smaller culture rather than a larger one. It may even be simpler to recreate an organisation than to influence a single individual's developmental psychology. But of course, even the overarching societal culture and the crucial societal institutions can evolve – which has occurred through history. The Nordic countries' culture can today probably in several respects be seen as 'more conscious' than that of many other countries in the sense that our cultures encourage us to become more aware about, e.g. climate and gender equality issues. Perspectives that many other cultures simply do not see.

Even during my lifetime, there have been considerable changes in culture. We have suddenly stopped being homophobic, stopped beating children in school and even in the home, have become feminists (well, to some extent). We have also become more distinctive individualists, and postmodern culture has seeped into more or less the entire media landscape. And everyone has started to talk about sustainability, indeed even arrange events where we race each other, in order to appear ecologically conscious.

Might a greater proportion of more conscious individual 'selves' start to collaborate with each other to propel new changes in societal culture? Can the norms actively and consciously be repudiated – for instance so that the political debate would give more space to agreement, openness for admitting mistakes and more respect for fact-checking and nuanced discussion? Surely, this would be of benefit to society's collective intelligence? Or would one be able to repudiate the norms so that inner development and meditation become more generally accepted – but by no means end up in the hands of the poorly thought-through New Age movements? Would one be able to make manipulation through sexist advertising and sweets at the check-out counter less accepted, so that people are less ashamed of their bodies and develop fewer self-harming behaviours and neuroses? Or just so that one generally becomes more cosmopolitan-minded and oriented towards sustainability and resilience? Would we generally be happier if we started each day at the office with a song or a poem? Or if the lunch break was a phone-free zone and the conversation revolved around what was beautiful? Would it be easier to handle our current complexity if we had stronger roots and developed deeper relations?

In order for a symbolic language, a culture, to be reproduced, a sufficiently large number of individuals must be located at the symbolic system's complexity level. Most can be located under this complexity level if the system should factor this in and develop 'scaffolding' (language, metaphors, schools, libraries, public service) that helps them function in society. But a significant 'culture-bearing' minority must personally be able to work and re-create at the culture's complexity level.

Thus, we must protect our symbolic world in the same way that we protect other common utilities, such as the environment. That is, we must focus on upgrading our cultural code!

As we saw in chapter 9, culture carries our common subjectivity – but it is also the role of culture to contribute to us being able to develop our individual subjectivity. Culture cannot develop your subjectivity for you. You have to do it yourself through your life experiences and use culture's symbolic tools for reflection and processing. But culture's symbolic world can provide tools, help and support. However, a less developed culture can of course hold us back.

In order for our society to grow socially, more individuals must reach a higher cognitive and empathic level. In order for this to occur, the individuals must be aided in their growth by culture. Thus culture and our common symbolic language must lead the societal development through cultivating the individuals' ability to understand and interpret our world. We could, inspired by Kegan's DDO, call such a societal culture a DDC: a Deliberately Developmental Culture.

Culture must thus in its supportive and developing role, lead the individuals and thereby also the market. We cannot expect that the developing culture will arrive as demand on the market. The religions understood this, and thus this is an important insight that we must try to integrate in our new thought perspective. Today this way of viewing societal culture is not particularly common.

Culture as a collective good

As previously mentioned, economists make a distinction between private and collective goods. Private goods are those that only can be consumed by the owner or very few people. If your friend eats your birthday cake, you will be without cake. The cake is a private good. Therefore it can also be bought and sold. If you have the money, you can buy a new cake, but then you must earn the same money by giving up some other private utility or working (i.e. sell your services).

But that your friend is running in the park, breathing the air, does not prevent you from doing the same. It may even be more fun to go jogging in the park if your friend is also doing so. We are now talking about collective goods such as parks, air and knowledge. Today a major discussion has flared up around these and in particular around 'commons' (woodlands and other things that people historically have shared, but also inventions and knowledge that are in the public domain), things that theorists and experimental business entrepreneurs imagine can guide us towards a fairer 'post-capitalist' society.

One way of approaching societal culture is precisely as such a collective good. Sometimes people wonder what education within the humanities really is good for. Why do we, with our hard-earned tax money, educate scarcely productive literary theorists and sundry professionals in culture snobbery? One answer may be sought precisely in how culture is developed as a collective good.

But it is, of course, not only the theatre, the opera and the snobby literary theorist who constitute 'culture'. Culture is, as has been noted earlier, the entire weave that our everyday lives, our habits, our language and common horizon of comprehension consists of – our symbolic world. Included here is, of course, both natural science and the ability to communicate this. Music and popular culture also contribute to associations, moods, shared emotions that are crucial for creating understanding of foreign cultures, for various situations in society, and perhaps often for the evolution of thinking itself.

A very important part of culture's development is connected with our common and socially negotiated definitions of what is considered 'good' culture. Can you win the Eurovision Song Contest by challenging established gender norms? Maybe so. Dana International, who is transsexual, did so in 1998. People having time, strength and possibility to delve deeper into such issues, is perhaps the only way for us as a society to chart some kind of direction for cultural development. Can our language be more clever, deeper and help us discover more nuances or perspectives? Can we become better at more accurately relating to the new, unwieldy phenomena that globalisation places before us? And – again – as a collective good, the market will never be able alone to provide the societal culture we all need to flourish.

More Conscious Societal Structures

Let us look a little closer at more conscious societal structures. How can we create societal structures that support both personal and cultural development? How do we, for example, consciously create constitutive rules of the market so that the market supports the flourishing of individuals, societies and the planet?

Today we have through science accepted that there is a need for experts within virtually everything pertaining to the material world. No politician or corporate leader would ever get the idea of themselves constructing the new bridge or a new aircraft. When it comes to the technological symbolic world, we put our trust in experts. As for the cultural symbolic world, we are today expected to construct our meaning-making and self-evolving symbolic world ourselves. A little bit like trying to build our own bridge with tree branches.

But changing laws and rules is easier said than done. Here we encounter the trickier problem that legislation around such things as the market's constitutive rules necessarily requires that all of us in society in some way must reach an agreement. This is not so easy if most are not even 'aware' of the issues.

Aware of what? Well, all the complex issues we have previously touched upon in the book (and other ones). Not least that society's institutions create many of the prerequisites for people's psychological development. If we stay within the search for security, validation and quest for success, or in defensive, opportunistic, flaw-oriented and simplified ways of thinking and acting, we also stay within socialised life. Assuming we can even get there – otherwise life revolves around attaining life's comfort.

But if the institutions are designed to better satisfy human needs and invite us to later stages of psychological development, more of us can live in deeper freedom. Such freedom does for most of us entail an endeavour to realise a unique individuality, but this invariably seems to result in a quest for the universal, for greater and more widely applicable values.

We may thus glimpse a chicken-or-egg causality dilemma: How can we create a conscious society without conscious individuals that can and want to create such a society, and how do we get conscious individuals without a society that supports us in a sensitive way? But it is also possible to view the issue in a different light: as a self-reinforcing historical development cycle. Individuals, culture and institutions reinforce each other bit by bit – even if the path is far from straight and unambiguous. It is of course true that the institutions are the hardiest, the most difficult to change. But once they do change, it usually happens with tremendous force. Just think of the effect modern trade law has had, or compulsory education.

When we talk of development of more conscious societal institutions, we should thus keep at least two thoughts in mind at once. One of them revolves around a dawning collective consciousness and resolve – or collective freedom to act – which thus is the general insight that society has the possibility and capacity to reshape itself. It can be transformed – from kingdom to democracy, from a capitalist to a post-capitalist society, from a parliamentary/representative society to a more profoundly democratic one. The other side of the coin is that the societal institutions constitute, or at least might constitute, collective support structures for the development of individuals, culture and subcultures (and their mutual interaction).

An important part of our individual consciousness is, as we have seen, our ability to take various aspects of our existence as objects of our will. When we succeed in attaining something as an object of our conscious will, our freedom to act increases; we can say that our consciousness has increased in scope.

In the same way we can view our society's ability to include various objects under its political will through political decision processes. Changing society's constitutive rules, for instance, does not fall upon our individual will. We can as individuals be fully aware of what needs to be done, but if we as a society in our collective decision processes do not have the ability to 'see' a problem, then nor do we have the ability to collectively act upon the problem. We would then have surrendered part of our common human freedom.

In such a case, as a society, we would be less conscious than we would have been if we had had the collective ability to see and act. But the increased consciousness in this sense does not necessarily mean that we make the 'right' decision. I am merely saying that we have the ability to make a decision on an issue. That we do not, because of our inability to exercise political will as a society, become 'force-fed' a 'decision' through failing to make a decision. In this way we have for instance gone from totally lacking an environmental policy to having one, or from completely lacking a gender equality policy to having an advanced debate about gender culture and the rights of the third sex.

* * *

What happens in an ecosystem when we increase its ability towards more complex self-organisation? When I am saying that we together must develop 'a more conscious society' I am thus referring to the combination of all three developments above, that is:

- more conscious individuals
- more conscious organisational and societal cultures
- more conscious structures in society

We must work at all these levels in the ecosystem simultaneously, and naturally the developments at the various levels support each other in continuously ongoing parallel processes of self-eco-organisation (see chapter 10).

With more complex self-organising individual consciousnesses, the organisational culture and society are better able to self-organise in a complex way. More complex systems give us more freedom, as we have seen, but also more responsibility to handle this freedom. With a more complex culture and society, individual consciousnesses are aided in developing complexity: deeper and more nuanced approaches within the world. And so forth in an upward spiral. But the spiral can also go in the opposite direction. The crucial insight is that the choice is ours and that a conscious common effort is required to attain the upward spiral.

Who Would Not Want to See a More Conscious Society?

This may sound like a rhetorical question, but it may be worth remembering that there unfortunately may be interests that have no wish whatsoever to see a more conscious society. Maybe they would even prefer a less conscious society. What interests would want us all to live our lives rather unconsciously and without reflection, merely following our programmed patterns? In whose interest would it be that most of us predominantly are passive and non-thinking?[3]

The first group that comes to mind is advertisers, marketers and the giant corporations that today dominate the world market. For them it is of course better if we continue to react to the impulses that their marketing is designed to awaken in us, without reflecting on it at all. That we continue to satisfy our emotional needs through consumption.

Another group might be our present politicians. They have no real interest in us gaining a more trenchant insight into the need for a system shift. Such an awakening would probably only lead to us voters seeing through their incompetence and their dependency on special interests, causing them to lose power.

Yet another group is, of course, many of the established religions whose power is based on our not being able to see that they have ceased to fill their original function – to help us and society evolve – and instead have become backward-striving power machines.

A final group might be established academics who have their entire careers invested in one or other of the old thought perspectives. Here a quote from the early quantum physicist Max Planck may be appropriate: 'A new scientific truth does not triumph by convincing its opponents and making them see the light, but rather because its opponents eventually die, and a new generation grows up that is familiar with it.'

As I mentioned, new values have taken hold during the last few decades. These new values, sometimes rather mockingly referred to as 'political correctness', are somewhat the equivalent of what previous generations would have called *Leitkultur*, the leading or guiding culture of society. Even if we are currently experiencing serious populist revolts, it appears as if now most of us – at least within the educated middle classes – are talking about gender equality, multiculturalism and environmental sustainability, even to a degree that it seems as if we are competing to appear the most politically correct.

But how exactly do such cultural changes occur? I would like to again stress the importance of mesolevel changes of organisations. It is becoming more and more clear that cultural change cannot be administrated as a top-down process. True cultural change happens in a bottom-up process, but top-down processes can help, putting conditions in place for this cultural self-organisation to happen. We are now starting to talk about 'self-organising' and 'purpose-driven' corporations.[4]

From the corporate sector we thus have evidence suggesting that cultural development can increase *efficiency*. On the other hand, it can even be said to increase *fairness* and *purpose* as well, given the more dynamic structures and enjoyable work conditions that often result from such changes. The three crucial aspects of society – *efficiency*, *fairness* and *purpose* – are thus co-dependent on the level of development of a culture.

The high level of development in the Nordic countries today has to a considerable degree been the result of the deliberate creation of institutions to support consciousness development in large parts of the population.

Lene Andersen and I describe in our book *The Nordic Secret*[5] how the unique progressiveness of contemporary Scandinavians has been the result of a deliberate effort, starting more than a century ago, to nurture personal consciousness development of all citizens. The cultural aspects of society in these countries have thus been the result not only of a number of changes on the institutional level, but also of a deliberate, and state sponsored, bottom-up process of cultural changes founded on an increased consciousness of the population. In fact, the Nordic welfare-model would probably not have been possible without the latter. A population that does not value equality, plurality and tolerance is simply not very likely to support a more progressive development.

There is little doubt that a culture cherishing gender and racial equality, ecological sustainability and social responsibility is more attuned to a hypercomplex multicultural reality that is on the brink of an ecological disaster and haunted by lasting social problems. To accommodate this new reality, more cultures beyond a few privileged pockets in the most developed parts of the world should evolve to embrace such values.

So how do we achieve this? Are not the populist reactions to exactly this multicultural reality, and to the increasing complexity of our world that we are now experiencing, proof of the fact that pushing these 'globalist' ideas and ideal will never work? To answer this, it can be helpful to look at how cultures evolve from one stage of a development to the next and to keep in mind that cultural evolution has to be a bottom-up process to work, but that this process can be – and has been – deliberately supported by society.

* * *

What I am getting at here is that we as individuals and collectives can develop the capacity to detach ourselves from the thought structures that unconsciously influence how we think and act. Our level of consciousness is in turn determined by an interplay between psychological, cultural and societal-structural developments. Very few of us manage to reach any higher levels of consciousness by ourselves. Even if we are adequately equipped by nature and our upbringing to develop our cognition, we remain underequipped to do so if we do not get access to the symbol-tools required to function on the higher level. The symbols, concepts and words obtained from our culture set the limits for what we can think and what we can do. Our language is thus a critical aspect that needs consideration if we are to grow both as persons and as societies.

LANGUAGE, A TOOL FOR DEVELOPMENT

Our consciousness is largely a social process stretching far beyond the brain. Our minds are intimately connected with each other through our shared symbol world, and the uniquely human symbolic language is to a considerable extent what enables our further psychological development. Thanks to our symbolic language we have been able to attain a reflective self-consciousness. Our language and culture are therefore intimately related, and the development of one of these is not possible without equivalent development of the other.

The streams of thoughts that constantly flow through our minds consist of words (and their contextual meanings) we have acquired from our social world. The words we use to describe the world in turn influence how we perceive and think about it, and the meaning we create from these is largely derived from the cultural context we have acquired them from. Accordingly, the modern idea of 'the individual' that shapes most people's idea of who we are is highly inadequate. Our thinking and agency are not entirely autonomous, but to a considerable extent dependent on the cultural context that has given us our language, the level of development of which in turn sets the limit for how far we can develop our individual consciousness. The idea of the transpersonal dividual, as described in the previous chapter, is thus a better term to describe who or what we really are. Psychology, culture and language are thus part of the same developmental process, and they all shape our societal structures and collective imaginary. Our personal evolution and development is thus closely interlinked with our collective evolution and development and vice versa. This is not something I have been the first to realise.

The psychologist Lev Vygotskij, whose now classic theories on cultural development and developmental psychology became known in the West only long after his death, took a particular interest in how language influences our personal development. According to Vygotskij, it is only when we as children start to acquire symbol tools from our environment that we can begin to gain knowledge and develop our thinking. Words help us create order in our perception of the world, and in ourselves, eventually becoming inner, inaudible speech where the words become tools for our thinking that allow us to govern our behaviour. In an unfinished theory building upon these insights, commonly referred to as 'cultural-historical psychology', Vygotskij proposed that language plays a role not only in psychological development but also in our cultural development.[6] Kegan has also emphasised the significance of language in our development, and argues that words can be used as tools to make us conscious about aspects within ourselves that we previously were unaware of, thereby enabling relations to those aspects as objects. By attaching words to something, we can extract it from ourselves and observe it with greater clarity. Words such as 'thought' and 'thinking' can help us reflect upon the fact that we are thinking, instead of merely being one with our thoughts, and a word such as 'values' can help us reflect upon what we value and strive for. Through symbols, we can name the context and meaning of a phenomenon, and thus enable it to become an object of our consciousness.[7]

Using words to name and describe phenomena and processes allows us to take a step back and observe these occurrences from a mental distance. The contextual meaning of the words can widen our perspective and increase the extent of our consciousness. If we do not have any words for what we observe, we will have great difficulties grasping what we experience. The fact that we use language to bestow names on things, and thereby increase our awareness of the world, or in a sense actually create the world, is the central theme of the creation myth in the Bible's *Book of Genesis*. In this narrative, the act of creation is explicitly followed by the naming of what has been created. The inclusion of this is not strange, because how else could we say that something has been created if we do not have words for what there actually is? With the initial act of creation, God creates something other than himself, or, if you will, becomes aware that there is an object; a world that now materialises itself through the differentiation between sea and land, day and night, and so forth. Thereafter, God tells Adam to name all the animals and plants so as to take possession of them.[8] The creation myth is not just intended as an amusing and entertaining tale in an age where no better explanations could be given, but contains an important message about the fundamental importance of the word, *logos*, in relation to our ability to relate to creation. The conceptual distinction of things from one another and the naming of them is, as we have seen, likewise considered a fundamental aspect of psychological development. Development entails ever finer distinctions and differentiations of that which previously remained undifferentiated and unconscious, but then becomes conscious object. The further we go, the subtler the distinctions, and the more of our internal and external world we can talk about. The creation myth in the Bible thus illustrates an ongoing differentiation process similar to those described in contemporary developmental psychology.

When we use symbols to bestow names on things, the more comprehensive and integrated a map of the world can be internalised in our minds. Symbols simply make us capable of taking more of the world into our mental possession. At the same time, language also takes possession of us humans. We become animal bodies, possessed by memes – or alien language 'spirits' – that follow a quite different logic than biology. These can in turn respond more or less well to our environment. Language enables not only knowledge and communication, but also delusions, conceited wishful thinking and chimeras of sundry kind. Often, the origin of these phenomena – from incorrect empirical assumptions to the most remarkable superstitions – is to be found within language's own peculiar logic, a logic containing its own agenda that reaches far beyond that of the individual thinking person. The words and concepts we use in daily speech often conceal a number of unarticulated ethical and cultural implications and assumptions that in turn affect our thinking and behaviour – for better or worse.

Hence, language can make us aware of new things, but it can also betray us in ways we remain unconscious of. Language is both an enabling and a limiting context that controls how much of the world we perceive and how we perceive it. As such, it is important that we take responsibility for developing our language in a desirable and sensible direction – especially now when the increase in the complexity of the world has begun to accelerate at such a pace that we cannot expect our current language to be sufficient tomorrow.

THE NEED FOR FURTHER CULTURAL DEVELOPMENT

In the same way we need theories about physics to understand the material world, we need theories about society to understand our social world. We needed neither of these worlds to understand on an abstract and analytical level during the Stone Age, when we evolved into the anatomically modern humans we are today. Our intuitive understanding of our physical and social environments thus only evolved to a level corresponding to the relatively low complexity back then. Evolution simply had no reason to bestow on us the ability to understand the theory of relativity or quantum mechanics, nor that of a global, hypercomplex, multicultural information society. Accordingly, to most people, complex societal matters remain impossible to grasp intuitively without assistance from suitable theoretical symbol tools. We still have the same Stone Age brains of our Palaeolithic ancestors and are therefore not evolutionarily 'wired' to understand any higher complexity than that of a life on the savannah. But in contrast to galaxies and atomic nuclei, which in our everyday lives rarely concern us and thus can safely be left to experts, society and culture concern us all.

If we want to understand and further develop our society, we must develop our symbolic language to a sufficiently high level corresponding with the current complexity of the world. But for that to happen it is not enough to change our society's exterior structures, it is also needed that we change its interior structures, our culture, to match its exterior complexity. In this respect our values play a particularly important role. Values can be said to constitute the very core of our culture. Right and wrong, how we prioritise, what we want to achieve, these are all at the centre of a culture. What people value obviously differs from person to person. You and I may have different views on what we consider the good life or whom we consider beautiful, but such personal preferences are not the greatest concern here. Sometimes quite the opposite: you take the apple and I take the orange. But when it comes to which kind of values we want at the centre of our culture, what we want to be the highest priorities in society, we cannot have too divergent views. Here we simply cannot agree to disagree. We may have different opinions on fairness, but for practical reasons we must agree on what constitutive rules shall apply in our society.

For example, if certain people do not consider murder or theft wrong, their values cannot be accepted to prevail by those who do not accept murder and theft. It is the same regarding environmental sustainability or racism. We cannot have one group protecting the environment and society's ethnic minorities, while another pollutes our world with dangerous chemicals and racial slurs. Values such as these are not something we only, or even primarily, hold to guide our own behaviour. Rather, we hold these values because we do not want ourselves and others to suffer from the negative consequences of others who do not respect these values. As such, they obviously need to apply to all. They cannot be individual, but must – by definition – be collective to seriously influence the functioning of society.

The values pertaining to society in turn depend on our level of psychological development. Criminal gang-members, for example, are often characterised by non-complex meaning making, usually the result of a poor upbringing stunting their inner growth. People adhering to multiculturalist and environmentalist values are on the other hand often characterised by high levels of complex meaning making, which has often come about from a privileged background. It is therefore critical that we ensure optimal conditions for people to develop their meaning-making capacities if we are to change the prevailing values in our culture in a more desirable direction. We simply cannot expect our culture to evolve without such measures. Hardened criminals will not become multiculturalists and feminists by exposing them to post-colonial gender studies. And neither will mainstream bourgeois careerists become environmentalists from reading the latest UN climate report. But an education system and labour-market that better facilitated their inner and empathic development could make them more concerned about societal issues beyond their own immediate self-interest. They could develop a more complex meaning making.

Then again, such changes to society's institutions require that the values we would want to cultivate are already present and prevail in a sufficiently large proportion of the population. If the dominant values limit us from making the changes required for a transition to a sustainable and more inclusive society, and this depends on lacking psychological development, the solution is thus to change society's structures to better facilitate personal growth. But making these changes may once again be obstructed by the dominant values. To change society's structures so as to cultivate more conscious individuals, the general public needs to be at an already sufficiently high level of consciousness to give the necessary political mandate.

Here we might glimpse a classic catch-22 dilemma: How can we create a more conscious society without more conscious individuals wanting to create such as society? The problem may appear unsolvable at first. But the nature of catch-22 dilemmas is that they only appear so from the perspective of a more linear conception of cause and effect. If that was not the case, we would still be riding horses, for example. Luckily (as an illustrative example of the illusory you-can't-have-one-without-the-other dilemma known as catch-22 goes), the absence of petrol stations at the beginning of the twentieth century did not prevent the automobile from becoming a widely available form of transportation. Similarly, the absence of environmentally aware citizens did not prevent us from suddenly having environmental policies and a public discourse permeated by concerns about sustainability. The current, almost complete, absence of concerns about life-long psychological development is therefore just as unlikely to prevent us from creating a more conscious society. The following will elaborate how such a system change could come about.

HOW DOES SYSTEMS CHANGE COME ABOUT?

The quantum physicist Max Planck once said that: 'A new scientific truth does not triumph by convincing its opponents and making them see the light, but rather because its opponents eventually die, and a new generation grows up that is familiar with it.'[9] It appears to be the same regarding a transition to a new thought perspective. While it is generally the younger generations who embrace the new ideas of the times, older generations tend to stubbornly remain loyal to the obsolete ideologies and thought-patterns of yore. It thus appears as though old thought perspectives can only be put to the grave – admittedly a tad morbidly – if they are accompanied by the mortal remains of those subscribing to them.

But do we really need to await our old-fashioned co-humans' departure from this world before we can anticipate a fundamental system change to occur? Isn't there anything we could start doing now? If we look at the patterns of how system changes generally come about, we might find a few clues as to what we can do to further a transition to a more conscious society.

All system changes start in the hearts and minds of a few individuals who independently, with luck and skill, succeed in developing their understanding to a higher level than their surrounding society and culture. This usually occurs in some of those fortunate individuals who grow up in a cultural environment with an exceptional abundance of highly sophisticated symbol tools. The more who grow up in such environments, the greater the number of people who reach beyond the current level of cultural development. When a sufficiently high number of such individuals are present and have opportunities to collaborate, they can start to support each other's work and together create a new symbol language that matches their new level of consciousness. Eventually, they will have produced a coherent symbol world that can influence the rest of society.

Once there is a ready-made symbol world available, those who are not capable of developing their original ideas and theories themselves can obtain the basics of the new thought perspective by adopting the symbol tools made by others. It requires effort to articulate the ideas for a system change, but it is not necessary to be an innovator to carry out the change itself. For instance, the world had to wait for the uniquely gifted genius of Newton to come along before we could start doing mathematical physics, but his equations can now be learned by an average college student. Similarly, no one came up with the idea of the theory of separation of powers before Montesquieu, despite modern notions of democracy being common prior to this, but every democratic government today employs an army of less brilliant lawyers (as compared to Montesquieu himself) to uphold this principle.

It is therefore not when a sufficiently high number of individuals spontaneously start thinking along the lines of a new thought perspective that a system change can come about, but rather once a critical mass adopts the ideas of the forerunners. This, however, does not have to be a majority of the population, far from it in fact. Only a minority of the population in the United States had attained a reasonably modern worldview at the time American democracy was established. Most remained within the religious thought perspective throughout most of the nineteenth century, but the activities of this initially small minority caused their numbers to consistently increase over the following many decades. The reason that this could happen in spite of the majority being in fundamental ideological disagreement with the modernist minority is that the latter had more powerful symbolic tools at their disposal to generate higher levels of efficiency, fairness, and meaning making. This simply made them better adapted to seize society's power structures. The religious majority may have despised their modern overlords' apparent materialism and godlessness, but the former could not resist the material advantages and efficient governance the latter brought about. In this way we can likewise expect that once a minority of pioneers have created a metamodern symbol world for others to adopt, the capabilities it will give the subsequent early-adopters in terms of better meeting the most stressing issues of our times, such as environmental sustainability and higher psychological wellbeing, will make them capable of winning political and economic power.

It is thus when a new and more complex symbol world has been developed and made available on the market place of memes that a new thought perspective becomes ripe for institutionalisation. First in culture, and from there it will transport itself into legislation, corporate and governmental institutions, and henceforth start shaping the thinking and behaviour of common people until they eventually become culture-bearers of the new symbol world themselves. How such a process might unfold has been proposed in a six-phase model known as the 'Two Loops Theory' that I will present in the following.

The Berkana Institute's 'Two Loops Model'

The Berkana Institute has proposed a model for how overarching systems shifts occur that can help shed light on how we could start developing a more metamodern society.[10] Here is a brief overview of the model:

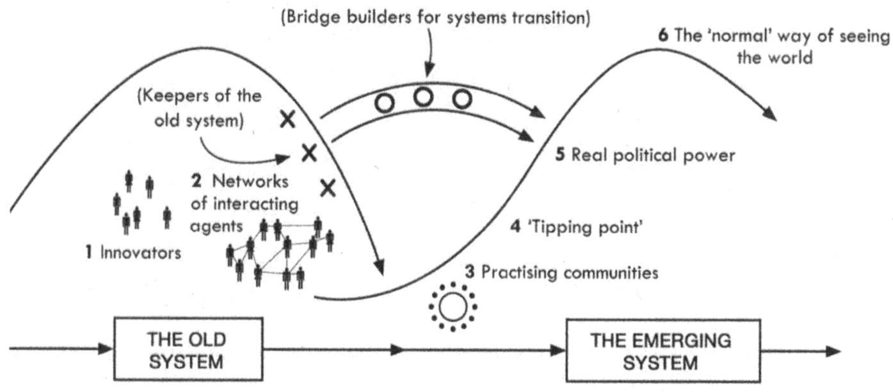

The Two Loops Model from the Berkana Institute.

When a social system starts to age and eventually approaches its inner limits – when, for example, further military conquests that a slave economy might depend on become unfeasible, or the oil deposits of an industrial economy start running dry, or a society just becomes technologically too complex for its current meaning making capacity – the social system faces a bifurcation point at which it either breaks down into chaos or manages a transition into a more complex, emergent new way of self-organising.

The Two Loops Model is an attempt to create a general description of such a successful transition. Below is a brief outline of the different phases described in this model and my comments on how they relate to a possible transition of our current society into a metamodern society.

1. As the old system reaches its apogee and highest degree of maturity, and ever more problems and limitations start surfacing, there first appear a few *innovators* – entrepreneurs, artists, philosophers, etc. – and other small groups that in various more or less pronounced

and conscious ways shape an alternative; solutions that touch upon and anticipate the next system's inherent logic. As the upcoming transformation gathers force – in thinking, emotions and wills – among the few individuals heading towards the next thought perspective (termed 'paradigm' by the Berkana Institute), it results in new ways of seeing the world and addressing our common problems. These views will eventually be institutionalised in parts of our culture, which in turn will help more people see the world from a higher level of complexity/consciousness. Hence, the transition to the metamodern thought perspective will begin in the inner world of a few individuals, W2, only later, when the time is ripe, to manifest itself in our socially constructed world, W3, so that it can be carried forth by future generations and shape our material world, W1. That is, increased consciousness in a few leads to a more conscious culture, which in turn leads to more conscious societal structures – which then leads to even more individuals with a higher level of consciousness.

2. Thereafter we will see the emergence of *networks of interacting agents*. As more initiatives surface and their key persons recognise each other, exchange ideas and methods and start to collaborate, the new thought perspective starts to crystallise as a force in society. An important part of this phase is the development of a new language and concepts that better enable the merging of various vantage points into fruitful dialogue and co-creation. Among such networks are a number of informal groups of people, whether they identify as metamodern, integral or other names used for ideas similar to those described in this book. The staff at the Berkana Institute have made it their explicit task to be a unifying force to help this interconnection on its way. My own initiative www.WhatIsEmerging.com is another effort to inspire, connect and explore what possibly is emerging in the form of a new thought perspective.

3. Thereafter the networks are gathered in more clearly *practising communities* that shape supporting subcultures in society. Some such contexts would in the case of a metamodern culture be, for example, the Burning Man Festival, the Syntheist Node in Stockholm and so-called 'TEAL organisations' described by Frederic Laloux in his book *Reinventing Organizations.*[11] Personally, I have founded Ekskäret Klustret in Stockholm and the Co-creation Loft in Berlin from the very same motivation of creating community hubs to promote societal developments based on this new, deeper understanding of our world.
4. During the fourth phase, the new thought perspective, which is now represented by various forms of subcultures, reaches *critical mass*, a tipping point from which the minority who adhere to the new thinking starts to influence society's mainstream culture. It might occur when roughly 5% to 10% of the population gravitate towards the new perspective, but it requires a much greater proportion of society's leaders – within politics, industry, culture – already adhering to it. When this happens, the prevailing cultural hegemony is upended, and the new thought perspective becomes more widely accepted, not necessarily as the only one, but at least as an established and influential one. This is a phase the transition towards metamodernism is yet to enter. The proportion of people gravitating towards this thought perspective is still too small. If we equate it with self-transforming mind, less than 1%, as mentioned in chapter 11, are currently capable of making this complex meaning and independently develop and replicate these complex cultural memes. However, current research may not provide us with an accurate estimate. Our current understanding of psychological development remains too limited to give us any good estimates. It is, however, absolutely clear that a broad awakening of consciousness is already under way, especially in the young generations approaching a possible early mid-life transition to self-transforming mind.

5. In the fifth phase the new thought perspective achieves *real political power* and can start influencing not only culture but also the societal structures that depend on political decisions. This applies to education, the market, governance and so on. It also tends to be associated with a counterreaction in the form of a few innovative individual thinkers attempting to go beyond the new dominant discourse by articulating the ideas for the next emerging thought perspective. With Phase 5 of one particular system shift follows Phase 1 of the next shift. This is the phase the postmodern thought perspective recently seems to have entered. Despite being a minority and even if it can be argued how much power those who gravitate towards postmodernism actually wield, the fact that multiculturalism, feminism and environmentalism have entered the political mainstream and affected political power to a considerable degree, at least in some countries, seems to correspond with the description of this phase.
6. Finally, as new societal structures have been created in accordance with the new thought perspective, it reaches the majority of the population, who, even in a socialised or self-authoring mind, start seeing it as *the normal way of viewing the world.* When this phase is complete, the new thought perspective can be said to have reached its final point of fruition. This was the case of modernity at the beginning of the twentieth century in the West, and is perhaps what we are currently approaching in our times with postmodernism. This usually coincides with the emergence of the first couple of phases pertaining to the next thought perspective.

As such, it seems as though the most developed parts of the world are now in the middle of Phase 1 or 2 of a metamodern system shift given the circumstance that postmodernism is well established.

The populist modern (or even pre-modern) political backlash that is currently under way is in fact a reaction against an over-confident postmodern, 'globalist' political elite. From their postmodern thought perspective, this elite is unable to see the necessity to meet and listen to the large part of the population that are absolutely unable to make meaning on a postmodern complexity level. The fact that this elite sometimes even refer to this part of the population as 'the deplorable' is not helpful.

With some goodwill, we might say that we are approaching Phase 3 in some pockets in the world. I certainly see this in Stockholm or in Berlin where, in my view, it seems like a large number of organisations and communities that could be described as metamodern have started to appear. The next phase in the development towards a metamodern society is thus the tipping point in which a larger proportion of the population starts gravitating towards this new mode of thinking and meaning making.

It is, however, very important to remember that the development of a more complex society is in no way given. The ability of the system to self-organise on a more complex level is dependent on the capacity of the components of the system (the individuals in a social system) to relate to each other in deeper and more complex (more conscious) ways. This ability to relate more deeply and more consciously can, as we have seen, be developed. Our societal culture can, as we will see, play an important role in supporting this development. Again, our personal evolution and our collective evolution are closely interlinked.

Now we also realise that in our efforts to usher in a new, more conscious, society we can do work on three interrelated levels: trying to work within the present system to support radical change, working on protesting against and dismantling the present system to make room for the new, or supporting the emergence of a new system. Work on all these three levels are important to facilitate the transformation.

HOW DO WE CREATE MORE CONSCIOUS SOCIETY?

We do not need to approach the issue of cultural and psychological development as a chicken-egg dilemma. Neither do we need to wait for older generations to retire and patiently await the day they are no more. As innovators, we can start straight away and begin influencing the culture we are part of.

We should not be ashamed of being in a highly privileged position from which we can influence our society in a direction that few still remain unappreciative of. If we believe we have the skills and insights that can facilitate the necessary development, it is actually our duty to break out from the social conventions that otherwise hold us back and take the responsibility to become the culture-bearing agents of tomorrow's society. As the Berkana Institute's model implies, there is always a need for some to take the first steps.

We have long accepted the rationalist view that there is a need for experts within virtually everything pertaining to the material and technological world. When it comes to the development of our symbol world in regards to technology and science we gladly put our trust in a few select experts. But as for the cultural symbol world, our postmodern view makes us reject all such notions. Instead, we are expected to construct our cultural symbol tools and our meaning making all by ourselves: a task most of us remain severely underequipped to manage.

And our societal culture and our collective imaginary are not a private concern. Just like the ecological environment, they affect all of us. And they should, like the ecological environment, concern all of us. I would like to stress again that our symbolic world and our societal culture is a collective utility that does not function on market terms. In the same way, we need to collectively agree on paying people to maintain our roads, we need to spend a share of our collective resources on funding the very experts who reproduce and develop our symbolic world. Supporting people who have the time, energy and skills to delve deeper into the complex mechanisms of our shared symbol world is perhaps the only way to guarantee that someone charts some kind of direction for the development of our society's collective imaginary. It is namely those who most competently master our symbolic language who can further develop it. By providing us with new words and contextual meanings, we can then use these symbols to describe the world more accurately and from more nuanced and diverse perspectives. In turn, this will give us the symbolic tools we need to participate in the journey of personal inner growth.

It Has Been Done Before

The idea to deliberately give the opportunity for many citizens to develop more complex meaning making is nothing new. My co-author Lene Andersen and I tell in our book *The Nordic Secret*[12] the fascinating story behind the high level of development in the Nordic countries as a result of such a large-scale endeavour. Industrialisation occurred relatively late in Sweden, a hundred years after that of the United Kingdom. Sweden was hence still amongst the most impoverished European peasant societies during the latter half of the nineteenth century. Many were starving, and a large part of the population emigrated, mainly to the US, to get away from miserable living conditions.

During the height of this emigration, in 1889, the twenty-nine-year-old atheist Hjalmar Branting, who later became prime minister in Sweden three times for the Social Democrats, and eventually received the Nobel Peace Prize as one of the initiators of the League of Nations, was sentenced for blasphemy because of a newspaper article he wrote criticising religion. From prison, Branting wrote an editorial in the Swedish newspaper *Arbetet* (literally 'Labour') that was published on 10 August 1889:

> But still at this moment, the Labour movement is unfortunately not strong enough to hold aloft a governing political party, which, aside from its purely socio-economic and political functions, could also serve as a provider of genuine culture to the people, one that could follow the ongoing spiritual development, shed light upon literature and art, popularise science: which, in a word, could represent in all aspects a party that takes pride in elevating humanity to a higher stage of devel-

> opment, not just in order to solve the 'matters of the belly' [material conditions], however necessary this is as a prerequisite for all else.[13]

So here we have an incarcerated atheist who thinks that cultural and spiritual development is more important than increasing material living standards and that the most important issue is 'elevating humanity to a higher stage of development'. Where did he – and many of his contemporaries in Scandinavia – get these ideas? Why has this been lost in the conventional historiography of the Nordic countries' path from some of Europe's poorest and most conservative countries to modern leading model societies?

If historians had gone deeper into this interesting part of the history of the Nordic countries, they would have noticed that Branting during his student years in Uppsala, along with his student friend Karl Staaff (who twice became prime minister for the Liberal Party), had established the society called Verdandi – still active today – which later became the point of departure for the great 'secular spiritual development project' ('*folkbildningsprojektet*' in Swedish). After an originally Danish concept, 'retreat centres' were established all over Scandinavia. Here, young adults with a few years of work experience could – later with state subsidy – spend up to six months with the expressed goal of finding their inner compass: to, speaking with Kegan, become self-authoring. At the beginning of the twentieth century there were about 100 such centres in Denmark, 75 in Norway and 150 in Sweden. A hundred years ago, about 10 per cent of each young generation participated in one of these six-month 'personal development retreats'.

The original ideas behind this vast programme came from the German philosophers of the nineteenth century, who took an interest in the significance of our inner development and how our subjectivity and meaning making has got the ability to develop throughout life. These philosophers called this life-long formation of self *Bildung*. The original German ideas were developed further in Scandinavia by, among others, Søren Kierkegaard, N. F. S. Grundtvig, Esaias Tegnér and Erik Gustaf

Geijer. During the latter half of the nineteenth century these thoughts constituted the main furrow within academic philosophy in the Nordic countries. But during the twentieth century, as we saw in Part 1, positivism and analytical philosophy would completely eclipse continental philosophy's focus on the inner world. Nowadays, even if these centres (*folkhögskolor*) still exist and continue to receive state funding, their original focus on inner, personal growth has been lost. They are now mainly used for adult education in a more general and conventional sense.

I am not proposing that we should go back to this original project. But we could let ourselves be inspired by the ways in which cultural and psychological development were made political priorities, and how it was possible to support the development of more conscious individuals in the past. And it is encouraging to know that this massive historical project was successful in supporting the dramatic – and in other places in Europe very violent and turbulent – transition from pre-modern to modern societies in Scandinavia. What can we learn from this when we now are in an equally dramatic societal transition? This time from industrial nation-states into a digital global world.

A young Hjalmar Branting around 1885.

THE HAND IN HAND OF DEVELOPMENT

Every new thought perspective also puts greater demands on people's personal psychological development in order to function well, which in turn influences the development of our common thought perspectives. Here we once again see an example of self-organisation at full strength: hand in hand. But it is important to realise that this development is not automatic, that both individual and collective efforts are required for it to start.

We are now facing a decisive step in human history. We are at a bifurcation, a *tipping point* or a phase transition, and the outcome of this phase transition is by no means clear. In order to navigate within this emerging landscape, new conceptual and existential maps are important. The lack of a developmental psychological perspective was one of Marxism's and socialism's great blind spots. They overestimated how much one actively could – and should – attempt to shape people's thought patterns, perspectives, emotions and behaviour. From a developmental psychological perspective, it is clear that major, jointly planned projects to reshape society and culture more towards solidarity cannot function if a large part of the population still have a need to follow powerful authorities and by necessity primarily think about putting food on the table.

Based on Kegan's layers of self-development, the table below shows a rough-hewn and simplified presentation of how the different levels of societal development, in terms of thought perspectives, make corresponding demands on people's psychological development.

Societal System	*Self-development*	*Explanation*
Religion *(the Axial Age, the agrarian, traditional society)*	*Kegan layers 2 and 3 – Instrumental and Socialised mind*	*People must be able to follow abstract norms, look to more long-term planning and the common survival of large groups.*

Societal System	*Self-development*	*Explanation*
Rationality *(the modern, scientific industrial society)*	*Kegan layers 3 and 4 – Socialised and Self-authoring mind*	*While many get through daily life merely by following modern society's norms, there is also a need for more independently minded people who question the system and develop new solutions.*
Postmodernism *(with the global market)*	*Kegan layers 4 and 5 – Self-authoring and Self-transforming mind*	*In order to function well in today's obscure reality, adults need to develop a high degree of critical thinking and find their own path in life. Ideally, they should also be flexible and able to continuously re-evaluate their assumptions about reality, creating complex modes of collaboration.*
Metamodernism *(the internet age and an unpredictable hypercomplex future)*	*Kegan layer 5 – Self-transforming mind*	*In order for humanity to handle the rapidly accelerating complexity of a global information society, many more adults must identify with more abstract and universal values and let these govern their lives. Such values must be cultivated and developed over time. Since the pace of change is accelerating, time is scarce, and societal developments cannot be left to chance but must be subjected to deliberate actions so as to keep up.*

The message is, simply put, that personal and societal development go hand in hand – W2 and W3, if you aren't tired of Popper yet. Note, however, that I am not saying that people in more developed countries are better or more civilised than others. A fundamental value here is namely that every human being has the right to be who they are – even the leadership of Saudi Arabia or the members of the alt-right movement. Self-development is *not* a moral order; it is a liberating process that can arise under favourable circumstances. Human beings are of equal worth, whether they have access to layer 5 or only layer 2 – each is every bit as much a sentient being whose dignity must be respected, even at taxing costs. And we each have the obligation to make the best moral choices available to us on our level of meaning making.

Often, societies find it necessary to legislate and instil a moral code that is above some of the society's members' meaning making. This could sometimes be absolutely necessary for the well-functioning of the society. But if a society's moral development is done more through such legislation than through personal development throughout the population, one will in any democracy eventually reach a breaking point – a populist backlash.

On the other hand, it would be utterly unreasonable – and dangerous – to allow the politicians in the most powerful nations to act from an ego-centric layer 2.[14] It is thus in our common interest that the leadership of nations, companies and other influential organisations is characterised by the later layers of development in Kegan's model rather than the earlier. This is both possible and necessary. We can and should make an active and conscious effort as a society to create favourable conditions for more people to be able to act from layer 5, as well as enable most adults to act from layer 4.

Developmental psychological models – which of course should be built on solid empirical work – are also a path to increased understanding and a more inclusive debate climate. The same demands cannot reasonably be put on everyone, even though we are equal under the law and have the same rights. The person who grows up in a home with parents and friends who are engaged in the surrounding world and have deep morals has remarkably different opportunities from a person growing up on the streets of Monrovia. Seeing phenomena such as the alt-right movement or ISIS from a developmental psychological perspective enables us to avoid harmful judgemental attitudes and delusional feelings of moral superiority. Instead, we see the psychological needs that have to be fulfilled for our fellow humans to develop and be able to participate fruitfully in our global society.

We can and should create a more well-considered and reflexive culture that is rich in opportunities and symbol tools for thinking about life's deeper issues, about what each one of us really wants to attain with our life, and what our unique contribution might be, so as to encourage personal growth. Unfortunately, our dominant culture today is still designed along the lines of the template of industrial society's demands and logics. In growing up, a person is merely expected to educate themselves and get a career to participate in the labour market and build a well-functioning household as a consumer. These are commendable endeavours. But they are insufficient to create the many conscious co-creators that in unpredictable ways will participate in the new local/global society and non-linearly help humanity become mature enough to take on its new, global responsibility: creating a more conscious society – hand in hand.

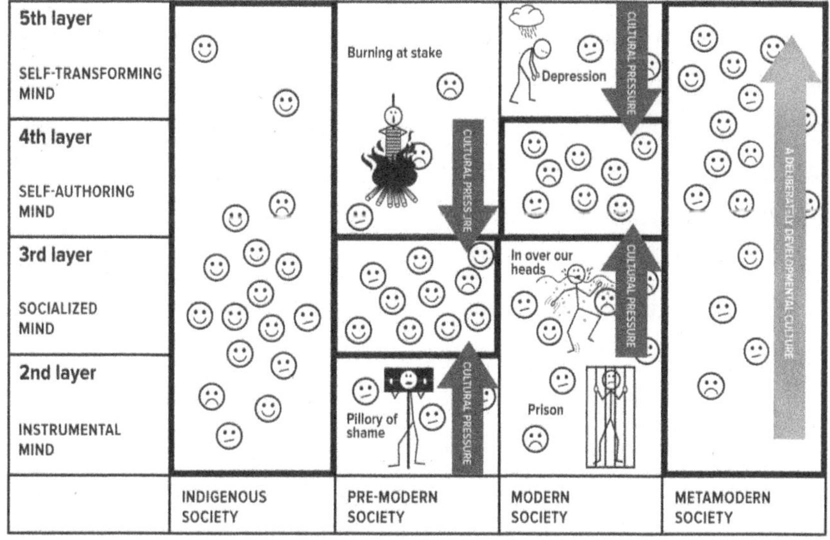

The indigenous society was able to provide a place for individuals on all different developmental levels. A metamodern society will do this again, but cannot just rely on human instinct to achieve this. The support of a Deliberately Developmental Culture will be necessary.

In the following I will present a few proposals as to how we – as culture-bearing innovators – can start influencing our society in ways to transcend the catch-22 situation we appear to be in.

MAKING OUR BASIC EMOTIONAL NEEDS A SOCIETAL PRIORITY

To make the development of a more conscious society a societal concern, we should begin by asking new questions that are perceived as relevant to the lives of ordinary people so as to convince them that the answers can improve their situation. Given that our psychological development, or the lack thereof, largely depends on meeting our emotional needs, I have chosen three such issues that should be given higher priority. These are fundamental psychological needs we all have (which many readers will probably recognise from Maslow's model of hierarchy of needs), but nonetheless remain largely absent as topics in our political debate. To actively promote them as central societal concerns could potentially be the starting point from which the idea that political measures should facilitate psychological development could eventually enter public discourse. So let's have a look at these and how we could approach the matter in a way that would make them politically relevant:

- **Belongingness / communion.** Far from everyone in modern societies feels part of a meaningful community. Many never get good and trustworthy friendships during childhood. We all know stories like this: the boy who spends his teens at home in front of the computer, fails to develop his social skills, cannot get a girlfriend and later cannot adapt to adulthood. When we send our children to school, there is no guarantee they will make friends and experience the social bonds with other people that are so crucial for their further development. The same also applies to adults. Many men lack deep friendships and walk a long, lonely path through life, never talking about deeper questions or feelings with anyone, even if they have jobs and family. Many women also feel alone and abandoned, especially as they get older, and never get to experience the loving relations and harmonious family life they wish for. Many adults simply experience long, difficult years of loneliness, involuntarily without life partners or other positive sexual relationships. And even in marriage, our relationships often lack true and deep-felt affection.

An absence of fulfilling social relations also characterises many people's professional lives, which may completely lack any rewarding interactions with others. Others struggle to even join the labour market and never get access to the social life a job can offer: the unemployed youth, the discarded elderly, the socially awkward and deviant. The lack of communion characterises so many people's lives, and the fear of social exclusion is often a driving force behind many decisions. Sadly, some of us die alone.

Accordingly, we should start asking new questions such as: how do we ensure nobody goes involuntarily through life without good friendships? How do as many as possible, if they want, get a loving life-partner? How can we make sure families stay together? How do we ensure that more people feel part of society, experience a sense of belonging at work or in their local community? That no one needs to age and die in loneliness? Here we need to consider a number of long-term efforts directed at all phases of life and venues for social interactions with others: from family life during preschool age, through childhood and adolescence in the education system and throughout adult life with all its relationships in workplaces, public institutions, civil society, and the care we are offered when we get too old to take care of ourselves. So many concrete situations can be changed to better facilitate positive bonds between people.

- **Recognition / self-esteem.** There are even more of us who never experience good self-esteem for a longer period. The good-looking girl, on the surface socially well-functioning and charming, often experiences serious doubts about her abilities to perform well enough in meeting society's expectations and beauty standards. Her doubts and insecurities can eventually turn into self-hatred and self-destructive behaviours. Many of us struggle through a long career without any real recognition to give us self-esteem. We all need recognition, some kind of confirmation that we are good people and that we are valuable to others, both privately and professionally. The lack of self-esteem is a societal problem of great importance. Many who struggle with low self-esteem do so because they are socially marginalised and lack opportunities to get a foothold in society, which often leads to anti-social behaviour and poor health that strains public expenditures. But lack of recognition also haunts the lives of many, on the surface, successful members of society. Low self-esteem creates suffering and deep bitterness in all social groups and is a driving factor behind many of our actions, which often does not lead to the most desirable outcomes. It can have negative effects on our relations, such as making us less considerate of the needs of others and constantly demanding others' recognition – and behaving badly when we do not get it – and compelling us to criticise others to compensate for our own lack of a positive self-image. Above all, low self-esteem can rob us of the courage to follow our dreams.

Today, however, if someone lacks self-esteem it is often regarded as a personal weakness rather than a social and political problem. We thus need to ask: what do we need to do in order to ensure that no one should feel like an unwanted or unsuccessful person? How can we make sure that people are not only tolerated, but actually loved, acknowledged and accepted? Here too, efforts are needed throughout all of society: to actively and consciously promote everyone to develop solid self-esteem from earliest childhood to the latest stages of our senior years. We should guarantee that all of our preschools, education institutions, workplaces and care services are guided by policies to provide social recognition and accept people as they are without anyone having to feel inadequate or as a failure without value to others.

- **Personal development / self-actualisation.** Even fewer people get the opportunity to live truly exciting and developing lives. How many do you know, for instance, who really follow their dreams in everyday life, who go their own way without asking anyone for permission? Many of us have creative and exciting professions, but most never make everyday life the beautiful adventure we know it can be. Many of us carry a deep desire to spend our lives on something truly meaningful, something where we give a unique and beautiful gift to our fellow human beings and the world. Sadly, too many of us feel that life just passes by, that what we basically wanted to create or contribute to is further and further away.

  We should therefore ask: what needs changing so that everyone can find good, meaningful purposes in life? How can we make sure that life does not become a meaningless hamster wheel? Or even worse, that people never get the opportunity to use their most valuable talents or feel that their lives matter? We need a more flexible work–life balance that does not lock us into particular roles we do not find meaningful or prevent us from chasing our dreams. Furthermore, people need increased support for their various individual projects of self-realisation. This would assist our personal growth and in turn make us better at handling many of life's most difficult and deepest crises.

So what would the results be if everyone – as far as it is practically possible – felt part of a warm and secure community, had good self-esteem and experienced meaningful self-realisation in their lives? How would social marginalisation, poor health and crime be affected? What would it do to our mental health? Would our needs for physical security and material well-being (the first two basic needs in Maslow's model) be more adequately met? Would it be unreasonable to suggest that society as a whole would become safer and more affluent and spend fewer resources on poverty reduction, crime fighting and medical treatments?

Initially we may not have all the answers about how to create this society, but the most important thing we can do is to ask these questions and make them relevant in our discussions about society. We may need a new symbol language to better talk about these as societal issues, but the fundamental prerequisites are already there with the fact that we are all hurting souls who share the same basic emotional needs.

A new system and a cultural change of the magnitude proposed here can never be the result of a pre-planned attempt at social engineering by a few gifted geniuses. It requires the contribution of us all. It is only together we can find the many small and big solutions. This can be done by increasing our ability to listen to all citizens, and thereby aggregate considerably more knowledge and viewpoints to improve society. This can take many different forms. A good start, however, would be to gather around new ways to talk about politics and societal development and experiment with different types of civic meetings to foster better conversations. This would in turn change our political culture, create a more inclusive debate climate, which would increase the odds of successfully creating the kind of society we want.

When our basic emotional needs have been sufficiently met, then all that remains is to immerse ourselves in purpose-driven endeavours and find meaning in the good we can do to others and the world. As such, the gains from a larger share of the population who do not struggle with unmet emotional needs could be immense.

* * *

The developmental process that initially appeared as a catch-22 dilemma can be initiated by a few individuals willing to make an active effort to develop our culture by advocating the values and new societal issues mentioned in this chapter. The gradual changes to our culture to occur from this will eventually make their way into the development of new social and economic structures, which will facilitate increased psychological development, which once again will develop our shared culture even further.

It thus may appear as an automatic process, but it will not occur without someone making deliberate efforts to change our culture. In order to ensure this process takes place to begin with, we need to develop a new symbolic language to make it possible to talk about psychological and cultural development. We need new words and concepts to assist this kind of thinking, a new symbol world to accommodate and form a meaning-creating context to make sense of the new complexity we are talking about, which in turn will promote the development of a new and more conscious political culture.

Although the emergence of new levels of complexity occur along the lines of certain regularities and developmentally determined patterns, the future remains far from predetermined. History has taught us that societal collapses and temporary regressions to lower levels of complexity are likely to occur if humans do not react in time. But precisely herein lies humanity's freedom. Humanity is not, as Hegel thought, via an idea-based deterministic development en route towards the ideal society, 'the realisation of the world spirit'.[15] Nor do we find ourselves, as Marx believed, in a materially determined development towards the ideal society: communism. Reality is much more complicated – and frightening – than that. Humanity faces collective existential choices. Just as Kierkegaard or Sartre indicated for the individual who stands before their existential freedom and who must take a leap of faith in order to go further, humanity stands before a similar *collective existential choice* and must take a leap of faith to decide its non-determined future. We must realise that we have this freedom – that we all play a crucial role in the world we create. We must summon the courage to act in accordance with this newly found freedom. It cannot be emphasised clearly enough: humanity is *not* running on auto-pilot towards the good society. Our collective imaginary is cumbersome, and if we do not nurture and develop it, it can easily produce Brexits or Trumps – or worse.

However, we should not, in Lenin's spirit, want to make ourselves the creator of society. Rather, we should make ourselves a *co-creator* of the processes that operate within the market, in politics and in day-to-day life. Hence, the choice is not between totalitarianism or neoliberalism, as proposed by Popper,[16] but between unconsciously or consciously created evolutionary processes.

The choice is ours.

Chapter 15

TOWARDS NEW METANARRATIVES

In this closing chapter I would like to highlight some of the main lessons from this book and point towards some promising directions. Ideally, I have been able to convince the reader that it is *we* who create the world, that we can influence the path we want the world to develop along. It is my hope that I have shared new perspectives that can assist us at this important crossroads in human history. It is up to you, the reader, how you will use these perspectives and ideas. It may not give you a list of new things to do when you wake up tomorrow, but it may have influenced how you interpret the world, the time we live in, your relationships and yourself.

In a way, it is an impossible task to share new perspectives. How does the experienced meditation teacher share their hard-earned spiritual insights? How does the designer share their sense of style? And how does a thinking and sentient being – which is the sense in which I wish to speak to you in this book – share their view of life, the human being, history and reality? Writing a book is, of course, a matter of one-way communication. But I hope that we can continue the conversation together in some form, that our paths cross in the great weave that is our remarkable, beautiful, crisis-ridden and mysterious present time.

You and I are part of the same great weave. We share symbols, we share deeply human experiences, and we both make impressions on society. But as we make our impressions and choose our paths, might we do so with a better common map for what society's development means? Can we see in ourselves and in each other how society develops, how society can grow and become more mature? Can we jointly create a more conscious society?

WE HUMANS NEED NARRATIVES

We humans need our narratives. This is how we make sense – how we make meaning – of the world and find direction. Postmodern philosophy has helped us understand that all narratives and so-called 'metanarratives' are human constructs and part of our collective imaginaries. Whether the metanarratives are about God, Science or the Market, they are all made up by us humans, for the benefits of us humans – or at least for some of us. They convey efficiency, power and meaning and they are at the core of our collective imaginary. It is our narratives that help us survive and flourish – as a collective and as individuals. We cannot live without our narratives. They create order and direction in our otherwise chaotic reality and life. This was the case when we gathered around camp fires in the Stone Age, and it remains equally so when we gather around internet discussion forums today.

Our collective imaginary must be anchored in an overarching narrative to give its constituent symbols a firm contextual foundation that furnishes meaning that ties the whole thought perspective it is derived from together into a coherent and accessible pattern. Our life force requires focus, and meaning is about focusing energy in an otherwise chaotic world.

A metanarrative is also needed to establish and articulate the principles from which the thought perspective draws its highest authority on truth that every thought perspective, as mentioned, inevitably contains – however abstractly conceived and implicit that might be.

We may not like the idea of an authority on truth, we may rephrase it and use the term 'epistemology' instead. But no matter how we phrase it, we need to make the conscious effort to articulate what our worldview considers valid beliefs and opinions. If we don't, we will risk blindfolding ourselves and thereby failing to see what is guiding our thinking and behaviour. If we refuse to acknowledge what has become our highest authority, we will lose the opportunity to hold it accountable. Every thought perspective has a fundamental flaw. Postmodernism's is that its internal thought structure, so beneficial in many other regards, has blinded its followers from acknowledging that their rejection of *all* authorities has inadvertently made the power of the market the highest authority. This is in turn the Achilles' heel that is the point of departure for the thought perspective to replace postmodernism; the metanarrative of what I have chosen to call metamodernism will therefore need to address this issue.

Metamodernism must in extension of this also create a new metanarrative that convincingly articulates a story about its own highest authority. This would need to answer why the preceding authorities are not based on sufficiently consistent claims of universality and how they contradict themselves. From a metamodern perspective, God, Science or the Market are no longer sufficient as narratives to provide us the objectives and meaning making we need in our complex world today. These lower levels of meaning making are simultaneously responsible for correspondingly lower levels of efficiency and fairness (expressions of power relations and empowerment). The new metanarrative to serve as a contextual framework for the metamodern thought perspective will therefore need to contain superior explanatory power regarding all three of these crucial aspects: consistency, meaning making, and its effect upon efficiency and fairness.

But what exactly is a metanarrative? A metanarrative might be linked to a thought perspective in the way the term has been used throughout this book, the overarching story that every society tells about the world and the human being's role in this – and the prevailing narrative about society itself. Religion created various overarching narratives about how the human being has a special role to play in a greater, enchanted world that stretches beyond our immediate perception. Modern science created many different small and big stories about how the world follows predetermined laws and that the human being has a random and arbitrary role in an indifferent Universe, but can still make this world their home by getting to know its alien, law-bound secrets. Postmodernism created a major story of the dissolution of all the grand human-made narratives, with a flood of minor tales in its wake where contexts, discourses, cultures and identities produce a non-cohesive multitude of experienced worlds that humans can only observe and participate in from their own limited perspective.

Metamodernism should therefore have a similar overarching story to tell about the world and our role in it. Additionally, it must clarify its own role to play in the world and in people's lives. Thus, a metanarrative is not exactly the same as a thought perspective, it is the story that a society tells about itself and its thought perspective.

The metanarrative is a large library of non-arbitrarily catalogued and interrelated narratives. Postmodernism believes that there is no such library. Metamodernism builds and organises the library of a thousand narratives: it organises its own metanarrative. Yes, there will be multiplicity, chaos and contradiction – yet higher orders are concealed within. Some narratives may be brought to the fore, tweaked, and used in different context. And the structure of each narrative. As such, it spites the authorities of old. No, God, Science and Market, you are not in charge – we are.

The metamodern mind, body and soul collects and interrelates the many narratives, looking for the inventors of new ones – for the co-creators of our age. It gathers some of the most abstracted and profound narratives and labels them as parts of the metamodern. Common to these different metamodern narratives is that – in a similar way as the previous thought perspectives – they provide a basic structure for how we might orient ourselves in the world and how new ways of creating meaning might arise. With the metamodern insights regarding evolution, self-organisation, complexity, individuation/integration and the transpersonal dividual, we can, I hope, sense some new patterns in people's thinking that today are gaining in strength and might eventually make their way into the metanarratives that metamodernism tells about itself.

By necessity, the new metanarratives and their perceived common sense must be more abstract than the previous ones. There are three reasons why that is:

Firstly, it is quite simply harder to fathom and incorporate a more complex thought perspective into one's thinking since it requires broader knowledge and coordination of more forms of understanding.

Secondly, it must be able to handle more complex phenomena, such as climate change or a global transnational world order, with highly advanced and rapidly evolving technologies, which need to be perceived and articulated in more abstract terms to be made intuitively comprehensible to our Stone Age brains.

Thirdly, a new metanarrative must be considerably more spacious than the previous ones. It must be able to discern opportunities for positive interaction between many people's vastly different worldviews, levels of psychological development and cultural backgrounds, not to mention different areas of knowledge. Once again this requires a higher level of abstraction in the symbol tools used to articulate the new thought perspective's metanarrative.

If I am accused of being too abstract in this book, I would respond that it is actually our new complex reality that demands this level of abstraction. To abstract is to pull out that which is most essential, to see patterns or governing principles in a thorny reality. Seeing the trees, indeed, but also creating a sense of what kind of forest we are strolling through.

We will, of course, for the foreseeable future have human beings that think, act and create meaning from very different levels of narratives – different stories about life and reality. The large majority of our fellow humans will still have religion, science or the market as their points of departure. Nonetheless the need for groups in all parts of society that understand each other on a more abstract level persists. Naturally, we cannot fully understand each other's areas of expertise, the specialised knowledge therein, or each other's unique experiences. But we might have better shared common sense as a starting point when we cooperate and communicate.

COMPONENTS OF NEW NARRATIVES

I think that any metamodern metanarrative has to be a story of stories. An evolving story of nested and interconnected stories on global, regional and local levels. We need narratives on all levels to make sense of the world: individual, family, local, national, regional and global.

All these narratives have to reflect many perspectives. Not just because we live in a multicultural world, but because evolution works through differentiation and integration and in a rapidly developing technological environment, we need a lot of differentiation for the cultural evolution to keep up.

But the narratives also have to be interlinked and nested within each other in increasing complexity and scope and be in healthy competition and cooperation with each other. And we have to acknowledge that this is an ongoing process. That no narratives are final. The narratives themselves need to evolve in the ongoing development of our world.

What is beautiful in this search for our new narrative about the human being and its world is that we will never complete it. It is an ongoing search without end – a never-ending proto-synthesis if you will. Any new narrative will have to be viewed only as a proto-narrative in this ongoing search process. It is yet another self-organising evolutionary process, with its own constitutive rules, which constantly challenges the narrative and keeps the dialogue alive. And the metanarratives will revolve around precisely this search for the great tales that manage to nurture and maintain *all* of our different stories and perspectives that in today's world are trying to outcompete and displace each other. Maintaining different perspectives from all of our human narratives might help us glimpse as many aspects of our world as possible.

But not to get lost in the postmodern hall of mirrors of perspectives, an artery in our new metamodern narratives is the direction. Religion had the union with the *divine*. Science had *progress*. The market and postmodernism struggle to create a positive direction in the story, but at least there was an effort to see the *individual's self-fulfilment* as a fundamental driving force.

Any new metanarrative must be one that is directed towards the global, sustainable society, and towards the human being's ability to attain self-realisation in two ways. We have already mentioned both of them – that we as *individuals* become responsible adults and as a *society* attain a higher level of freedom and responsibility than we have known so far.

With our new insights, we can now affirm that it is not, as the Middle Age philosophers thought, a case of using human *logos* to understand God's *telos* in nature. Instead it is about using *logos* and *eros* to create *human telos* in our collective imaginary and in this way build in greater consciousness in our society.

Here, developmental psychology, *Bildung* philosophy or an increased spiritual sensibility may chart a way forward. It seems to be the case that the human being will develop towards a higher level of consciousness given favourable circumstances. Such consciousness entails a higher level of cognitive complexity and self-awareness; increased capacity for empathy and extended circles of belonging. This in turn entails a lower degree of defensive, deficiency-based self-interest, and a more abstract identification with the world, society and nature. In this way, our solidarity is deepened and extended to comprise a greater number of sentient beings in more ways. The abolition of slavery, the introduction of democracy and human rights, the emergence of the welfare society and increased gender equality can all be seen as steps in this direction towards a more conscious society.

Again, I am by no means arguing that a positive development towards a more self-aware global human is predetermined or automatic. Throughout world history we have repeatedly seen how decisive both individual and collective human decisions have been in shaping the future. But with a higher level of psychological and cultural development we boost our chances and our freedom to make crucial decisions – both individually and collectively. There is good reason to believe that if we do not reach higher levels of development, this century will see even more burdensome crises – and unfortunately also catastrophes.

The human being's most complex and decisive issue in the new metanarrative is therefore our personal, psychological development – and a corresponding development of our shared culture and societal structures. This is the most important project in human history today. It started many thousands of years ago, but it has only just begun. When the complexity in our society increases, the process might get caught in a blind alley – just as it has done now – and must be rebooted again.

MY PROTO-NARRATIVE

I do not want to propose new metanarratives that blindly praise the human being at the expense of the rest of the biosphere and the Universe. That the human being develops also means that the understanding we have had of ourselves is surpassed. As early as in Nietzsche's writings, we might sense such a perspective: when the human being really grows up, when we *truly* realise that God (all our 'gods', new and old) is dead, then we become something other than the human being that we hitherto have known. A new metanarrative might therefore harbour an undertone of *post-humanism*, a theme that has become frequent among many contemporary philosophers. The term 'post-humanism' can trigger negative associations, but its purpose is not to dehumanise us or hollow out our human dignity. Rather, post-humanism means that the human being no longer sees itself as the measure and meaning of everything, but that we are parts of a greater reality and evolutionary process.

As stated before, we live in a complex and rapidly developing time and therefore need many, interlinked proto-narratives. Any metamodern narrative that I might embrace will have to be a proto-narrative that needs to be open to reinterpretation and reformulation as I mature and the world around me changes. If I, in a socialised mind, too deeply define myself from a specific, static narrative, I will hurt myself and possibly those around me. I should strive to hold my narrative lightly and see the possibility of change. If I do need a pre-fabricated narrative to internalise from my culture, it has to be a narrative around change and growth – that we as individuals and society are on a developmental journey and that change and growth is the new normal.

We should on all levels go from a belief in a fixed externally given metanarrative to an internally generated and lightly held proto-narrative.

My contribution to these framing stories can be told on three levels – Personal, Collective and Universal – that are of different complexity, depth and reach and therefore will resonate differently with us depending on where we are on the life journey of maturation and consciousness development. They all take their starting point in the rapid technological development we are experiencing right now.

We are living at a very critical time

The exponential technological growth that we discussed in chapter 11 gives rise to opportunities and challenges on a scale that humanity has never faced before. Never before in history has humanity gone through such fundamental change in framing conditions.

Even though throughout history humanity has seen many major shifts in technology, like the invention of farming or industrialisation of production, we used to be able to adapt to new technologies between generations. Older generations could, if they wished, remain with previous technologies and the new generations would adapt. You could remain a farmer for the rest of your life, but your children might decide to move to the city and become factory workers. This was the experience of most human beings in the past. Technological change, if it happened at all, occurred from one generation to the next. The pace of change allowed for the older generation to literally die out without embracing the change. Then, what was once novel could be embraced fully by their children and became a new norm.

We now live in a world where disruptive change happens many times within our lifetime. A typical fifty-year-old person living in the developed world today will have experienced several major technological shifts during their lifetime, changes that meant new structures in social life, work life, in access to information, and in meaning making. They have, for example, lived through the transitions from landlines, mainframe computers and letters to the World Wide Web, smart phones, the Internet of Things and the rise of Artificial Intelligence. Unlike in the past, such shifts have not been something that could be ignored and left for the next generation to embrace. Our brains are not wired for this and the world we have created has become very complex and very rapidly changing. Consequently, we suffer stress from confusion and loss of ability to make meaning.

New technology and new ways of life now impact every part of the earth and the scale of human impact on our planet is so great that geologists have concluded that we have created a new geological epoch which they have named the Anthropocene.

While anthropogenic ('human-made') climate change is the poster child, there are many other consequences of both our sheer numbers and the way we interact with the biosphere that are equally significant and damaging.

We are transcending the boundaries of a safe operating space for humanity with respect to most of the key indicators identified by science. These range from land use, fresh water cycles and biogeochemical flows of nitrogen and phosphorous, to atmospheric aerosol loading, chemical pollution and ocean acidification.

The latest scientific insights suggest that our failure to respond at sufficient scale and with sufficient urgency, means that we are already at a stage where, at best, we may be able to stabilise the natural systems on which we and our civilisations depend for our existence. Restoring them, we are told, may already be beyond our reach.

History has shown us many examples of civilisations collapsing from over exploitation of nature – the Mayan Civilisation of the Americas and the Roman Empire in Europe and North Africa to name but two. The difference is – this time the consequences are global.

As stated before, we can try to understand these challenges, and frame a narrative around them, on three levels: Personal, Collective and Universal.

Personal Level

The story on this level can be told from a strictly personal, individualistic and instrumental perspective. This is a story that can easily resonate with a majority of the population in the West and it goes something like this:

In this rapidly moving world it is impossible to know what specific skills we ourselves and our children need to develop in order to just be able to keep up with change. If you spend three years learning to programme and code, chances are that in five to ten years coding and programming are done exclusively by Artificial Intelligence. Therefore, we need to focus more on the fundamental life skills that we in chapter 12 called *transformative skills*. By focusing on developing our capacity for compassion, perspective taking, complex sense making and self-knowledge, etc. we will be better prepared as individuals to meet a future we can know very little about, apart from the fact that it will be even more complex and rapidly developing.

As the world around us becomes more and more complex we have to evolve our thinking and being in the world. We have to evolve our minds and we understand that this will be a lifelong challenge. By focusing on developing transformative skills, we will be advancing in the different dimensions of consciousness development we explored in Chapter 12. This will result in a general increase in consciousness in society.

Collective Level

On the Collective level, we expand our horizons in time and space and go from our individual lives and lifelong development to that of civilisations. We go from a perspective of ten to fifty years to a perspective of 100 years and beyond.

Here the narrative is that our modern worldview has given us extraordinary development but is no longer able to help us in the next step. The complexity of our challenges demands a response at the level of changing our paradigm – our collective imaginary. The task is urgent as we are at a bifurcation point where collapse is also a real possibility.

Humanity has reached the end of the currently dominating civilisation and worldview, and we need to collectively move on and give room for the birth of a new civilisation.

As we rapidly approach this bifurcation point, our individual minds as developing complex self-organising systems interact with the developing complex self-organising systems of our societal culture and institutions. The unavoidable phase-shift could go in two directions: the emergence of a more interconnected, more complex and more conscious society; or the disconnect, breakdown and fragmentation of our human world.

The ability of any developing complex self-organising systems to find new stability in higher states of complexity depends on the ability of the individual parts of the system to begin to relate in deeper and more complex ways. Developing the transformative skills mentioned above would therefore not just be important for individual consciousness development and the individual's ability to adapt, but also – importantly – be crucial for the support of the collective transformation of society.

The way we view the world is, as we have seen throughout the book, important for the way we make meaning and therefore act in the world. Early in life we download our worldview form our surrounding culture. A shift in worldview is therefore much more dependent on a collective cultural shift, rather than just individual developmental efforts. Starting to collectively deepen and widen our worldview will therefore also be an important contribution to a successful societal transformation. We have throughout the book been exploring blind spots in our currently dominating Western worldview; areas where our limited understanding today will have to be deepened in order to see the world in different and deeper perspectives necessary to successfully meet our current challenges.

One way to get an overview of these blind spots discussed throughout the book could be to gather them under five headings:

Our view of ourselves	*from separation, to connection and relationship*
Our view of the world	*from a world of things, to a world of evolving processes*
Our view of our mind	*from rational and fixed, to a constantly evolving living system*
Our view of society	*from something given, to something socially constructed out of our thinking and acting today*
Our view of our lives	*from a focus on material success as an end in itself, to a focus on purpose and meaning*

The shifts of perspective above that we have been exploring throughout the book are becoming more and more accepted and applied in academia and in social activism. But many academics, organisations and projects today only use one or two such new perspectives.

As the complexity of the context is so high, all five shifts of perspective must be applied in our understanding to every aspect of our human world, including the interconnection of these aspects, in order to activate the potential for deep change.

Organisations or projects that disregard one or two of these insights and shifts are more likely to face significant systemic pushback from blind spots in their approach.

If we do not achieve a transition to a new worldview, it seems probable that the forces we have set in motion, especially within the natural world and the biosphere, will tip us into a collapse.

Universal Level

We could stop our story at the collective level. All the important insights for increasing the probability for a successful next step in human history are there and we can find meaning in life through consciously participating in the creation of a better world. But as we mature, we might slowly start to realise that we are an integral part of the Universal evolution and story we started to explore in chapter 1 and our story can again be expanded to even wider perspectives.

Throughout human history, from the Renaissance to the scientific revolution, to the Enlightenment, to full-blown modernity and its postmodern critics, we can see a similar pattern emerging. Our palace in the Universe has been pushed farther and farther into the periphery of reality itself; we are no longer God's chosen children, not at the centre of the world, and even our emotions, thoughts and choices are – according to latest research – beyond us. At the same time, in what seems to be a strange and wonderful paradox, each time we are dethroned by the history of science, we rise above our previous understanding and become more intimately involved as self-conscious co-creators in the Universe. At the same time as we realise our insignificance in the Universe, our sense of agency and responsibility for our world and its place in the Universe increases.

We have now the uniquely human possibility to self-consciously see the interaction between our Personal evolving meaning making and the evolution of our Collective imaginary. An interaction that takes place within – and is a unique expression of – the Universal evolution of cosmos. By this self-consciousness we now also have the opportunity to align our personal purpose and meaning making with the 13.8 billion-years-old evolutionary impulse of the Universe. This alignment of the Personal, Collective and Universal evolutionary processes is the maturity that we need to participate in the world in a more responsible and meaningful way. And in some remarkable way something greater than ourselves, perhaps not God but at least a deeper, universal meaning, has slipped in through the back door.

I began this book by using the Big Bang and evolution at the Universal scale as a springboard. Although it might have seemed grandiose to connect our own history to the birth of the Universe, we can now see that the Universal story offers a perspective from which to see ourselves and our future as part of a greater and deeper unfolding and development.

It has been somewhat poetically observed that we are nothing but stardust, that we are made up of the same kinds of particles that we share with all celestial objects. This metaphor serves to illustrate that we are the result of the same fundamental evolutionary process that began with the Big Bang. The story I have told in this book takes its starting point in my own background within a Western, natural science, materialistic worldview and investigates the strengths and limitations of this approach. This is the language I, and many other in the West and elsewhere, are most familiar and comfortable with. I could instead have started from the point of *panpsychism*, the view that consciousness or mind is a universal and primordial feature of all things, but that would have been a less intuitive story for most Western readers. The origin of the Universe and the primordial forces and principles that still govern it are beyond human metaphors and understanding, so whatever language we chose to describe them, it will always be an anthropocentric projection. The end point of this book would still have been the same.

The main reason to connect to our cosmic origins is therefore not to explain the physical mechanisms that gave rise to biological thinking creatures like ourselves. In a time where the divine creation myths of yesterday have lost their explanatory power, and with that the beauty of our origins to be derived from there, seeing our everyday lives and accomplishments as parts of the history of the Universe could make us feel like the descendants of the great mother Big Bang – a perspective from which we could find renewed meaning and a sense of connection to all of creation. A 'modern creation myth', as proposed by the historian David Christian,[1] with its point of departure going back to the very beginning of what we have an understanding of, could be the foundation of a new shared metanarrative needed to foster a stronger feeling of belongingness and interconnectedness to all of human kind and the natural environment we all share.

If we see ourselves and others – despite our differences – as intimately connected and ultimately part of the same all-encompassing reality, the result could be that we started to experience a higher and more inclusive level of solidarity and compassion.

The scientifically explored Universe, with its unfathomable astrophysical dimensions, leaves us very few messages about the meaning of life. No divine commandments are written in the starry skies and no gospel rings through the quiet, cold expanse of the cosmos. Instead, it invites us to something else: to see the mystery of existence and our own situation in a wider world.

Sometimes I hear friends late at night, as they gaze at the sky perhaps after a drink too many, talk about how small they feel in the great Universe. But I do not feel this way. I feel that we are part of a seemingly boundless self-organising Universe where life, consciousness and intelligence can flourish and observe this remarkable world and give it meaning. We are meaning-making creatures in a Universe that otherwise would be void of meaning. In this unique position it is actually the heavens that need us in order to be looked upon, and in some peculiar way recognised for the beauty and mystery they contain.

* * *

What comes after God, Science and the Market? Naturally I cannot know what will happen or what kinds of development awaits. But I can say what I wish for and what I think we can achieve together. We have already come so far that if we distributed humanity's resources fairly so that everyone has their basic material needs met, we could go further and attain a society that supports every human's personal growth and further psychological development; a society in which so many compassionate, curious and free-thinking humans are born, who from a deep-rooted conviction in their hearts and minds will co-create a civilisation to manifest the highest known expression of the Universe's self-organising adventure.

Seeing the Big Bang as intimately connected with every daily occurrence is not to lapse into reverie and close one's eyes to the suffering in the world and the difficult challenges that confront us. On the contrary, it could be a narrative that helps us fully recognise and create meaning from the fundamental condition of tragedy pertaining to all existence, while endowing us with the ability to see the beauty that permeates all aspects of creation – from the small and mundane to the vast and spectacular. Our capacity for collective meaning-creation and collective imaginaries is not just something that makes us uniquely human, it is also our strongest asset to increase our chances for survival. In an increasingly complex world, our ability to create meaning is decisive for whether we face a dignified future or a tragic collapse.

When we reach a point where we can intuitively sense that everything is connected in one great self-organising process, with billions of component processes that have been given emergently different properties through evolution, and have become aware of the collective imaginaries fabricated by previous generations so that we can disembed ourselves from them, then it is time to take one more step in the development of our consciousness by throwing away *all* our symbol tools and other chimeras of our analytic mind so we do not risk mistaking them for reality. At least just for a brief moment. Don't worry, they will still be where you left them. Throw away the thought perspectives. Throw away the metanarratives. Throw away Kegan's layers and Popper's worlds. Throw away the efficiency, power and meaning aspects of our society. Throw them all away, for they don't really exist. They are merely symbols and metaphors. The only thing that exists is an indivisible and extremely complex whole of infinite parts in constant co-evolution.

And while we are in the process of discarding such non-existent imaginaries, maybe we should also throw away our individual self. Now we understand that this is also just a construct that we have been given by evolution to passably navigate this indivisible whole. There quite simply are no individual selves.

Something happens inside you when you really understand that you, your life and your actions are an integrated part of a constantly ongoing evolutionary process that eternally leaves traces in the future. Your way of viewing the world and yourself becomes irrevocably altered. You experience what the ancient Greeks called *metanoia* – a permanent inner transformation. There is no way back. You will then realise that you have a role to play in the evolution of the Universe – something that you can now choose to do self-consciously.

To self-consciously contribute to society's development thus becomes a source of meaning in your life. You will start seeing yourself as an agent and a link in the great co-created evolutionary process of the Universe. Your self-consciousness will be shifted from yourself as an individual to all of humanity and to the evolutionary process that has been ongoing for billions of years, and which at this moment – when you and I are alive and active – is at one of its most critical stages ever. During this century, the direction for the future of humanity will be decided by the *collective existential choices* that confront us. And the important insight – which both obligates and liberates us – is that the future lies in *our* hands.

NOTES

Introduction

1 Christian, David (2004). *Maps of Time: An Introduction to Big History*. University of California Press, p. 505.
2 Spier, Fred (1996). *The Structure of Big History: From the Big Bang Until Today*. Amsterdam University Press, p. 13.
3 See e.g. Schuster, Heinz Georg (1995). *Deterministic Chaos: An Introduction*. Wiley VCH.
4 Bar-Yam, Yaneer (2002). 'General features of complex systems', *Encyclopedia of Life Support Systems*. EOLSS UNESCO Publishers.
5 Johnson, Neil (2009). *Simply Complexity: A Clear Guide to Complexity Theory*. Oneworld Publications.
6 Weaver, Warren (1948). 'Science and complexity', *American Scientist*, 36: 536.
7 Stevenson, Betsey and Wolfers, Justin (2008). 'Economic growth and subjective well-being: reassessing the Easterlin Paradox', *Brookings Papers on Economic Activity*: 1–87.
8 Interview with Stephen Hawking (2000). *San Jose Mercury News*, 23 January.
9 The line between the two admittedly remains fuzzy. It is not immune to conceptual confusion or tricky, deviant in-between occurrences. To put all living systems in the same category, while using terms such as 'agency', 'strive for self-maintenance' and 'consciousness' to differentiate their unique properties, may strike one as conceptually odd when that even pertains to primitive single-cell organism whose behaviour even may appear somewhat mechanical. Dividing up the scale to make room for two categories to differ between single-cell and multicellular organism could easily have been made, but to simplify the terminology I have chosen to refer to both kinds as 'complex systems'. Similarly, at the other end of the middle-scale, it can be debated whether a human institution (a company, government, etc.) is best understood as a complex system or a chaotic one. On one hand they seem to have deliberate built-in rules for self-maintenance (often in easily comprehended written form), but on the other they certainly do not give rise to any whole in terms of something akin to a consciousness. They also seem to be governed by both a regulatory core of self-maintenance like in complex systems and self-organising rules relating to its constituents as in chaotic systems simultaneously; and the degree to which one or the other is more prevalent can differ from institution to institution. Once again, I have omitted making any further differentiation to serve the purpose of simplification and brevity.

10 Although complexity science and chaos theory study many of the same phenomena and the two methods largely overlap, a rough-hewn differentiation between chaos theory and complexity science that is commonly made is that the former studies systems that are deterministic whereas the latter studies systems that are not. A central concern in chaos theory is how the behaviour of systems is determined by its initial conditions. The emergent phenomena that complexity science give considerable attention are not even in theory deterministic. However, since both methods are applied to the same phenomena it says more about the different approaches than the system themselves.

11 Capra, Fritjof and Luisi, Pier Luigi (2014). *The Systems View of Life: A Unifying Vision*. Cambridge University Press, pp. 144ff.

12 Mayr, Ernst (1982). *The Growth of Biological Thought: Diversity, Evolution, and Inheritance*. Harvard University Press, p. 63.

13 Another way of understanding different levels of complexity is how entities on the higher levels can be said to be indeed 'higher' by how they subordinate their lower-level components. Complexity arises through processes where previously independent entities get 'locked' into an overarching structure that can be said to limit their 'autonomy' so as to maintain the structure. For example, atoms lose their autonomy as independent atoms when they become part of a molecule; they no longer behave exactly how they would outside it. The structure of the molecule organises the atoms in a more ordered fashion vis-à-vis each other, but this is at the expense of their own more 'chaotic agency'. It is the same when molecules become part of an organic cell. Here, their behaviour gets limited to a number of patterns that give rise to the organism's metabolism. Atoms and molecules do retain their specific properties – atoms do not cease to bond just because they become part of a molecule and neither do the laws of thermodynamics cease to apply when molecules form organic matter – but the new structure they have become part of transcends these properties, without negating them, which makes it behave in ways to give rise to emergent properties on the higher level of the overarching structure that could not have appeared if they had remained independent. Of course, these ordered patterns are only visible if we see the overarching structure, the whole greater than the sum of its parts. Studying an individual component in isolation of this will not reveal the higher order it has become part of. To understand an emergent phenomenon, it thus needs to analysed on the level of complexity pertaining to its order.

Chapter 1

1 Chaisson, Eric J. (2001). *Cosmic Evolution: The Rise of Complexity in Nature*. Harvard University Press, p. 11.

2 Christian, *Maps of Time*, p. 34.

3 NASA/WMAP Science Team, http://map.gsfc.nasa.gov/media/121238/index.html.

4 Christian, *Maps of Time*, p. 507.

5 Goldilocks conditions refers to the Earth seemingly at the perfect distance from the Sun in order to sustain oceans of liquid water for life; just as Goldilocks, in the story of Three Bears, found the porridge that was just right.

6 Sadi Carnot wrote only one book in his lifetime. It was published in 1824 and had the rather lengthy title, *Réflexions sur la puissance motrice du feu et sur les machines propres à développer cette puissance*, in English 'Reflections on the Motive Power of Fire and on

Machines Fitted to Develop that Power'. Carnot formulated the principles that the 'fall of heat' from a high temperature to a lower is where the work in a machine comes from and that the correct way to analyse a heat engine is by analysing it as a thermodynamic cycle, also known as the 'Carnot cycle'. These ideas became crucial for the theory of thermodynamics and his book is considered the founding work of the field.

7 Spier, Fred (2010). *Big History and the Future of Humanity.* Wiley-Blackwell, p. 49.

8 Erwin Schrödinger published *What Is Life? The Physical Aspect of the Living Cell* in 1944. It was based on a course of public lectures in Dublin the previous year and written as a work of popular science for the lay reader. The way life appears to contradict the second law of thermodynamics became known as 'Schrödinger's paradox', although Schrödinger himself pointed out that there was none.

9 Christian, *Maps of Time*, p. 510.

10 Spier, *Big History and the Future of Humanity*, pp. 31–32.

11 Spier, *Big History and the Future of Humanity*, p. 30.

12 Schrödinger, Erwin ([1944] 1992) *What Is Life?* in *What Is Life? The Physical Aspect of the Living Cell*; with, *Mind and Matter*; and *Autobiographical Sketches*. Cambridge University Press, p. 77.

13 Christian, *Maps of Time*, p. 80.

14 Chaisson, *Cosmic Evolution*, p. 134.

15 The higher power density of a human brain than e.g. the sun of course sounds counterintuitive. Keep in mind that power density is the rate of energy flux per unit volume. So even if the sun if of course hotter than the brain, the brain expends more energy per unit of volume. On a related topic, the concept of entropy has interestingly also become increasingly used within neuroscience. For instance, it has been suggested that the 'entropy' of the patterns of brain activity increases under e.g. psychedelic states. See Carhart-Harris, R. L., Leech, R., Hellyer, P. J., Shanahan, M., Feilding, A., Tagliazucchi, E., Chialvo, D. R., Nutt, D. (2014). 'The entropic brain: a theory of conscious states informed by neuroimaging research with psychedelic drugs', *Frontiers in Human Neuroscience*, 8: 20.

16 Schrödinger, *What Is Life?*, p. 73.

17 Of course, stars are born from the spoils of other stars – an estimation is 275 million stars born per day in the observable Universe as a whole. Such reproduction, however, does not carry with it genetic codes or acquired behaviours.

18 Christian, *Maps of Time*, p. 81.

19 Spier, *Big History and the Future of Humanity*, p. 59.

20 Villarreal, Luis P. and Witzany, Guenther (2013). 'The DNA habitat and its RNA inhabitants: at the dawn of RNA'. *Sociology*. 6: 1–12.

21 Spier, *Big History and the Future of Humanity*, p. 78.

22 Emiliani, Cesare (1995). *The Scientific Companion: Exploring the Physical World with Facts, Figures, and Formulas*, 2nd edn. John Wiley, p. 151.

23 Humphrey, Nicholas (1992). *A History of the Mind.* Chatto and Windus, p. 97.

24 Gärdenfors, Peter (2003). *How Homo Became Sapiens: On the Evolution of Thinking.* Oxford University Press, pp. 18–19.

25 Adapted from MacLean, Paul D. (1968). 'Alternative neural pathways to violence', *Alternatives to Violence.* Time-Life Books, p. 26.

26 Gärdenfors, *How Homo Became Sapiens*, pp. 22, 59.
27 Nagel, Thomas in Honderich, Ted (ed.) (2010). *The Oxford Companion to Philosophy*. Oxford University Press, p. 637.
28 Russell, Bertrand (1910). 'Knowledge by acquaintance and knowledge by description', *Proceedings of the Aristotelian Society*, New Series, 11: 108–128.
29 Koestler, Arthur (1967). *The Ghost in the Machine*. Hutchinson.
30 Christian, *Maps of Time*, pp. 153–155. Spier, *Big History and the Future of Humanity*, p. 125.
31 Gärdenfors, *How Homo Became Sapiens*, pp. 227–228.
32 Christian, *Maps of Time*, p. 166.
33 Gärdenfors, *How Homo Became Sapiens*, pp. 84–97.
34 Dunbar, Robin (2005) *The Human Story: A New History of Mankind*. Faber and Faber, p. 70
35 This idea has been proposed by Härd, Ingemar (2011). *Efter fem miljoner år av tystnad: språkets uppkomst*. Ordfront, p. 238.
36 Spier, *The Structure of Big History*, pp. 129–130.

Chapter 2

1 Christian, *Maps of Time*, p. 178.
2 Diamond, Jared (1999 [1997]), *Guns Germs and Steel: The Fates of Human Societies*. Norton, p. 39.
3 Christian, *Maps of Time*, p. 182.
4 Christian, *Maps of Time*, p. 178.
5 Brown, Cynthia Stokes (2007) *Big History: From the Big Bang to the Present*. The New Press, p. 60.
6 Diamond, *Guns Germs and Steel*, pp. 39–40.
7 'Collective imaginary' is sometimes also referred to as 'social imaginary' or just 'imaginary'.
8 Christian, *Maps of Time*, p. 178.
9 Christian, *Maps of Time*, p. 179.
10 Mithen, Steven (1996). *The Prehistory of the Mind: A Search for the Origins of Art, Religion, and Science*. Thames and Hudson.
11 Christian, *Maps of Time*, pp. 172–173.
12 Christian, *Maps of Time*, p. 173.
13 Casanova, José (2012). 'Religion, the Axial Age, and secular modernity in Bellah's theory of religious evolution' in *The Axial Age and Its Consequences*. Bellah, Robert Neelly and Joas, Hans (eds.). The Belknap Press, p. 199.
14 Harari, Yuval Noah (2014, originally published in Hebrew 2011). *Sapiens: A Brief History of Humankind*. Vintage, p. 23.
15 Harari, *Sapiens*, p. 41.
16 Harari, *Sapiens*, p. 37.
17 Wright, Robert (2001). *Nonzero: The Logic of Human Destiny*. Vintage, p. 24.
18 Again, see Harari, *Sapiens*.
19 The 'Dunbar limit', as it is known.
20 Gottschall, Jonathan (ed.) (2006). *The Literary Animal: Evolution and the Nature of Narrative*. Northwestern University Press.

21 Harari, *Sapiens*, pp. 26–31.
22 Thompson, John B. (1984). *Studies in the Theory of Ideology.* University of California Press, p. 6.
23 Steger, Manfred B. and James, Paul (2013). 'Levels of subjective globalization: ideologies, imaginaries, ontologies', *Perspectives on Global Development and Technology*, 12(1–2): 23.
24 Sartre, Jean-Paul, ([1936]2010). *The Imaginary: A Phenomenological Psychology of the Imagination*. Routledge Classics. p 90.
25 Thompson, *Studies in the Theory of Ideology*, p. 24.
26 Spier, *The Structure of Big History*, p. 113.
27 Mcneill, John Robert and McNeill, William Hardy (2003). *The Human Web: A Bird's-Eye View of World History*. Norton, p. 13.
28 Wright, *Nonzero*, pp. 36–38.
29 This idea has also been proposed by Everett, Daniel (2012). *Language: The Cultural Tool.* Profile Books.
30 Inspired by Berger, Peter L. and Luckmann, Thomas (1966). *The Social Construction of Reality: A Treatise in the Sociology of Knowledge.* Berger and Luckmann's theory on social constructions will be presented in further detail in chapter 9.
31 Lent, Jeremy (2017). *The Patterning Instinct: A Cultural History of Humanity's Search for Meaning.* Prometheus Books.
32 Christian, *Maps of Time*, p. 189.
33 Ingold, Tim (2000). *The Perception of the Environment: Essays in Livelihood, Dwelling and Skill.* Routledge, p. 42.
34 Willerslev, Rane (2007). *Soul Hunters: Hunting, Animism and Personhood among the Siberian Yukaghirs.* University of California Press, p. 24–27.
35 Piaget, Jean ([1926] 2002). *The Language and Thought of the Child.* Routledge.
36 Bellah, Robert N. (2011). *Religion in Human Evolution.* Belknap, Harvard University Press, p. 117.
37 Capra and Luisi, *The Systems View of Life*, pp. 308ff.
38 Christian, *Maps of Time*, p. 145.
39 Christian, *Maps of Time*, p. 146.
40 Christian, *Maps of Time*, p. 146.
41 Christian, *Maps of Time*, p. 147.
42 See e.g. Dawkins, Richard (2006). *The God Delusion.* Bantam Books, pp. 189–201; or Blackmore, Susan (1999). *The Meme Machine.* Oxford University Press, pp. 24ff.
43 For an engaging further exploration of this phenomenon, see Gleick, James (2012). *Information: A History, a Theory, a Flood.* Fourth Estate.

Chapter 3

1 Christian, *Maps of Time*, p. 210.
2 Spier, *Big History and the Future of Humanity*, pp. 144–145.
3 Christian, *Maps of Time*, p. 222.
4 See e.g. Cohen, Mark (1989). *Health and the Rise of Civilization.* Yale University Press, pp. 132, 139; or Coatsworth, John H. (1996). 'Welfare', *American Historical Review*, 101(1) (February): 2.

5 Harari, *Sapiens*, p. 87.
6 Christian, *Maps of Time*, pp. 223–224.
7 Sahlins, M. (1968). 'Notes on the Original Affluent Society', *Man the Hunter*. DeVore, Irven and Lee, Richard Borshay (eds.). Aldine Publishing Company, pp. 85–89. (Compare with Marx's notions of pre-agrarian communistic production, for example).
8 Spier, *Big History and the Future of Humanity*, p. 149.
9 Spier, *Big History and the Future of Humanity*, pp. 97, 146.
10 Famously noted by Jared Diamond in *Guns Germs and Steel.*
11 Christian, *Maps of Time*, p. 242.
12 Spier, *Big History and the Future of Humanity*, pp. 152–153.
13 Elias, Norbert (1982). *Power and Civility (The Civilizing Process: Volume II)*. Pantheon Books, pp. 229–333.
14 Spier, *Big History and the Future of Humanity*, pp. 158–159.
15 For more, see Spier, *Big History and the Future of Humanity*, pp. 151–152, 158–159; Christian, *Maps of Time*, pp. 268–271.
16 McNeill and McNeill, *The Human Web*, p. 81.
17 Christian, *Maps of Time*, p. 275.
18 Christian, *Maps of Time*, p. 261. Spier, *Big History and the Future of Humanity*, p. 159.
19 Anderson, Benedict (1983). *Imagined Communities: Reflections on the Origin and Spread of Nationalism*. Verso.
20 See e.g. Diamond, Jared (2012). *The World Until Yesterday*. Allen Lane; or McNeill, W. H. (1999). *A World History*. Oxford University Press.
21 Christian, *Maps of Time*, p. 287.
22 Christian, *Maps of Time*, pp. 264–265.
23 Christian, *Maps of Time*, p. 248.
24 Wright, *Nonzero*, p. 93.
25 Spier, *Big History and the Future of Humanity*, pp. 163–164.
26 Harari, *Sapiens*, pp. 138–139.
27 Graeber, David (2011). *Debt: The First 5000 Years*. Melville House Publishing, pp. 38–39.
28 Graeber, *Debt*, pp. 214–215.
29 Wright, *Nonzero*, p. 105.
30 Assmann, Jan (2012). 'Cultural memory and the myth of the Axial Age', in *The Axial Age and Its Consequences*, p. 395.
31 Assmann, 'Cultural Memory and the myth of the Axial Age', p. 380.
32 Assmann, 'Cultural Memory and the myth of the Axial Age', pp. 389–390.

Chapter 4

1 Wright, Robert (2009) *The Evolution of God*. Little, Brown. p. 90.
2 Bellah, *Religion in Human Evolution*, p. 175 ff.
3 Wright, *The Evolution of God*, p. 91.
4 Jaspers, Karl (1953). *The Origin and Goal of History*. Routledge.
5 Roetz, Heiner (2012). 'The Axial Age theory: a challenge to historicism or an explanatory device of civilization analysis? With a look at the normative discourse in Axial Age China' in *The Axial Age and Its Consequences*, pp. 249–250.

6 Wittrock, Björn. (2012). 'The Axial Age in global history: cultural crystallizations and societal transformations' in *The Axial Age and Its Consequences*, pp. 104–105.
7 Runciman, W. (2012) 'Righteous rebels: when, where, and why?', in *The Axial Age and Its Consequences*.
8 Christian, *Maps of Time* p. 319.
9 Spier, *Big History and the Future of Humanity*, pp. 162–163.
10 Dalferth, Ingolf U. (2012). 'The idea of transcendence', in *The Axial Age and Its Consequences*, pp. 146–147. (From: Jaspers, Karl ([1953] 2010). *The Origin and Goal of History*. Routledge, p. 219).
11 Armstrong, Karen (2005). *A Short History of Myth*, Canongate Books.
12 Wright, Robert (2009) *The Evolution of God: The Origins of Our Beliefs*. Little, Brown, p. 246.
13 Wright, *The Evolution of God*, pp. 229–320, 251.
14 Armstrong, *A Short History of Myth*, p. 78.
15 Jaspers, *The Origin and Goal of History*, p. 219.
16 Dalferth, 'The idea of transcendence', p. 147.
17 Armstrong, *A Short History of Myth*, p. 39.
18 Armstrong, *A Short History of Myth*, pp. 76–77.
19 Plato's *Apology* (38a5–6).
20 Armstrong, *A Short History of Myth*, pp. 90–92.
21 Sacks, Jonathan (2011). *The Great Partnership: God, Science and the Search for Meaning*. Hodder and Stoughton, pp. 57ff.
22 Armstrong, *A Short History of Myth*, pp. 96–97.
23 Sacks, *The Great Partnership*, p. 61.
24 Tarnas, Richard (2010). *The Passion of the Western Mind: Understanding Three Ideas that Have Shaped Our World View*. Pimlico, pp. 179ff.
25 Sacks, *The Great Partnership*, p. 66.
26 See Hume, David (1739). *A Treatise of Human Nature*. Wikisource, pp. 469–470.

Chapter 5

1 Graeber, *Debt*, pp. 275–281.
2 See e.g. Diamond, Jared (2012). *The World Until Yesterday*. Allen Lane; or McNeill, *A World History*.
3 Söderberg, Johan (2008). *Vår världs ekonomiska historia*. Del 1. SNS Förlag, p. 52.
4 Mankiw, N. Gregory (2007). *Macroeconomics* (6th edn). Worth Publishers, pp. 22–32; Greco, Thomas H. (2001). *Money: Understanding and Creating Alternatives to Legal Tender*. Chelsea Green Publishing.
5 Mankiw, N. Gregory (2008). *Principles of Macroeconomics*. Southwestern Cengage Learning, pp. 338–339.
6 Wright, *Nonzero*, p. 97.
7 Wilson, Charles ([1958] 1963), *Mercantilism*. Routledge and Kegan Paul, p. 10.
8 Carruthers, Bruce G. and Nelson Espeland, Wendy (1991). 'Accounting for rationality: double-entry bookkeeping and the rhetoric of economic rationality', *The American Journal of Sociology*, 97(1) (July): 31–69.
9 Lane, Frederic C. and Riemersma, Jelle (eds.) (1953). *Enterprise and Secular Change:*

Readings in Economic History. R. D. Irwin, p. 38. (Quoted in 'Accounting and rationality'.)

10 Wright, *Nonzero*, p. 100.

11 Ferguson, Niall (2008). *The Ascent of Money: A Financial History of the World*. Penguin, p. 72.

12 Tarnas, *The Passion of the Western Mind*, pp. 231–240.

13 Complete quote: '*Reason is the Devil's greatest whore*; by nature and manner of being she is a noxious whore; she is a prostitute, the Devil's appointed whore; whore eaten by scab and leprosy who ought to be trodden under foot and destroyed, she and her wisdom ... Throw dung in her face to make her ugly. She is and she ought to be drowned in baptism ... She would deserve, the wretch, to be banished to the filthiest place in the house, to the closets.' From Martin Luther, Erlangen Edition of Luther's Works, volume 16, pp. 142–148.

14 Tarnas, *The Passion of the Western Mind*, pp. 253.

15 Tarnas, *The Passion of the Western Mind*, pp. 272–375.

16 The phrase originally appeared in French as 'je pense, donc je suis' in *Discours de la Méthode Pour bien conduire sa raison, et chercher la vérité dans les sciences* (1637), known as simply *Discourse on the Method*, and later in Latin in *Principia Philosophiæ* (1644) (Eng. *Principles of Philosophy*).

17 Cited by Galilei in 'Letter to the Grand Duchess Christina' (1615).

18 Tarnas, *The Passion of the Western Mind*, pp. 366–380.

19 Andersen, Lene R. and Björkman, Tomas (2017) *The Nordic Secret: A Story of European Beauty and Freedom*. Fri Tanke.

20 Christian, *Maps of Time*, pp. 393–398.

21 Christian, *Maps of Time*, p. 414.

22 Christian, *Maps of Time*, p. 416.

23 See Sturgess, R. W. (1966). 'The Agricultural revolution on the English clays', *Agricultural History Review*; Mingay, G. E. (ed.) (1977). *The Agricultural Revolution: Changes in Agriculture 1650–1880*. A. and C. Black; or Overton, Mark (1996). *Agricultural Revolution in England: The Transformation of the Agrarian Economy 1500–1850*. Cambridge University Press.

24 Christian, *Maps of Time*, pp. 358–359.

25 Christian, *Maps of Time*, pp. 359–360.

26 Engels, Friedrich (1847). *The Principles of Communism* (German: *Grundsätze des Kommunismus*). Principle 7.

27 Marx, Karl and Engels, Friedrich (1848). *The Communist Manifesto*.

28 Marx, Karl (1843). *Critique of Hegel's Philosophy of Right*. Introduction.

Chapter 6

1 See e.g. Stephen, R. C. (2004). *Explaining Postmodernism: Scepticism and Socialism from Rousseau to Foucault*. Scholarly Publishing.

2 See e.g. Tarnas, *The Passion of the Western Mind*, pp. 362–365.

3 Original quote: 'There is no such thing as society, there are individual men and women and there are families.' Margaret Thatcher, 1987.

4 See e.g. Jones, Daniel Stedman (2012). *Masters of the Universe*. Princeton University Press, p. 85 ff.

5 Lyotard, Jean-François ([1979] 1984). *The Postmodern Condition: A Report on Knowledge*, translated Geoff Bennington and Brian Massumi. University of Minnesota Press.
6 Hughes-Warrington, Marnie (ed.) (2005). *Palgrave Advances in World Histories*. Palgrave Macmillan, p. 175.
7 Anthony Giddens famously coined the term 'late modernity' in *Modernity and Self-Identity: Self and Society in the Late Modern Age* (1991).
8 Hughes-Warrington, *World Histories*, pp. 175–176.

Chapter 7

1 Nietzsche, *Will to Power*, *KGW* VIII I, p. 138.
2 Nagel, Thomas (1986). *The View from Nowhere*. Oxford University Press.
3 Brown, Callum G. (2005). *Postmodernism for Historians*. Pearson Education, pp. 6–7.
4 Jameson, Fredric (1991). *Postmodernism, or, The Cultural Logic of Late Capitalism*. Duke University Press.
5 The blog is called 'Ens Et Potum' (Latin for 'being and beverage') and the post's title is 'What the fuck is structuralism and who the fuck is Jacques Derrida?' https://ensetpotum.tumblr.com/post/126037327408/what-the-fuck-is-structuralism-and-who-the-fuck-is.
6 de Saussure, Ferdinand ([1916] 1971). Cours de linguistique générale. Payot.
7 Lyotard, J. F. (1988). *The Differend: Phrases in Dispute*. University of Minnesota Press.
8 See e.g. Foucault, Michel (1972). *The Archaeology of Knowledge and the Discourse on Language*. Routledge.
9 Derrida has argued that 'Deconstruction is not a method, and cannot be transformed into one', Wood, David and Bernasconi, Robert (1988). *Derrida and Différance* (Reprinted edn). Northwestern University Press.
10 Cilliers, Paul (1998). *Complexity and Postmodernism: Understanding complex systems*. Routledge, p. 80 ff.
11 Brown, *Postmodernism for Historians*, pp. 10–11, 30.
12 Manning, Patrick (2003). *Navigating World History: Historians Create a Global Past*. Palgrave Macmillan, p. 235.
13 'Il n'y a pas de hors-texte'. Derrida, Jacques (1967). *De la grammatologie*. Les Éditions de Minuit, pp. 158–59, 163.
14 Iggers, Georg G. (2007). *Geschichtswissenschaft im 20. Jahrhundert: Ein kritischer Überblick im internationalen Zusammenhang*. Vandenhoeck and Ruprecht, pp. 102–104, 124–125.
15 Own Translation of 'In den Diskurs der Zeit einzubetten'. Iggers, *Geschichtswissenschaft im 20. Jahrhundert*, p. 107.
16 First introduced in *Prolegomena zu einer jeden künftigen Metaphysik, die als Wissenschaft wird auftreten können* (1783). See Kant, Immanuel (1902). *Prolegomena to Any Future Metaphysics*. Translated by Paul Carus. Open Court, § 52c.
17 Brown, *Postmodernism for Historians*, pp. 46–47.
18 The term 'theory of relativity', based on the expression 'relative theory' (German: 'Relativtheorie'), was used for the first time in: Planck, Max (1906), 'The measurements of Kaufmann on the deflectability of β-Rays in their importance for the dynamics of the electrons', *Physikalische Zeitschrift*, 7: 753–761. In the discussion section of the same

paper, Alfred Bucherer used the expression 'theory of relativity' (German: Relativitätstheorie) for the first time.

19 Sokal, Alan (2008). *Beyond the Hoax: Science, Philosophy and Culture.* Oxford University Press.

20 Sokal, Alan D. (1996). 'Transgressing the boundaries: toward a transformative hermeneutics of quantum gravity', *Social Text*, 46–47, pp. 217–252.

21 Iggers, *Geschichtswissenschaft im 20. Jahrhundert*, p. 62.

22 Brown, *Postmodernism for Historians*, p. 31.

Chapter 8

1 First introduced in: Smith, Adam (1759). *The Theory of Moral Sentiments.*

2 See e.g. Stiglitz, Joseph (2002). 'There is no invisible hand', *Guardian*, 20 December; or Fullbrook, E. (2009). *The Ontology of Economics: Tony Lawson and His Critics.* Routledge.

3 Lundmark, Robert (2011). *Mikroekonomi: Teori och tillämpningar*. Studentlitteratur.

4 Björkman, Tomas (2016). *The Market Myth*. Fri Tanke, p. 47.

5 See e.g. Wilkinson, N. and Klaes, M. (2012). *An Introduction to Behavioral Economics.* Palgrave Macmillan.

6 See e.g. Lipsey, R. G. and Lancaster, Kelvin (1956). 'The general theory of second best', *Review of Economic Studies*, 24(1): 11–32.

7 Own translation, from: Rydberg, Viktor ([1891] 1996). 'Den nya grottesången' in *Dikter*. Atlantis.

8 Habermas, Jürgen (1979). *Communication and the Evolution of Society.* Beacon Press, pp. 164–165.

9 Own translation, from: Strindberg, August ([1883] 1995), 'Esplanadsystemet' in *Dikter på vers och prosa* i *Samlade Verk 15. Nationalupplaga*. Norstedts.

Chapter 9

1 Popper, Karl (1980) in Ashby, E. et al *The Tanner Lectures on Human Values*. Cambridge University Press.

2 Own translation of 'Mit jedem Sprechakt bezieht sich der Sprecher gleichzeitig auf etwas in der objektiven, in einer gemeinsamen sozialen und in seiner subjektiven Welt.' Habermas, Jürgen (1988 [1985]). *Der philosophische Diskurs der Moderne*. Suhrkamp Verlag, p. 365.

3 Thanks to the philosopher Åsa Burman for this example.

4 Berger, Peter and Luckmann, Thomas (1966). *The Social Construction of Reality: A Treatise in the Sociology of Knowledge.* Penguin Social Sciences.

5 Berger and Luckmann , *The Social Construction of Reality*, p. 67.

6 Berger and Luckmann , *The Social Construction of Reality*, p. 60.

7 Berger and Luckmann , *The Social Construction of Reality*, p. 76.

8 Berger and Luckmann , *The Social Construction of Reality*, pp. 110ff.

9 Berger and Luckmann , *The Social Construction of Reality*, p. 113.

Chapter 10

1 Björkman, Tomas (2016). *The Market Myth*. Fri Tanke. p. 124.

2 US Copyright Office, 'Circular 1: copyright basics', pp. 5–6.
3 From an online article in the *Independent* the 27 October 2015 titled 'George Orwell's estate sent copyright notice to man selling t-shirts with "1984 is already here" on them'. http://www.independent.co.uk/arts-entertainment/books/news/george-orwells-estate-sent-copyright-notice-to-man-selling-t-shirts-with-1984-is-already-here-on-a6710926.html.
4 From an online article on VG247 12 May 2017 titled 'Alan Wake is being pulled from steam and the Xbox Store after this weekend'. https://www.vg247.com/2017/05/12/alan-wake-is-being-pulled-from-steam-and-the-xbox-store-after-this-weekend/.
5 This has also been proposed by Ostrom, E. (2003). 'How types of goods and property rights jointly affect collective action', *Journal of Theoretical Politics*, 15(3): 254.
6 Illustration taken from: Björkman, *The Market Myth*, p. 133.
7 For more on sociocracy: Endenburg, Gerard (1998). *Sociocracy: The Organization of Decision-making: 'No Objection' as the Principle of Sociocracy*. Eburon; or Buck, John and Villines, Sharon (2007). *We the People: Consenting to a Deeper Democracy*. Sociocracy.info Press. For more on holacracy: Robertson, Brian J. (2016). *Holacracy: The Revolutionary Management System that Abolishes Hierarchy*. Portfolio Penguin; or https://www.holacracy.org/.
8 For more information, see Alaska Permanent Fund Corporation's website: http://www.apfc.org/.

Chapter 11

1 Jordan, T. and Andersson, P. (2010). 'Att hantera de svårlösta samhällsfrågorna. Göteborgs stad och Tryggare mänskligare Göteborg' [Managing the wicked issues of society. Published by City of Gothenburg and the Organization Safer and More Humane Gothenburg], http://www.tryggaremanskligare.goteborg.se/pdf/publikation/Att%20hantera%20de%20svarlosta%20samhalls%C2%ADfragorna_web.pdf.
2 Inspired by Jordan and Andersson, 'Att hantera de svårlösta samhällsfrågorna. Göteborgs stad och Tryggare mänskligare Göteborg'.
3 After Kegan, Robert and Laskow Lahey, Lisa (2009). *Immunity to Change: How to Overcome It and Unlock the Potential in Yourself and Your Organization*. Harvard Business Press.
4 For an exhaustive overview, see Young, Gerald (2015). *Development and Causality: Neo-Piagetian Perspectives*. Springer.
5 After Kegan, *Immunity to Change*.
6 Ontology (the doctrine of being, from the Greek word *ontos*, 'being', and *logi*, 'doctrine') revolves around how the world is fundamentally constituted: what are the traits that condition its nature? This pursues the world as it is. What really exists? Matter, ideas, consciousness, energy fields, gods – and what do these then consist of? These ideas are the backbone of metaphysics. Kant realised that we will never understand the world's ontology entirely.
7 Epistemology (the doctrine of knowledge, theory of knowledge, from the Greek word *episteme*, 'knowledge', and *logi*, 'doctrine') is the study of how we can acquire knowledge of the world. What are the best paths and methods to understand the world and ourselves? This question is connected to our conception of the world's ontology: its

nature. If we, as René Descartes did, believe that matter and consciousness are two ontologically distinct component parts of the world, we will probably believe that we need various ways to approach the understanding of these domains. If we instead have an essentially materialistic ontology, we may believe that a reductionist natural scientific stance can provide us with complete knowledge of the world.

Chapter 12

1 See e.g. Taylor, E. W. (2007). 'An update of transformative learning theory: a critical review of the empirical research (1999–2005)', *International Journal of Lifelong Education*, 26: 173–191; or Loevinger, Jane (ed.) (1998). *Technical Foundations for Measuring Ego Development*. Psychology Press.

2 See e.g. Taylor, E. W. and Cranton, P. (2012). *The Handbook of Transformative Learning*. Jossey-Bass.

3 See Laros, Anna, Fuhr, Thomas and Taylor, Edward W. (eds.) (2017). *Transformative Learning Meets Bildung: An International Exchange*, Sense Publishers.

4 Andersen and Björkman, *The Nordic Secret*.

5 Skar, Patricia (2004). 'Chaos and self-organization: emergent patterns at critical life transitions', *Journal of Analytical Psychology*, 49: 243–262. Capra and Luisi, *The Systems View of Life*, pp. 252ff.

6 See Vygotskij, Lev (1978). *Mind in Society: Development of Higher Psychological Processes*. Harvard University Press.

7 Papert, Seymour (1999). 'The century's greatest minds', *Time Magazine*, special issue, 29 March, p. 105.

8 Hesse, Janina, and Gross, Thilo (2014). 'Self-organized criticality as a fundamental property of neural systems', *Frontiers in Systems Neuroscience*, 8: article 166.

9 Stephen, Damian and Dixon, James (2009). 'Dynamics of representational change: entropy, action, and cognition', *Journal of Experimental Psychology*, 35(6): 1811–1832.

10 A good introduction to the model: Commons, M. L. and Pekker, A. (2008). 'Presenting the formal theory of hierarchical complexity.' *World Futures*, 64(5–7): 375–382.

11 Own translation, from: Tranströmer, Tomas ([1993] 2011) *Minerna ser mig, i Dikter och prosa 1954–2004*. Albert Bonniers förlag, p. 489.

12 Kegan, Robert (1994). *In Over Our Heads: The Mental Demands of Modern Life*. Harvard University Press.

13 Elfhag, Kristina (2019). *Livsutvecklingens Psykologi*. Fri Tanke.

14 Kegan, *Immunity to Change*, p. 17.

15 Kegan, *Immunity to Change*, p. 28.

16 Basseches, Michael (1984). *Dialectical Thinking and Adult Development*. Ablex Publishing Corporation.

17 Kegan, *Immunity to Change*, p. 28.

18 Mead, George Herbert (1967). *Mind, Self, and Society from the Standpoint of a Social Behaviorist*. The University of Chicago Press, pp. 173, 174.

19 German: 'Wo Es war, soll Ich werden'.

20 See e.g. Abrams, Jeremiah and Zweig, Connie (1991). *Meeting the Shadow: The Hidden Power of the Dark Side of Human Nature*. Tarcher.

21 Based on Kegan, *In Over Our Heads*.

22 Elfhag, *Livsutvecklingens psykologi*. p. 31.
23 Jordan, Thomas. Unpublished lecture material. Gothenburg University 2016.
24 Pepperberg, I. (1992). 'Proficient performance of a conjunctive, recursive task by an African gray parrot (*Psittacus erithacus*)', *Journal of Comparative Psychology*, 106(3): 295–305.
25 See e.g. Taylor, Edward and Cranton, Patricia (2012). *The Handbook of Transformative Learning: Theory, Research, and Practice*. Jossey Bass.
26 Elfhag, *Livsutvecklingens psykologi*. pp. 205–220.
27 Taylor, 'An update of transformative learning theory', p. 179.

Chapter 13

1 Nealon, Jeffrey (2012). *Post-postmodernism, or, The Cultural Logic of Just-in-time Capitalism*. Stanford University Press.
2 As Frederic Laloux posits in *Reinventing Organizations* (2014).
3 The formulation used throughout Ken Wilber's work.
4 Habermas, Jürgen (2008). 'Secularism's crisis of faith: Notes on post-secular society', *New Perspectives Quarterly*, 25: 17–29.
5 Reder, M. and Schmidt, J. (2010) 'Habermas and religion', in Habermas et al. *An Awareness of What Is Missing: Faith and Reason in a Post-Secular Age*. Trans. Ciaran Cronin. Polity. pp. 1–14.
6 Used by Robert Kegan, *In Over Our Heads*.
7 Used by Hanzi Freinacht (2017). *The Listening Society: A Metamodern Guide to Politics, Book One;* and the (2019) *Nordic Ideology: A Metamodern Guide to Politics, Book Two*; and also in Andersen and Björkman, *The Nordic Secret*.
8 Gilles Deleuze coined the term 'dividual' to explain the mechanisms of a 'control society' in an article titled 'Postscript on society of control' (1992).
9 As derived from holons, insightfully found in Koestler, *The Ghost in the Machine*, but also in wider literature on 'Holacracy' as an organizational type.

Chapter 14

1 Nouwen, Henri (2011). *Spiritual Formation: Following the Movements of the Spirit*. SPCK, pp. 5–12.
2 Kegan, Robert and Laskow Lahey, Lisa (2016). *An Everyone Culture: Becoming a Deliberately Developmental Organization*. Harvard Business Review Press.
3 Thanks to Jonathan Rowson for insights.
4 Laloux, Fredric (2014). *Reinventing Organizations: A Guide to Creating Organizations Inspired by the Next Stage in Human Consciousness*. Nelson Parker.
5 Andersen and Björkman, *The Nordic Secret*.
6 Vygotskij, *Mind in Society*.
7 Kegan, *In Over Our Heads*.
8 Genesis 2:18–20.
9 Planck, Max (1948). *Wissenschaftliche Selbstbiographie. Mit einem Bildnis und der von Max von Laue gehaltenen Traueransprache*. Johann Ambrosius Barth Verlag, p. 22, trans. F. Gaynor (1949) in *Scientific Autobiography and Other Papers*. Philosophical Library, pp. 33–34 (quoted in Kuhn, Thomas S. (1962). *The Structure of Scientific Revolutions*. University of Chicago Press).

10 For more information see Berkana Institute's website: https://berkana.org/about/our-theory-of-change/
11 Laloux, *Reinventing Organizations*
12 Andersen and Björkman, *The Nordic Secret.*
13 Own translation of: 'Men ännu i denna stund är tyvärr icke arbetarrörelsen stark nog att kunna bära upp ett organ, som förutom sin rent social-ekonomiska och politiska afdelning äfven kan göra tjenst som bärare till folket af äkta kultur, som kan följa den fortgående andlige utvecklingen, belysa literatur och konst, popularisera ^: som med ett ord kan i alla riktningar representera ett parti, som berömmer sig af att vilja lyfta menskligheten till et högre utvecklingsstadium, icke blott att vilja lösa "magfrågan", hur nödvändigt detta än är som förutsättning för allt annat.' Branting, Hjalmar (10 August 1889). *Arbetet* (literally trans. 'The Work').
14 Andersen, Lene Rachel (2017). *Testosteroned Child. Sad: Or the Dawning of a New Renaissance?* Det Andersenske Forlag.
15 Hegel, G. W. F. (1807). *Phänomenologie des Geistes* (*The Phenomenology of Mind*).
16 Popper, Karl (2002 [1945]). *The Open Society and Its Enemies.* Routledge.

Chapter 15

1 Christian, *Maps of Time*, pp. 1–11.

BIBLIOGRAPHY

Abrams, Jeremiah and Zweig, Connie (1991). *Meeting the Shadow: The Hidden Power of the Dark Side of Human Nature*. Tarcher.

Andersen, Lene R. (2017). *Testosteroned Child. Sad: Or the Dawning of a New Renaissance?* Det Andersenske Forlag.

Andersen, Lene R. and Björkman, Tomas (2017) *The Nordic Secret: A Story of European Beauty and Freedom*. Fri Tanke.

Anderson, Benedict (1983). *Imagined Communities: Reflections on the Origin and Spread of Nationalism*. Verso.

Armstrong, Karen (2005). *A Short History of Myth*. Canongate Books.

Basseches, Michael (1984). *Dialectical Thinking and Adult Development*. Ablex Publishing Corporation.

Bellah, Robert N. (2011). *Religion in Human Evolution*. Harvard University Press.

Bellah, Robert Neelly and Joas, Hans (eds.) (2012). *The Axial Age and Its Consequences*. The Belknap Press.

Berger, Peter and Luckmann, Thomas (1966). *The Social Construction of Reality: A Treatise in the Sociology of Knowledge*. Penguin Social Sciences.

Björkman, Tomas (2016). *The Market Myth*. Fri Tanke.

Blackmore, Susan (1999). *The Meme Machine*. Oxford University Press.

Brown, Callum G. (2005). *Postmodernism for Historians*. Pearson Education.

Brown, Cynthia Stokes (2007). *Big History: From the Big Bang to the Present*. The New Press.

Buck, John and Villines, Sharon (2007). *We the People: Consenting to a Deeper Democracy*. Sociocracy.info Press.

Capra, Fritjof and Luisi, Pier Luigi (2014). *The Systems View of Life: A Unifying Vision*. Cambridge University Press.

Chaisson, Eric J. (2001). *Cosmic Evolution: The Rise of Complexity in Nature*. Harvard University Press.

Christian, David (2004). *Maps of Time: An Introduction to Big History*. University of California Press.

Cilliers, Paul (1998). *Complexity and Postmodernism: Understanding complex systems*. Routledge.

Cohen, Mark (1989). *Health and the Rise of Civilization*. Yale University Press.

Dawkins, Richard (2006). *The God Delusion*. Bantam Books.

Diamond, Jared ([1997] 1999). *Guns Germs and Steel: The Fates of HumanSocieties*. Norton.

Diamond, Jared (2012). *The World Until Yesterday*. Allen Lane.

Dunbar, Robin (2005) *The Human Story: A New History of Mankind.* Faber and Faber.
Endenburg, Gerard (1998). *Sociocracy: The Organization of Decision-making: 'No Objection' as the Principle of Sociocracy.* Eburon.
Elfhag, Kristina (2019). *Livsutvecklingens psykologi.* Fri Tanke.
Elias, Norbert (1982). *Power and Civility (The Civilizing Process: Volume II).* Pantheon Books.
Emiliani, Cesare (1995). *The Scientific Companion: Exploring the Physical World with Facts, Figures, and Formulas, 2nd edn.* John Wiley.
Foucault, Michel (1972). *The Archaeology of Knowledge and the Discourse on Language.* Routledge.
Ferguson, Niall (2008). *The Ascent of Money: A Financial History of the World.* Penguin.
Freinacht, Hanzi (2017). *The Listening Society: A Metamodern Guide to Politics, Book One.* Metamoderna.
Fullbrook, E. (2009). *The Ontology of Economics: Tony Lawson and His Critics.* Routledge.
Gärdenfors, Peter (2003). *How Homo Became Sapiens: On the Evolution of Thinking.* Oxford University Press.
Gleick, James (2012). *Information: A History, a Theory, a Flood.* Fourth Estate.
Gottschall, Jonathan (ed.) (2006). *The Literary Animal: Evolution and the Nature of Narrative.* Northwestern University Press.
Graeber, David (2011). *Debt: The First 5000 Years.* Melville House Publishing.
Greco, Thomas H. (2001). *Money: Understanding and Creating Alternatives to Legal Tender.* Chelsea Green Publishing.
Habermas, Jürgen (1979). *Communication and the Evolution of Society.* Beacon Press.
Habermas, Jürgen ([1985] 1988). *Der philosophische Diskurs der Moderne.* Suhrkamp Verlag.
Harari, Yuval Noah (2014, originally published in Hebrew 2011). *Sapiens: A Brief History of Humankind.* Vintage.
Hegel, G. W. F. (1807). *Phänomenologie des Geistes.* Projekt Gutenberg.
Hughes-Warrington, Marnie (ed.) (2005). *Palgrave Advances in World Histories.* Palgrave Macmillan.
Hume, David (1739). *A Treatise of Human Nature.* Wikisource.
Humphrey, Nicholas (1992). *A History of the Mind.* Chatto and Windus.
Iggers, Georg G. (2007). *Geschichtswissenschaft im 20. Jahrhundert: Ein kritischer Überblick im internationalen Zusammenhang.* Vandenhoeck and Ruprecht.
Ingold, Tim (2000). *The Perception of the Environment: Essays in Livelihood, Dwelling and Skill.* Routledge.
Jameson, Fredric (1991). *Postmodernism, or, The Cultural Logic of Late Capitalism.* Duke University Press.
Jaspers, Karl (1953). *The Origin and Goal of History.* Routledge.
Jones, Daniel Stedman (2012). *Masters of the Universe.* Princeton University Press.
Johnson, Neil (2009). *Simply Complexity: A Clear Guide to Complexity Theory.* Oneworld Publications.
Kahneman, Daniel (2011). *Thinking, Fast and Slow.* Farrar, Straus and Giroux.
Kant, Immanuel (1902). *Prolegomena to Any Future Metaphysics.* Open Court.
Kegan, Robert (1994). *In Over Our Heads: The Mental Demands of Modern Life.* Harvard University Press.

Kegan, Robert and Laskow Lahey, Lisa (2009). *Immunity to Change: How to Overcome It and Unlock the Potential in Yourself and Your Organization.* Harvard Business Press.

Kegan, Robert and Laskow Lahey, Lisa (2016). *An Everyone Culture: Becoming a Deliberately Developmental Organization.* Harvard Business Review Press.

Koestler, Arthur (1967). *The Ghost in the Machine.* Hutchinson.

Laloux, Fredric (2014). *Reinventing Organizations: A Guide to Creating Organizations Inspired by the Next Stage in Human Consciousness.* Nelson Parker.

Lane, Frederic C. and Riemersma, Jelle (eds.) (1953). *Enterprise and Secular Change: Readings in Economic History.* R. D. Irwin.

Laros, Anna, Fuhr, Thomas and Taylor, Edward W. (eds.) (2017). *Transformative Learning Meets Bildung: An International Exchange.* Sense Publishers.

Lent, Jeremy (2017). *The Patterning Instinct: A Cultural History of Humanity's Search for Meaning.* Prometheus Books.

Loevinger, Jane (ed.) (1998). *Technical Foundations for Measuring Ego Development.* Psychology Press.

Lyotard, Jean-Fran.ois ([1979] 1984). *The Postmodern Condition: A Report on Knowledge.* University of Minnesota Press.

Lyotard, J. F. (1988). *The Differend: Phrases in Dispute.* University of Minnesota Press.

Mankiw, N. Gregory (2007). *Macroeconomics (6th edn).* Worth Publishers.

Mankiw, N. Gregory (2008). *Principles of Macroeconomics.* Southwestern Cengage Learning.

Manning, Patrick (2003). *Navigating World History: Historians Create a Global Past.* Palgrave Macmillan.

Mayr, Ernst (1982). *The Growth of Biological Thought: Diversity, Evolution, and Inheritance.* Harvard University Press.

McNeill, William Hardy (1999). *A World History.* Oxford University Press.

McNeill, John Robert and McNeill, William Hardy (2003). *The Human Web: A Bird's-Eye View of World History.* Norton.

Mead, George Herbert (1967). *Mind, Self, and Society from the Standpoint of a Social Behaviorist.* The University of Chicago Press.

Mithen, Steven (1996). *The Prehistory of the Mind: A Search for the Origins of Art, Religion, and Science.* Thames and Hudson.

Nagel, Thomas (1986). *The View from Nowhere.* Oxford University Press.

Nouwen, Henri (2011). *Spiritual Formation: Following the Movements of the Spirit.* SPCK.

Piaget, Jean ([1926] 2002). *The Language and Thought of the Child.* Routledge.

Popper, Karl ([1945] 2002). *The Open Society and Its Enemies.* Routledge.

Sacks, Jonathan (2011). *The Great Partnership: God, Science and the Search for Meaning.* Hodder and Stoughton.

Sartre, Jean-Paul, ([1936]2010). *The Imaginary: A Phenomenological Psychology of the Imagination.* Routledge Classics.

de Saussure, Ferdinand ([1916] 1971). *Cours de linguistique générale.* Payot.

Schrödinger, Erwin ([1944] 1992). *What Is Life? in What Is Life? The Physical Aspect of the Living Cell; with Mind and Matter; and Autobiographical Sketches.* Cambridge University Press.

Schuster, Heinz Georg (1995). *Deterministic Chaos: An Introduction.* Wiley VCH.

Sokal, Alan (2008). *Beyond the Hoax: Science, Philosophy and Culture.* Oxford University Press.

Spier, Fred (1996). *The Structure of Big History: From the Big Bang Until Today*. Amsterdam University Press.

Söderberg, Johan (2008). *Vår världs ekonomiska historia. Del 1.* SNS Förlag.

Spier, Fred (1996). *The Structure of Big History: From the Big Bang Until Today.* Amsterdam University Press.

Spier, Fred (2010). *Big History and the Future of Humanity.* Wiley-Blackwell.

Stephen, R. C. (2004). *Explaining Postmodernism: Scepticism and Socialism from Rousseau to Foucault.* Scholarly Publishing.

Taylor, E. W. and Cranton, P. (2012). *The Handbook of Transformative Learning.* Jossey-Bass.

Tarnas, Richard (2010). *The Passion of the Western Mind: Understanding the Ideas That Have Shaped Our World View.* Pimlico.

Thompson, John B. (1984). *Studies in the Theory of Ideology.* University of California Press.

Vygotskij, Lev (1978). *Mind in Society: Development of Higher Psychological Processes.* Harvard University Press.

Wilkinson, N. and Klaes, M. (2012). *An Introduction to Behavioral Economics.* Palgrave Macmillan.

Willerslev, Rane (2007). *Soul Hunters: Hunting, Animism and Personhood among the Siberian Yukaghirs.* University of California Press.

Wilson, Charles ([1958] 1963). *Mercantilism.* Routledge and Kegan Paul.

Wright, Robert (2001). *Nonzero: The Logic of Human Destiny.* Vintage.

Wright, Robert (2009). *The Evolution of God: The Origins of Our Beliefs.* Little, Brown.

INDEX

Page references in *italics* indicate images.